Kadesh, 1275 B.C.: The ... outnumbered and outs... Mutwallis. His solution: Hire mercenary charioteers.

Savage's Station, West of Richmond, Virginia, 25 June 1862: General McClellan has the Confederates on the run, but there is something strange and menacing coming up the rails from Richmond. The first armored engine-propelled gun in history was invented by General Robert E. Lee! And it changed the course of history.

Flers-Courcelette, France, 1916: Escorted by a cluster of New Zealand infantrymen, a clanking nightmare appears out of the murky dawn with machine guns rattling. The Germans run for their lives as the machine plows down the previously impregnable barbed wire, straddles uncrossable trenches, and begins mowing down the enemy with relentless ease. The first tank assault of World War I is a smashing success!

The Egyptian Desert, World War II: Three British Matilda tanks roll steadily forward and over a sandy crest. Their squadron commander transmits a quick contact report over the radio and gets down to the business at hand. *Italian tanks. This can be serious because it has been learned that while the 37mm gun of the M11 cannot break the front of a Matilda, the newer Italian M13 with its 47mm gun can. . . .* With a whine of motors, the turret swings and the gunners shout, "Identified, sighting." The tank commander reaches for his binoculars and instructs: "Driver, steady. . . . Gunner, *fire!*" And a flash of fire bellows out of the muzzle into the not-quite daylight.

Books by Ralph Zumbro

Tank Aces
Tank Sergeant
The Iron Cavalry

Available from Pocket Books

THE
IRON CAVALRY

RALPH ZUMBRO

POCKET BOOKS
New York London Toronto Sydney Tokyo Singapore

An *Original* Publication of POCKET BOOKS

POCKET BOOKS, a division of Simon & Schuster Inc.
1230 Avenue of the Americas, New York, NY 10020

ISBN: 0-671-01390-4

First Pocket Books printing December 1998

10 9 8 7 6 5 4 3 2 1

Front cover photo credits: background © Robert Frerck/Historical
Artifacts/PNI; inset, Kulik Photo

Printed in the U.S.A.

Acknowledgments

The scope of this book is partially due to the contributions of a number of interested researchers who, having read some of my previous efforts, have enthusiastically jumped aboard. First and foremost is my good friend, Major Bill Schneck of the RD&E Center at Fort Belvoir, and the two ladies who gave of their time at the Van Noy Library, Phyllis Cassler and Lynn Fenster. Between them, they found much of the material for the Civil War chapter and contributed materially to several others.

Judy Stephenson of the Armor School Library at Fort Knox obligingly searched through many old volumes of *Armor* magazine, even back into the 1800s, and found dusty history volumes written in the interwar years. She also came up with some of the Civil War information, and her research added to the understanding of the tank-cossack integration in Russia.

The staff of *Armor* magazine also helped me with essential information. They include Lieutenant Colonel Terry Blakely, Jon Clemens, Vivian Oertle, Mary Hager, and their staff artist, Jody Harmon, who provided previously unpublished photographs, especially of the Russian Shermans.

My thanks also to Major Generals Stan Sheridan and Ronald J. Fairfield Jr., who keep coming up with extremely valuable connections from their wide range of military friends.

Ernst Furstner, formerly of the German army, has served on the Russian front and in the Afrika Korps and sent me several letters that gave me a richer "feel" for those campaigns.

Lieutenant Colonel Rolf Meyer of the German army provided invaluable assistance in the creation of the study of Villers-Bretonneux, the first tank-vs.-tank battle in history, because the German side has never been published in English. He also introduced me to Lieutenant Colonel Günther Guderian, the German liaison officer at Fort Bragg who, with the cooperation of his father, Heinz Günter Guderian, a historian and son of the general who originally created the Panzer Corps, checked that part of the manuscript for historical accuracy. I am grateful for their interest in this project.

The secretary for the Rolls-Royce Enthusiasts Club in Britain, Peter Baines, sent me a copy of the extremely rare book *Steel Chariots in the Desert* by S. C. Rolls, which opened up the entire armored side of T. E. Lawrence's desert battles.

Mr. E. J. McCarthy, senior editor at Presidio Press, Novato, California, gave me a very necessary copy of *Zhukov*, by Captain William Spahr, just when it was needed for a critical segment, the battle of Nomonhan.

David Fletcher, librarian for the British Tank Museum at Bovington, England, gave of his time to check the accuracy of several books and extracted information about the little-known armored battles after the Dunkirk evacuation.

Anita Dodd, librarian for the Douglas County Library, in Ava, Missouri, was my connection with the library system, through interlibrary loans, and facilitated much of the long-range research for the book.

My editor, Tris Coburn, helped me with the original layout for the book and then turned it over to Max Greenhut, who ably edited the rather large manuscript, carrying it through to completion. Their editorial skills are greatly appreciated.

Last, but definitely not least, my lovely wife, Louise, carries a precision-grade word processor in her head, which made this writing job a lot easier for all concerned.

My many thanks are due to all of those people who gave of their time and knowledge as this work progressed. Their contributions are greatly appreciated.

Finally, there is a correction that must be made to chapter 12 of my previous book, *Tank Aces*. On page 165, the episode of Captain Samuel Herbert Roth near Crailsheim, Germany, was mistakenly credited to an article in *Military* magazine. It should have read: "From an article in *Armor* magazine by Mr. John E. Armstrong, entitled 'A Routine Mission,' in the January–February 1995 issue." I regret the omission of credit to him for my adaptation of his very fine article in that publication.

Contents

INTRODUCTION

*The great generals have always aimed at decisive warfare.
To that end, they have always seen to it that the ratio of
their fast troops compared favorably with their slower
ones. Alexander, at the start of the war with Persia, commanded 32,000 foot soldiers and 10,000 horsemen. Hannibal at Cannae, had 40,000 dismounted and 10,000
mounted troops. Fredric the Great at Rossbach went into
action with 27 infantry battalions and 45 cavalry squadrons. These few figures indicate that the great leaders
maintained mobile elements comprising one sixth to one
quarter of their entire strength. Similarly, modern units
can be of decisive value only if their strength is in due
proportion to that of the whole army. . . . There will
always be men eager to voice misgivings, but only he
who dares to reach into the unknown will be successful.
The man who has been imaginative and active will be
more leniently judged by the future.*
—MAJOR GENERAL HEINZ GUDERIAN, quoted from an
  article in the *American Infantry Journal,* November 1937

We cannot say that we were not warned.
This book will be a unique look at history, through a

soldier's eyes instead of a conventional historian's. This writer has been a paratrooper, an artilleryman, and a tanker. I served in the famed 69th Armor in Vietnam and went through the Tet experience and many others in a Patton tank. Having to brain hostiles with a cannon tube and shoot them off a wingman's back creates a different attitude in a historian. I have served in every crew position in a tank—in combat—and have gone on foot patrol with our infantrymen. You will be looking through a soldier's eyes, not those of an academician.

In his book *The Face of Battle*, John Keegan suggested that "the treatment of battle in fiction is a subject almost untouched by literary critics, but one which the military historian, with his specialized ability to check for veracity and probability might well think of tackling." This can now be done for the battles of antiquity. Enough research is now available for a writer who has smelled the smoke of battle to send a fictional observer back three thousand years and plant his point of view in the middle of a swirling chariot battle as the "tankers" of that age do their work.

The mobile armored fighting man is one of history's decision makers. As far back as the Bronze Age, we find lists of armored "chariotries" that went into battle for city-states such as Carchemish, Troy, and Ugarit, sometimes towing strings of skirmishing infantry with them. The concept was probably invented in the fertile mind of some nomadic raider who used a stolen farmer's cart to haul his plunder back to the barren steppes that were his home. Once the connection was made that the cart could also carry supplies and arrows on the next raid, military evolution was off and running.

Literally running, for the nomads were horse herders who used the horses for food and sometimes as pack animals. They also rode them, but the mounted archer had not yet evolved. When the nomads saw tame cattle being used to pull two-wheeled carts, it took no stretch of the imagination to harness the fleeter animals of the steppes to the new wheeled carriers. Very quickly, they found themselves riding the carts into battle. As the technology evolved, the wheels grew lighter and the pace of battle grew faster.

A decorated box dating back to 3000 B.C., from Ur of the Chaldees, shows heavy four-wheeled war carts with spear throwers and quivers of javelins drawn into battle by teams of wild asses. Ahead of the battle wagons, infantrymen are wearing armored cloaks and are carrying battle axes and pole weapons and herding naked captives before them. It is also worth noting that many of those spear quivers were angled so that the infantrymen could get at them easily.

The next great leap was the invention of the compound bow, launching arrows from a mobile, lightly armored platform, and so the concept of the armored fighting vehicle, which could carry supplies and firepower into battle, was born. The horn-backed bow had a greater range than normal wooden bows, and an archer equipped with one could kill his foes before they could reach him—if he could carry enough arrows. Those old charioteers did not charge at first. Instead they roamed the flanks of opposing armies and killed their enemies with impunity. Then, with their opponents disorganized, they joined the squads of infantry to protect their horses and tore into the main body of the enemy. At short range, many of them used the heavier javelin weapons to break armor that was made of boiled leather and bronze plates.

They were the "tankers" of their age, and nomad groups of mercenary charioteers were part of the forces that brought down some of the great civilizations of antiquity. The first of the armored knights of antiquity rode chariots, not warhorses. The concept of a mobile, protected weapon platform has proved to be one of the great military innovations, be it in the form of an ancient chariot, the armored knight of the Middle Ages, or modern fighting machinery.

The concept of a vehicle-carried projectile launcher dates back much further than is currently recognized. Alexander of Macedon used portable catapults to cover river crossings, and Julius Caesar's solution to swirling Celtic cavalry was "Sixty Ballistae per Legion, mounted on chariots." Two thousand years later, American soldiers and Russian cossacks were towing machine guns into battle on wagons.

With the advent of the internal combustion engine and armor plate, the task of battlefield bully was taken over by the tank, in all its many variations. History, however, seems to concentrate on the grand, sweeping battles, such as Cambrai, El Alamein, Yom Kippur, and now Desert Storm, probably because tracking down old soldiers is hard work—especially the ones who are five thousand years in the grave.

The little battles at the fringes of the larger wars are part of history too, and they have lessons to teach that are directly relevant to the period of small wars that we are now entering. They are also direct, exciting accounts of military derring-do, not dry historical number crunching. Both the Christian Bible and the Mahabharata of ancient India contain stories of the classic chariot warriors of antiquity. The tales of those old warriors and their "chariots of iron" are in this book, along with those of their modern descendants, the tankers and the armored cavalry.

The key to battle, however, is the intelligent use of combined arms. While the infantry is the base, or what is called the Queen of Battle in chess terms, the armored mobile force is the King of the Killing Zone. This modern concept dates back much further than is usually suspected, and this book will look very carefully at that relationship. Artillery, from the catapult to the cannon to the dive bomber, has recently been seen as the third leg of the battlefield triad, but there is one forgotten member of the mobility team: the combat engineer, the sapper, or the pioneer. These are the breaking-and-entering specialists, the bridge builders, and the road makers. They are here, along with the tankers, out on the fringes of the larger wars.

Although the classic tank assaults of World War I are known, not much has been written about the American tankers, or the French tank assaults, or the German reaction, which was originally to use captured Allied equipment. The Germans also built and sent into combat 20 of their own tanks and triumphed in the first tank-vs.-tank combat in history. That story is here, told from the German side as well as the British. Here also are the "female" machine-gun tanks and their cannon-armed "male" protectors.

Almost unknown are the activities of His Majesty's Land Ship Detachment (HMLD) in the Gaza Strip in Palestine in 1916. The second and third battles for the city of Gaza,

against overwhelming numbers of Turks, involved eight orphaned tanks commanded by Major Nutt, and they have
almost disappeared from history. Their story has been captured in this book, taken directly from Major Nutt's battle
log.

The first long-distance armored raid in history is here, the
rescue of a group of survivors of a British warship that had
been torpedoed, the crew given to Sennusi tribesmen for
safekeeping. Four months later it was necessary to send a
squadron of Rolls-Royce armored cars after them, with extreme prejudice. Those armored cars eventually wound up
working for T. E. Lawrence, and that story is seen through
the eyes of Lawrence's driver, Sammy Rolls.

Throughout the period between the two great wars of the
century, there were little potboilers that included tank action. Many nations were involved in these mechanized shiva-
rees, and their stories are here. The French and British had
many small actions during that period, and there is even a
tank detachment in the Foreign Legion. To this day, Legion
tankers are active in Africa, from Chad to Botswana.

At the same time, the Russians and the Japanese were
experimenting with their first crude tanks. They would be
fighting against each other in Manchuria before World War
II "officially" began.

In the Mideast, the British were using armored cars in
desert battles, and in Africa, the Italians used tankettes
against the Ethiopians and Somalis until the British ran
them out. There were even battles that pitted nomad horse
cavalry against these primitive tanks . . . and the tanks did
not always come out on top. Although World War I witnessed the birth of the armored fighting machine, the 1920s
and '30s were the experimental decades.

In the Spanish civil war, both the Russians and the Germans used the conflict to battle test their new, modern hardware, resulting in quite a few tank-vs.-tank actions, which
taught lessons that immediately went onto the drawing
boards. Oddly enough, the Germans and Russians were co-
operating at this point in history, and the German tank
school was deep inside Russia, away from prying Western
eyes.

At Nomonhan, Manchuria, General Georgi Zhukov gave the Japanese such a shellacking that the story has been expunged from their public history, although it is studied—very thoroughly—in their staff college. This was also where the Japanese learned that they could shove swords into the vision slits of those primitive tanks and decapitate the drivers. This was where General Zhukov learned how to operate tanks along with horsed cavalry. That secret art has almost been lost, but it is in this book. For all of our dependence on machinery, it can be demonstrated that the horse still has a place in battle. All through World War II, cable dispatches coming out of Russia detailed the Russian tank experience, and not one of those stories has ever seen popular print. Many of them are in these pages.

The CBI (China-Burma-India) theater also generated many small-scale tank actions. Although most of the tanks used were American, the crews were not. Chinese and Indians and Sikhs and Australians went to war in machines that came out of the Baldwin locomotive works in Lima, Ohio, and out of the Chrysler and Cadillac tank plants in Detroit.

The Korean War generated many adventurous tank actions, such as the drive to the Yalu and the retreat from the Chosin Reservoir. There again, the stories of the little actions where one or two tanks turned the tide of a battle, rescued infantry, or served as artillery, have been lost until now.

Twenty years after Korea, Vietnam began to generate many low-level tank actions. This writer was a tank commander and was in quite a few of them. What is *not* generally known is that Vietnamese tankers also fought in armored vehicles all over that nation. They now have an organization in California, and a few of their stories are here.

The wars in South Vietnam and Africa during that experimental period were a laboratory experience that has remained largely unknown to the greater armor community. Although it was learned as early as World War I that air and armor are natural partners, it was not until the Panzers linked up with the dive-bombers that the generals were turned loose. Even then, fuel couldn't be provided fast enough to keep the tanks going. Korea started off as a war of motion and then congealed in stalemate. In the Republic of Viet Nam (RVN), however, the link between air and armor became ever closer. Now, for the first time, a gunship could hover over a working tank, and a CH-47 could bring it fuel and ammunition.

The copters' lift capability was evolving to not only feed the tanks but lift them as well. Those stories too have never been told. In Africa, the Russians finally did it—they learned to move assault guns behind an enemy with heavy-cargo choppers, and the lesson has been allowed to go unlearned. In Afghanistan, they did it again and were ignored by the theoreticians. This, however, is where we are headed in the twenty-first century, the linking of light armor with heavy-lift capability. It promises to be an exciting ride.

CHAPTER 1

First of the Breed

EASTERN JORDAN, 1275 B.C.

THE ANCIENT DESERT OF EASTERN JORDAN SHOOK FROM DIS-
tant concussions as the three soldiers crept down narrow,
dusty stairs into a gloomy tunnel. The dark crevice in the
side of a rocky outcropping had been opened by the explosion of a land mine when their escorting tank detonated the
hidden weapon. At first they had thought it to be one of
Hussein's military works, but the narrow passage in the
earth was older than that, far older.

Ahead of them their lights speared through draping cobwebs, and small things screeched and skittered in the gloom.
Behind them they could hear clanks and curses as their
mates worked on their mine-crippled tank out in the desert
sun, with a battle raging around them. Down here, though,
they seemed to be walking farther back in time with each
step downward.

The dust of millennia dropped from the rough stone walls
and crunched underfoot as they walked nervously down
stairs hewn out of living rock. The very air seemed stale, as
if it had been down here a long time without being breathed.
With each tremulous step, the hackles on Sergeant Edwin
Lamb's neck rose another degree. His crook-necked flash-

light flickered over the lichened, age-grimed walls as he stopped and turned.

"This for certain ain't one of Sa-Damn's underground works," he hissed to the two soldiers behind him. "Not this far into Jordan."

"Hell, I don't even think it's military," Private Jensen half whispered back. "Feels more like a tomb, like the ones they keep finding around here. Roman, mebbe . . . mebbe even earlier."

"Well, if it ain't military, let's get the freak outa here," Specialist Four Brooks suggested in an urgent, quavering voice. She held a video camera and a pistol, while the other two were armed with the M-16A3 carbines carried by the Dragoon Infantry of the newly formed UN Military Interdiction Force. The Beretta 9mm was in her right hand while her left rested on the camera, where a strap kept it resting against one well-curved hip. Annette Brooks was an Army combat recorder, and she'd come along with these two on a hunch. She was now beginning to regret her intuition. As the dust moved in the lights, she began to imagine ghostly forms in the dark shadows.

Another series of thuds, nearer this time, jolted some more dust from the wall. Her eyes detected the motion and then picked out a form as her camera light swung to it, and she hissed, "Sarge, right above that recess in the wall—isn't that some kind of lettering?"

Lamb, eyes darting left and right, reached up and brushed the area where the wall and the low, rough-hewn ceiling met, wiping the dust away, revealing a deeply chiseled series of wavy marks. "Probably some old Arab tomb," he guessed as he stepped forward around a curve. Then he stopped dead in his tracks. He'd run into a stone wall, literally. The passage was blocked by a gigantic granite slab.

Like many of the U.N. force, which was actually an American battle group on loan to the world's debating body, Sergeant Lamb was well educated, working on his masters in archaeology, which was why he'd joined this unit in the first place, and why he'd volunteered to lead a scouting party down this hole. Neither his personal finances nor those of his little midwestern college could finance field research.

Three years of Middle East military service would have to do, and Edwin Lamb had spent much of his leave time working in various digs there.

Earlier that day, the Abrams tank to which his mechanized infantry section was attached had hit a mine and since then they'd been jacking new sections of tread into its tracks. One of the Dragoons, just poking around, had found this newly exposed hole, and the tank commander, Sergeant First Class Wilson—a portly, nervous individual who took no chances—had wanted a look-see and a report. Lamb had volunteered and now he found himself entering not an Iraqi bunker, but some ancient enigma. The dust and cobwebs reeked of undisturbed millennia.

Clipping his flashlight to a band on his webbing, he began probing the roughly dressed stone in front of him. "Well, hell," he said, "nothing ventured, nothing gained. Give a shoulder, Jensen, and we'll see if it moves." Slinging his carbine, Jensen none too enthusiastically stepped beside his sergeant and put his shoulder to the stone while Brooks swung up the video camera. Nervously, she spoke into the radio that was part of her helmet.

"Three-two Tango Charlie, this is Brooks. We've hit a stone wall, literally. This is a tomb, not a bunker, and Sarge is going to— Eek!" Her video light showed her the picture of the stone vanishing, down, fast, and the two men falling forward into blackness. Then a monstrous thud shook dust loose from the ceiling and almost suffocated her.

"Hey, Brooksie," came TC's (tank commanders) instant, concerned voice, "what's loose down there?"

Licking her dry lips, Brooks had to give her unwilling feet individual orders to move forward through the swirling murk. Step by dreaded step, she caught up to Lamb and Jensen, whose lights were darting around a room full of wonders.

"We're okay, Sarge," she answered in a hushed tone, "but this *is* a tomb, and it's full of—"

Lamb's helmet radio cut in, his excited voice interrupting her. "There's a chariot down here, Wilson. Looks like some old warrior's grave. There's a few mummies standing in the chariot and even a horse's mummy and weapons all over.

But get this: Mosta this stuff is *bronze,* 'ceptin' for the chariot wheels and a scaled brigandine that're iron. This is an *old* site. Tactical situation permitting, better get the chaplain and the antiquities crew over here ASAP."

There was a longish silence and then the answer, seeming to echo down the passage, came back. "That's a rog, Lamb. The battle, such as it was, has passed us by and it'll be a while before that last probe of Saddam's is combat-worthy again. We kind of roughed 'em up a bit and I can see at least twenty burning tanks from here. Hold in place down there and don't touch nothing. There's a bird on the way."

Annette Brooks had originally joined the army for combat duty, but after the press had found out what really happens to female POWs in Arabic hands, there had been some changes made in the table of organization equipment (TO& E). She was in a combat zone but not, most of the time, at risk. Very soon the entire tomb was lit up and Brooks, followed by a pair of very attentive soldiers, was busily scanning the whole place from several angles. One man drew their attention to an entire wall directly behind the chariot that was covered with a strange semi-alphabetic writing "Hey, what's this?" the man asked, "looks like a whole book in stone."

After one look, Lamb whistled and then said, "I'm no expert on ancient scripts, muscle-powered weaponry being my specialty, but that looks like new kingdom Egyptian script, the demotic alphabet the scribes invented to replace hieroglyphics, about 2000 B.C. You two," he snapped, indicating a couple of tankers, "dust off that wall and set those lights over to the left, on that casket, and give her a little contrast. Brooks, that may be the most important find in here. Information is always more precious than hardware. Scan that wall, twice or more, if you got time, with separate cartridges. We take no chances at all with this information, and we smuggle some copies out ASAP!"

She nodded, feeling her piled hair moving down inside her commo helmet, threatening to escape, and began to scan the wall, a few lines at a time. Behind the lens, her mind was wandering again. *Watch yourself, Netty, he ain't real handsome, but he's got a way about him. Do you want to*

*get attached to a professional soldier and then have to stay
home and tend kids while he goes adventuring. There ain't
no such thing as a Mom and Pop Army—or would you be
a professor's lady?*

"Heads up. Brass arriving," a voice echoed down the passage, and at Lamb's nod, she again changed cartridges, dropping one between her generous breasts, slipping one to
Lamb and one to Jensen, as they heard the clatter of arriving
feet. Suddenly the underground crypt was full of personages,
and the troopers were trying to make themselves small. At
Lamb's nod, Jensen, with the master tape, slid out the door
and up the stairs. That was one on the way out, two more
to go.

The first man into the room was the battle group's all-
faith chaplain, Captain Curtis, who doubled as their antiquities expert, his studies in comparative religion having given
him some knowledge of older cultures. The second was The
Man. Major Ulysses Tecumseh Butler, commander of this
little task force, had come to check out the site. Like many
competent commanders, he'd studied history, using it like a
line on a graph to predict future political contretemps.
"Have you people got all this recorded?" he asked Brooks,
who nodded vigorously, feeling stray locks of hair sneaking
out of her "fritz" helmet. Butler then turned to query his
chaplain, who had a bemused look on his face as he puzzled
out the carved inscription over the heavy war chariot. "Problems, Mike?" he asked. Generic Chaplain Michael Curtis
nodded as he made notes on the pad that always rode in
his left breast pocket. "Have to get those tapes bounced
back to some university in the States," he said, "but if phar-
aonic curses work, it's a good thing we're all military. Here's
roughly what it says—I'm interpolating some of this, but it
won't be far wrong." With one last glance at the wall, Curtis
swung his rimless spectacles up on his forehead and began
to read from his notebook:

*To ye who have entered my tomb and broken the sleep
of the ages, a warning and a greeting. Know that I,
T'Chad, of the city of Tobrug, have been made an Egyptian noble of the warrior class and having fought wars*

from Libya to the battle of Kadesh under Pharaoh Ramses, named the second, in the chariot division named after the god Ptah, and have earned the same protection for my grave as the great Pharaoh himself. The curse of Ptah hovers over my bier.

If ye be plunderers or seekers for curiosity, ye shall die before this moon is over, and slowly. If ye be of the warrior class, then you are well-come, for I am the first of a new breed. I was the first to buy black metal from the sons of Tubal-Cain and set iron tires to the wheels of my war chariot instead of those of bronze, and the first to use an axle of iron. I fought in great battles, grinding all who came against me under iron-shod hooves and iron wheels. My chariot, my stallion, and my weapons are before ye and my story is on the wall beside ye.

A great Seer, whose soul has roamed the millennia between the arrivals of Marduk, which decides the ends of our world ages, has told me of thee, that ye would one day, toward the end of an age, come in great fire-spewing iron chariots. Sit, be welcome, and read my legend, for ye are the sons of my spirit. AND YE HAVE WAR BEFORE THEE, BEFORE THINE SOULS CAN JOIN MINE IN THE GREEN VALLEY BE-YOND DEATH, WHERE WARRIORS REST AND MAIDENS DANCE.

"Well, won't that just fry yer ever-lovin' circuits?" one soldier commented. "Just how old is this grave, sir?"

"About thirty-two-hundred years, give or take a century," Butler answered. "Now get your butts out of here. Your tank is fixed and this two-bit war is about over. The Jordani-ans have got an antiquities team on the way and will proba-bly want to confiscate all the tapes too. How many copies did you people make?"

"Three, Sir," Brooks and Lamb said in unison. "One is already smuggled out and one is Islamic-proof," Jensen added with a pointed look at Brooks's bosom.

"Good. There'll be a jump in rank for all concerned with this little escapade," Butler said with a grin. "As soon as we get a usable translation, you people will be the first to get a copy, that I promise. Now move it, troops."

Just over three weeks later, in a rocky, brushy valley south of Amman, Jordan, the troopers of the tank Dragoon section were gathered around a campfire, getting ready to give themselves a small celebration. The most recent of Saddam Hussein's aggressions had been violently slapped back into its own borders and the new, American-operated U.N. force had proved itself capable of taking on all comers.

Maintenance on the tank and the two personnel carriers was on schedule and the rumor factory had foretold a movement back to their base in Egypt. Better yet, a new UN ruling had said that Islamic prudery could not be enforced inside a UN military compound or perimeter. The three armored vehicles, parked at the corners of a triangle, were legally such a perimeter and the tankers and their infantry were going to make the most of that fact. Sergeants Wilson and Lamb had declared party time.

Beer had been dropped off by the supply truck that brought their parts, rations, and mail. One of the infantrymen had grown up in the restaurant business, so a bartered lamb and issue rations were undergoing a radical transformation behind his vehicle. Several musical instruments had surfaced from various storage places and an impromptu band was warming up to play for the forty-odd troops in the compound. Brooks and two other women had cooked up some entertainment of their own and were getting into costume. The word had gotten around, and small groups of tankers and infantrymen were filtering in from other laagers in the area.

One of the other lady soldiers, a commo tech, could sing pretty good country, and looked really good in a show skirt, but Brooks had promised to put on a show that would "have you barbarians dreaming about Tel Aviv and thinking seriously about lady camels." She'd spent some leave time in Cairo and picked up belly dancing as her form of oriental aerobics." She'd just gotten stripped down to breast shields, a concho belt, and harem pantaloons when a hummer pulled up and Major Butler and the chaplain got out.

"Eeek!" she squealed, hands suddenly clenched into fists in front of her mouth, as Butler's eyes caught her. Annette was already beginning to think of herself as PFC Brooks when she heard the chuckle in the major's voice. "At ease, troops. I heard about this shivaree and decided to invite myself because those translations I promised you came in, right on schedule. The chaplain here has been ordered not to be offended. We've brought a projector, screen, and something a little bit stronger than issue beer. Are we welcome?"

"Yes, *sir*," Sergeant Wilson said. "But what's with the projector? Have the university people made a video of those inscriptions?"

Nodding his head as Curtis set up a standard six-foot screen, Butler answered, "Right. Modern computer imaging never ceases to amaze me. We sent those tapes to the University of Nebraska, which does a lot of military history work, and they turned an animation program loose on the university people. The basic visual imaging was taken from those old *Ben-Hur*-type movie spectaculars, so don't be surprised if some familiar faces show up."

"All *right*, Sir," Lamb said enthusiastically, "but we better get the food first, Major, if this's going to take a while. Specialist Five Kane's got some goodies fixed up behind the ACAV (Armored Cavalry Assault Vehicle). This way, please. We've got a lamb on a spit over a charcoal pit."

Shortly, mess kits in hand, bottles and glasses resting in the sand beside them, the assembled troopers were looking through a window in time. Before them on the screen, a lean, muscular man of medium build, with snapping black eyes and black curly hair, stood on a beach. Behind him, to his right, an azure sea rolled off into the distance. To his left, a steep, almost clifflike hill rose sharply several hundred feet. It was crowned with a mud-brick village surrounded by olive trees. To the older members of the audience, the man on the screen resembled an actor named Cornel Wilde. Presently, he began to speak, in a slightly gravelly tenor voice.

"My name is T'Chad, youngest son of T'Chad the harness maker, who lives in that village. I was born here, but born restless. After learning my father's trade, I decided to follow his footsteps and go adventuring and maybe earn a small fortune before settling down. This village has never had a name of its own, only being thought of as near the market town of Calneh, where we sold our fish, olives, goats, and leather. At the seawall of Calneh, many ships put in during the summer sailing season and the far-traveled tales of the sailors decided my initial course.

"At the age of sixteen, I took my father's hammered bronze axe, cut down a tree of gopherwood, and carved an oar. Being young and strong, I would apprentice myself to a merchant ship as an oarsman and man before the mast. Setting off to market, I put my new, varnished oar, inscribed with my name, in the oar rack outside a quayside wine establishment and went within to find a captain who needed a strong back and a willing mind. As luck would have it, a ship in port was one hand down, an older sailor having, as the saying goes, swallowed the anchor stone and quit the sea that very week."

The picture froze for a moment and Butler cut in with an explanation. "The instructions that came with this disk say that the man's whole Bronze Age life is here, through several ships, several seagoing adventures, and literally hundreds of little chariot battles, so tonight we're just going to hit the high spots and get to the battle where he was, for all practical purposes, knighted." Butler tapped a new code into the disk player and a short parade of ancient ships flickered across the screen.

First, a round-bellied merchant ship with only a dozen oar ports on each side, a single mast, and a pair of steering oars was shown. This was followed by a series of ships of its type, some larger and better kept, some smaller and distinctly seedy. One ship, small, many-oared, and very well kept, hoisted a black sail with a skull in its center. From then on T'Chad seemed to have switched from merchantmen to warships, for the only time the big-bellied ships were depicted was as convoys or prizes. After several of these oar-powered warships, the picture began to move again, and a small bireme was seen entering a busy port and, using its seaward set of oars as sculls, sidling crabwise up to a stone quay with bronze mooring rings embedded in its wall. A

caption appeared across the bottom of the screen: THE CITY/
STATE OF TOBRUG, CYRENACIA, NORTH AFRICA, 1300 B.C. +
50 YEARS.

Again T'Chad, older, somewhat heavier, and obviously
more a man of the world, stood before them. He was now
wearing a sword at his side, and dressed in the rich accoutre-
ments of a wealthy warrior. A cargo slave from the ship
stood behind him to carry his baggage.

"Having now had my fill of the sea," he said, "I determined to see just what lay behind those ports which I had
visited these past ten years. I was now rated as a petty officer
and could command a berth on any ship as lead oarsman
or ship sergeant, and had a small personal wealth, enough
to tide me until I found a post to my liking. For the last
time, I racked my oar at a seaside hostel and went within,
this time to sell it to a likely lad.

"Again, the luck which the gods have seen fit to bestow
on me at odd times came to my aid and I found that likely
lad, who volunteered the information that this city, named
Tobrug, was soon to be at war with another city-state,
named Lukk, over its boundaries, and was in dire need of
chariots and those who could fight and repair them. Remembering that I was a harness maker, I determined to go a-
soldiering.

" 'One last thing,' the boy said as he shouldered my now
worn but still varnished oar. 'Take your service with one of
the mercenary bands,' he said, 'instead of the city chariotry.
For when the war is over, the mercenary will go his way to
find another, while the city soldier will spend the rest of
his term polishing and parading.' This seemed to me to be
intelligent advice and I took it in good faith."

Again, Butler stopped the disk for a moment to explain
what had been done. "You'll note that all you've seen so
far has been personal narrative, and that's how they put in
T'Chad's personal notes. In the actual stories, though, the
scriptwriters at the university decided to switch to third-
person narrative to improve the flow, so here goes."

The picture showed T'Chad, still followed by a slave from
the ship, who carried his sea chest, approaching one of the
chariot camps outside of the city. There were several hun-

dred light chariots drawn up in a large circle, each with a small tent beside it and a pair of men working on either the chariot or their weapons. He saw no one spending idle time. In the distance, a huge horse herd, guarded and controlled by mounted youths, grazed. Spying a burly individual of about his own age working on a wheel with some help from another, smaller man, he walked up and asked a question.

"Greetings, charioteer. My name is T'Chad, and word is that there are posts to be had here. To whom might I make inquiry?"

The man, a blond Scythian who seemed inclined to portliness but apparently was fighting it well, turned and said, with a scar-twisted smile on his face, "Well, I'm Jobeb. Me and my buddy Elric, here, are just one chariot pair, but we own our chariot and one horse. Our captain, Joktar, is a Philistine and a righteous sort. He's got four chariots that he owns, beside the six that he's hired for this war, including us. He's allowed that he could use another man or two, but only if they know chariots. . . .Where have you fought, and for whom?"

"I have fought when need be," T'Chad replied, "and you'll not find a much better man with javelin or sling, but most of my fighting's been at sea. I'm a newly beached sailor, looking for a war to try on for size."

As the man's grin began to die in disappointment, T'Chad added hastily, "But I was raised a harness maker, apprenticed to my father, and you'll not find too many as good as I with leather and cordage."

At that, Jobab stopped what he was doing, set down his grease pot and brush, and grabbed T'Chad's sword strap as if to hold him captive. "Captain Joktar," he yelled, turning about and dragging T'Chad with him in his excitement. "Take up a collection and double the offering to the priest of Ishtar. He's here; the sacrifice was accepted."

"Who, what, which?" issued from a large, ornate tent as a small, waspish-looking man with a worried expression on his face emerged, slipped a sword belt over a shoulder. "Make sense, Jobab."

Jobab, who wore a broad but pointed beard, a kilt, and sandals, said, "T'Chad here is a landed sailor, harness maker, rigger probably, and says he can hold his own with a sling and javelin." Some of the worry began to leave the man's face as he looked T'Chad over. "If you're a sailor, you know knots and cordage and can also repair canvas," he stated rhetorically. T'Chad nodded, mentally cataloging his skills like a slavemaster trying to sell prime merchandise.

"Yessir, as Jobab said, I grew up a harness maker and can also do decorative leatherwork, and even tan and work my own leather. You find me a dead horse or goat and not much will go to waste. I've got my own knives, awls, and needles there in the chest behind me, and some woodworking tools as well. I can steam and bend hardwood for ship's timbers and could probably help your wheelright too."

"Damn, boy," the older man said, "I'm beginning to believe in the gods again, but you'd better be able to cover your story, or it'll be the worse for ye." Turning his head, the captain yelled, "*Lara,* get your buns out here, and bring the roster, we've got a harness maker."

"Yes, master, a female voice answered from within the tent, and a slender, well-formed woman of about a score of years emerged, bearing a rolled papyrus scroll. She wore only a short tunic that showed her legs off to good effect, a collar, a bell on her left ankle. "Never put what you can buy or capture on the payroll," Joktar said, as the woman unrolled the scroll and took a writing feather out of her long brown hair. A small earthenware inkpot swung from the single sash that held her garment to her, and she pulled its wooden stopper and dipped her quill.

"Put this man, T'Chad, on the payroll as a temporary sergeant," the captain said. "Bunk him in one of the two-man tents, and give him the get-it-done-yesterday list."

"Yes, master," the woman said, with a look at Joktar that told T'Chad that her collar was only symbolic. The two had obviously been soul mates for quite some time and her voice was a caress to the ears. She gave T'Chad a small smile and said, "Follow me please, m'lord, to your tent." She turned gracefully and walked off, barefoot, with a tiny bell tinkling at each step.

Grinning now, T'Chad followed that delightful form down the row of tents, in turn followed by the ship slave. He'd been a gentleman of leisure for almost five whole hours, and already he was beginning to see advantages to this way of life. Being able to take a luxury like the little item walking in front of him on campaign was surely one of them. He wondered just how many of the billets in a chariot company would be filled by such temptations. Clerks for certain, seamstresses and laundry also, cooks maybe, but pony messengers almost certainly. He decided that he might just need an assistant or gofer.

The next morning, he got a good look at the selection of chariots in Company Jokter and saw why the captain had been worried. With a major campaign in the offing, much of the harness was simply worn out, some of the wheel rims were showing signs of wear, and the wooden tires on the metal spokes were showing stress cracking. Some of the rims would have to be recycled for smaller wheels or traded off to a bronzeman, but that wasn't his department anyway. The bronze traders were a specialized lot and Jokter had several individuals whom he was allowing to make competing bids for the company's business.

The wheels would take the longest, T'Chad thought, so he examined the ones on Jobab's chariot first. The long-hafted, six-spoked hubs were made of cast bronze and turned on a bronze axle. They were held in place by a large washer, which itself was anchored by a long peg, shaped much like a ship's belaying pin. The problem was that the outer wheel was wood, held to the spokes by wire and another cast fitting, over which a bronze rim had been shrunk. Many of those wooden rims needed to be replaced and re-shod, so the first thing T'Chad did was find a carpenter to make him a steam box so that he could soften wood enough to take the standard curve of a three-cubit wheel. That being started, he asked Jobab to use the chariot to go to market for harness leather in the nearby city.

"Sure," Jobab said. "We've done all we can without new rims and harness anyway. We own one horse that gets us around, and that'll be all we need for a shopping run anyway. . . . Elric?" The smaller man nodded and trotted off toward the horse park on the valley floor.

Suddenly the picture on the screen stopped, and Butler

said, "Okay, that got us started and there's a lot more here, but it'd take a week or two to get it all out. He soldiered all across North Africa, Egypt, and down into the Indus civilizations, and eventually got command of a mercenary company of his own and plugs into the history we know at the battle of Kadesh, about 1275 to 1300 B.C., depending on whose chronology you're using."

Butler keyed the player again and the screen began to show a scene eerily like their own. The panorama was a night view of a military camp on a dry, lightly forested plain. Like their present camp, there were clusters of military vehicles next to small tent clusters with cooking fires burning in their centers. Also like their current scene, an almost full moon dominated the sky. Where tarps were slung from the hulls of tanks and APCs (Armored Personnel Carriers) in their present on the screen chariots were gathered in round clusters with their team shafts lashed together in the center, making a star out of the two-wheeled war machines. A tarp had been spread over the wooden shafts, and the soldiers of the day were going about their normal evening tasks. Some were cooking, some greasing axles or oiling leather. Many were resting, or looking at the stars as if to divine the morrow's events.

As the view focused on one camp, a woman was dancing to the music of a drum, flute, and lyre before a dozen or so warriors who were roasting a goat. "Geez, Sarge," one man said to his NCO, "that's kinda spooky—they're just like us. How long has this been going on?" Lamb, overhearing the question and feeling Annette suddenly snuggle closer, shuddering with the weirdness, answered with a distant tone in his voice as he sent his memory back down what he learned in his college years—through five thousand years of history.

CHAPTER 2

KADESH, 1275 B.C.

"SINCE THE BEGINNING OF TIME, JONESY," LAMB SAID REflectively, "Soldiers *are* history, since the first younger son had to pick up a rock and bounce raiders out of his tribe's berry patch. Ever since monogamy and tilled land, the concept of civilizations had had to be fought for—and we still haven't gotten it straight. That bunch on that screen out there don't know it, but they're headed straight for the dark age that took down Troy and Mycenae—"

"Shhh, genius, and watch," Annette whispered in his ear, and after a self-conscious look at the chaplain, he focused and looked at the screen.

After a scan of the camp, the view had singled out a pair of chariot clusters on either side of a larger tent with an emblem post in front of it. On top of that post was the cast bronze sea-dragon head that T'Chad had taken as his emblem, and inside the tent, T'Chad slept lightly, on a bearskin laid over piled rushes. A brazier supported on a tripod warmed the tent with glowing coals and a small oil lamp sputtered with a fitful light. Suddenly his eyes snapped open. At the same time the tent fly was pulled open and one of his two sentries hissed, "Hoofbeats, single horse, south, coming fast." Drawing his longsword, one of the few actual steel weapons available, T'Chad jammed it into the ground, pressed his ear to the hilt, and affirmed his henchman's statement.

He heard the faint drumming and looked off to the south, from where a messenger from an Egyptian camp would be arriving. He became instantly on guard. Night news was *never* good news. Scanning south, he saw two red coals beneath the stars. Sentries had uncovered their guard fires and thrown grass on them to reveal the location of the fast-drumming hooves—they came directly from Kadesh. "Light our beacon and pass the word—quietly—for the company commanders. Brain anybody that speaks above a whisper." The word had gotten around and the camp was already bustling with the quiet, deadly efficiency of trained soldiers. Someone else had gotten nervous and he saw hostlers heading out for the horse remuda.

A sudden light flared as coals were thrown into a bundle of straw on a pole and the area in front of the tent became light with flickering shadows. Into this scene an exhausted horse cantered, fell to earth, and dumped an Egyptian scribe, scarcely more than a stripling boy, to the ground in front of the charioteer officers. Forcing himself to his feet, the boy stammered out his message.

"Th-the Hatti . . . Mutwallis has the chariotries of eighteen Hittite cities at old Kadesh and only the Corps of Amun is with His Majesty. . . ." The boy dropped, and at a gesture from T'Chad, two men picked him up and took him into the command tent. Already a pair of old women of the regiment's camp followers were attending to him. A military unit in those days was a small village on the march.

Looking around, T'Chad could see that all of his important subcommanders had arrived and were squatting in a semicircle around his relit council fire. He looked at them, needing time to think, and asked for a report from his second officer, an Egyptian adventurer, a bastard son of a general, whose keen vision had given him a combat nickname of Horus "The Hawk" Horemheb. "Hawk," T'Chad said, "It's going to hit and splatter,—what is our status? Mercenary company first, then the Egyptians, then the city troops."

Hawk, taller than T'Chad, younger and leaner, with lighter, almost blondish hair, said, "As of right now, we're at full mobility, all wheels trued and lubed, all horses rested, all quivers full. We can move when ready—but eighteen cities, that's got to be over three thousand chariots."

"We won't have to fight all of them, Hawk," another of the captains cut in. "After all, the whole Egyptian army's coming up. You've got five companies of ten each, and so have the Egyptians, and our Amurran squadrons did pretty fair last year." Hawk nodded, some of his worry subsiding. "We've got fifty chariots in our mercenary squadron, the city chariotry of Ullaza and Byblos add up to fifty more, and Mutwallis, even with good spying, probably doesn't know about the Egyptian squadron that came by sea into Simyra last week. So we're at a strength of a hundred and fifty chariots ready to roll. Not enough to fight a host, but enough to decide a battle, if they're well used."

" 'Well used' being the important point," T'Chad said, and hearing a rustle behind him, he turned to see the young messenger being led out by Lara, Jokter's widow of some years now. Gratefully the lad slid down to the pillow she placed for him, took a drink of wintered wine, and began to talk. The boy wore the headdress and belt of a military scribe in the division named after the god Amun.

"I am Nakht, scribe, driver, and acolyte to the vizier Meketre, and we were sent to warn you of what has transpired near Kadesh. I am most afraid that our young Pharaoh has been shamefully misled by the wretched fallen ones of Hatti and is in serious danger. As you know, we have marched up from Tanis and Kantara in the Delta of the Nile, using the coast forts and the way of Horus to move quickly to Gaza. We came up the valley of Zorek, through the mountains and the valley of Quina at Megiddo, where Thutmose, named the third, triumphed two centuries ago, and then up the Bekaa Valley, past Baalbeck, and down the valley of the Orontes, fording it several times. We were a month on that road.

"As we approached Kadesh, which has revolted from the

empire, we met two desert Bedouins of Shasu, who assured
His Majesty that the Hatti were not yet assembled and were
still far to the north at Tunis. Being fully taken in, we re-
joiced and set up our camp at a point this side of the Orontes River, north and to the west of new Kadesh, on its
mound. We are based where our young Pharaoh's father,
the magnificent Seti, had encamped. Yesterday morning our
scouts rousted out two more of the wretched Bedouins
sneaking about our shield wall, counting men and chariots.
Being just the one division, we have but five hundred vehicles and five thousand Ph'rr, the running infantry. We could
not afford that knowledge escaping.

"One of His Majesty's viziers, my master Meketre, became suspicious and had them captured and beaten with
canes on their soft parts. After some hours of this, and being
asked whose men they were, they admitted, 'The entire host
of Hatti is assembled at Old Kadesh, across the River Orontes, and are furnished with their infantry and their chariotry
carrying their weapons of warfare and they are more numerous than the sand of the riverbanks. See, they stand ready
to fight behind Kadesh the old.' This filled the Pharaoh and
his viziers with much dismay and many messengers have
been sent out.

"The Hatti did not attack yesterday, Lord T'Chad, but
they will assuredly do so this day, and morning is only hours
from now. Unless the gods intervene, we are doomed. We
have brought all the baggage of the army, and Pharaoh's
princes and princesses and his golden throne, and all the
accouterments of his army—which is not yet here. The division named Amun and the Sherden mercenaries which are
His Majesty's bodyguard were still building their shield wall
when we left."

"Easy, boy," T'Chad said quietly, "I've been fighting
these people since before your father was a gleam in your
grandfather's eye. Egypt has an army with a few mercenaries. The king of Hatti has a motley collection of fractious
allies. Some are headstrong, some greedy, and many un-
skilled. All are jealous of each other. Egypt, according to
the letters given me by Captain Kawab, who brought one
of the squadrons of the division P'tah by sea, has told me

that Divisions P'tah, P're, and Seth are following by one day's march, so as to keep good grazing ahead of them, what of them?"

"We have sent messengers, sire, the Pharaoh's own viziers in swift chariots to urge them to haste, one to each division, but if they are dealt with as we were, I have doubts that they will survive. We were three chariots, Lord T'Chad, and I myself was driving the chariot of Meketre, Pharaoh's senior vizier. We had two heavy three-man chariots with a driver, three horses, and two archers each as escort, to get through against all odds. But suddenly a hail of arrows cut us down and we were attacked by Scythian mercenaries. But here is the worst part: They were *riding* larger horses than any save yours, and *shooting the long composite chariot bows from horseback,* a thing never seen before!

"They rode us down and shot my master and his escort, and I escaped only by cutting a horse loose and riding him till he died at your feet, Lord T'Chad." Reaching into a tubular wooden container strapped to his waist, the boy, obviously still at the end of his tether, handed T'Chad a short scroll and then his eyes rolled back in his head. Gently, the women took him away as the men began to talk in quiet but intense tones, trying to figure out just what could be done about this mess.

One thing could be done quickly, T'Chad decided, and spoke one word: "M'Bonga." Where there had been a darkness in the circle of men, three white circles appeared, as if lit by some mystical force, as the captain of the mercenary Nubian archers opened his hooded eyes and grinned. While he and his hundred had been hired as running infantry for some of the chariots, they preferred independent action where possible, and could run as long and far as most horses. Good trackers all, they made excellent scouts. The black man stepped forward, a short feather plume nodding in his plaited hair. He held a strung recurve bow and was wearing a leopardskin kilt. A leather belt and a diagonal colored cotton shoulder strap supported a short bronze knife, a sack of possibles, and a full quiver of obsidian-headed arrows. A small pouch of food swung from a strap over his left shoulder. The Nubians prided themselves on being ready to fight or travel at all times.

"Take such of your men as you need," T'Chad said, "leaving a guard for your women, and screen out south and east toward where an ambush would be. We are going to have to be creative, and don't need surprises. Pull them in as we go by and you'll have a chance to get in on the battle. It might be a bit 'iffy,' so Scout us an escape route too—due south might be a good idea."

"Done," the Nubian said, and ghosted off on bare feet. Chad turned to one henchman and one henchwoman. Old Jobab, crippled and limping from age and wounds, could no longer handle a chariot, but he had fallen naturally into the job of camp commander and knew what was coming next. "You want us to take the dependents and go set up a base and hide?" he asked.

Lara, spokeswoman for the camp followers, wives, dancers, cooks, and laundry girls, replied, "The word is out, Chaddie, and the girls are moving."

"Right," T'Chad said. We are in the valley of Elutheros, west of the lake of Homs, and there is a wooded marshland southwest of the lake, where the Orontes flows into it. Take your column there, set up low and quiet, and don't draw attention to yourselves. Now let's see what Hawk and the 'regimental wizers,' have come up with." He turned to where his senior captains had been conferring and, from the looks on their faces, the news was not good.

Captain Kawab had the Egyptian report first, working from the papyrus message that T'Chad had given him. "The plan, according to this," he said, "was to come up from the Gaza in four groups, two on either side of the Bekaa Valley, leapfrogging so as to always hit good pasture. Apparently, with himself watching, Amun outdid itself and got into the old campground at Kadesh a day early, for once. P're should be only one march behind, but fording the Orontes takes time. P'tah and Seth are on the western side and will probably not make it into action this day. If anybody is going to bail Amun out, it is going to have to be us. The only question is, will canny old Mutwallis do something stupid? He doesn't, often."

Kawab sat down as Hawk spoke tersely. "Each Egyptian division is self-contained, five hundred chariots, five thousand infantry runners, assorted donkey and ox transportation. That's *all* Ramses has with him right now, save for a few hundred Sherden, who are about worth two other men because of their size and their iron longswords. He's also made a target of himself with that baggage train. Those carts must be simply creaking with loot—not to mention all those relatives and offspring of his. The man's already sired enough sons to officer a regiment, and they'll all be up for ransom."

Hawk squatted near the fire and looked at a potsherd upon which he had been scratching numbers with a piece of charcoal. "The host of Haiti, under Mutwallis and Hattushilish, totals a thousand all by itself. Pitassa brings another five hundred, as do the combination of the city-states of Wilusa, Mire, and Hapalla. Each chariot with supposedly two or three crew, according to type, and up to eight runners each, depending on recent casualties and desertions. You can be assured that with the amount of loot in Ramses's camp, enlistment just took a leap. Most of those johnnies don't get paid unless there's loot, you know."

He went on down the list: "Ugarit, Carchemish, Mitanni, Aleppo, Nuhashshe," until his listeners were groaning. "Worst-case scenario, thirty-seven hundred chariots, and about forty thousand assorted runners, strong-arm types, archers, slingers, and whatnot milling around them. . . . Gargh."

"That's about what we all feel," T'Chad said, "but the gods got us into this one, and maybe they'll let us out. You all know the situation. None of this would exist if the Almurrans hadn't decided to throw their lot in with Egypt after the Hittites got hardnosed about taxes and tariffs." He looked over at the Almurran captain, who was looking a bit pained, and continued. "We were working for Almurra, so we got stuck holding the bag until Ramses sent an army up here last year. In the meantime, Mutwallis has been politicking, putting a host together, and now we have to live with it. Your Almurrans have to fight for your cities, the Egyptians can't abandon Ramses, and if we fade out, we'd never get another contract. All we can do is give it our best and look for an out—And pray for P'tah and P're to get here soon. The only good sign that I see out of all this is that Mutwallis didn't attack yesterday. That just might mean that he isn't at full strength yet either.

"One thing for certain: this is going into the scrolls alongside Thutmose at Megiddo—or Sargon at Sumer, for that matter. . . . All right get them moving. You know the night drill: The horses'll need rest about moonset, and then we move slowly by starlight, after they wake again. We have to get there soon, but with animals rested and bowstrings tight."

The morning of the tenth day of the second month of the spring season of the fifth year of his reign was a bad one for the young Pharaoh of the two kingdoms of Egypt. He'd been soundly tricked by the older king of Hatti, Mutwallis II, and was anxiously awaiting the results of the messengers to his rapidly approaching divisions. He had arrayed his units as well as possible, under the circumstances, but he could see many things that could go wrong. The division named after the god Re, for instance, could have been ambushed before it got to the plain of Kadish. He looked to the south only to see, not an organized host approaching, but a few panicked stragglers driving blown teams—P're had been hit, then.

Ramses, known as the Second, after his grandfather, whose short rule had been overtaken by his father, the Great Seti, looked to his shield wall, to his archers, and to his charioteers, who were waiting beside hitched but rested teams, as the first of the fugitives came in. The men spread panic wherever they went and if he hadn't needed the news so desperately, he would have had them beheaded. Pharaoh gave quick, terse orders that all of the refugees were to be isolated and that only the highest rankers be brought to him. The order did no good.

The panic continued to spread, and the story told him by the survivors left almost no hope. The messenger sent to P're had gotten through and the division had quick-marched most of the night. They were tired and somewhat numb when they went by the woods along the little tributary named Mukadiyah, which adjoined the southern end of the hill upon which Kadesh rested, its white walls and towers gleaming in the morning sun.

With only the rumbling of chariot wheels as a warning, they had been hit by a chariot force of Hittite heavies that had cut them in two and then started chewing on the pieces. What should have been only a reconnaissance in force had not been able to resist the temptation and had streamed into the P're in a seemingly endless stream of attacking regiments. Looking at the north end of Kadesh town, above the union of the Orontes and its tributary, Ramses fancied that he could see the brightness of the sun reflecting off the gold and glitter of the vantage point of Mutwallis. How the wretched Hittite must be gloating now.

They must have been busy during the night, as they'd obviously gotten a force from behind the city of Kadesh, south around the fields, and then across both the Orontes and its little tributary. Then, and this was Ramses' only hope, they must have been surprised by an outriding Egyptian scout, and with no chance to organize, had impulsively charged straight into the middle of the marching column of P're, scattering them and driving all their troops and squadrons to the winds.

There were now swirling little dogfights going on all up and down the plain, and obviously, whatever Mutwallis had planned, this was not it. The Egyptian watchmen, mounted in specially constructed towers at the corners of the camp, now sent runners to the palace tent with its golden throne and worried ruler. "Sire, Sire," one of them shouted, "we are undone, P're is vanquished, and the Hittite van has circled and is coming at the western wall of the camp." Ramses himself jumped to a vantage point to see that the man's report was true.

Mutwallis must have intended a forceful reconnaissance, for the chariot formation was coming at a canter, but without its running infantry. A glance back at the hill of Kadesh baffled Ramses, for there was a huge force of infantry, with no hope of entering the battle, milling at the base of the mound. "Mount up, mount up," Pharaoh shouted, and at that, his own driver, who was named Menna, trotted the golden chariot up and handed Ramses the scaled blue battle crown called the Kheprish, with its flanged sides and the golden war asp at its front. Already Ramses wore his scaled, gold plated brigandine armor and his two horses, named Victory-in-Thebes and Mut-Is-Contented, were prancing in their bronze scaled armor. They were warhorses and, true to the breed, were anxious for battle. His quivers were full both with arrows and javelins. The young warrior king was ready, but his men were not.

The psychology of being outnumbered had been working on them during the night and the obvious panic of the survivors of P're had finished them off. When the Hittite van broke down the western shield wall, many of them panicked, their chariots taking off in all directions, leaving the infantry to fend for themselves. These, linking up with the Sherden mercenaries, began to try to save what of the camp they could. They set up a new shield wall across the middle of the camp and moved all the noncombatants that they could inside the smaller peremiter.

Meanwhile, the Hittites, stupefied by the amount of wealth they had discovered, got distracted and began to loot. At this time, Ramses, utterly beside himself with fury, broke through the shield wall of Egyptian infantry and Sherden, and began to loose his arrows with a cold precision. For a time, he was alone, going through quiver after quiver, seemingly protected by the gods, for no arrow touched him, although his shield bearer Menna was wounded and dropped off the chariot. Tying the reins around his waist to reassure the horses that he was still there, Ramses controlled them by voice and continued to drill Hittities while his officers finally began to rally the scattered forces of Division Amun.

By this time, the Hittite looters were beginning to stream out of the camp, some being chased by Sherden, some attacked by returning elements of the Amun Division, some trying to skulk off with captured gold or women. Ramses' generals prevailed upon him with a plan, for he had proven his bravery and, by it, given his officers a chance to rally the rest of Amun, for only those caught in the western part of the camp had exploded outside. On advice of his officers,

Ramses took the remaining segment of Amun out of the eastern gate of the camp, circled north of the rectangular field fort, and began to sweep down on the retreating Hittites, who were now driving somewhat blown horses and hauling loot.

By now, discrete elements of P're were coming in from all directions, and small parties of archers and slingers were skulking around looking for someone to kill. When the avenging hosts of Amun, with fresh horses and full quivers, began to swoop down on the Hittites from the north with a Golden Pharaoh at their head, they panicked into full retreat. At this point the battle of Kadesh was a swirling mess and it was due to get worse. Mutwallis, standing on the hill at the north end of Kadesh, had a much smaller force than history has credited him with, or he could have eaten the Egyptians alive.

His entire strength was not fully with him that day, and he had sent out only what he could afford as a reconnaissance in force. His allies had been credited with hundreds of chariots, but their entire force was not yet in place. If he had had the entire thirty-seven hundred he had been promised, there would have been no battle, only a massacre. Instead, his reconnaissance force spent itself on P're, and then got distracted by looting, and then Ramses came around on their backs. A running battle was streaming southward, back toward the original ambush site.

Now the eastern side of Ramses' camp, the richer side into which all the wealth had been compressed, was empty and unguarded save for infantry archers, and what was left of the Sherdana. Whether Mutwallis gave the order or whether the kings and princes of half the cities of Anatolia couldn't resist the urge to pillage will never be known, but suddenly the command banners of half the royalty of the Hittite empire began to leave the mound of Kadesh and charge into the Egyptian camp. When they arrived, they overwhelmed the defenders and began to loot the palace tent, capture Pharaoh's children and cousins, and were in the process of breaking up his golden campaign throne when a deep-throated war horn sounded and the mercenaries began to move in. They had been paid Pharaoh's gold and they were honest tradesmen.

The small regiment of mercenaries, city chariotry, and professionals from P'tah had agreed that T'Chad, as the most experienced leader, should command and, adapting to the natural daily pattern of the horses, had moved at a quiet march during the night, resting when the horses rested, quick-marching when the animals were ready. Now, with the sun fully up, some were munching dried meat, some unwrapping Egyptian-style fruit-nut cake from palm leaves or eating dried nuts. No one was stuffing himself, just re-stocking bodily reserves. There was dust on the horizon from several directions and the messengers began coming in.

The first was a boy of the regiment, too young as yet for combat, but light enough to ride a swift pony and use his young eyes well. He reined his trotting mount alongside the banner that marked the command chariot and shouted, "City chariotry of Sidon, Sire; their messenger's not far behind me. Their colonel asks information. My mount is still fresh."

Nice and concise, T'Chad thought, *and the boy doesn't want to get sent back when things are warming up.* "Tell him the battle has started, but to rest his horses; we'll pick him up on the way by. And send his own scouts south to pick up P'tah, when they come up along the mountains of Lebanon." With a quick wave, the boy was gone, to be replaced by a girl who rode as if she were part of the pony. Her high, clear voice could cut through battle where a man's roar would be lost. She'd been far out south and her pony was lathered and wild-eyed.

"My Lord T'Chad," she cried in anguish. "P're is broken and scattered to the winds, the Pharaoh fights alone like a wounded lion, and his chariots desert his camp."

He nodded, absorbed the news, and then said, "Get a remount—quickly—and go back, but only to the camp." And she too was gone.

One of M'Bonga's blacks trotted up almost leisurely. Placing a hand on the chariot to pull himself along, the Nubian reported in a low, almost melodious voice, "The Hatti have made the mistake we prayed for this morning. They have stopped to loot the rich camp of Amun. The young Pharaoh has come back to his senses and counterattacked to the north. Another force of the Hatti have begun to ford the river to the north of Kadesh. They look to have a lot of gold on them and carry many banners. The way south is fairly clear for an organized host." The Nubian looked questioningly at T'Chad, who suddenly grinned back. Regardless of the odds, he was going to take the chance.

"Find a chariot, one of ours, sweep up all the scouts you can find in that direction, and get me information. We are going to jump right into the middle of this." The Nubian answered the grin and sped off down the line of advancing chariotry to find a friend with whom to seek glory. The small regiment had been advancing in three columns, at a quick walk to save energy and allow the infantry to keep up. T'Chad was lead chariot in the center column, with a small cluster of the youthful riders alongside him. Now he signalled to a pair of them, a boy and a girl who normally rode together. "One of you to each column," he snapped. "They are to follow the direction of the chariot which will have a black rider."

With a sudden rattle of hooves, a chariot peeled out of line and took off slightly to the southeastward of their line of march and then the whole formation began to curve after them. For long minutes, there was no news, only the dust and smoke of battle on the horizon and the rapidly enlarging dots of swirling chariot clusters riding alongside each other and trading javelins, arrows, and sling stones. As always, T'Chad's stomach began to feel like it was full of butterflies. Then he spotted the arriving cluster of messengers.

There were several of the Nubians, some of the regiment's child messengers, and a chariot liaison from the city chariotry of Sidon, who spoke first. "You are known from of old, T'Chad of Tobrug. If you command here, we will obey. We have ninety chariots of the Hittite pattern, large horses, a driver, and two archers and also javelins."

Nodding, T'Chad turned his attention to a girl who seemed to be ready to be relieved of scout riding, before some warrior classified her as booty. "The Pharaoh does well," she said. "He drives the Hatti back through the stream, he is picking up chariots and runners of P're and increasing his strength."

Again T'Chad nodded understanding and turned to the senior of the two Nubians. "The Hatti are now across the river in force," the man said, "and are into the camp that Ramses left in the hands of the infantry of Amun and the Sharden, and are looting it. They are more than we, but are out of their chariots and digging for gold."

That was all T'Chad needed—a totally unfocused enemy force. *"Form line of battle,"* he roared as his blood began to pulse. "Battalion Jokter center, facing the camp. Chariotry of Sidon to my rear as second wave. Chariotry of Ullaza/Byblos to the right, Chariotry of P'tah to the left nearest the river. Messengers to commanders, scouts out to flanks and rear, move it. Advance on my signal."

Men, chariots, boys, and some young girls scattered to obey. All sensed that history would be made this day.

The line cantered forward, with the runners now holding on to the chariots, each to his assigned team. This way, each chariot would be able to tow enough runners into battle to protect them in close combat. They did not yet, however, charge. "Hawk," T'Chad yelled to his second in command, "What can you see of the shield line? Is it down or do we need to send someone?"

"It is down. The fools have taken it down," was the welcome answer, as they came in arrow range.

T'Chad reached down into a leather sack in his chariot and drew out a sea-triton horn, spiraled a full cubit long and knobbed around its curled length. A trumpet mouthpiece had been set in its end with melted resin, and this he put to his lips, blowing a long two-toned blast. The line stopped as if it had hit a wall and every bowman nocked an arrow. Eagerly they looked at the central chariot of the front line. "Fly the gulls," T'Chad ordered, and every bow loosed at once.

Like rising birds of prey, the bronze-headed, gull-fletched flock rose, arced, and fell on the swarming camp. Suddenly the swarming became more purposeful as men rushed to their neglected defenses. The mercenaries had been hoping

for this, because indiscriminate arrow rain would hit friend—
as many as were left—as well as foe. While the camp swirled,
the horn sounded again and the chariot line advanced. Now
arrows began to fly out of the camp and strike shields, some
sticking in the armor of both horse and man. Again the horn
sounded an order and the line turned and stopped. Now the
chariots shielded the horses and the armored archers stood
beside their drivers and launched bolt after bronze bolt into
the ranks facing them—Ranks that wore much gold and carried banners of command.

"By the gods of ancient Sumer," Hawke shouted. "By the
beard of Sargon, that's nobility in there, looting Pharaoh's
camp. The buggers came out to get the best themselves. Kill
off or capture this lot and we've *got* them."

Old P'tah be praised, you are right," T'Chad shouted back
as he emptied his first quiver. "They're fading. *Mount wheel!
Charge!* Again the battle triton sounded, now a rippling note
as T'Chad tongued the mouthpiece, and with the infantry
clinging desperately, the teams were whipped up to full
charge. A man couldn't take this for long, but long wasn't
needed. T'Chad had gauged his distance accurately. The
dash was only a hundred yards and they were in the thick of
it. Company Joktar hit the camp like a hooved and wheeled
tornado, iron wheels and axles breaking those of wood and
bronze. Long iron swords broke the short bronze sickle
swords of the age, and the slingers went joyfully to work.

Long ago, the runners had learned to work with the chariots and, while infantry battles seethed around the embattled
chariots, the archers, protected from clubs and blades, shot
their enemies down by the score, by the drove, and then by
the hundred. T'Chad, temporarily clear of assailants,
watched almost casually as his slingers worked. Dropping a
lead missile, which had been cast with a hieroglyphic insult,
into a pouch, a slinger who had been born a thousand miles
away on a Balearic island whipped his thong up, over, and
down. The missile entered a man's breast and the flesh
closed over it. Then a spear whizzed past the slinger, and
T'Chad lifted his arm and drove a short javelin into the
assailant.

The slinger shifted to close-combat mode. Drawing a large

stone from his ammunition pouch, he knotted his thongs
and drew a short obsidian dagger. A Hittite ally approached
in a crouch, shield forward, curved sword held low for an
underhand slash. The slinger feinted with his dagger, drawing the sword out of line. Then the almost unnoticed sling
arced up under the high-held shield and caught the swordsman's testicles. The man doubled up and the sling, really
picking up speed now, arced up, over, and down, halfway
into the man's skull. The slinger ripped a golden armlet off
his late adversary, slipped it on his own arm beside several
others, and went carefully about searching for more prey.
The mercenary, as always, was his own paymaster.

Yet these troops were disciplined, long ago having learned
the value of teamwork. Behind the chariots came a group
of lighter infantry whose job was collecting arrows and javelins from friend and foe alike. Most of these were apprentice
warriors, sons of the regiment, just learning their grizly
trade. Hittites were now streaming from the camp. Some
were trying for the nearer, western end, but the city chariotry of Ullaza, backed up now by more and more assembling
Egyptians from Amon and P're, had set up their own shield
wall and had blocked that exit. Chariots and spearmen were
escaping to the east, into Pharoah's path as he swept up
from the south.

The mercs and the chariotry of Sidon were fighting in
close combat mode now, line abreast, with the heavy, shield-
carrying swordsmen almost shoulder to shoulder ahead of
the horses. Above the infantry's shields and helmets, a rain
of arrows and javelins flew into the now wild-eyed retreating
Hittites. Gold and plunder forgotten, all these greedy lord-
lings wanted was escape.

A feminine shriek from the remains of the throne tent
drew T'Chad's attention, and slashing the cloth with his
sword, he dismounted and stepped in. Rescuing one of
Ramses' sometimes delectable young female relatives could
bring its own reward.

That, however, was already in hand. A Hittite had been
hacking the golden latticework from the throne and a linen-
clad woman of some rank had taken it upon herself to brain
him with some ceremonial instrument. The armored man

had simply shrugged off the blow and swept her up, just as Hawk came in the other side of the palatial framed tent. He'd left his chariot and driver to keep watch outside—and do a bit of looting.

The Egyptian girl, young, raven-haired, and quite pretty, was now crouching on the floor, looking up from between the legs of the man who was trading thrusts for cuts with her erstwhile captor. In a very few seconds, the duel was over and Hawk was lifting the girl to her feet.

She'd been won in battle and after one quick appraising look, Hawk said, "I am mercenary, second commander to T'Chad of Tobrug, in the employ of the Pharaoh. This ape here, his chariot, and his possessions are now my plunder by right; guard it for me until I return, in the name of Pharaoh." Then he cocked his head for another look. "If you are not noble, or owned by a noble, you also are plunder." She gave him an arch look and said, "Charioteer, I am noble, and of the family of Ramses, but I may still be plunder—and I will guard your property in my uncle's house until you return for us."

At that point, chuckling at the Hawks' pretty predicament, T'Chad got out of there and back to business. By now, the camp was clear and there was a perfect cauldron by the river as one Hittite lordling after another was ridden down and made to surrender to Pharaoh or his minions. In the far southern distance, gallopers from the advancing Egyptian divisions were appearing, and across the river, more gallopers from the assembling Hittite reinforcements were arriving at Mutwallis's camp. Tomorrow, he mused, might be the worst one he'd seen yet, but he'd found a bit of glory today, by the light of the gods.

Sunlight reflected off gold and caught his eye as two of the finest horses he'd ever seen pulled abreast of him, pulling a golden chariot driven by a wounded, bandaged driver, and that carried a haggard figure in a blue war crown, a man whose eyes held many more years than the last time they'd met. Past the chariot of the Pharaoh of upper and lower Egypt sped another vehicle, but T'Chad's suddenly misty eyes couldn't focus on it.

"Hail, friend of my father," came a clear, imperious baritone. "When I was a child, you fought with us against the Libyans, and my father offered you power and position, do you remember?" The ghost of a smile tipped the corners of the royal lips.

"Aye, Lord, do I remember, but I was young, and a whole world beckoned."

Pharaoh nodded, the grin widening. "And now you have again earned Egypt's gratitude these twenty years later and are a bit wiser, and I would sit and hear your tales of far lands and sea voyages and chariot duels with the knights of Mohenjo-Daro. Will you accept the nobility of Egypt as your Captain Hawk has?"

T'Chad's eyes now swept in Pharaoh's wing rider and saw the Hawk with a bemused expression on his face, driving a Hittite lordling's chariot with an Egyptian princess in his arms and golden plunder at his feet. One does not lightly turn down the offer of a god-king named Ramses. "Aye, Lord of Egypt, Nubia, Syria, Canaan, and Libya, I will accept thy offer."

Thus ended the battle of Kadesh, and the mercenaries did indeed go into the history scrolls and onto the tomb carvings of Ramses the Great. They were the mysterious Ne'arim, the first mention of mercenary soldiers in all of history, and saviors of the first battle in all of history for which we have a complete record. Their exploits have been graven in stone by a living god, but neither they nor their Pharaoh were to know that their age was ending. They had won their place in the history of a cycle that was nearly completed. Their time is close to the time of legends. Mycenae, Mohenjo-Daro, Hatti, dynastic Egypt, all would disintegrate into a time of chaos when the explosion of an island named Thera in the Aegean Sea disrupted their trade and let loose the barbarian raiders, whose depredations brought on a dark age from which would rise Persia, classic Greece, another, weaker, dynastic Egypt, and finally Rome and our own times.

Our new, iron-using civilization, like the age of bronze before us, has been muscle-powered, whether by man or animal, for the majority of its history. The soldiers of

Ramses and Mutwallis would have fit comfortably, with no retraining necessary, into the armies of Alexandar, Hannibal, Caesar, and most of the early Dark Ages. Even the armored knight was presaged by the armored chariot over two thousand years earlier.

By the end of the period we define as the Middle Ages, knowledge was again on the march, and this time there were two developments that would change the course of history. The first, gunpowder, was a predictable outgrowth of advancing technology, and was essentially a development of Greek fire and imported Oriental formulas.

The second is a still-unmastered tool, which is yet causing international disruption when used by unscrupulous people. With the invention of the printing press, for the first time in human history, ancient, arcane knowledge was let loose on the whole population and there was hell to pay. For with knowledge came also the social engineer, who claims to know better than the populace what is good for them. From the ancient theories of philosophers who had never gone to war, never built a home, never forged either a tool or a weapon, or conned a trading ship across treacherous seas, came the inane political dogma that today drives men to war—for the good of all mankind, of course. From unwashed prophets and seers, not honest tradesmen, came religions that drive otherwise honorable men to war, and now threaten Armageddon. In this book lies the record of the struggle that threatens, yet again, to inflame the world. And this time it will be with weapons that even the gods are afraid to use.

REFERENCE SOURCES

The Barbarians of Asia, Stuart Legg, Dorsett Press.

The End of the Bronze Age, Robert Drews, Princeton University Press.

Qadesh, Mark Healy, Osprey Books.

The Hittites, J. G. Macqueen, Thames & Hudson.

"Ambush at Kadesh," Robert C. Sahr, *Military History,* August 1994.

The Military Horse, Sue Simmons, Roydon Publishing.

Strong's Exhaustive Concordance of the Bible, James Strong,
   Riverside Book and Bible House.
The Companion Bible, Kregel Publications.
Egypt, Land of the Pharaohs, Time-Life Books.
The Art of Warfare in Biblical Lands, Yigal Yadin, McGraw-
   Hill.
National Geographic magazine, March 1977, December
   1982, December 1987, June 1988, April 1991, and Janu-
   ary 1997.

CHAPTER 3

The Armored Knight

WAR SEEMS TO BE THE MAIN BUSINESS OF HUMANITY, AND TO quote Mark Twain, "No single piece of real estate on this globe remains in the hands of its original inhabitants." There are many areas on the globe that, like Canaan and the Gaza Strip, seem to be fated to be host to perpetual war. The North of France along the course of the Somme River is one of these. Saxons, Celts, Romans, Franks, Norsemen, Normans, French, Germans, English, and lately, Americans have all shed blood on those low, rolling chalk hills that are seemingly made for war.

When the Roman Empire began to falter in the late third century A.D., its influence slowly left the provinces. In the wake of that withdrawal came chaos. Roman Britain was left to fend for itself; then Iberia, then Gaul, then the German provinces, and finally Rome itself felt the barbarian hammer. But with the invasion of the barbarians from the east came one gift. Attila may have brought devastation, but he also brought the stirrup, the final link in the equipage of the armored knight of the Middle Ages.

During what we call the Dark Ages, from the end of Old Rome to about the end of the first millennium, tiny, dark,

proto-Christian Europe was oppressed. Hammered by
Norsemen from the seas, even London and Paris were besieged. From the southeast, Musselmen barked at the gates
of Constantinople and tore Byzantium from its age of su-
premacy. Across the vast grass seas of the steppes, wave
after wave of nomad horsemen swarmed across what was
left of the old Roman Slavic provinces and into Europe.
Even the Mediterranean Sea was no safe barrier, for Moorish invaders, Mohammedanized descendants of the Vandals,
crossed the Strait of Gibralter and conquered the Iberian
Peninsula. Eventually Spain would be born there, but not
yet. The wave of Islam rolled up the highlands of Castille,
across the lands of the Basques, and was finally staggered
to a halt by Charles Martel and his grandson Charlemagne
in the south of what is now France, in the late eighth century. In 732, Charles "the Hammer," Martel brought the
Moors to a bloody halt, and in 777, Charlemagne set up the
Spanish Marches as a barrior between Islam and
Christianity.

For a time, France stood alone against all the invaders of
Europe. For those dark years, all that would be Western
civilization rested on the shoulders of the armored knights
of ancient Gaul. With Vikings in her rivers, Huns coming
out of the Teutonic forests, Moorish horsemen cantering
through the Pyrenees, and no hope of help from England,
which was not yet born, France needed what we now call a
"technological breakthrough."

The destitute, half bandit, half warrior of the Dark Ages
was a far cry from the feudal noble as he shivered in his
log house, behind a log palisade and tried to figure out how
to keep the Norsemen from running off with the crops that
his few followers had grown. Eventually, though, the technological breakthrough came, in the form of stirrups, lances,
chain mail armor, and larger horses.

While light skirmishing cavalry and mounted archers had
swayed the course of nations, the heavily armored mounted
man had never been the dominant factor in ancient battles
for one reason. The more weight one puts on top of a horse,
the easier it is to fall off, unless one has a saddle and stirrups. That it was done is known, for the Parthians, ancestors

of present Iranians, wore scale armor as early as 400 B.C. and even armored their horses. Thousands of years earlier, even chariot horses were armored. An armored man on an armored horse is a historical fact. The inference that must automatically be made is that horses existed that were big enough to carry the load.

When succeeding waves of Eastern horsemen swept through an area already contested by Rome and the Parthians for control of the trade routes with China, they brought with them the stirrup, and probably larger horses. Unfortunately, civilization was regressing just then, due to corruption and a welfare state on the Italian peninsula. With Rome weakened both internally and externally, yet another wave of conquerors swept through the Middle East and out onto the world stage. Islam was here to stay and to sway half the world.

Now the stage was set for a contest between armor and missile, between infantry archer and armored knight, and between the archer and the swordsman. When the Crusades pitted them against each other, lessons were learned that bear heeding to this day. In close quarters, the heavy slugger, the armored axeman on a great warhorse, will best the light archer. In open going, he can't even get within cursing distance of the scimitar-wielding warrior and has to suffer clouds of arrows and insults. There the matter rested for several hundred years, while each side developed its various versions of civilization. More and more, Islam turned inward on itself while Europe began to face outward to the world. And all the time, a set of nasty shocks were being prepared for the now all-powerful armored knight.

In the year 1066, England was so weak and so corrupt that an adventurer who would come be known as William the Conqueror gathered up a few fellow noble bandits and, almost by invitation, displaced King Harold and began what is now known as the Norman Conquest. Unwittingly, he also displaced several thousand Anglo-Saxon noblemen who, driven to desperation, took up their ancient weapon, the longbow, originally of Welsh origin. The exploits of Robin of Locksley may be legend, but the archers who went back to France several hundred years later are one of the pivot points of history. Here, finally, for the first time in all history, was a weapon that one man could afford, and could build with his own hands, that would smash the armored aristo-crat, or any other foe, from his saddle. Heretofore, expen-sive, all-powerful weaponry had kept the common man in his place. He had worked for an armed aristocracy, and his land, produce, even his women had been subject to the weaponmaster. With a few exceptions, such as democratic Greece and republican Rome, this had been the pattern of history—Even if Greco-Roman culture did rest on a slave base. For this reason, the great bow as a weapon deserves a closer look. Even today, an archer can find a place on the field of battle. No quieter method of removing sentries exists and a flaming arrow can put fire where you need it. In a straw roof, for instance. The longbow is the leveler, the com-mon man's revenge, for its secret is that it can be made by anyone with a few tools.

The weapon that took down Sumer and earlier civiliza-tions was the compound bow, made of wood, horn, and sinew, created by a master craftsman and taking sometimes as many as five to ten years to age in the craftsman's shop while its various glues set and the varnish cured. This was the weapon first of the chariot warrior, then of the horse archer of the steppes. This was the weapon that would be the proudest possession of that warrior and that would allow him to dominate the open plains, even against the armored knight. It was, however, expensive, thus limiting the num-bers of effective warriors to the number of bows the few craftsmen could produce.

The longbow, however, required only access to a yew tree, and the knowledge that yew is unique among woods. The outer sapwood pulls and resists tension, the inner heartwood pushes and resists compression, exactly like the laminated parts of the compound bow. Once this is known, and the bow stave is cut, the wood need only be cured for three years in a loft, or, in an emergency, first under running water and then over a slow fire, and a bow can be made. The weight, or draw, of the bow is limited only by the strength of the archer, and draws as heavy as 170 pounds have been recorded. Howard Hill, who did the archery for the original

Robin Hood movie, used a 140-pound laminated bamboo longbow and took all five of the big game animals of Africa with it. With just one improvement, this was the weapon that would change history.

The broad hunting arrow point was perfect for slicing holes in flesh, but it couldn't pierce chain mail. A bodkin dagger, however, could. The word *bodkin* is simply Old English for "needle," and a hardened needle point became the bodkin arrow. A blacksmith would forge a few dozen of these needle points, six inches long by a little over half an inch across the base and triangular in cross section, with a hollow for the arrow shaft. Then he would pack them in charcoal and burnt leather in a small iron box and set that under the burning charcoal in his forge. For several weeks, the arrowheads would lie in the heat as he worked, absorbing carbon in their outer layers and becoming much harder than the mild wrought iron from which the chain mail, or even plate armor, was made.

The longbow and the case-hardened bodkin point were two parts of a weapon, but there was a third part that has lain hidden by history, until the British commandos began to give survival lessons and the last secret of the yew tree emerged. The leaves, berry coverings, and the sap, especially in spring, contain taxine, a deadly nerve poison, known as far back as Celtic times. While this is not mentioned in formal histories, it would be strange indeed if the archers of Old England had forgotten this bit of Celtic lore.

Now the weapon system was complete, and the stage was set for the confrontation between the armor of the French knight, which had grown steadily heavier, and the longbow, which, in another of history's cycles, was about to bring infantry to the fore, as in Greek and Roman times. Just as the Normans had adventured into England to carve out a domain, so the English kings periodically adventured into France, seeking territory and plunder. By the middle of the fourteenth century, the nobility of England and Europe had grown so set in their ways that the aristocratic warlords had ceased to be able to learn unless their lessons were written in blood. . . . This was now about to happen. Crécy, Poitiers, Agincourt, the names still ring down the centuries.

When English King Edward III invaded France in 1346, he faced an overwhelming superiority of numbers in the form of French chivalry, who unfortunately for them, knew only one way of war: Line up and charge, get into a melee, and earn as much "glory" as possible by getting bragging rights on conquered adversaries. The French, whose plan of battle had been case-hardened by three hundred years of success, had absolutely no concept of the role of infantry, except to serve the needs of the knights. Against them were pitted archers who had been practicing since childhood and who had been killing Scotsmen for most of their lives. The longbowmen of England could easily be called the first modern professional infantrymen, and they did murder at Crécy.

What Edward III did was this: He tempted and harried and insulted the French until they charged straight into a prepared position full of professional archers. Worse, they charged in piecemeal fashion, against the orders of their King Philip VI and his knight-marshal, John of Valois.

The English had set up their supposedly defensive position across a road between the little villages of Crécy and Wadicourt in the traditional three medieval "battles" or units of about regimental strength. Edward had dismounted most of his men-at-arms (knights and mounted auxiliaries) and set them to protect his archers. He had set two battles forward and kept the third, smallest one in the rear as a reserve. His little army totaled just 11,000 men. Against this force, almost 60,000 Frenchmen were coming, mostly armored knights on horseback. Theoretically, he was already dead. In the forefront of the right-hand English "battle" was a seventeen-year-old boy, Edward, who would later be known as the Black Prince of Wales. At that time he was under the tutelage of older knights who had been on crusade and were exposed to the more mobile eastern form of war. Just then, though, they were facing the medieval military mastodon, the plate-armored knight of France, over 300 pounds of man, armor, and weapons, strutting on a barded 2,000-pound horse.

It would have been a glorious sight, knights by the thousands, each in full armor on a snorting charger, itself a formidable engine of war, carrying its own armor. Each lance carried a knightly pennon and each shield carried the coat of arms of a chivalrous house, grown rich with hundreds of years of successful plunder in foreign lands—and neighborly disputes and extortions from local merchants. King Philip looked over the English formation from a vantage point, saw something unfamiliar, and wisely gave orders to wait and attack the next morning, after he'd had time to analyze this novel line of archers.

His knightly warriors, however, thought differently. On receiving the orders, they noted that the troops behind them were still moving, and decided that they were being deprived of the honor of opening the fight. They pressed on toward the quiet English line, gradually speeding up and focusing their attention on the dismounted knights and their grounded lances. The line of archers were infantry and beneath contempt. The first shots were loosed by Genoese mercenary crossbowmen and did some damage to the English. The Genoese, however, were tired from marching all day and weren't really fit for battle. They were simply driven into position and made to loose their bolts at the stationary English line.

Suddenly a war horn sounded and from one part of the English line a flock of goose-feathered, cloth-yard (36 inch) arrows lofted in a cloud that is said to have blocked the light of the sun where it passed. A contemporary historian said that the cloth-yard arrows fell like snow. While the crossbowmen were cumberously winding up their weapons for the next volley, they were slaughtered by the hundreds, and fled the field of battle carrying their wounded. This behavior so enraged the flower of chivalry that some of the knights actually charged in among the crossbowmen and began killing them . . . for cowardice? And all this time the English arrows were falling on both knights and crossbowmen.

Finally, after much arguing and pushing about for the most honorable positions, the knights began to charge (at about 10 to 15 miles per hour) in disconnected groups, right into the sleet of arrows. They barely reached the archers, and in no instance did the English line move a foot backward. History was written in blood and steel that day, as the solid line of infantry cut down the armored knights with a wooden weapon—and an armor-piercing bodkin point that may have carried the ancient Celtic arrow poison. The English had put themselves where they *must* be attacked, like a thorn must be removed from sensitive anatomy, and then picked their own killing zone.

Ten years later, at Poitiers, in the west of France, it happened again. Another French king, John this time, with a son named Philip, came against a vastly inferior English force commanded by Edward, the Black Prince of Wales, who was now twenty-seven years old and had become a general in his own right. He knew a bit about maneuver warfare and used some of his noble cavalry to bait the French into a killing zone in front of massed archers. King John now determined that if dismounted men could hold the flanks at Crécy, then there must be something good about the technique. Dismounting all but three hundred of his knights, he sent them on foot behind the rest into the English position.

The result was that the French king and his son attacked directly into an "offensive defense" position and were shot to rags by the archers yet again, then hit in the flank by a small unit under the Captal de Buch, one of Edward's trusted subordinates. At this point, their army began to come unglued and the king and his son were forced to surrender and ransom themselves. At this point, the French simply gave up, shut themselves up in their castles to regroup, and left the English free to harry the countryside. They also left the field of battle to the newly emerging breed of professional soldier.

Slowly, the art of war began to change as men like Charles V of France and his high marshal, Bertraud Du Gesclin, fought a series of running skirmishes and put maneuver back into a type of warfare that had devolved into three centuries of head-to-head contests. Gradually they wore the English down to the point where their noble "leaders" could again come out of their castles for one last try, at Agincourt, north of the Somme, south of the town of Dunkirk, west of a little town named Flers, and northwest of a place called Villers-Bretonneux—where, in about 500 years, tank would fight tank in two world wars.

Less than an hour's drive from the D-Day beaches, English King Henry V landed a small army of about 10,000 men on the morning of 14 August 1415. His landing site was the open beach, about three miles west of the town of Harfleur, near the mouth of the Seine. At that time in history, the French and British had been at war for a hundred years and England had dominion over part of the north of France centered on the port of Calais. Henry's objective seems to have been to win back some of the continental possessions that had been retrieved by the French in the past thirty years.

After taking until late September to reduce the fortress town of Harfleur, Henry had lost his summer campaigning season, but seemed to want to have one final battle, just for the record. His plan of march was to have taken him from Harfleur to Calais, but the few usable fords across the Somme River were held by an ever-growing group of French knights, who were spoiling for a fight. Finally, by pulling off a fast forced march, he got ahead of them and crossed the Somme, heading north for Calais. In so doing, he marched across the plain of Santerre, where on 18 August 1918, the first large-scale tank action would take place.

Henry's mostly infantry army was heading for safety at about 18 miles per day, but on 25 October 1415, his little force, now worn down to about 6,000 men, mostly archers, found, according to record, 25,000 Frenchmen, mostly armored knights, across the road to Calais, and were forced to give battle just east of the little town and castle of Agincourt. Six thousand men, of whom 5,000 were foot archers, against more than four times their number of mounted armored knights—how could they have even dreamed of surviving, let along triumphing?

At Agincourt, Henry faced a French nobility reborn but "having forgotten nothing and remembered nothing." King Henry was one of the few medieval tacticians (strategy in the Roman or modern definition would have to wait a century) who could maneuver rapidly and who used light mobile forces. His marching infantry could cover 17 to 20 miles per day, and he once covered 320 miles in 18 days, which was unheard of in those times, as it implies that, in a day where maps were a novelty, he had scouts out and knew where he was going. With that tiny, almost pathetic force, he determined to face the high marshal of France and all his newly emboldened knights. The man must have had something up his sleeve in order to try something that crazy—or are the numbers off? There are valid suspicions about the accuracy of medieval records.

Fortunately, for Henry, the French were their own worst enemy. They had somehow developed the mind-set that there was something more honorable about dismounting their cavalry and chose to fight on foot. . . . That is the traditional view. This writer suspects that they didn't want to lose expensive horses or get shot off of them wearing upward of 60 pounds of armor. If there really were coats of taxine on those arrows, almost nothing would survive the impact—and the casualties were all out of proportion to the numbers involved. The English king is quoted by William Shakespeare as saying, "And gentlemen in England now abed shall think themselves accursed they were not here. And hold their manhoods cheap whiles any speaks that fought with us on St Crispin's day." If that statement and the odds of 6000 against 25,000 are accurate, King Henry had a military ace of some kind up his mailed sleeve.

Henry chose his position well, along a road and between two woods that channeled any French attack right across freshly plowed, rain-soaked fields, which would have slowed charging horses, let alone dismounted men carrying broadswords and heavy mail and breastplates. First, the archers cut long poles from the woods and drove them into the ground at an angle, forming a barricade known as an abatis. Then they waited for the French assault, which didn't come. The French were still waiting, apparently trying to figure out what they were supposed to be doing without their horses.

The French leadership at this time is a bit difficult to define. Earlier in the century, Charles V and Du Gesclin had used hired knights and mercenaries to wear down the English. Now, however, Charles VI, also known as "The Silly" due to his unfortunate tendency to come mentally unglued at important times, was the king. The French body of knights, in no way to be distinguished by the word *army*, was nominally commanded by Constable D'Albret and the Dauphin, who would later become Charles VII. In actuality, the unruly mob of ironhats was on automatic pilot. D'Albret was so harried by the varying suggestions and orders of the noble dinosaurs that he cannot really be held responsible for what happened.

Finally, by pulling up his defensive stakes and moving forward to longbow range, about 300 yards, Henry got the French to charge on foot, up to their ankles in mud. The still-mounted cavalry wings of the French force got to him first, of course, and died first. Their horses couldn't charge into sharpened stakes embedded in the ground and the bowmen stood behind the stakes and shot them out of the saddle and killed their horses. The cavalry never broke the English line, and when they broke and retreated, they charged right through their own line of dismounted knights, who were charging on foot into that murderous sleet of bodkin points.

Almost completely exhausted, the attacking knights fell in among the unarmored archers and a vicious hand-to-hand battle followed, with the archers pounding on knightly armor with the mallets used to drive in their abatis stakes. Some of them were so exhausted that they were beaten to death with mallets or stabbed through the chinks in their armor— or were they dying of arrow poison?

The heaps of armored corpses were taller than a man's height, according to eyewitness accounts, and suddenly the French knights became so frightened of *something* that they surrendered—in some cases up to ten times each, eagerly seeking out some Englishman with authority to accept them, just to avoid being shot at. The next morning, under the supervision of the Bishop of Arras, the local peasantry began the enormous task of burying 6,000 armored knights. Henry V had brought only 5,000 archers to that battle, and if the normal four-to-one wounded-to-dead ratio prevailed, the army that King Charles VI of France brought to that battle suffered over 50 percent casualties.

So ended the reign of the mounted knight . . . for a while.

The English didn't have things all their way, though. What Agincourt forced on the French was a close look at reality. The Dauphin, Charles VII, had finally learned to his sorrow

that the brain of the armored knight was just as impenetrable as the armor of his helmet. As a result, French military
thinking, already altered by Bertrand Du Gesclin's mobile
tactics and semiprofessional soldiery, began to evolve away
from the glory of the knight and toward modern warfare.
The mind-set that caused this action was the French attitude
toward their villeins. They were not about to create a French
equivalent to the independent longbowmen. Charles VII
simply wanted an army that would fight efficiently, and set
about the task in a logical manner.

First, at the instigation of his mistress, Agnes Sorely, he
hired professional soldiers—men whom he could trust to
obey orders and not go stupidly hunting "glory" into a rain
of missiles. Next he began to develop his own answer to the
longbow, the culverin.

As is known, the cannons of the time were crude, stone-
throwing bombards of use against fortifications but hardly
suitable for mobile warfare. The tubes were rough castings,
or worse, built-up guns of iron bars with shrunk-on hoops.
What was needed was a strongly cast gun with a bore that
would seal behind the cannonball to create pressure for
long-distance accurate shooting. France already had a decent
metalworking industry and King Charles put his foundrymen
and metalworkers to work on developing a better, more accurate bore. The mechanicians succeeded beyond all his expectations, and this is the true beginning of the industrial
age. By trueing the beds of their old lathes and making their
bearings out of metal instead of wood, they finally got their
accuracy within .001 of an inch—And the Machine Age
was born.

Never before in history had mankind actually needed a
long, straight hole machined to perfect dimensions. The
French cannon-boring lathe led directly to modern machinery. Not only were light, field-mobile cannons made possible,
the smooth sealing bore made steam engines and ultimately
our internal combustion engines possible. The trail leads
smoothly from the need for a gun to outrange the longbow
to the auto in your driveway, or the engine and the cannon
in a tank. At Formigny on 15 April 1450, the English were
defeated, for now the cannons outranged the bow. By that

date, the culverin was a wheeled, aimable weapon with an elevating screw.

According to author Sir Charles Oman, the English under Sir Thomas Kryiel and Sir Matthew Grough had arrived near the town of Formigny, near modern Caen, after taking Valognes and forging across the fords of the Vire and Douve Rivers. Their force consisted of about 4,500 men, of whom half were archers and the rest the billmen who protected the archers in hand-to-hand work. Against these came the Count of Clermont with 600 "lances." A medieval lance was the unit of armed men under the command of one knight. That might be the knight, an armed squire, a few hired men, and maybe a page. The little cluster could run from five to ten men, and in this case the total force was about 3,000—and a pair of new mobile culverins of 20-pound rating, or about 4-inch bore diameter.

The English, who were bound for Caen, should by all rights have taken the offensive immediately, but by now the "defensive offense" was set in concrete. . . . This is what General Heinz Guderian, hundreds of years later, would call "military decadence." They set up in a curving formation with a small stream at their backs and orchards on their flanks. Three groups of archers, each of 700, were the main force, and on each flank were stationed a "battle" of billmen with their ferocious hooked poleaxes. The French had finally learned and only skirmished with the English while their master of ordnance, Giraud, worked his little cannons into place on either side of the English formation.

The English were then neatly enfiladed by what may have been the first accurate cannons in history. From outside the range of the longbow came 20-pound cannonballs that tore great gaps down the length of the English line. Even a grounded and rolling cannonball will rip a man's foot off. While no formal account specifies its use, case shot, bags of harquebus balls in leather bags, had already been invented. The English couldn't take the barrage and suddenly one of the groups of archers charged out and tried to take the cannon that was murdering them. Though they reached one of the guns, they were attacked by a group of dismounted French knights. In the resulting melee, the archers couldn't

work effectively. Worse, while all this was going on, the
other cannon, protected by another French "battle," continued to rip holes in the English formation.

Then there came the hammering of hooves as the counts
of Richemond and Laval arrived with another 1,200 men at
arms. When this attack hit the now madly fighting infantrymen, Lord Gough immediately cut his way out with his
knights, abandoned his friends, and eventually reached Bay-
eux. Kryiel, now surrounded, was literally annihilated. Possibly a few hundred archers escaped, and Sir Kryiel was
captured and forced to pay ransom. The next morning, the
heralds, whose duty it was to keep track of such things,
counted nearly 4,000 English corpses on the battlefield.

This battle, though small and insignificant, was one of history's hidden pivots, for here was the first time that the
cannoneers broke a small army. Not only had the cannon
broken the archer, it would finish destroying the armored
knight and even, at Marignano in 1515, would finally blast
the Swiss phalanx from the field of battle. Here was the
beginning of the evolution that would eventually lead to a
commander who could say, "It is with artillery that one
makes war"—Napoléon Bonaparte.

REFERENCE SOURCES

The Profession of Arms, General Sir John Hackett,
   Macmillan.
The Art of War, C. W. Oman, Cornell University Press.
The Face of Battle, John Keegan, Military Heritage Press.
War Through the Ages, Lynn Montrose, Harper & Brothers.
Henry V, William Shakespeare.
Military History, Cowley and Parker, Houghton Mifflin.
Technology and War, Martin Van Crevald, Free Press.

CHAPTER 4

The War Wagons, Early 1400s
JAN ZISKA AND THE HUSSITES

IN THE EARLY FIFTEENTH CENTURY, THE BLOSSOM OF EUROpean knighthood was being pressed like a flower in a book.
In the west, at places like Crécy, Poitiers, and Agincourt,
the English longbow had plucked knights from the saddle.
South of France and Germany, the Swiss had rediscovered
the Greco-Roman phalanx, and used it so successfully that
they regularly charged formations of knights—On foot.
These, of course, are the historically known reasons for the
demise of classic chivalry, but there was a third, Eastern
threat: the cannon-armed war wagons of Jan Ziska.

In Bohemia, five hundred years before its time, there existed a force of cannon-firing armored wagons, drawn by
captured, armored warhorses and crewed by a fighting elite.
The war was religious in nature and had been going on since
1420. Once started, it drew the knights of Europe like moths
to a candle flame, with about the same results.

Most knights fought for glory or the hand of a maid. The
problems were that wealthy merchants were almost insuperable competition for the ladies and, due to changes in military methodology, the price of glory was all too often death.
Each year, though, the knights of Christendom would take

ship or trail and flock to the lands of Eastern Europe, to
fight alongside the Knights Templar. Their "glory" was the
sacking of the still-pagan villages of what would become
Russia and Poland.

When the Bohemians converted to Eastern Orthodoxy,
they were still considered fair game and the Templars kept
the pressure on. Finally, the order was disbanded by the
Pope, but still the German knights fought their wars of
expansion. Then came a time when three Popes contested
for the Holy See and Roman Catholicism became the most
corrupt religion in history. In Bohemia, a hundred years
before Martin Luther, Jan Hus rebelled and began to preach
a return to the simpler religion of Jesus and the disciples.
He renounced indulgences, purgatory, and some of the more
onerous practices of the Church, such as monastic celibacy.
After some years, he gained quite a following, even among
the nobility.

Once the Catholic Church got its difficulties worked out
however, the Pope and the Holy Roman Emperor, Sigismund, decided to do something about this puritanical up-
start. Jan Hus was given a safe passage to a neutral city in
Switzerland, given a chance to promote his beliefs to the
prelates, and summarily burned at the stake. After due consideration, the Pope also declared a crusade against the Hussites. This, of course, started a vicious little religious war
and knights flocked in from all over Christendom. Unfortunately for the crusaders, the Hussites had found a champion,
an aging petty noble named Jan Ziska, who'd been to the
wars and had a few ideas of how to destroy armored cavalrymen. It took him a few years to perfect his wagon system,
but when he got the bugs out, it was a murder machine.
And not least because it was independant of the countryside
and could feed itself.

While the knights were the fighting jaws of the military
animal, its belly and tail were as necessary to the beast as
its teeth. Like modern fighting machines, the armored knight
needed supplies: meat for the men, and oats and grass for
their mounts. While the elegant knights took their ease or
practiced with their weapons, swarms of armed foragers
stripped the peasant-farmers of their year's crops. It is only

in legend that medieval chivalry did not make war on the civil population. In actuality, they stripped the food from the land like a plague of tin-plated locusts and left the people to starve through the winter on their leavings. The only thing left to the peasants after the passage of a feudal host were well-fertilized fields and pregnant daughters.

It is also only in legend that knightly hosts exceeded 30,000, let alone the 300,000 knights and men-at-arms accorded to some gatherings. The land available simply wouldn't support such numbers. Proof of this exists in reports from the College of Heralds at the time. When a participant of the host that invaded Bohemia in 1421 claimed to be a member of an army 100,000 strong, a letter from one of the heralds estimated "4,000 knights and serving men." In 1426, when Sigismund called for an army of 6,000 "lances," his princes told him that such an army could not be assembeled in Germany, nor fed in Bohemia.

Jan Ziska had reinvented another military necessity, the combat ration. Half his people at any given time were home growing food for his army, while his opponents had to live off the land. Thus he could campaign at will, even in winter, while the crusaders had to go home to regroup. The medieval powers that be never did figure this one out, and it was not until the time of Gustavus Adolphus that the practice became standard.

The valley was long and dotted with little villages. Green hills rose from its sides and here and there, the first tinges of fall were beginning to dot the forest. At the western end of the valley, where a dirt road rose to meet the hills, a host had gathered. Knights from England, France, Italy, and Germany were assembling for their annual go at the heretic Slavs of Eastern Europe. The gently sloping land was a forest of gaily colored tents and pavilions, each marked by a fluttering banner with the heraldic device of the knight over whose tent it flew.

Three knights sat at a trestle table in front of a red and gold tent. Over the tent flew the hound and hartshorn emblem of the House of Somerau, whose battered old chieftan, Baron Karl von Somerau, had come to the wars. Von Somerau was a largish man with dead gray eyes and close-cropped gray hair. His hands were large and corded and worked slowly as he talked. As host, he sat with his back to the tent, facing his two friends, Sir Martenot de Chavennes, a French knight banneret, and Sir Roland of Highwood, an Englishman and the youngest of the three.

"What does anyone know of this knave Ziska?" Martenot was asking. "He seems to have burst on the scene out of nowhere." Martenot was of medium build, dapperly handsome, and wore a thin mustache. He directed his question at both his companions. While the German's methodical mind considered the question, Roland, tall, lean, and sandy-haired, answered thoughtfully, "My father was at Agincourt in 1415, twenty years ago, and before I left England, he mentioned that there'd been a Ziska with King Henry's forces, a mercenary cannoneer, I believe. Possibly he is the same? That would make him quite old."

"Ja," Karl said, "the Hussite commander is mine own age, about three score, blind in one eye from youth, shot in the other mit an arrow last year. Ve have stories of him from Tannenburg and before. He vas mercenary against Tatars. That must be where he learned the wagon tricks. Those heathens always fort up in the wagons when they get caught. Ach, being outfought by a blind man on a farm cart is an insult. This time we do it right. We clean out this nest of heretics once und for all."

Roland wasn't overly sure about that. "This Ziska may take a little more 'cleaning' than anyone's thought," he said. "Stories have been filtering back from that fortress they've built, the one they call Mount Tabor. Apparently Ziska knows some siegecraft. He's been raiding the local castles and fortified monasteries, blowing their gates with petards and running off with stock, weapons, iron, gold, and slaughtering the good brothers. That's probably what drove his Holiness to proclaim the crusade. We are urged to kill all heretics and confiscate their posessions."

Martenot nodded agreement, his long black hair shining in ringlets, as he lifted a silver cup of the baron's fine wine. "I heard that story too, also that he drills his people constantly and has militarized the whole compound at Tabor.

Even children run messages and women sew powder bags. There's a Jewish colony near there, and they tell of the constant thundering of those wagons at practice, and the constant booming of cannons. Apparently Ziska's got his men-at-arms aiming their hackbuts [matchlock harquebuses] from the shoulder like crossbows."

"*Ja,* I know some of those Hebrews also," Von Somerau said, "and Ziska is going to be more dangerous yet this year. How many men he's got we don't know, but he's been building special wagons, not using old farm carts. Let's chust see, now." His eyes went out of focus as he peered back into his memory and then snapped back as he found what he was looking for and began to recite. "Each wagon carries two axes, two pickaxes, two hoes, two spades, und two shovels. The men on board are two handgunners, six crossbowmen, two flail carriers, four men mit halberds, two shield handlers, and two drivers who is also armed. In each, one man commands."

A girl, obviously impressed from some local village, brought them a ceramic jug of wine and began to fill their goblets. As she passed Martenot, his hand wandered under the peasant skirt and the girl stopped, eyes wide and staring. Then she gasped, flinched, and began to sob helplessly. "Well, now," Martenot said, grinning as he sipped his wine, "the papal bull did say 'all possessions.' Are you a possession, little one?"

The girl, who couldn't have been much past puberty, nodded, sobbing. "I have been given to the son of our village hetman and will be married in the spring."

"We will see about that, my flaxen-haired pretty," Martenot said, not unkindly. "You might just end your days in a French castle."

"Please, no" was all she said.

Growly old Somerau came to her rescue. "Ach, no rape under my tent. . . . Chentlemen—if you have to have your fun, do it elsewhere, and remember that rape is fleeting, while what a woman gives freely is lasting. Now fill mine jug, little one, while I tell these boy-knights what we is facing."

Unabashed, Montenot de Chavennes removed his hand, and the girl, positively glowing at the old baron, filled his goblet. Roland of Highwood looked first at Montenot and then at the girl's face and filed that one away in his memory. . . . One could learn more than battle skill from that old knight.

"The Taborite wagon system is goot," Karl said. "They can shoot on the move, und they can fort up so fast you don't want to believe it. We *got* to get them before they hook up the wagons. What they do is to charge in a tight formation, get up on some hill, und then chain der wagons together, mit ironbound pavises in between. Lances won't penetrate, and they got iron flails on six-foot poles. Is goot luck the Ziskites can't charge in wagons. Is also goot luck their nearest formation is fifteen miles away. Tomorrow we kill them all . . . We hope."

The younger knights were soberly absorbing this information and nodding agreement when a small body of horsemen came clattering into the encampment in some haste. The men were Wallachian mercenaries who were used by both sides as scouts, and their light horses were lathered. While the great chargers of the armored knight could approach a ton in weight; the lighter mounts of these horse-archers ran to about 800 pounds and were fast and long-winded. The archers wore long tunics, boots, and high-crowned felt hats. Bows and quivers were slung from their saddles and they carried short curved swords.

"They look excited," Roland said, pulling speculatively on his lower lip. "Possibly they have found a group of Taborites closer than we knew. If so, our Florentine Condottiere will soon be sending the runners out. Time for us to arm ourselves, I think."

"Yes, my English friend," Maretnot said, "and possibly their scouts have already found *us*. . . .Pages, esquires, to us, saddle the destriers, array our armor and weapons—and where's old Karl? Down for a nap?"

The old German had disappeared into his tent and the clank of weaponry could be heard. At that time, the war horns sounded and messengers began to streak in all directions from the command pavilion of Philippo Scolari, known to history as Pippo Scano, a vicious mercenary commander, now in the service of Sigismund, Holy Roman Emperor and principal executor of the crusade. Pippo Scano and Jan Ziska had met before, at Prague in 1423, and the Florentine had lost humiliatingly. Now he thirsted for revenge against the heretics and their aging, blind leader. What he could not have known was that Ziska was a born engineer, and there was a totally new type of wagon in the Hussite table of organization.

The other thing that changed history was Ziska's blindness itself. While the great commanders of history from Genghis to Napoléon have always surrounded themselves with eager young officers and have taught them the necessary skills, this was not normal medieval practice. Ziska, no longer able to see his adversaries, was forced to teach his methods to all his commanders. This, of course, created independent battle groups all over Bohemia.

Roland and Martenot were sitting on their mounts giving orders to their squires, pages, sergeants, and the small group of lighter-armed, mounted men who attended them. When the host moved, the heavy armored knights would be in the lead, each followed by successive waves of more lightly armed, more mobile men-at-arms. They stopped talking and stared with some interest at the German contingent of their little group cantering up. Old Karl's lance of warriors looked like something out of the past.

Von Somerau was not heavily armored and was not mounted on a heavy charger. Instead of full plate armor, he wore a thick back and breast plate armor on his upper arms and thighs, and all this connected by double-woven chain mail. The type of armor was about a hundred years out of style, but about 30 pounds lighter than the suits of full plate. A modern expert would have called it transitional. Instead of a ton of horseflesh, Von Somerau was mounted on a tall roan with a cream mane and tail. The horse was 17-hands tall at the withers if it was an inch, and had legs that looked like it could run like the wind. The rest of Von Somerau's contingent was likewise armed and mounted for speed.

"*Mon Dieu,* my old friend," Martenot said, "have you raided your grandfather's armory? And why are you riding a racehorse?" Roland of Highwood characteristically said nothing, preferring to listen, watch, and learn. What he heard made him faintly nervous.

"Well, we know that plate armor won't stop bodkin points or handgun bullets or light cannon shot," Von Soumerau said, his voice echoing a bit in the visored helmet. As the other two nodded, he continued, "So why wear and haul what can't protect you? For three generations now, der knights of Burgundy have been eating Swiss pikes, der Normans is English pincushions, and the Prussians could use their breastplates to strain cheese. What we wear will stop anything a man can swing and mine gelding is faster than a charger by twice. Today we—"

There was a clatter of hooves and then a messenger mounted on a native pony skidded to a halt and delivered a rehearsed message.

"Sires, the infidel host is five miles off and coming at a trot. They have six horses to the wagon and are coming in columns which fill the valley. We are to form the host from hill to hill as deep as can be found, and prepare to charge . . . but only on Pippo Scano's signal, on pain of death." The boy cringed at that and took off for the next group before he could be struck.

Both Sir Roland and Von Somerau looked sideways at Martenot de Chavennes, but the Frenchman had learned, or at least those who taught him had learned from thousands of lost battles, the folly of the lone charge into a missile-armed army. Martenot only nodded understanding and then the long trumpets sounded "to horse," a signal no knight needed to hear more than once. Looking to the headquarters pavilion on its rise, they could see Pippo Scano, the Italian mercenary to whom the emperor and the Pope had committed this crusade, standing in his favorite pose.

Scano was in full, gaudy Florentine armor of wonderous complexity, standing in front of his page and warhorse with the heavy eastern scimitar that he favored in his right hand. His left hand held the tip, the blade crossing in front of his hips. He was not yet helmeted and his face, cruel yet sensuous, was framed by short, thick black curly locks of hair. As the horns fell silent, his squire placed a visored, plumed helmet on his head. Slipping the curved Turkish blade into its scabbard, Scano swung into his saddle and took the pennoned lance the squire offered.

The horse he rode was fully armored from chanfron to crupper, and while the observers knew that it was a giant, white-starred bay stallion, nothing could be seen but four heavily muscled legs churning along under the weight of horse armor, man, and man armor. From up close, those hoof beats would have sounded like hammer blows as the modern medieval military mastodon clattered by. . . . Unfortunately, Knighthood was about to be deflowered yet again.

Slowly yet smoothly the host formed, with very little of the usual jostling and arguing for positions of honor that had previously been a feature of a medieval battle line. There were no stolid battle groups of pike-armed infantry here, nor deadly silent lines of death-dealing longbowmen. Only an almost silent line of heavily armed and armored knights walking forward into a golden fall afternoon. Ahead of them, a series of darkening dots on the horizon advanced under a cloud of dust. When they came to a waiting halt, a steady rumbling sound could be heard, as if a mighty host were approaching, but only those dots were visible.

Roland, Martenot, and Von Somerau were, for the present, still riding stirrup to stirrup. Time enough to separate and go to their little units of nobility and followers, for now they took each other's counsel. "Well, we know that they were 15 miles away this morning," Roland said, "and unless their heresy also includes sorcery, which I have not heard of, Ziska's just moved whatever size force that is fifteen miles in just over half a day and is offering battle."

Something was bothering Martenot, but he could not quite pin the idea down as he watched the dots become four columns of wagons and some light cavalry, coming straight for them at a steady, almost impossible speed. The columns were about one hundred yards apart and seemed to be composed of several hundred wagons, each full of crossbowmen, gunners, and whatnot, and attended by more of that light skirmishing infantry—and there were a lot of them. The holy host's own scouts were galloping for life now, with that prowler cavalry hot on their heels.

Martenot turned to ask a question of Roland but the Englishman raised an armored hand and pointed at Von Somerau. The old German had that unfocused look again and they knew that someplace back in his mind a small machine full of facts was whirring like a mechanical clock. The gray eyes focused and the quiet words shattered their world.

"Destriers!" Karl hissed. "Der heretics is pulling der wagons mit armored warhorses. Ach, I now remember in 1423, when Sigismund thought the campaign was over, the Hussites charged and we tried to ride over der rivers of ice. Most drowned, and the Hussites chust laughed and came out and brought back the chargers and let the knights drown or freeze." His voice became normal again and he said, "The page said six horses each wagon—that explains his speed. We got to go *now,* but whoever charges first will get shot, as he should for breaking ranks like at Agincourt." Von Somerau's head swiveled and his eyes focused on a bachelor knight in his retinue. *"You.* Heinrich. You tell Pippo Scano der heretics is pulling der wagons mit chargers. *Raus mit, schnell, ghennen und sprechen."* The last came in a roar that seemed to have force enough itself to bridge the half mile between their small group and the leader of the host.

Handing his lance to a squire, the young knight whirled his horse and sank in his spurs with a shout.

As the knight took off, Roland again filed a fact. The young knight was armored well enough for combat, but mounted well enough to outdistance anything he could not outfight—and had enough rank that his message would not be argued with.

Roland of Highwood was very grateful that old Von Somerau was a friend, for he would not like to face an army trained and commanded by a man whose ancestry went back past the days of legend. Von Somerau could trace his family line back to ancient Eturia, before the Romans came over the Alps, and there were things in his memory that spoke of old knowledge.

The message seemed to do no good. Heinrich was back in ranks and Roland, Martenot, and Von Somerau were back with their own family groupings before the advance was ordered, and still those infernal war wagons came at that steady, menacing speed. The last of their scouts had either made it to friendly lines or been shot down by horse-archers and still there was no order to charge. Was Pippo Scano going to treat the advance of the war wagons like another mounted host? As a matter of fact, yes.

Somewhat nervously now, Karl looked upon the advancing wagon host. From the front wagons, flags were being raised and lowered as whoever was in charge gave orders. Several wagons down the line relayed the signals as various maneuvers were carried out. There were four lines of wagons, the outer of which were somewhat longer. The inner lines of wagons seemed to be slightly different, but he couldn't be sure. Suddenly those inner lines turned toward each other and seemed about to collide. Pippo Scano now must have seen the danger, and the war horns sounded.

Slowly the great line of knights began to canter forward—one does not get jackrabbit starts out of a horse the size and weight of a modern Clydesdale, carrying a fully armed knight. In less than a minute, though, the entire host of about a thousand knights was at full gallop—About 15 miles per hour. In that period of time, though, the center two lines of wagons had become an ironbound wooden redoubt. The harness tongues had been swung inward and the vehicles chained together. Shields connected them and boards had been swung down from the wagon boxes. Above the impromptu fortification, fuse smoke curled ominously as the gunners waited. But what of the oncoming wagons? Karl wondered. They should have forted up long before. The long lines began to veer inward to the shape of a large V pointed toward them.

As the line of chivalry approached the line of wagons, handgun fire began to erupt from the war vehicles, saddles began to empty, and the knights began to realize that all was not well. Being shock troops and infighters only, they did not have a missile weapon among them. Karl could see only one way of disabling those fearsome, rumbling four-wheelers: Kill the horses. Regretfully, he lowered his lance toward the withers of a plunging bay, first of its team, and got a second bad shock. The horse was barded. It was still wearing knightly armor. His lance glanced off the horse and he lifted it to one of the occupants of the war wagon.

A halberdier swung desperately at the tip of a lance but failed to intercept the point and Karl's aim was true. He took the head and helmet clean off a Hussite, just as an awful thunder erupted from the side of the wagon. These were not pistols, but cannons. Long tongues of flame shot before and behind him and his eyes registered what was, to him, doom. The wagon was armed with a row of serpentines, muzzle-loading cannons of about 1.5-inch bore on each side. The roar of the serpentines was almost continuous now and the field was filling with smoke; screaming, wounded knights; and riderless horses. This was no battlefield, it was the plains of Hades.

Now Ziska's outriding cavalry, more Wallachian mercenaries and some mounted Hussites wearing their chalice emblem on their surcoats, were simply trotting into the battle and rounding up the free horses. . . . Cheeky bastards, he thought, but there was absolutely nothing he could do except shift his course toward the next wagon on the oncoming V. Split by the hail of pistol fire and the armored horses, the knights were filtering through the gaps in the wagons and being broken up by massed cannon fire. Pretty soon they'd all be inside the Hussite formation and something began to form at the back of old Von Somerau's mind, something that he didn't like at all. Then the next wagon took his attention.

This time he ignored the armored horses and aimed his lance at the man in the center of the vehicle, the one who was yelling at the rest of them. *Must be its commander,* he thought, and lightly roweled his mount with one spur. The gelding instinctively sidestepped and a crossbow bolt whizzed harmlessly by as Karl's practiced eye and aim speared the man in the chest—and also ripped the lance from his hand. All of that wagon's cannons were muzzle up as their gunners frantically swabbed the bores and dropped powder bags into them. The knights were inside the big V now and the war wagons were getting progressively farther away to the sides, and Karl had time to look around. What he saw was appalling.

Fully a quarter of the knightly host was down, unhorsed, wounded, or killed. Without missile weapons they were helpless. Many were trying, usually unsuccessfully, to cap-

ture a stray horse. Here and there a loyal horse had stopped
for its master and some knights were helping each other
cumbersomely into their saddles. Karl was relieved to see
that most of his retainers still lived and that his friends were
coming to him. Martenot seemed to be listing to one side,
and blood leaked from joints in his right leg armor. He still
held his lance, but the point was broken off. Roland also
was reining his horse toward them, waving to his somewhat
shrunken party. Two of the English knights were missing,
but surprisingly all of their sergeants were present. More
evidence, Karl thought, that heavy armor was outdated.
Speed and maneuverability was the key to survival.

His two friends reined up facing him and the three threw
up their visors. Martenot was white-faced while Roland had
a healthy flush. Suddenly he too went white-faced. "God in
heaven," he said. "The heritics have reversed. Here they
come again." Two of Martenot's men-at-arms had closed in
on him and were now holding him erect in the saddle. The
blood leaking from his armor was a stream dripping from
his boot, and his horse, a youngish stallion, was prancing
nervously.

Von Somerau, who'd been facing east toward the laager
of the two middle lines of wagons, began to get very nervous. He'd seen quiet activity in the mobile fort. The teams
were being hitched up and the wooden shields were surrepti-
tiously being removed. "Now what?" he wondered as he
swung his head back westward. Suddenly he began to understand. The wagons of that V were a *lot* closer together. A
sudden thunder of hooves to the east confirmed his worst
suspicions. The first group of wagons was shaking itself out
into a line.

"We got to get out of here *schnell,*" he snapped, "or we
get caught like fish. They can lock up those wagons mit us
inside—been done before. You, Roland, get Martenot out
and see to that leak before he bleeds to death. Get him to
that Genoese surgeon. For him this war is over." Reluctantly, the small party of mounted men obeyed the senior
knight, not wanting to lose honor, but seeing the wisdom of
his orders. Von Somerau, for his part, placed his cluster of
three knights, six armed squires, and about a dozen ser-

geants between Roland, the wounded Martenot, and the on-coming wagons. A quick glance east confirmed his guess. The wagon fort was now a solid line of linked gunports, waiting with fuses lit.

The mobile V was coming at a gallop and Karl anxiously eyed the narrowing gap between one arm of the formation and the stationary line. Once the two groups of Hussites were within effective cannon or handgun shot, the trap would be effectively closed, and his men were moving just too damn slow. What could he do? Now, somewhat desper-ate, he searched the wagons with anxious eyes, searching for a weakness. Even the driver wasn't vulnerable—the reins went into a slot in the front of the high wagon box . . . the high, unstable, wagon box.

"*Du*, Heinrich," he snapped, now speaking German again, "give me that lance." He almost ripped the weapon out of his nephew's hand. "You, Sergeant from the south of der Barony—Jodl, isn't it? When I blind the driver, you better be alongside the lead horse. You grab the reins and turn them sharp to the right and we tip them over, understand?" As the man nodded sudden understanding, old Von Som-erau launched himself in the most important charge of his life. If that trap closed with them inside, they were all doomed. They'd be shot down like highwaymen.

His tall roan gelding had recovered its wind and was mov-ing considerably faster than the Hussites could have guessed. In only seconds the warhorse was at a gallop, and before the wagon crew could react, the lance tip had gone straight into the driver's vision and rein slit. Karl let go of the lance and fancied that he'd heard a shriek from inside. Now, look-ing up, he saw the next team coming straight at him, with pistols and crossbows aimed at him from the top of the fighting compartment, and they were only feet away.

Desperately he reined the gelding to his right, at the wagon box, where a hole would appear if Jodl had suc-ceeded. If he'd failed, Karl would first hit the side of the wagon and then be ridden down by the next one. *I'm getting too old for this,* he thought as a picture of a mangled suit of armor underneath iron-shod wheels appeared in his mind.

I get out of here alive, this is my last war. Better I stay home and raise grandchildren.

It worked! The rear of the war wagon suddenly wasn't there anymore and he shot through the gap as astonished yells issued from both the wagon and the following vehicle, which promptly crashed into it. Now laughing almost hysterically in relief, Karl joined his sergeant as they cantered away from the temporary gap and toward their group of fellow escapees. Behind them, the roar of the serpentine cannons swelled to a thunderous crescendo, smoke rose over a killing field, and the orange glow of the muzzle blasts began to flicker in the gathering autumn evening. Suddenly there was a thumping blast as some wagon's powder went off. It wasn't over yet. The wagons had stopped, unhitched, and were forting up again. They had trapped hundreds of knights and lighter cavalry.

All around the wagon line, scattered groups of knights and retainers were forming assault lines on foot, giving their horses to pages and sergeants and beginning to at least try to attack the monstrous creation that was murdering their noble comrades. Suddenly one wagon swung back and a horde of light cavalry came charging out. They were a mix of Wallachian horse archers, hastily armed farm boys, and the light prowler-cavalry that Ziska had trained up in the Tartar fashion.

Karl had by now gotten into a patch of woods and linked up with Roland and their wounded French knight. Martenot lay on a litter made of a pair of saplings cut with swords and attached to his warhorse. His wounded leg was exposed to the hip and the removed armor was hanging from his saddle. The wound, a bad gash from where a bullet had pierced the armor, had been covered with a dressing made from someone's surcoat. The bleeding had stopped, but he was still deathly pale. His squire stood nervously by, looking anxiously at the melee forming up outside the wagon wall.

Roland was standing by his charger. His squires had been busy, as there were a dozen or so lances leaned against the lower branches of a spreading oak tree. "Shouldn't we be going to their aid, Karl?" he asked. "My God, what an awful thing. The heretics don't even give quarter or take surren-

der. Just listen to those guns, and look at the flashes. It's
like thunder and lightning in there."

"*Ja*, that's just what it is," Karl answered. "The men inside is already dead. All we can do is form up and hit them
horse archers and light horsemen like old times. . . .*Vas ist?*"

A lathered pony bearing an English page galloped into
the little grove that hid them, and skidded to a rump-down
halt. "My lords, the camp is under attack too," the messenger gasped. "There are more of those light cavalry and
they're looting us, killing the women and craftsmen. The
town is ablaze. I don't know who torched it. The camp is
full of refugees and they're being slaughtered."

Von Somerau's mind, long used to snap decisions, sorted
out his priorities. One, the men in the trap were beyond
hope. Two, this battle was lost and no one knew where their
alleged commander, Pippo Scano, was or if he even lived.
Three, they would badly need those supplies, wagons, and
their servants, men-at-arms and armorers, to get out of here
before winter.

"Jodl, Fritz, you go with this messenger," he commanded
two of his sergeants. "Go around the wagon fort and collect
all that you can. We go to the camp *now*. Switching back
to his accented English, he rapidly brought the French and
English parties up to date. "So, best we go to the camp now,
before they burn it too and steal all we got." Seeing assent
in the other man's eyes, he detailed a small party to escort
Martenot, who was drifting in and out of consciousness.

The rest of the group, about twenty of them, trotted off
toward the wreckage of their camp. Smoke from the burning
village was drifting through the gathering gloom and small
fires were starting in the dry autumn foliage. *This*, Roland
thought, *must be what hell is like*.

The scene in the camp wasn't quite as bad as the messenger had painted it, but bad enough. There were perhaps
300 light cavalry loose in there, grabbing loot, raping camp
followers, loading plunder wagons, rounding up horses, and
generally having their way with the camp. Unfortunately for
them, they had just reverted to the type of war that the
knights were born for. They were caught dismounted, disorganized, and in some cases dishabille.

One group was looting expensive rugs, clothing, and some gold from Roland's tent, another was loading a cart from Von Somerau's pavilion, and Martenot's palatial wagon was already on fire when the party of battered knights came upon them at full gallop, lances couched and swords loose in their scabbards. With a wild yell, Roland spitted a dismounted looter, let the lance twirl down as his horse passed the man, pulled the tip out, and with a practiced skill, swung it up in time to knock a half-armored man off a horse in front of Von Somerau, who'd already lost his lance and was laying about him with a heavy battleaxe. Reining his heavy destrier around to help the German, who seemed to be besieged by a swarm of armed footmen, Roland received another lesson from the old knight.

That big, fast roan gelding had been trained to fight too. The horse seemed to be bucking under old Karl until one saw what his hooves and teeth were doing. A spearman came running at the German knight from the front and got his head kicked in by a steel-shod hoof. Von Somerau beheaded a man with a backhand sweep of that heavy axe, and at the same time the roan put both forehooves on the ground, aimed his hindquarters, and knocked an armored man twenty feet with a double kick. Roland spitted another attacker with a lance and almost lost his face as the roan's teeth snapped shut just inches from his open visor.

War horns sounded from several quarters of the camp as more parties of surviving knights came charging sporadically. Suddenly, as quickly as it had started, the melee was over and the surviving looters were running for their lives. Looking up the slight rise to where Pippo Scano's lavish tentage stood, they could see that he still lived—and that he was directing the folding and packing of his tent and equipment.

"That's a good idea, mine friends," Von Somerau said, looking around at the half-wrecked camp. "Ziska's men won't attack at night, but sometimes they pursue for days. Supplies for a month in the wagons they got, even grain for the horses. The war this year is over—we go home."

The next morning, the Hussites didn't seem disposed to pursue. They'd spent the night fighting the fire in the half-destroyed village and all that could be seen around the rapidly shrinking camp were mounted scouts—probably making sure that the knightly host was really on its way. Over half the knights' number hadn't returned and there was a little internal plundering going on as some of the knights made sure that anything they'd lost was replaced.

Roland, Martenot, and Von Somerau would ride together until they were close to the Rhine River, where the old German would turn south to his castle and holding in Bavaria. Martenot's squire had just made sure that the French knight was comfortable in a canvas-covered wagon, and Roland and Von Somerau were mounting up when a small voice addressed Karl.

"Do you have a home for me, sir knight?" Looking down, he saw the girl who'd been serving them in the camp. Her clothing was in tatters and her eyes were red and brimming with tears that streaked the soot on her face. She was barefoot and her gray peasant dress was ripped off level with her knees. "My family is dead, my home is burned, and the boy to whom I was to be wed is dead," she said. "There is nothing here for me anymore and I do not want to live with the Hussite puritans. . . . Please, my lord?"

Old Von Somerau's iron visage cracked in a wry smile and he nodded shortly, holding out a fist to her. Understanding, she first kissed the fist and then grabbed it with both tiny hands. Effortlessly, he pulled her straight up and she twisted her body as she rose, settling behind his saddle, legs to his right, arms around his waist. She made a pretty picture sitting there, and Roland, admiring her, commented, "What a woman gives freely is lasting, eh, Karl?"

"Ach, Englander dumkopf," Von Somerau growled with a half grin. "Grandchildren her age I got, and a good wife. We put this one to work in der castle and one of der boys will find her. We go, mine friends." Kneeing the big roan gently, he led their little cavalcade into the line of departing knights. Their time was almost over and history was closing in on them.

After the Hundred Years' War, the day of Jan Ziska, and the time of the Swiss pikemen, changes began to blow in the wind. Changes that would begin a new age as shocking in its historical effect as that wrought by iron and the mounted warrior. For all of the Middle Ages, European society was ruled by the armored knight and his "lance," or band of armed retainers. The peasantry was kept in its place not so much by armed force as by lack of organization and lack of training, except on one small island—England.

Picts, Celts, Romans, Saxons, Danes, Norsemen, and Normans—it seems that for several thousand years, any warlord who could see that tempting mass on Europe's sea horizon put a few bullyboys on a raft and invaded. Each conqueror added his genes to the native pool, and eventually legendary kings united those warring tribes into a nation that has been invasion-proof for a thousand years. A nation that ended the domination of the armored knight and his half-bandit retainers.

In what would eventually be Great Britain, the freedoms that we now enjoy were being born in the form of the armed citizen. Long centuries before Mao Tse-tung stated that "political power flows from the muzzle of a gun," political power hung from the points of English bows. In Europe, the armed noble and his retainers easily dominated the peasantry, but in England the longbow, with a bit of carburized steel on the tip of its cloth-yard arrow, would set off a course of events that would trigger our own age of steel and technology. When the barons of old England extorted the Magna Carta from King John at Runnymede in 1215, history began to swing in a new direction. The Magna Carta and the later English Bill of Rights are two of the ancestors of our Constitution.

Oddly enough, it was the attitude of French chivalry that was the pivot. When they were driven from the field of battle by longbow-armed infantry, they weren't about to arm their peasantry. Instead, they took the newly invented cannon-style artillery and began to refine it to the point where, as we have seen, only a pair of culverins were sufficient to win the battle of Formigny. The British knights and archers simply couldn't stand the galling of accurate cannon fire and broke their positions, allowing a French victory and starting an arms race.

Two significant results came from this race. One was the

sudden need for massive amounts of iron ore to build the
newly effective cannons. This immediately caused an increase in deep mining activity, which needed both pumps
for water and blowers for ventilation. The second was that
the accurate machining necessary for accurate gunfire made
the creation of cylindrical bores possible. From these two facts
arose the possibility of the steam engine and the internal combustion engine and our own age. The Renaissance, the Industrial Revolution, the age of steam, and the age of the atom
are the direct result of the need for accurate weapons.

The other devastating product of the Middle Ages was
the invention of the printing press and the resultant spread
of knowledge, especially military knowledge. While the first
works printed by Gutenberg and his associates were theolog-
ical and speculative in nature, such as the Bible and the
works of Boccaccio, the military texts were not long in coming. This gave rise, in the early 1500s, to a class of military
professionals. While Plato, Aristotle, and Marcus Aurelius
were being printed, so were Thucydides, Xenophon, Polyb-
ius, Vegitus, and a host of others. At the same time the
Renaissance witnessed the establishment of the first real universities, it also hosted the first military academies.

Knights were on the way to becoming officers in national
and mercenary armies and the "sergeanty"— the high-ranking
peasants who gave military service for land tenancy—were on
their way to becoming the noncommissioned officers who
would convert the serfs to the Prussian and Napoleonic infantry—until machine guns, cannons, barbed wire, and poison gas
began to slaughter them by the millions.

REFERENCE SOURCES

Military History magazine, August 1996.
Tank, Macksey and Batchelor, Ballantine Books.
The History of Land Warfare, Kenneth Macksey, Two
    Continents.
History of the Art of War, Vol. III, Hans Delbruck, Univer-
    sity of Nebraska Press.
Engineers of the Renaissance, Bertram Gille, MIT Press.
Medieval Warlords, Tim Newark, Blandford Press.
French Chivalry, Sidney Painter, Cornell University Press.

CHAPTER 5

America and Technical Warfare
1861–1865

THE YEARS SLIPPED AWAY IN DECADES AND THEN CENTURIES and still the demons that plagued Europe drove men to die for, among other things, religion. Steadily the weapons of war became more deadly. The Renaissance brought technical advance at the cost of human life. The knight became an officer and the alchemist became a scientist. First gunpowder made it easier to arm an infantry soldier, then cannons became mobile, then came men like Gustavus Adolphus, Fredrick the Great, Napoléon, and Bismarck.

At the same time, the new scientists were discovering a technology that, like that of Archimedes in the third century B.C., could easily be adapted to warfare. And by this time, a new breed of human was assembling a new kind of nation, in relative isolation, far across the Atlantic ocean. They wanted no part of Europe's wars, but their roots were in Europe's technology and England's freedoms. The combination of knowledge and the freedom to use it would change human history in ways no man could have predicted.

The smooth cannon bore begat first the steam engine; the first working engine seems to have been that of Edward Somerset, who created a steam fountain pump to give Raglan Castle its own water pressure in 1650. In 1698 Thomas Savery began the commercial use of steam power to drain water from the mines, and was followed closely by Thomas Newcomen in 1705, Brighton in 1718, and James Watt in 1784.

By that time the new machinery had already attracted the military, and by 1760 a French artillery officer named Nicolas Cugnot had invented a crude steam traction engine. It was not effective, but it was a step. Next on the road to mechanization was Richard Trevithick, who introduced high-pressure steam and compact engines. By 1804, he was not only manufacturing stationary engines but was creating what was probably the first steam locomotive. It pulled ten English tons of iron to a distance of 9.75 miles on the tram road from Penydarren to Abercynon.

The Industrial Revolution and the steam age was off and running, and by this time the rifle and the breech-loading cannon were already under development. In the American Revolution, the Pennsylvania long rifle and the Ferguson breech-loader had already made their marks on history.

The development of truly independent mechanized travel—the internal combustion engine—goes back a bit farther than is popularly known. In 1678, a French inventor came up with a gunpowder pump that exhausted a chamber by explosion and then pulled water out of a well with the resultant vacuum. By 1688, the vacuum was being tested to operate a piston by Christian Huygens. Gunpowder fuel feed, however, was a bit of a problem. By the late 1700s, the invention of illuminating gas baked out of coal made more progress possible, and by 1791, an Englishman, John Barber, was running a crude steam turbine on gas, air, and water.

By 1794, Robert Street was running a piston/flywheel engine on light oil with flame ignition. By 1847, a 20-horsepower hot/tube ignition engine was invented by a man named Drake. By the time of the American Civil War, the steam engine had reached a level of efficiency that made railroads and some free-ground traction engines possible, and infernal combustion was past its infancy and beginning to be put to work.

Breech-loading rifles were in development, and revolving weapons were off the drawing boards and in the holsters of soldiers and adventurers. The Parrot rifled cannon was in existence and enough horsepower was available to haul respectable amounts of armor. All that remained was to assemble a vehicle that would self-propel both armor and firepower. The inventor was General Robert E. Lee, of the Confederate States of America.

In many ways, our Civil War was the act that validated the Constitution and made us a nation. Before that war, each separate state thought it had the right to secede at will. After 1865, we were one of the great nations of history. We were the first nation to have an electronic nervous system and arteries of steel, in the form of telegraph lines and railroads. It was those two systems that made the war of the Southern rebellion the first of the modern wars. Morse code messages could be sent at the speed of light and troops moved as fast as 60 miles per hour—assuming of course that no roving cavalryman had cut the lines or blown the tracks.

Due to our wars with the Indians and the need for long mounted marches, such as the march of the mounted riflemen from Fort Leavenworth to Fort Vancouver in 1849, our cavalry was the best in the world. Men who had fought in the first of the Indian Wars and the Mexican War were very capable of thousand-mile mounted journeys. This changed the art of war. In Europe, wars were still fought relatively formally on agreed-upon fronts and fields of battle, by nations about the size of Montana. In America, a 200- or 300-mile raid behind enemy lines was nothing unusual, and the destruction of a railroad was almost considered a sporting event—even if that railroad was armed and armored.

The conflict started in Charleston Harbor, South Carolina, when Edmun Ruffin emplaced a shore battery and on 12 April 1861 opened fire on Fort Sumter. Oddly enough, the first American-built, scheduled passenger railroad run also originated in Charleston, on 25 December 1830. . . . Two years later, the city also witnessed America's first boiler explosion when the locomotive *Best Friend* let go in the railroad yards, 17 June 1832.

When the Civil War began, Virginia had almost 1,500 miles of track, all in good repair, and of several track widths. Three of them operated generally east-west on a five-foot gauge (still common in Russia), but the majority ran north and south on a standard track, and the remainder were short-run, narrow-gauge logging and local railroads. Like the local citizenry, the owners of the railroads had varying sympathies and would sometimes, under duress, serve both sides of the war.

The rails themselves were of varying capacities. Some were modern T rails, some only wooden stringers laid on wooden ties with strap iron laid on top of heart-oak rails. Virginia's ten railroads had 180 operating wood burners, ranging in size from 9 to 31 tons. Rolling stock was 158 passenger cars, 67 mail and express cars, and almost 2,000 general freight cars. This was the biggest network of Southern railroads. Either of the two largest Northern railroad systems owned more than all of Virginia's railroads put together.

Very early in the war, Southern sympathizers began to pressure the railroad operators to cease transporting Northern goods and troops. Reluctantly, John Garret of the Baltimore & Ohio agreed to stop the transport of troops but continued to move goods. When General "Stonewall" Jackson observed trainload after trainload of coal moving into Baltimore, he began to take steps. On 22 May 1861, Jackson's troops laid a trap at Harper's Ferry and nabbed 50 of the B&O's locomotives along with 350 cars of various types. For the remainder of the war, the B&O would get "preferred attention" from Jackson.

The first combat movement of troops in history took place on 18 July 1861, when three little puffing wood burners pulled 10,000 Confederate troops in a mix of flat, box, and passenger cars from Piedmont Station to Manassas. After the battle, it was almost inevitable that the first ambulance train would be created. The wounded were placed on mattresses on straw pallets in the boxcars at first, but by October there were formal ambulance cars, converted from passenger cars, in service on several of the railroads.

Later in the year, General Joseph E. Johnston created the

world's first purely military railroad by laying five miles of track between his base at Centerville and Manassas. The rails themselves were extorted from the B&O by Stonewall Jackson, as usual. By the middle of 1862, the Confederates were outnumbered by the vastly larger Union forces under McClellan. They were also facing the superior mobility conferred by the much larger and better maintained and organized northern rail network. General Herman Haupt, an engineer officer, had been put in charge of the system and showed a genius for the work, developing an organization that outlived the war and became the basis for the growing national system.

Not only were the trains used to move troops and matériel, sometimes individual locomotives were used as mobile scouts. To a generation raised with diesel locomotives, this may seem impossible, but one who has grown up with steam engines knows that the steam loco can be almost silent at creeping speed, when running free. They can also suddenly reverse direction and vacate the area at 60 miles per hour, which is a handy capability when suddenly confronted with Confederate horse artillery. The drill then would be for the locomotive to go back to its base, hook up to a train of cars full of cavalry and infantry, and return to the scene of action.

At the Battle of Savage Station, however, something new was added. General Johnston had been severely wounded at the Battle of Seven Pines and could not remain in command. He was replaced by General R. E. Lee, who in introducing himself to his new command referred to it as the "Army of Northern Virginia," the name by which it went into history. Lee, outnumbered, was thinking furiously about how to tilt the odds a bit. Eventually, he conceived the idea of mounting a rifled 32-pounder naval cannon on a railroad car and armoring it with boiler plate.

The guns of that day had no recoil mechanism and, if too large for a solid or swivel mount, had to be allowed to roll backward to lose their recoil energy. The problem was simple with field guns, but on shipboard, the guns had to be restrained with heavy ropes called breechings. Hence, Lee assigned the job to the Confederate navy. Their guns were better adapted to working in close quarters. Also, the rifled guns had much better range than the normally available 12-pound howitzers or Napoleon-style six-pounders. The "pound" system of rating guns, still used in some nations, refers to the weight of iron ball that the cannon would shoot.

At Savage Station, ten miles east of the existing border of Richmond, a series of battles had been going on over the use of the Richmond & York River Railroad. The Battle of Oak Grove took place on 25 June 1862, the battle of Seven Pines on May 31–June 1. On 29 June, both sides were in place for a culminating battle. Savage Station was the residence of a planter whose house and barn were on the south side of the railroad. On the north side of the single tracks were a group of Negro cabins and a peach orchard, which had already been used as a military cemetery. Mr. Savage's barn had already been converted to a hospital, but many of the wounded Confederates were housed in tents farther south of the actual battle.

While the two preceding battles had driven the Confederates slowly back, they had had time to prepare positions across the railroad. To the north about one third of a mile from the tracks, were Anderson's and Toombs's Brigades, the Cobb's Brigade, and a battery of two nine-pounders under a Lieutenant Hart. South of the railroad and to the west of Savage Station were Kershaw's Brigade, Semmes's Brigade, Kemper's battery of six guns, and the 17th and 21st Mississippi Regiments comprising Barksdale's Brigade. Behind a high bridge over the railroad, Confederate General MacGruder had set up his HQ, with one regiment from Barksdale's Brigade.

Facing them, only on the *south* side of the tracks between the Williamsburg road and the rails, was a large Union force under Generals Franklin and Sumner. The centerpiece of this force was an artillery park comprising three batteries under lieutenants Pettit, Hazzard, and Osborn, seven guns in all. On the battle line facing the Confederates were Burns's Brigade, Gorman's 1st Minnesota, and Brooks's Brigade. As the Union troops began to move forward, this is how General Franklin described it, quoted in *Battles & Leaders of the Civil War:*

As we rode over the open field, we saw a group of men come out of a wood on the north of the railroad but some distance from the place where we expected to find [General] Heintzleman. I thought they were our men, but General Sedgewick looked at them more closely, stopped and exclaimed, "Why those men are rebels!" We then turned back in as dignified a manner as the circumstances would permit. But we had hardly started when they opened up with a field piece, keeping up a lively and uncomfortable fire. A second piece soon joined the first and they kept up the fire until silenced by our batteries. This ludicrous incident prevented what might have been a disastrous surprise for our force. A few minutes afterward, before we had reached our troops, the signal officers reported the approach of a force on a railroad car on which was mounted a rifled cannon, from the direction of Richmond.

This gun was being pushed slowly forward by a locomotive and was under the command of a Lieutenant Barry, presumably of the Confederate navy. The car is described as "protected from cannon fire by a sloping roof in front, covered by plates of iron through which a porthole had been pierced." One of the few books on the subject, *Victory Rode the Rails* by George Turner, has the following to say:

The battle at Savage Station supplied the setting for something new on rails. While the Federals were struggling to hold off the attackers until they could complete the destruction of their stores and ammunition, shells far too heavy to be fired from any ordinary fieldpiece began falling on them from the direction of Richmond. . . . This was the debut of the railroad battery built by the Confederate Navy at the request of Robert E. Lee.

It was also about as far as General McClellan could get his brand-new army that year.

Confederate General Robert E. Lee seems to have been the first man in history to put mechanical motive power to an armored cannon, predating the British invention of the tank by 53 years, and finally fulfilling the dreams of Leonardo da Vinci and the promise of Jan Ziska. While the Confederate rail battery was not, in the proper sense of the word, a tank, due to its unarmored engine, Lee's invention deserves to be put in direct line of ancestry.

This action set off an immediate arms race and soon some rare and wonderful contraptions were riding the rails. Construction and repair trains were created, with steam-driven winches to lift locomotives back onto the rails and armored cars to protect the repair crews. Engineers, firemen, and brakemen were so often fired at that it became necessary to boiler-plate the cabs, as the following letter from the Official Records of *The War of the Rebellion* indicates:

Washington D.C. October 9, 1862
To Colonel D.C. McCallum, Director of Military Records

Dear Sir:

I have been thinking over the subject of locomotives. It is one which, at the present time and in view of future requirements of the service, demands especial attention. Experience has shown that on engines, men are targets for the enemy; the cabs where they are usually seated have been riddled by bullets and they have only escaped by lying down on the footboard. It will be necessary to inspire confidence by placing iron cabs (bullet proof) upon all or nearly all of engines and the necessity will increase as we penetrate farther into the enemy's territory.

Again, it is desirable that the smaller and more delicate portions of the apparatus should be better protected than at present, and I would be pleased if you could give to the plans of which I spoke to you recently, a careful consideration. It seems to me that they are peculiarly well adapted to military service. I hope you will investigate the proposed improvements. . . .

Yours truly,
H. Haupt, Chief of Construction and Transportation

South of the Bristoe Station, the night of 26 August 1862 turned out to be a bad one for the harassed B&O. The Confederates had stacked the rails with crossties and logs. When they heard the rumble of a freight engine, they lit the creosote-soaked ties and soon a burning pyre blocked the tracks. The engineer, with more courage than sense, opened the throttle of the little wood burner, named *Secretary,* and took his train straight through the roadblock, throwing burning ties and logs among the waiting Confederates.

Now somewhat frustrated and out of firewood, the Southerners found a switch to a siding and partially opened it. Very soon after their mechanical meddling, the big freight locomotive *President* hit the switch points, jumped the tracks, and took half its long train down the embankment, with the Rebels firing their weapons into the tumbling mess. Shortly thereafter, an engine named *Red Bird* plowed into the remainder of the *President*'s cars and was wrecked as well. The Confederates burned both trains, salvaged and repaired the locomotives, renaming them the *General Stuart* and the *Mars.* The captured engines served the Southern cause for the remainder of the hostilities.

As the war progressed, so did the technical innovations. After the battle between the Erickson-designed USS *Monitor* and the CSS *Virginia,* more armored batteries called railway monitors began to show up on battlefields and add their bit to the carnage. Heavy mortars, protected by shields made of crossties covered with sections of boiler plate or even railroad track, were created for siege work, setting the pattern for the giant railroad guns of World War I. Self-powered steam cars, with internal engines and passenger seating, had been designed for interurban commuting but were commandeered for scouting, message carrying, and even as mobile headquarters.

Even the modern armored personnel carrier and the infantry fighting vehicle had their precursors in the age of steam, as armored troop carriers with their sides pierced for cannons and rifles were used by both sides. Assaults on bridges and strategic points were made by using sacrificial engines loaded with explosives or by loading a car with rock and explosives and simply turning it loose at the top of a hill with a lit fuse.

Sometimes a battle would be started by a complete armed train. The order of march would place the locomotive in the center of the train, with an armored cannon car on each end and armored troop cars called rifle cars between the power source and the firepower cars. Some of these trains substituted railroad repair cars for some of the rifle cars and the engineer repair train was born.

And so was the railroad mine. These were usually artillery shells and could be either command-detonated or triggered by a percussion device set off when the engine's weight pressed the rail down a sufficient distance. This caused the engineers to start loading flatcars with enough rock to set off the explosion before anything sensitive rolled over the mine. Even handcars were pressed into use as rolling weapons, due to their relative silence. Many were used to inspect for disconnected rails and mines, which in those days were called torpedoes, but some were made into gun platforms.

Nothing, however, was safe from maurading cavalry, and the master of horse artillery, Nathan Bedford Forrest, was known as the "Tiger in a Saddle" due to his harassment and destruction of railroads. Forrest's famous quote, "Get there first and hit them with the most," is typical of the man who, orphaned in childhood, took over the management of his family, went into business, provided educations for his sisters and brothers, bought a plantation, and made himself the wealthiest planter in Kentucky. When the war came, Forrest enlisted as a private but, finding a talent for the work, soon asked to be allowed to raise a force of cavalry.

It may have been Forrest who began the demise of the saber as a cavalry weapon, for his chief of artillery John Morton quotes him as saying that the weapon was a "dangling, clattering appendage," and Forrest preferred that his men be armed with two Navy Colts and a Sharps carbine each. Remembering that a mounted man has to "reverse lead" his target, one can imagine what a cavalryman with twelve shots in his revolvers can do to a group of men with single-shot muzzle-loaders. It was for his use of mobile artillery, however, that his name is revered by modern soldiers.

Forrest followed the example of Gustavus Adolphus and Napoleon with his preference for sending large-bore guns into battle before risking his troopers.

Forrest also had a genius for making war support war. After using his own finances to purchase the original equipment for his new cavalry force, he converted the Union army into his own personal supply depot. Two of his first acquisitions were a pair of rifled three-inch-bore Rodman guns, which could outrange most other weapons of the time, with considerable accuracy. Once he had these two "breaking and entering tools," he could say with confidence, "I never worry about a battle as long as I have Watson and his Rodman guns with me." Captain Watson was to play a leading role in the development of Forrest's tactics and became an expert gun handler in his own right. At the Battle of Brice's Crossroads on 10 June 1864 the guns went in first, and Watson's account is worth quoting in some detail.

U. S. Grant had decided for about the third time to finally do something permanent about "that Devil Forrest," and had sent General Sturgis with 6,000 men and 16 guns to eliminate Forrest's approximately 2,500 cavalrymen and eight guns. Sturgis, more than somewhat overawed by Forrest's reputation, on the recommendation of General Washburn took an additional 2,000 men and a huge wagon train of supplies. Unfortunately, the excess of supplies made it impossible for Sturgis to match Forrest's maneuverability. John Morton's combat autobiography, written partially in third person, states the following:

> General Forrest, calling a council that night with General Buford, Colonel Rucker and Chief of Artillery Morton, stated that both refugees and scouts reported that the enemy had passed Ripley and were on their way to Guntown, burning and pillaging as they went. It was decided to concentrate all available forces and get between the enemy and Tupelo, giving General Lee time to fall back to Okolona, where it was expected Chalmers would join him. Three days rations were ordered and before dawn of the 10th, the troops were in motion in the direction of Pontotoc, passing through

Baldwin. Only a few miles had been covered when scouts brought in word of the presence of the enemy on the Ripley-Guntown road, only eight miles from the intersection of the confederate line of march. . . . General Forrest decided to engage them at the crossing known as Brice's Crossroads, the store, dwelling and plantation and the junction being on the property of a family named Brice.

Forrest, with his usual violence and verve, immediately threw what troops he had with him straight at the Federals, without waiting for the rest of his brigades, and sent word back to his artillery to move up as rapidly as possible— which wasn't overly rapid, as their horses were almost exhausted and the mud that time of year was downright thick. Finally, Morton got his guns up the last rise and over the crest looking down into a cauldron at what General Stephen D. Lee described as the "critical hour of the battle."

At that point in the battle, the Confederates were retreating from the superior Union firepower and Morton was directed to place two batteries to relieve a pair of Confederate brigades, those of Rucker and Lyon. He immediately got into an artillery duel with a pair of Rodman guns sited in front of Brice's house, and after smothering them with firepower, captured the two-gun battery with a short, sharp cavalry action, putting the gun crews and their infantry to rout. Immediately, the guns, along with the rest of the Confederate artillery, were turned on the Federals, who were beginning to fade back toward the bridge over Tishomingo Creek, just north of the Brice compound. Suddenly an advancing army had been thrown back by one thing: firepower.

The Federals had too much of everything and no place to maneuver. Infantry, cavalry, cannons, and supply wagons were in a hopeless snarl and Morton's and Rice's gun batteries tore into them mercilessly. The teamsters and unwounded soldiers cut draft horses loose and rode them out of the carnage. Behind them Forrest's men were heaving wagons out of their way and off the bridge over the creek. The Federals had been surprised, smashed, and routed, while the Confederates were still organized and under central command—Forrest's. Sometime in here, the Confederates seem to have acquired fresh gun horses, or they could never have pulled off what happened next.

The Rebels had been on the move since 0500 and it was now 1630. The Federals were on the run and a lesser general would have been content to hold the field of battle. Forrest, however, knew that he had reinforcements coming, and at this point, he seems to have had the only cohesive artillery force in the area. Calling his artillery chief to him, he said, pointing to his rear where Bell's and Buford's Brigades were trotting up in a long gray double line, "John, do you see that column coming up the road yonder?"

"Yes General," was the reply.

"Well, I am going to take command of that column and move across this field in front of us and strike their column over yonder on that parallel ridge. We'll double them up on the road right up yonder where that piece of artillery is. And when you hear Gause sound the bugle for the charge, you take your artillery battery and charge right down the road and get as close as you can. Give 'em hell right up yonder where I'm going to double them up."

No one had ever done this before, in all the history of warfare. Before this, any artillery, whether muscle-and-spring-powered or powder-driven, had always been escorted by some sort of close-in infantry or cavalry force. Morton's exec and the commander of his own battery, Captain Rice, who'd come up at just this time, simply didn't believe what he'd heard and had to be reassured that Forrest hadn't taken leave of his senses. Forrest had not snapped; instead he'd sent his cavalry through the woods to the sides of the road upon which his guns were to charge and had them dismount. They would be covering Morton's and Rice's assault with their carbines.

Horse holders were setting up picket lines and most of Forrest's cavalrymen were slipping forward to the Union lines—each one with a Sharps breech-loading carbine and a pair of revolvers. Morton ordered his guns loaded and limbered up, and when bugler Gause sounded the charge, he led his teams in a wild race toward the Union line. The Union forces bravely set themselves—probably shocked beyond belief at what was coming—but at only 60 yards' range, the guns wheeled in a half-circle, and as the teams shuddered to a halt, the crews unlimbered the trails of the cannons and dropped them to the ground even as the gun layers spun their elevation screws and hand-spiked the guns into alignment.

With an unholy roar, two batteries of mixed six-pounders, 12-pounders, and Rodman guns spit a mixture of canister, ball shot, and exploding shell into the Union ranks. They couldn't take it. To quote Morton, "No mortal could support the incessant terrible fire of the artillery at short range." The solid shot ripped great gaps in the infantry line and knocked down horses. Explosive shot smashed hastily-thrown-up breastworks and threw men and parts of men and screaming horses dozens of yards. The canister, bags of pistol balls shot from the guns, easily duplicated the effect of a modern machine gun. Flesh and blood cannot face such firepower without armor.

The Rebel gunners never faltered. As each piece fired, the double-ended swab went into the barrel, one end wet to quench sparks, the other dry to remove the moisture. As the swabber left, powder and ball were rammed and a cap put on the nipple. Those guns could fire faster than a muzzle-loaded rifle and each time they let loose, *pounds* of metal, not ounces, went downrange—and the Confederates were steadily rolling those guns into the Union position by hand.

The Federals fell back on another battery, but Morton had already limbered up his guns, displaced forward, and was blazing at that one. Already six guns had been captured and put to work against their former owners. Canister screamed into the rapidly disorganizing Federals and now the Rebels were beginning to encounter abandoned supply wagons. They restocked their own haversacks with Union supplies and rehitched Union horses to their artillery. Bedford Forrest was in his glory. "Come on, men," he shouted. "In a rout like this, two men are equal to a hundred; they will not stop to fight."

It should be noted here that riding alongside men like J.E.B. Stuart and Forrest and percolating throughout the

Confederate brigades was a Prussian observer, a Major Heros von Borcke. He kept detailed notes and his book, *Two Years in the Saddle*, would later be fully absorbed by a Lieutenant Erwin Rommel, who also learned the use of artillery in the battle line—in his case, the 88mm flak gun.

By 0100 on the 11th, Morton's artillery was in bivouac and the semi-starved Confederates were joyfully plundering the Union wagons. The dried meat and cornbread was dumped out of their haversacks to be replaced with ham, bacon, cheese, and coffee. One of Morton's gunners, an Irish corporal named Charlie Brady, had found a bottle of Federal whiskey and was riding a captured gun-horse in high spirits, singing "The Girl I Left Behind Me" at the top of his Irish lungs.

Of this battle, General Forrest said to Morton, "Get 'em Skeered and keep the Skeer on 'em."

The guns won that battle, as they would win the battle of Harrisburg to follow. All through the war, the complaint of Federal officers was that they could find no way to move troops as fast as the Southerners, but Forrest made them set a record—in retreating. The Federals' retreat from Brice's Crossing to Collierville took 36 hours; it had taken them nine days to cover this distance without the proper incentive.

These episodes prove the superiority of big-gun firepower in close combat, but Forrest took one hell of a chance of a platoon of infantry or a squadron of cavalry coming out on the flanks of his unprotected gunners. Normally, Forrest rode with his "Critter Company," as he called his escort cavalry, and his preferred position of command was near his artillery commander so that he could affect the course of battle by sending horse artillery where it would do the most damage. While no SOP (Standard Operating Procedure) from that command has survived, one would suspect that those guns rode loaded, half with case shot and half with shells. Certainly it was shell-firing guns that gave the armored trains the most trouble.

In June 1864, General Jubal Early was operating in central Virginia and received orders from Lee to send an expedition to Point Lookout, Maryland, with the idea in mind of releasing 25,000 or 30,000 Confederate prisoners known to be held

there. Early instructed B. G. Johnson, whose brigade included both Virginia and Maryland regiments of cavalry and
the Baltimore light horse artillery.

We pick them up on 31 July 1864, in the words of Mr.
Robert E. Zell, printed in the July 1920 issue of the *Confederate Veteran*. The Confederates had been trying to extort
money and rations from the Marylanders of the city of Han-
cock, and were in the process of falling out over it when a
Federal cavalry unit under a General Averell arrived and
began to shell them:

> Averell's cavalry charged our rear guard and drove it
> in and the fight became general in the main street of
> Hancock. During this my horse was killed under me
> and I was saved from capture by Lt. Will Reed who let
> me get up behind him and ride out to the western part
> of town where General Johnson let me have one of
> his led horses. McCausland and Johnson placed their
> batteries and drove the Federals back. We moved on
> toward Beavansville, Md. with General McCausland in
> the advance. When nearing the forks of the road leading
> to Cumberland the generals held a council and decided
> that as the enemy was in large force near Cumberland,
> we could take the direct road to Oldtown Maryland, on
> the Potomac River. This crossing over the river and
> Baltimore and Ohio Railroad was well guarded and we
> knew we would have to cut our way through to get
> back to Virginia.
>
> We reached this point about daylight on August 2,
> and found the Federals in force there. They had burned
> the bridge over the canal and had taken a strong posi-
> tion in a blockhouse and on a hill opposite the ford in
> the river. They repulsed the dismounted charge of the
> 8th Virginia Cavalry, attached to the Maryland Brigade,
> owing to their having to swim the canal. We then
> brought up two more regiments and they protected the
> bridge until we had constructed a temporary bridge on
> which to get our four pieces over.
>
> One Gun of the Baltimore light artillery was placed
> in position and fired several shots when we saw a train

coming from Cumberland. It was an odd looking train and set the boys to guessing as no troops were in sight. This was the first iron clad train of which I can find any record. [Not quite, Mr. Zell.] The Federals had built it to use along the Baltimore and Ohio Railway to protect it from raids of the Confederate Cavalry. When it arrived in front of our position we saw that it was composed of a locomotive and six cars covered with railroad rails. Two of the cars had rifled guns inside with holes to fire through while the other cars had numerous holes for infantry firing.

They began a rapid firing and General Johnson had his horse killed under him by the explosion of a shell. He ordered Lieutenant McNulty of the Baltimore light artillery to put some shells into the armored train. Corporal McElwee sighted his gun and the first shell hit the boiler of the engine at the smokestack, blowing up the boiler. This stopped the train. The second shot from the same gun went inside a porthole on one of the armored cars and exploded, killing three of the enemy; the rest of them crawled out on the opposite side at the same time we landed two more shells in the cars containing the infantry and they all left the train and took to the woods. [The man knew his gun.]

We then gave our attention to the blockhouse on the opposite side of the ford of the river. General Johnson sent a flag of truce asking them to surrender, which they refused; but after our shells hit the blockhouse twice they put out a white flag and surrendered.

Already, in our own Civil War, we are beginning to find action that sounds as if it came out of some of the wars of the twentieth century. The next stop will be the birth of modern armor in England, in 1916. We will, however, be finding light cavalry blowing up railroads as time progresses, and in some of the most unexpected places.

REFERENCE SOURCES
The Lore of the Train, C. Hamilton Ellis, Cresent Books.
Reminiscences of Gen. Herman Haupt, Herman Haupt, Arno Press.

Yonder Comes the Train, Lance Phillips, Galahead Books.
Tank, Macksey and Batchelor, Ballantine Books.
Victory Rode the Rails, George E. Turner, Bobbs-Merrill.
The Northern Railroads in the Civil War, Thomas Webber, Greenport Press.
The War of the Rebellion, Vol. XXXVI, No. 3, U.S. Department of Official Records.
Battles & Leaders of the Civil War, Vol. II, Century.
America's Civil War, September 1996.
The Confederate Veteran, July 1920.

CHAPTER 6

Wheels and Tracks
THE BIRTH OF THE ARMORED FORCE

One: Britain

AS WE HAVE SEEN, THERE ARE CYCLES IN HISTORY AND IN technology. Because the human body is neither armored like an armadillo nor as large and powerful as a gorilla, we have had to use our large brains to survive a hostile world. The history of human strife has always been a contest between projectiles and armor. We have the example of Agincourt, which led to the development of accurate machined cannon bores, which made steam engines possible. This, in turn, made deep mining possible and led to the whole Industrial Revolution.

Cannons and muskets had also eliminated the armored warrior, because neither a man or a warhorse could carry enough armor to ward off steel-headed arrows, let alone bullets. We have seen the invention of the armored train, but that Civil War creation was limited to prelaid tracks and couldn't roam the battlefield like the medieval knights. To put an armored man back into battle required two more inventions: the internal combustion engine and the Caterpillar track.

The reason tanks had to be invented is best illustrated by a horrid little story told to a British Captain Everest at an

Australian field hospital at the small city of Abbeville in late 1916. Abbeville is less than an hour's automobile drive from the historic battlefield of Agincourt, and what happened at the Belgian city of Ypres in 1916 again proves the danger of fossilized, aged leaders facing new weapons. Five hundred years after the slaughter of the French aristocracy, inane leaders were again shoveling young men into a cauldron. Captain Everest was a British tanker whose tank had been sent to break a deadlock, and he'd been wounded in the process: the speaker was an Australian corporal.

While I and others were taking supplies into the line at Ypres [the Australian told him], we waded through mud all the way. It was necessary to keep following the leader strictly in line, for one false step to the right or left meant falling into dangerous and deep mud-holes [waterlogged, pulverized dirt in shell craters, with the sucking power of quicksand]. One of our men was unfortunate enough to step out of line and fall into one of these mud-holes. Knowing from past experience that quick action was needed if we were to save him from sinking, we got hold of his arms and tried to pull him out. This did not produce much result, and we procured a rope and managed to loop it securely under his armpits. He was now gradually sinking and the mud and water reached his shoulders.

We tugged at that rope with the strength of desperation, in an effort to save him but it was useless. He was stuck fast in the mud and beyond human aid. Reluctantly the party had to leave him to his fate, and that fate was—gradually sinking inch by inch and finally dying of suffocation. The poor fellow now knew he was beyond all aid and begged me to shoot him rather than leave him to die a miserable death by suffocation. I did not want to do this, but thinking of the agonies he would endure if I left him to this horrible fate, I decided that a quick death would be a merciful ending. I am not afraid to say, therefore, that I shot this man at his own most urgent request, thus releasing him from a far more agonizing end.

The power of long-range, indirect-fire artillery to pulverize land is second only to the atomic bomb. Indeed, the masses of explosives used in World War I can be measured in actual kilotons, just like modern tactical nukes. The only thing missing would have been the radiation. That particular skill of the gunners, the ability to lob shells to a calculated destination, was a new skill in World War I, having been created just a few years before. The old generals, who'd already done their personal combat in much earlier political land grabs, had never been under the guns themselves, and knew not what they'd created.

Barbed wire, machine guns, poison gas, and vast trenchworks were new to the art of war and they were killing a generation of loyal, patriotic young men who were willing to die for their causes. Worse, much worse, were the perfumed generals who sent men off to die in hells that they never visited. When a British general named Kiggel made his *first actual visit to the battle zone,* late in 1917, he broke down in tears and said, "Good God, did we actually send men to fight in that?"

The old armchair generals never led from the front like the more aggressive commanders of history, and that was their failing. They never breathed the sickly coppery smell of freshly shed blood, never saw a battalion dismembered and turned to hamburger by distant guns, and never choked on chlorine gas—with a few notable exceptions. One was Brigadier General Sir Hugh Ellis, who became the first tanker general, who rode a tank named *Hilda* into the first grand tank assault at Cambrai. Before the tank could be ridden into battle, however, it would have to be invented, and that story is an interesting one. It starts in the air.

On a cold, rainy afternoon, over the flat autumn countryside of Belgium, a Sopwith biplane was in trouble. Riddled with bullet holes, but with its pilot unwounded and its engine turning smoothly, it ran out of fuel twenty miles from home. At that time in history, October 1914, the British Expeditionary Force (BEF) had not yet been reinforced and was withdrawing toward the port city of Dunkirk—just as it would twenty-five years later. The military mind is very slow to learn, even when the lessons are printed in blood.

This was the early part of World War I, not long after the assassination of Duke Ferdinand and his wife, and firm lines were not yet established. Infantry and cavalry patrols crisscrossed the land, and a pilot unlucky enough to crash-land behind enemy lines had an excellent chance of filtering out through the as yet unhardened MLR (main line of resistance). The Germans were rushing across Belgium in an attempt to cut the British off from Dunkirk, and already the city of Antwerp was beginning to feel the sting of German artillery.

Flight Lieutenant R. L. Marix had been assigned to carry out one of the first air raids into enemy territory, the bombing of the giant zeppelin sheds at Düsseldorf. From just 600 feet, he'd dropped his bombs into the shed that contained the German's newest and biggest airship, the Z.IX, a zeppelin craft that had already participated in the first air raids in history, on the city of London. In retaliation, the War Cabinet had ordered the Royal Naval Air Service, which owned the only long-range planes in the world at that time, to retaliate. The airships, being inflated with hydrogen gas, naturally exploded and burned quite nicely.

Lieutenant Marix, justifiably quite pleased with himself, somehow forgot that an infantry rifle can reach 600 feet quite easily, and his Sopwith soon became riddled with rifle bullet holes, several of which obviously found his fuel tank. Cold, wet, and 20 miles from a warm fire, Marix searched desperately for a level spot in the wet, dismal countryside below. He was now a prisoner of gravity and aerodynamics. His choices were limited by just how far his collection of wire, spruce, and cloth could glide. Finally, he spotted a long brown strip of earth, a freshly plowed field, and swung his gliding airplane toward it. He had a few anxious moments lining up for a landing, because he had to land parallel to the furrows instead of across them to avoid a crack-up. Finally his Sopwith bounced to a shuddering halt. Now all he had to do was avoid swarming German foot and mounted patrols, and walk all the way to his base at Antwerp!

After some miles of walking, he came to an isolated farmhouse and managed to pursuade the farmer to loan him a bicycle. This was, of course, faster transportation, and prom-

ised to get him to the city in a few hours—if he could avoid
the Germans. He suddenly spotted a German patrol and
quickly dove, bicycle and all, into a ditch. Marix was slowly
working his mind around to surrendering when he heard the
rattle of machine gun fire and, raising his head out of the
ditch, saw an armored angel of rescue coming for him.

His squadron had a small fleet of Rolls-Royce automo-
biles that they had militarized by installing long-range fuel
tanks and machine guns. They were used for local transportation and for daring dashes through the patrol zone to rescue downed pilots. Marix, however, had thought himself out
of the reach of these first mechanized patrols. The people
disdainfully referred to as "those rude mechanicals," however, had been busy. These particular Rolls had been fitted
with armor made of boiler plate from a steel mill in Antwerp, and the bullets from the German Mauser rifles simply
bounced off while the machine gunners cleared the Germans
from the area and picked up Marix.

As has been recorded many times, the British navy was
involved in the creation of the first armored vehicles, but
several individuals seem to have slipped through the cracks
of history. The name of the innovator who armored the first
Rolls was Commander C. R. Samson, who'd been in the
RNAS (Royal Naval Air Service) since it had been formed
in 1908. He'd been in on the first bombing experiments and
had flown the first plane equipped with a wireless. So, when
it became necessary to send a flying unit to France, Samson
was the natural choice to command it.

With the BEF Royal Naval Air Service under pressure
from the Germans, and London already under zeppelin attack, First Sea Lord Winston Churchill decided that a naval
air presence on the French coast would cause a necessary
diversion. On 27 August 1914, Samson landed at Dunkirk
and proceeded to operate against the zeppelins, scout over
German lines, and generally make a pest of himself. It was
during this period that he and an army general named Aston
cooked up the scheme of armoring their motorcars.

The innovation was an instant success, and working
through his commanding officer, a Commodore Sueter, Samson sent drawings back to the Rolls factory where the mili-

tary cars were being made. Once these cars had evolved to
fully operational armored vehicles with protected turrets,
their fame began to spread and attracted the attention of
General Sir Henry Rawlinson. Orders quickly went to the
Rolls Company, and the Dunkirk Armored Car Brigade was
created. Eventually, it grew into two dozen squadrons of
about eight cars each and their attendant Ford supply trucks.

By December 1914, however, the war was beginning to
lock up, the wire was going up, the trenches were being dug,
and the great guns were beginning to pulverize Europe.
Since the new armored cars were unable to operate past the
trench line, they were shipped back to England, where they
immediately generated much interest and, in the case of Colonel E. D. Swinton, a British engineering officer, considerable thought. What, he wondered, would happen if those
turrets were sitting on tracks instead of wheels? In the back
of his mind, a germ of an idea created by a science fiction
writer named H. G. Wells was slowly percolating.

In 1903, Wells had published a short story called "The
Land Ironclads" in the *Strand* magazine. He'd created an
iron beast a hundred feet long, which was steam-powered
and crossed trenches by the means of huge wheels. The story
had been widely read and no mechanically inclined person
in England could have been ignorant of the concept. At any
rate, when the armored cars proved to be such a success,
not only were they used in other theaters, Winston Churchill
and Swinton decided to build their own Land Ironclad. As
First Sea Lord Churchill had been well aware of the operations of "Samson's boys."

Colonel Swinton had originally come into contact with the
armored car unit by a rather circuitous route. War correspondents had been proven to be militarily unsafe because
they leaked vital information like a machine-gunned water
tank. As a result, they'd been forbidden from the war for
the first few months. Due to public pressure, though, *some*
information had to be given to the press. Due to Lord Kitch-
eners's violent dislike of reporters, a serving officer had to
be selected for the unwanted job, and fate fell on a hapless
engineer named Swinton. He was assigned to cover the war
for the press and wrote under the nom de plume of "Eyewit-

ness." During this period, he was exposed to the raid-and-slash type of war of the Dunkirk Armored Car Brigade.

Before the war, he had been exposed to a report on a track-laying machine designed by a Mr. Hornsby, and then had promptly forgotten the concept. In the meantime, with interest in England dying out and interest in America growing rapidly, Hornsby had sold his interest in track-laying machines to his nearest competitor, Holt, Inc. Holt was now selling tracked prime movers to most of Europe, and examples were pulling guns and wagons over many of the battlefields. Swinton could not have avoided seeing them.

Now, with the Wells story percolating in his engineer's mind, he put the concept of the armored car and Caterpillar tracks together and began to talk with Lieutenant Colonel Maurice Hankey, the Secretary of the Committee of Imperial Defense. By early 1915, the war was beginning to eat men and horses to no progress, and Hankey sent a long memorandum on the subject to Churchill, who began to lean on Prime Minister Asquith.

After much politicking, a Landship Committee was set up at the Admiralty, because the army at that point, wasn't interested. The chairman was one Tennyson D'Eyncourt, the director of naval construction. Slowly, the pioneers of the tank were assembling. Next came a banker named Albert Stern, who, fascinated by the concept, offered his services and was appointed secretary of the Landship Committee. Swinton, who was frustrated by the lack of army interest, heard of the naval effort and called in Stern, who was now a temporary lieutenant.

"Listen, Stern," he said, "this is the most extraordinary thing I have ever seen. The director of naval construction appears to be making land battleships for the army, who never asked for them and are doing nothing to help. You have nothing but naval ratings doing all your work. What on earth are you, a mechanic or a chauffeur?"

"A banker," Stern replied. Swinton was completely baffled, but at least he now had a contact within the naval effort. This was a good thing for the tank, because at the time the Admiralty was beginning to wonder what their interest in a land battleship really was. One of the designs had grown to 300 tons, mounting 12-inch naval rifles, just like Wells's science fiction design. It never got beyond design stage, of course, but when the concept began to shrink down to more modest levels, about 30-feet long and about 30 tons in weight, engineering began to approach reality. At just the time that one of the Sea Lords of the British Admiralty said, "Caterpillar landships are idiotic and useless. Nobody has asked for them and nobody wants them." The Admiralty squelched the project and cut the funding, turning the armored car squadrons over to the army, who suddenly found a need for them in the colonies. In lands where, a thousand or more years ago, crusaders had fought Saracens, the armored man had returned in another of history's long cycles.

Fortunately, Seuter, who was army, managed to retain No. 20 Squadron, which became the foundation for the new tank corps. Swinton, who had returned to France, was now relaying semi-frantic requests from the front for something to break the deadlock, and the War Office began to show much more interest in the landship project. The spring offensives in early 1915 had failed utterly, producing nothing but literally millions of corpses. On 1 June 1915, Swinton had sent in a memorandum on the need for "Machine Gun Destroyers" on tracks. Suddenly, money began to flow to the tanks and it was not long before the Landship Committee had an office, directors, and two engineers, a William Tritton and Lieutenant Walter Wilson, a naval officer who was transferred to the army with the rank of major.

The track design was acquired from Holt, and sample chassis were ordered. Tritton and Wilson had a working model by 11 August 1915, and it has gone into history as "Little Willie." For the first few years, the tanks were sometimes called "Willies," and this probably gave birth to the expression, "a case of the willies." Little Willie was driven by a 105-horsepower Daimler engine and was capable of two miles per hour. Steering was accomplished by throwing one of the tracks out of gear. The boiler-plate body rested on nine-foot tracks that had been shipped over from America.

The next tank was considerably larger than Willie, and went through several name changes. It was first named Centipede, then Big Willie, and then simply Mother. She was 33 feet, eight inches long, eight feet wide, and eight feet tall. She was also powered by a 105-horsepower Daimler engine and weighed 28 tons. By changing the gearing of the engine, she was capable of 3.7 miles per hour. Mother's teeth were a pair of six-pounder, or 57mm, guns firing from sponsons that bulged from her sides and that could be retracted for rail travel. Her tracks would last just 20 miles before requiring major work.

The problem of what to call her went through several stages, as the obvious names, such as Land Cruiser or Landship gave the game away. Since she was roughly rhombic in shape, resembling a squashed parallelogram, several code words were proposed. They went from Cistern, through Container and Water Reservoir, to simply Tank. So Mother became a Tank. In the parlance of the time, a gun-armed tank was called a male and a machine gun tank was a female, so Mother was the victim of an armored sex-change operation.

Now would come the production of the many and varied versions, and improvements, and the training of the crews. As we will see, the first tank assault in history took place at the little French village of Flers, in the center of a zone of historic battles that date back past Roman times. It was more or less a success and the lessons of that battle were taken to heart by the instructors at the brand-new tank school.

While the tank school was operating, though, the original Mk-I tanks and the original armored cars would be found out and fighting all over the Middle East and down into the African colonies.

Two: France

The creation of the French tank corps was apparently independent of the British program, at first. As with the English, and later the Germans, the powers that be initially put as many stumbling blocks in the path of the armormen as possible. At first, a Major Boisson, working with a mechanically minded minister of the National Assembly, J. L.

Breton, came up with the idea of converting Filtz farm tractors into machine gun carriers, but this scheme failed due
to mobility problems. At the same time, a Colonel J. B.
Estienne, a known artillery officer, saw the British use of
the Holt artillery tractor and came to the same conclusion
as Colonel Swinton: Here was something good.

After a certain amount of politicking and letter writing,
Estienne was given leave to try to find a technical concern
that would build a few pilot models. Renault at first turned
him down, so he turned to M. Brillié at the Schneider works,
and working with an engineer named Deloule, and even the
works director, M. Courville, they hammered out the design
for the Schneider tank in only a few days; the design
showed it.

The main gun of the Schneider tank was a short 75mm
cannon that was mounted on the left front of the hull with
a traverse of only 20 degrees, and the two side-mounted
machine guns were unprotected and could be knocked off
in heavy woods. At 13 tons and 70 horsepower, it wasn't
exactly overpowered and could make only 3.7 miles per
hour. Basically it was an armored box sitting on a Holt chassis, and, since the hull overhung the tracks, was not good at
trench crossing. Unfortunately, once the French commanding general, Joseph Joffre, had been won over to the concept, the bureaucrats struck.

Schneider was given a contract for 400 vehicles and then
Estienne was summarily transferred back to his old artillery
command at Verdun. There seems to have been a little bit
of collusion going on, for the War Ministry then awarded a
contract for 400 more tanks to Schneider's competitor, the
St. Chamond Works. Then in mid-1916, the French high
command learned that the British were also building tanks
and recalled Estienne from the front, sending him to England as a liaison officer.

After learning what the Brits were up to, he returned to
France and began to build a plan, probably based in part
on conversations with Swinton, for a massive, war-winning
assault with the combined tank forces of both nations. The
Germans seem to have been completely ignorant of what
was coming.

By the middle of August, the first group of tanks was ready and Estienne, now a general, was put on command of the Artillerie D'assault, and assigned barracks and a maneuver area at Fort Trou d'Enfer at Marly le Roi. Several things were discovered very quickly. First, the armor was not proof against the German "K" round, which could be fired out of a machine gun or even a standard Mauser rifle. Second, and worse, was that the heavy tanks, Schneider at 13 tons and St. Chamond at 23 tons, were too heavy for any kind of cross-country mobility.

The first French tank assaults would have to be done with the existing tracked boxcars, but Estienne immediately approached Renault again, with his own reconsidered design. This eventually resulted in the Char Légers, or FT-17, the celebrated six-tonner, which, like the Rolls armored car, fought in the rest of World War I and through the experimental decades, right up through 1940.

About this time, though, pressure was being applied to the budding tankers of both Britain and France to throw their tanks into battle. To quote Major General Heinz Guderian, "The same people who tried to block the development of tanks were now yelling the loudest for them." In France, Estienne and his backers were able to resist the pressure, but in England, General Haig and his cronies had considerably more clout, and long before the French tanks were ready, and with only 50 Mk-I British tanks manufactured, the 32 of them that could be made to run were thrown into battle at Flers, 15 September 1916. The first Schneider hadn't even been delivered yet and the surprise was thrown away. The French, including Estienne, were furious, but the cat was now out of the bag.

Fortunately for all concerned, the German commander, General Ludendorff, considered the new vehicle strictly a terror weapon and wasn't really worried. He did, however, authorize a research committee, coded A7V, to dig out a Holt tractor that he knew was in storage somewhere, and start experimenting. He also put out rewards for the capture of repairable British machines, and the first few German tank units into battle were mounted in Mk-I British machines, while the A7V committee began to work on the Holt chassis.

Three: Germany

The German approach was much the same as that of the French. They took the basic American chassis and put an iron box on it. There were, however, radical differences as well. One of the reasons for this was that, unlike the French, the A7V committee already had some idea of what was needed, due to their having been on the receiving end of the first tank assault in history. So of course they came at the project differently. Specifically, they figured out how much weight would have to be moved, and applied enough horsepower to the chassis.

Their engineers were a cross-section of German industry and included Herren Gossi, Sunck, and Knoop of N.A.G. From Daimler came Herr Schippert, and Nallinger and Lohrmann of Benz. From Durkop came Herren Hartman and Wulfert. From Hansa-Lloyd came Almers and lastly, Professor Hoffman of Bussing. As you would expect of a machine designed by a committee, the basic A7V tank was uninspired, being the result of compromises, but it was also one of the most effective designs of the war.

The designers farmed out the work to a group of subcontractors and the parts began to roll in. From Daimler-Benz came the four-cylinder, sleeve-valve, 100-horsepower engines, two per tank, making the A7V the most powerful and fastest tank of the war. From Adlerwerke came the gearboxes, which allowed the tank to make a bit over eight miles per hour and to pivot-turn in its own length.

Caterpillar-Holt of Budapest shipped the tracks and Brass-Herstett provided the bogie wheels and suspension. In this the Germans were far ahead of the British and French, who were still using unsprung American track designs—all right for logging, but unsuitable for high-speed operation. Radiators, armor plate, machine guns, and cannons all came together at a rapid rate, and by the first of October 1917, the first running A7V was demonstrated to the kaiser by *Sturm Bataillion Rohr,* which was an experimental pioneer unit commanded by Captain Willie Rohr, a distinguished career officer with quite a lot of professional experience. His Sturm battalion was designed to experiment with combined arms at the most basic level, and had its own shops for repair and innovation. So, in the German Army, as in the French and British, the engineer was father to the armored force.

Since the basic support organization of the Allied tank units seems not to have survived the test of time, we will use the German TO&E. This will allow a close look at just what was necessary to keep a unit of five primitive tanks running, away from central shops.

The tank crewmen: one officer commander, one driver, one riding mechanic, twelve machine gun crewmen, one cannon pointer, and two cannon loaders. Theoretically, there should have been 18 men in each tank. In practice, there were always a few venturesome hitchhikers and the total was usually over 20. When a tank stalled or ditched, they acted like dragoons and got out and protected the vehicle while the German "rude mechanicals" got their mount going again. This meant that there were 90 official crewmen for just five tanks.

The rest of the vehicle complement shows quite a bit of forethought on the part of Captain Rohr. There were two passenger cars, one light truck, and one motorcycle. There were two shop and supply trucks with trailers, and one fuel truck with trailer. There was also a field kitchen on a trailer, and one truck with driver and spare parts for each tank. I have personally seen a headquarters section of this general type keep 17 M-48A3s, and over 20 M-113s in operation, in RVN.

The total personnel roster, including the top soldier and assorted ordinary soldiers, came to 171 men and included quite a few specialists. There were cooks, clerks, a tailor, and a shoemaker, as well as drivers, reserve drivers, mechanics, and a technical sergeant for the shop truck. These men all came from different branches of the German army and had to be trained as a cohesive unit before entering combat, of course. But as will be seen, they did quite well, considering the rush job that was done on them.

REFERENCE SOURCES

Tanks & Weapons of World War I, Beekman House.

Cambrai, Bryan Cooper, Stein & Day.

Tanks and Trenches, Edited by David Fletcher, Alan Sutton Publishers.

Tank Commanders, George Forty, Firebird Books.

Achtung-Panzer!, Major General Heinz Guderian, trans. Christopher Dreffy, Arms and Armor Press.

Tank, Macksey and Batchelor, Ballantine Books.

Sturmpanzerwagen-A7V, E. S. Mittler & Sohn, Herford and Bohn.

Tanks Advance, Gordon Beckles, Wilson, Cassell & Co.

Iron Fist, Bryan Perrett, Arms and Armor Press.

CHAPTER 7

The First Tank Assault

FLERS-COURCELETTE, FRANCE, SEPTEMBER 15, 1916

THE TECHNOLOGY OF WAR HAD FINALLY SURPASSED THE fighting power of human flesh. Barbed-wire entanglements stopped bayonet charges and machine guns slaughtered infantry regiments in such numbers that many were simply written off the books, never to be raised again. Artillery dropped shells into fortifications in such numbers that their weight could be measured in kilotons. Mortal human flesh could not survive and the "Great War" was grinding the youth of a whole generation of Europeans, Britons, and Americans into the dust of history. Something desperately needed to be done to break the deadlock and get the war over with, and it was just about to happen.

General Sir Douglas Haig was not one of Britain's better field commanders. His idea of the art of war was to pulverize the enemy with kilotons of explosives and then feed men into the resultant churning Hades until something gave. He had been feeding men into the cauldron known as the Battle of the Somme and was deadlocked and losing both his army and his military reputation. While news reporting was severely restricted, no one could hide the millions of casualties and deaths that were being shipped back to England. When most of a generation of young men quit writing home, people began to wonder. "Just what is this war about, anyway?" Feeling the pressure, Haig made a decision to send in all the tanks that England owned—about 50.

Tankers frequently complain that infantry officers don't know how to handle tanks, and they are right. At the outset of tank combat, they were sent into an infantry killing ground too few, too soon, and too spread out to do much good. However, very important lessons were learned, by the tankers if by no one else, and that was all for the good. Fortunately, they made so little impression on the battle as a whole that they were written off as a mechanical novelty and forgotten by fossilized commanders on both sides. While Haig blew the secrecy of the tank in 1916, the armored monster was so new and so little known that by the time it was used "en masse" at Cambrai the surprise was again almost total. At Flers, the first use of heavy armor was devastating and this is where the Germans coined the term "tank terror."

The Delville Woods, near the town of Flers, had been broken down to a forest of blackened, shredded stumps by artillery, and the ground resembled the surface of the moon more than any earthly landscape. Unless one imagines what the scenery of Hades might look like, with broken souls chained to barbed wire and tortured by eternal fires. The day before, at dawn, the British had tried to dislodge a regiment of Bavarian farm boys turned soldiers, and the machine guns had cut the British down. Most of a proud regiment lay dead or dying on the shell-turned, smoking, grassless dirt of no-man's-land.

In July, Sir Douglas Haig had thrown 60,000 lives away in an attempt to break that line, and since that time, the Germans had been strengthening their defenses. The defense lines in front of the villages of Combles, Morval, Flers, Martinpuich, and Courcelette had all been steadily improved and thickened with yet more trenches, bunkers, and wire obstacles. There were overlapping machine gun fields of fire, endless belts of wire, concrete fortifications, and deep, shell-proof dugouts. The Germans expected that any further British attempt would be as expensive as the July effort, but

General Haig had some new coin to gamble with—just not quite enough of it. The first thing he did was soften his objective with 15 kilotons of explosives, or about the equivalent of the Hiroshima bomb. It took him three days, but then the bombardment was followed by a heavy rain, which filled most of the shell craters with a tanker's eternal enemy—mud.

Both sides regularly put out night listening posts in no-man's-land, and pulled them in at dawn. Sometimes raiding parties crept out to assassinate the other side's pickets, sometimes to plant mines, but on this morning, the German pickets heard mechanical sounds issuing from the British lines and duly reported back by field phone. No notice was taken by their commanders because both sides were using motor transport to augment their horse-drawn supply wagons.

At 0500 hours, escorted by a cluster of New Zealand infantrymen, a clanking nightmare lurched out of the muddy, smoking dawn with machine guns rattling from its bulging side sponsons. The German farm boys took one look and suddenly weren't there anymore. First, the gray rhombic shape had crushed their supposedly impregnable wire down; then, straddling their uncrossable trenches with daunting ease, the tank, numbered D-1 but named *Dracula*, of the Heavy Section, Machine Gun Company, began to murder them with relentless ease. Worse, it was bulletproof; the copper-jacketed lead projectiles from their Mauser rifles bounced off the riveted armored sides and whined away into the gathering light. The appearance of *Dracula* was a complete and total surprise.

Lieutenant Arnold, in command of the tank, gave this story in his after-action report.

It was now half light; we were getting along better and were amongst the infantry who were in turn advancing and sheltering in shell holes as our creeping barrage gradually lifted. The German shelling was severe and one felt comparatively safe inside the tank. The German front line trenches had been shelled practically out of existence and I think the infantry met little opposition there. And DRACULA reached the parapet first. A row of German heads appeared above the parapet and looked—no doubt with amazement—at what was approaching out of the murk of the bombardment.

To the defending Germans it must have been as if some ancient pagan battle wagon out of legendary times had come back to haunt them for their recent military misdeeds. A German war correspondent sent back this report of the assault:

> When the German outposts crept out of their dugouts in the misty morning and stretched their necks to look for the English, their blood was chilled in their veins. Mysterious monsters were crawling toward them over the craters. Stunned as if an earthquake had burst around them, they all rubbed their eyes, which were fascinated by the fabulous creatures. . . . One stared and stared as if one had lost the power of their limbs. The big monsters approached us slowly, hobbling, rolling rocking, but always advancing. Nothing impeded them: a supernatural force seemed to impel them on. Someone in the trenches shouted, 'The devil is coming,' and the word was passed along the line like wild-fire.
>
> Suddenly, tongues of flame leapt out of the armored sides of the iron caterpillars. Shells whistled over our heads and the sound of machine-gun fire filled the air. The mysterious creature had yielded up its secret as the English infantry rolled up in waves behind the "Devil's Coaches."

An entire section of well-fortified, well-manned trenches had been cleared by one primitive tank in less than an hour. As far as is known, the machine named after the legendary Vlad Dracula was the first tank to fire in battle.

Inside the tank, the yammering hell was only slightly less unbearable than outside. There was very little room to move about, as most of the interior space was taken up with machinery. Those early tanks weren't compartmented and the great clattering engine took up most of the center of the hull. The crew shared space with the engine and it was not a cozy roommate. Whirring machinery could suck in a body part in an instant, and the unshielded exhaust both overheated the crew and leaked carbon monoxide.

Only a few naked light bulbs, powered by the engine's electrical system, and a few vision slits provided illumination. Those vision slits were provided with narrow glass prisms that had a nasty habit of shattering when hit by a bullet, of which there were plenty, all aimed at the new "bullet magnet." The noise was so intense, especially when the tank was taking thousands of incoming rounds, that it could shatter a human eardrum. In all this, men were still expected to fight and shift and steer. One of the first tankers, William Divall, a transplanted sailor, wrote this letter to his sister:

> As the tanks travel over the front trench, the troops rub their eyes in wonder at their strange, cube-impressionist coats of many colours. The deck of the tank rolls and pitches like a torpedo-boat in a storm. But we are all old hands. A.B.'s in fact—and we come safely through it without sea-sickness. Hun bullets are rebounding from our tough sides like hail from a glass roof. We just crawl over the embankment, guns and all, it is not necessary to fire a shot. Two or three Huns are brave enough to creep on the back of the tank from behind. We open a small trap-door and shoot them with a revolver. . . .
>
> By this time the fumes from the hundreds of rounds which we have fired, and the heat from the engines and the waste petrol and oil have made the air quite oppressive and uncomfortable to breathe. . . . We make a fairly difficult target as our way lies between numerous tree trunks and battered stumps, also much barbed wire. We are battling bravely with the waves of earth we encounter. . . . The last trench proves to be the worst, for just as we are crossing a large hole, our bus stops. I believe the sparking plugs have ceased to sparkle and it is in a very awkward place as the tree stumps now prevent free traverse of our guns.

Divall and his crew got their "bus," restarted, finished their part of the battle, and pulled back for supplies, ammunition, and a maintenance break. Then as now, while everybody else rested, the tankers worked on their mounts.

Tank D-17 *Dinnaken,* under Lieutenant Hastie, rolling at its maximum speed of four miles per hour, flattened the wire, spanned the trenches, and rumbled up the main street of Flers, which was used as a garrison by the invading Germans. A British soldier who was there reported, "The tank waddled on with its guns blazing and we could see Jerry popping up and down, not knowing what to do, whether to stay or run. . . . The Jerries waited until our tank was only a few yards away and then fled—or hoped to. The tank just shot them down and the machine gun posts . . . just disappeared."

Another British soldier wrote in his war memoir: "Wounded? Who cares about being wounded? There was that old D16 groaning and grumbling along, poking her big nose here and there. She stopped now and then, as if unsure of the road, then plunged on over everything. I can still see her great big head, coughing like a hippo. But the best of it was how the Tommies went on, following her—actually cheering! There hasn't been anything like her in this bloody war before. Let's have more of them, I say."

Out of 50 machines to start the attack, only 32 actually reached the battle zone, due to various mechanical problems, and even these began to fall by the wayside or ditch in the soupy mud. Of the tanks in contact with the enemy, many were taken out by artillery; where they stayed in packs, they were successful; where they stayed with their infantry, they survived and prospered. Lieutenant Arnold now continues his account:

We soon covered the mile or so to Flers and on my right, I saw DINNAKEN [Hastie], on the road into Flers. The New Zealanders immediately set about consolidating and took possession of a sunken road which leads out of the village to the northeast. I sent off a pigeon with a message to Corps HQ. It was now about 8 a.m. Things were quiet except for spasmodic shelling and it was a lovely morning. Not liking the look of the German observation balloons, I withdrew DRACULA behind the shelter of a belt of trees. There we made tea and filled up with petrol from the reserve which we carried in a box on the stern wheels. . . . I moved our position occasionally as from the incidence of shelling, I felt sure we were visible to one of the German sausage balloons.

A bit later, an infantry commander sent me a message, "Counter attack brewing, and could I do anything about it?" We emerged from our lair and went out to the front. We were rewarded with the sight of long lines of Germans advancing in open formation and opened fire with our portside Vickers guns at about 900 yards range. It was impossible to tell just what effect our fire took but it certainly checked the advance. DRACULA cruised around for a while in front of the village and then came under what seemed to me to be direct fire from a field gun. . . . One shell in particular missed us by inches. . . . We had taken aboard a badly wounded New Zealander and putting the village with its trees between us and the immediate front, we made tracks for the slight rise that intervenes between Delville wood and Flers.

In a skirmish for a section of the works known as the Gird Trench, a portent for the future took place. A lone tank rocked and clanked forward against heavy machine gun fire, knowing that the 77mm field pieces behind the trench line could easily kill their tank. But they had an ace in the hole, in the form of an artillery observer who had an unbroken telephone wire. Minutes before picking up with a strange infantry battalion, they'd found the observer and his telephone, and had requested special fires. This may be the first time in history that a tank had the chance to request its own covering fire.

The tank advanced confidently, with the Tommies stalking warily alongside. Would this work? From the sky came a rising series of moans and shrieks and the trenchworks exploded in fire and thunder. With a cheer the first tank/

infantry/artillery team in history surged into the works just
as the prearranged concentration ceased. The astounded, demoralized Germans wavered, tried to find the nerve to face
this lone tank and its handful of infantrymen, but suddenly
there was another sound from the sky: the roar of a Le
Rhone engine as a lone Sopwith Camel fighter plane came
down on a strafing run. The pilot, coming back from a frus-
tratingly boring patrol with full ammo racks, had seen the
fight and couldn't resist the chance to strafe some Germans.

The first-ever use of armored, track-laying tanks on a
battlefield had been a success, more or less. As usual on the
advent of a new weapon, neither the commanders nor the
accompanying troops seemed to quite know what to do with
it. The originators of the tank, men like Winston Churchill,
Ernest Swinton, and J. F. C. Fuller, had originally imagined
a mass attack of hundreds of the metal monsters along a
vast line of offense, accompanied by charging infantry with
horse cavalry for exploitation. They got none of this. Instead
the tanks were sent out spaced along the infantry lines, not
as a cohesive unit. Even then, conservative estimates are
that the use of those few already obsolescent Mk-I tanks
saved at least 20,000 casualties, which would have been the
cost of doing the job the "old-fashioned way." And in England, the Mk II and III tanks were in production, and the
Mk IV was already on the drawing boards.

Hindsight, of course, is always 20-20, and the military habits of generations are almost impossible to break. Even
knowing that the shells would churn the land into a quag-
mire, Haig couldn't prevent himself from the traditional
three-day "prepping." The result was that the tankers spent
more time pulling each other out of holes than in attacking.
The few which did get to their objectives, like *Dracula* and
Dinnaken, showed what they could do, and began the learning curve that continues to this day. The romp of *Dinnaken*
through the town of Flers was the ancestor of the stunning
victory of the tankers in Operation Desert Storm.

When those first primitive tanks got out past the line of
villages behind the defensive works, though, things began to
come unglued. No one had yet figured out that it would
have been a good idea to neutralize the German 77mm field

gun batteries, and once the tanks got back to the gun line, they were helpless because most of them were females. In the peculiar British mind-set of the day, tanks armed with machine guns were females, and tanks armed with cannons were males. A tank with both machine guns and cannons was called a hermaphrodite.

The gunnery procedures were also rather primitive, due to the tanks having been sent in before the crews were properly trained. In order to designate a cannon target, the commander in his cupola had first to spot the target with his binoculars in all the battle smoke, explosion, and general confusion. Then he had to drop down, get the attention of the proper gunner, and point out the target. Next, he had to get the attention of a driver, a brakeman, and two gearsmen, and get the tank swung so that the gun could bear, and then stop long enough for accurate firing.

As a result of this problem, when the female tanks had broken the German lines, they were almost defenseless against the artillery and many were taken out by the 77mm dual-purpose gun, which was the direct ancestor of the famed 88. Worse, the Germans very quickly figured out that by putting an observer with a telephone in an observation balloon, they could keep track of the armored thrust and counter it with indirect remotely fired artillery of major caliber. The guns, directed by telephone, could be talked onto targets that they could not see. Warfare was suddenly getting a lot more complex than the minds of the old horse-oriented generals could comprehend and it would take a new generation to fully utilize the new weapon. Those men were already in the trenches, learning. Their names were Erwin Rommel and George Patton.

The slashing armored raids of World War II could easily be called the echo of the American Civil War. Erwin Rommel studied those lightning cavalry raids endlessly, but he also studied the use of heavy firepower, and identified one glaring flaw in contemporary German tactics, which he set out to rectify. Somehow, in all the years since our Civil War, one of Napoleon's maxims had gotten lost. "It is with artillery that one makes war," the emperor had once said. What he was referring to was the use of direct-fire heavy weapons with infantry and cavalry, a technique first used by the Romans and resurrected by Jan Ziska back in the 1500s. It had been used by Napoleon and by American armies in the Civil War, the vast majority of whose leaders had studied at West Point.

The concept was put back into European minds by one Heros Von Borcke, a Prussian cavalry officer who was an accredited observer with the Southern forces during 1860–64. His book, *Two Years in the Saddle,* was one of Erwin Rommel's favorite texts. A copy, with Rommel's name in it, was found in a bunker in Normandy by an American GI in 1944.

When Rommel extracted that bit of information from the writings of Von Borke, he began moving his 77mm direct-fire guns and the heavy Maxim machine guns up with his infantry and blowing his enemy's obstacles out of the way. By war's end, his Italian adversaries in southern Austria were on the run and Rommel's infantry could sometimes walk fully erect across fields where they once had to crawl along under withering streams of machine gun fire. After the first world war, Erwin Rommel wrote a book in which he set down his experiences and conclusions. That book, of course, is the famous *Infantry Attacks,* which was eventually read by George Patton, who in World War I was in command of the first of the American tankers in the Ardennes and was getting his own baptism by fire.

Patton, however, had another source of knowledge, which went back—directly—to the Civil War. George Patton's grandfather had been a Confederate officer, and young George was a frequent visitor at his grandfather's house in his younger years. Another guest was a retired lawyer for the Southern Pacific Railway, John Singleton Mosby. As a boy, George Patton was exposed to the experiences of the great cavalry raider, and when other boys were playing ball, George was getting replays of cavalry tactics made famous by a man who had studied Alexander of Macedon, Genghis Khan, and Oliver Cromwell. The stage for the great tank battles of World War II was being set—this time by men who understood machinery as well as horseflesh and infantrymen.

The problem with older, overly revered sources of military maxims, such as Vegitus, Clausewitz, and Oman is that they were born and studied on the wrong side of the Industrial Revolution. Even such a simple machine as a breech-loading rifle was sufficient to unhinge their time-honored methods. The generals who sent millions into the Somme had apparently never even heard of Pickett at Gettysburg, let alone self-propelled killing machines. Yet the information was available. After the American Civil War the first of the machine-age wars, the U.S. War Department had sent an official history to every major European military academy and war college, who all, with one exception, ignored it. Helmuth Von Moltke, the greatest German marshal of that century said, the Civil War "was a war of one armed mob chasing another—an experience from which nothing of value can be learned." The exception was Russia, and we will meet our Civil War generals again, coming out from behind Stalingrad. The Crossack cavalry thundering alongside T-34 tanks had read of J. E. B. Stuart, John Hunt Morgan, and Phil Sheridan.

REFERENCE SOURCES

Tanks and Trenches, David Fletcher, Alan Sutton.
Cambrai, Bryan Cooper, Stein & Day.
"With the British Army Cheering on Behind," Richard S. Faulkner, *Armor* magazine, March–April 1995.
Tank, Macksey and Batchelor, Ballantine Books.
"A Company of Tanks," Major W. H. L. Watson, *The Strand* magazine, 1922.

CHAPTER 8

The First Tanker's School

AS WE HAVE SEEN, WHEELED ARMORED CARS COULDN'T HAN-
dle trenches and were sent abroad to work in the colonial
wars, saving back only No. 20 Squadron to act as a training
cadre. The tracked tanks were rushed into battle at Flers-
Courcelette, half trained and underequipped, into a hellhole
full of gas shells and soft, tank-trapping mud. They had
proven themselves, however, and the knowledge deficiency
was now to be rectified. Two schools were to be set up, one
at Bovington in England, and another in a forward area
in France, where the few combat-experienced tankers were
patching the wounds of Flers and digesting their experiences.

Brigadier General Sir Hugh Elles, an engineer officer, had
by now been given command of the newly created Tank
Corps and told to build a fighting force of the new war
machines. The lines of battle having now been stabilized by
gigantic trenchworks and the new tanks being very short-
ranged, Elles picked a location quite close to the front for
his forward base. On 18 November 1916, the force took up
residence in the village of Bermicourt, which is so small that
it doesn't appear on most maps. Bermicourt Chateau is near
St. Pol on the road from Montreuil to Arras, and it was

simply a large chateau surrounded by a few farmhouses whose owners walked out every day to work their fields. At some time in the past, it had been taken over by an order of nuns and their charges. Now it was to become the temporary home of the British forward tank school.

First, however, there had to be a small reorganization of the fledgling training command. The reason that no one has ever been able to keep track of British tank unit designations is that the first four companies of the provisional battalion at Flers were now designated as battalions and kept their alphabetic designations for a time. They now became A, B, C, and D battalions, with numbered companies. Effectively, the tank *Dracula* had become a battalion commander's vehicle. The men who'd been through the hell of the Somme at Flers suddenly became veteran instructors . . . one battle, but they were all Elles had.

The call had gone out for volunteers and they came in by the droves. Regardless of the opinions of reactionary senior officers, those who'd seen armor in action wanted in on the new kind of war. There were men from cavalry and infantry, machine gunners and artillerymen, even some fliers who wanted the new experience. There were seamen who'd helped build the tanks and bombadiers from the Royal Naval Air Service. And of course, No. 20 Armored Car Squadron. . . . *This* collection of mechanized miscreants they moved into a French nunnery?

The first morning parade must have looked like a military zoo. There would have been Scottish kilts, army infantry khaki, cavalry riding breeches, and naval and air force blue, sprinkled with the uniforms of colonial regiments from Australia, New Zealand, and India. There was apparently one totally American crew also, commanded by Captain James A. McGuire and his midwestern warriors. The name of their tank was *Judge Jefferies,* and it bore the picture of a hangman's gibbet on its bow.

Something of the atmosphere of Bermicourt can be gotten from a letter from Major W. H. L. Watson, who was posted to command a company of tanks. The letter later appeared in a magazine of the time:

On parade, the company looked like a motley crew, as indeed it was. Men from different battalions knew different drill and some of the less combatant corps knew no drill at all. The company lived in a rambling hospice built around a large courtyard. The original inhabitants consisted of nuns and thirty or forty aged and infirm men who, from their habits and appearance, we judged to be consumptives.

The men were trained in the elements of tank driving in the appalling winter of snow, rain and mud, while officer's courses were held at Bermicourt. Very few tanks were available for instruction, and so dummy tanks were provided. Imagine a large box of canvas stretched on a wooden frame. There is no top or bottom, it is about 6 feet high, 8 feet long and five feet wide. Little slits were made in the canvas to represent the loopholes of a tank. Six men carried and moved each dummy, lifting it by the cross-pieces of the framework. For our sins, we were issued with eight of these abominations.

We started with a crew of officers to encourage the men, and when the first dummy tank waddled out of the gate, it was immediately surrounded by a mob of cheering children, who thought it was an imitation dragon or something out of a circus. It was led away from the road to avoid hurting the feelings of the crew and to safeguard the ears and morals of the children. After colliding with the corner of a house, it endeavored to walk down the side of a railway cutting. Nobody was hurt, but a fresh "crew" was necessary. It regained the road when a small man in the middle stumbled and fell. The dummy tank went back to the carpenters for repairs.

We persevered with those dummy tanks. The men hated them, they were heavy, awkward and produced much childish laughter—the dummies became less and less mobile—one company commander mounted them on wagons drawn by mules. The crews were tucked in with their Lewis guns and each contraption, a cross between a fire engine and a triumphal car in the Lord

Mayor's Show, would gallop past targets which the gunners would endlessly endeavor to hit.

Oddly enough, some of these wheeled dummy tanks went to war as the first decoy tanks in history. Wheels were built inside of them and donkeys were harnessed ahead of the wheels, but inside the superstructure. History does *not* record whether there was a volunteer driver or simply a carrot inside to give the animals direction. At any rate, the Society for the Prevention of Cruelty to Animals would never have approved.

Eventually they got their first real tanks and began their training in earnest. A Sergeant Littledale recorded his first impressions in a magazine article after the war:

> There is not one of us who will ever forget his first ride; the crawling in at the sides, the discovery that the height did not permit a man of medium stature to stand erect, the sudden starting of the engine, the roar of it all when the throttle opened, the jolt forward and the sliding through the mud that followed, until at last we came to the "jump" that had been prepared.
>
> Then came the forward motion which threw us off our feet and caused us to stretch trusting hands towards the nearest object, usually at first, a hot pipe through which the water from the cylinder jacket flowed to the radiator. So, down and down and down, the throttle closed, the engine just barely ticking over, until the bottom was reached, and as the power was turned on full, the tank raised itself to the incline like a ship rising on a wave, and we were all jolted the other way, only to clutch again at things which were hot and burned, until at last with a swing over the top, we gained level ground.

Those early tanks had no protection from the heat of the engine, no powered ventilation, and unsprung tracks The axles of the road wheels were bolted to the hull and the tracks were solid steel. When the tracks hit something solid, the jolt was transmitted, undampened, to the crew. Another man, Richard Haig, when he reported to the school in late 1917, was impressed by the tiny area in which he was expected to live and fight:

We looked around the little chamber with eager curiosity. Our first thought was that seven men and an officer could never do any work jammed in such a confined space. Eight of us were jammed in here, but we were standing still. When it came to going into action and moving around inside the tank, it would be impossible. In front are two stiff seats, one for the driver and one for the officer. . . . Two narrow slits serve as portholes through which we looked ahead. In front of the officer is a map board and a gun-mounting. Down the middle of the tank is the powerful petrol engine, part of it covered with a hood, and along each side a narrow passage along which a man can slide from the officer's and driver's seats to the mechanism at the rear. There are four machine gun turrets [sponsons] two each side. There is also a place for a gun in the rear, but this is rarely used. "Willies" do not often turn tail and flee.

Along the steel walls are numberless ingenious little cupboards in which stores and ammunition are stacked high. Every bit of space is utilized. Electric bulbs light the interior. Beside the driver are the secondary gears by which the machine is turned in any direction. All action inside is directed by signals, for when the tank moves, the noise is such as to drown a man's voice.

This was the machine that was to change history at Cambrai, later in the year 1917. For the modern reader, a comparison to our own experiences is easily made.

The track suspension was roughly equivalent to that of a D-8 bulldozer, only without the return rollers. The treads simply slid over (hopefully) greased steel runways. The engine horsepower was 100 to 150, depending on the model. That is about equivalent to a six-cylinder auto engine, certainly not equal to a standard V-8, which can reach over 300 horsepower in normal configurations.

The engines were hand-cranked, magneto-fired, and ran

at 1,000 rpms, due to an extremely long stroke and primitive valve timing. As to the driving and crewing experience, try to imagine being inside a trash Dumpster with an unmuffled stock car engine, and rolling on unsprung tracks while being shot at—for days at a time. Your only view of the outside world is an unarmored slit through which a bullet could arrive at any time.

The machine gun firepower was about what a squad of light infantry can deliver today, but those heavy-barreled guns were served by a 25,000-round supply. Their six-pounder cannons had about a 2.5-inch bore and threw a four-pound projectile in several versions, armor-piercing, canister, and high-explosive. They carried 200 rounds for this weapon, but could fire accurately only when the tank was stopped, making it a perfect target.

Their armor plate was between 6mm and 12mm in thickness and was held together by rivets that tended to pop off and strike crew members when hit by a bullet on the outside. For modern reference, one-half inch equals 12.5mm and a modern armor-piercing rifle bullet can get through 6mm of side plate quite easily. . . . The armor-piercing bullet had been invented by the Germans in 1916, not too long before the first tanks were used. The battle of Cambrai promised to be quite interesting. First, however, there was one last gasp for the now ancient Mk-I. Eight of them would be shipped to Gaza in the Holy Land, where armored, crewed vehicles have been contesting the right of way since the days of the Hittites. Then, as now, the contest was over the security of trade routes through the area. Then, as now, the problem was the unstable rapaciousness of the denizens. *Palestinian* comes from the word "Philistine," and the inhabitants of the land that is now Israel have been a problem since there has been history.

REFERENCE SOURCES

Cambrai, Bryan Cooper, Stein & Day.
The Fighting Tanks, Since 1916, Jones, Rarey & Icks, National Service Publishing Co, Washington, DC.
"With the Tanks, " H. A. Littledale, *Atlantic Monthly*, December 1918.

CHAPTER 9

Armored Cars in the Desert

EARLY IN THIS CENTURY, ITALY, THE LAST OF THE PRESENT European nations to consolidate in modern form, decided that it needed a few foreign possessions, and quietly shipped a few "peaceful agrarian colonists" off to Libya, which was then a province of the empire of Ottoman Turkey. The land was ill-governed and the local religious sect, the Senusis, were in the process of defying the sultan of the dying Ottoman Empire. Turkey itself, vegetating under a corrupt and decadent theocracy and vacillating between either a German or British alliance, wasn't looking at its possessions very closely. As a result, the sultan was taken completely by surprise when Italy declared war on his nation.

In 1911, claiming that its Libyan colonists were being mistreated, Italy bombarded Tripoli and landed a force of 50,000 troops with modern weapons. Specifically, they had nine aircraft (two small airships, two Berloits, three Nieuports, two Farmans, and a pair of Etrich Taubes). The armored car detachment consisted of a pair of barrel-hooded, turreted Bianchi cars armed with a single machine gun each. This, just before World War I in 1912, as far as is known, is the first use of mechanized armor in any war, and they don't seem to have been used much, except against local strongpoints. The airships, though, caused squalls of outrage from the Turks because of their "inhuman" practice of dropping hand grenades on the troops below.

This army did, however, manage to extort Libya from the sultan—and attract the attention of Mohammed es Senussi, who, like the Mahdi before him, claimed descent from Fatima, the daughter of the Prophet, and was building an empire out of the oasis deep in the southern deserts. The aims of the Senussi Brotherhood were the simplification of Islam and the restoration of fertility to a ravaged land. This inevitably brought them into contact with the French in Tunisia, the Italians in their own land, and the British in Egypt. Now North Africa, like Palestine, was a powder keg with a short fuse.

The British had been watching the rise of the Senussi cult rather closely as they were pan-Arabic in scope, much like today's Islamic fundamentalists. However, the British seemed to get along with the Senussi, who were expanding their influence into Egypt, which was then a British protectorate.

Once World War I spread to Britain's colonial possessions and protectorates, and under the influence of German gold and Turkish flattery, the Senussi saw an opportunity not to be ignored, and began to expand their activities into undergarrisoned Egypt, which action began to seriously aggravate the British commander, Lieutenant General Sir John Maxwell. All it would take to light that fuse was one match, and it would soon be struck: Enter German submarine U-35, under Lieutenant Commander Waldemar Kophamel.

The Germans, who had won the diplomatic courtship of Turkey, were cruising at will along the coasts of North Africa, landing cargos of small arms, machine guns, and light artillery, arming the tribes to insurrection against their colonial overlords. They also brought Turkish military instructors to teach the use of the new weapons. U-35, commanded by Kophamel, had dropped off a load of these supplies and, before returning to Istanbul for another cargo, took time off for some ship hunting.

Five sea-miles out into the Gulf of Sollum, he sighted

smoke and dived. Shortly, he sighted the hull and twin fun-
nels of HMS *Tara* and began his approach. In civilian life,
the *Tara* had been the SS *Hibernia,* a railroad ferry. Now,
requisitioned by the Royal Navy, she had been armed with
three small cannons and was used as an armed boarding
vessel. Her mission was the waylaying and inspecting of the
cargoes of neutral ships, which legally made her a warship
of the British Navy.

Inside the conning tower of his tiny submersible, Kophamel feverishly looked through his book of silhouettes and
came up with first *Hibernia,* then *Tara,* and informed his
executive officer that "we have a warship, small, but a warship." Measuring the height of *Tara*'s mast against a scale
in his periscope, Kophamel estimated the range. This information was transmitted to the forward torpedo room and
the gyros were set to intercept the unsuspecting British
warship.

Kophamel took her with a beam shot on a clear day,
putting a single torpedo into her. The *Tara* immediately
began to go down on an even keel, giving the crew time to
launch their boats and perform a classic abandon-ship drill.
All would have been well, had not Kophamel been a gentleman of the old school, who thought the honorable thing to
do would be to rescue the survivors of the *Tara* and escort
them to safety.

Calmly, the commander surfaced his U-boat in the middle
of the cluster of lifeboats and chivalrously offered to tow
them to the nearest port. That port was Bardia, the one that
U-35 had just left, and Kophamel turned the care of his
prisoners over to the senior Turkish officer, Ja'far Pasha—
who turned them over to the Senussi for safekeeping.

Captain Gwatkin-Williams and the officers and men of the
Tara, and the survivors of another ship's crew, the transport
Moorina, were promptly hustled out into the desert to an
unknown destination, and when word of this got back to
Egypt, the fuse had burned down short. That action would
eventually generate the first long-range armored raid in history. Before that would happen, though, the sputtering stalemate between the British and the Senussi would have to
become a full-fledged war. It didn't take long.

The Senussi leader, Said Ahmed, who succeeded old Mohammed es Senussi, had fallen under the influence of two Turkish officers, one of whom had been trained in Germany. These two, Nuri Bey and Ja'far Pasha, had arrived with gold and honeyed words and the enhanced reputation of the Turkish army, which had defeated the British at Gallipoli. Using the exploits of Commander Kophamel and the U-35 as examples, they even managed to convince the Said Ahmed that the British were losing control of the sea. Said Ahmed took the bait and told his followers to march. On 17 November 1915, the world war found North Africa.

Without warning, a jihad was declared and the Islamic troops were again on the march. The port of Sollum had to be evacuated, then Mersa Matrūh came under attack. Sidi Barani was attacked but held. This was Italian Libya, remember, and in that war, Italy was on the Allied side. A large percentage of the British/Egyptian Coast Guard were Senussi and deserted to the enemy. Maxwell, in the meantime, had sent a high-ranking envoy to the Said Ahmed to inquire after the health of the crew of the *Tara*. Said Ahmed at first denied any knowledge of the affair. Then, under a little more diplomatic pressure, he admitted that the prisoners were being held "somewhere in the interior" and would say no more, feeling safe under the sultan's and Germany's alleged protection. At just this time, a very experienced armored car unit was arriving in Egypt. It was known as the Emergency Squadron, Royal Naval Air Service Armored Car Division.

As can be inferred from the designation, the unit was one of the first of its kind, having been put together by the Royal Navy, which had remote air squadrons to protect. The menace of submersible warfare was finding one of its natural enemies on its track. American-made flying boats with open cockpits, biplane wings, and primitive aero engines were lifting off the waters of quiet bays and remote islands to sweep the seas for prowling U-boats like the U-35.

Since the bases of these patrolling seaplanes were often some distance from the nearest British army base, they needed their own protection. The navy and Rolls-Royce motor company came up with a design that survived almost unchanged for thirty years. The Rolls was uncomfortable, cramped, and hot, but it was also extremely rugged and reliable, and that made all the difference.

The big slow-turning Rolls engine was hand-cranked in the first models, which meant that someone had to get out of the vehicle and start the engine, even if they were under fire at the time. This job usually fell to the driver, as the vehicle commander and gunner had more important work at the moment. The armament, a Vickers .303-caliber machine gun, was reliable and rugged but tended to run out of water at inconvenient times. The crew were supposed to be three—a driver, gunner, and commander—but in practice was usually only two, the driver and a commander/gunner—who needed to be relatively small men, as the interior quarters were quite cramped.

The turret was hand-operated, requiring good shoulders, and when firing forward, the hot cartridges would fall directly down the driver's back, which gives some idea of the interior tightness. Directly behind the turret was an open cargo bay with toolboxes on the sides—about like a modern pickup truck, except that the car was plated with three-eighths-inch armor and weighed three and a half tons. This was the armored beast that would begin to change history.

This was what would be called in American parlance, a "Hot Outfit." These gents knew they were good, having been involved in fighting in Flanders and having been selected for mechanical expertise as well as individual bravery. They could fight, and as important, they could keep the machinery running and the guns clean. Many had been horsed cavalry and there was a good leavening of a new breed of soldier . . . an armed mechanic with a fighting machine. These were the men referred to by an older generation as "those rude mechanicals."

The link with airplanes and armor was also being forged, as the fledgling RAF became the flying eyes of the armormen. In the middle of January 1916, a patrolling two-seater biplane, with no radio, spotted the Senussi trying to occupy yet another town. The Muslim sect had set up a camp at Halazin, 22 miles south of Mersa Matrūh, on the coast. Wheeling in the air above the encampment, the pilot eagerly brought the news back to his base. In those days, a pilot's only means of communication was to write a message on a sheet of notepaper, secure the message with a ribbon, tie the other end to a rock, and drop it in front of the armored cars. Or, if possible, land on a road and deliver the information in person.

General Sir Alexander Wallace's health was failing at this time and he'd had to turn the command over to a successor, Major General William Peyton, who decided to use South African infantry, light cavalry, and the new armored car brigade to kick the Senussi out. The commander of the Senussi and Turkish forces was the German-trained Turkish officer Ja'far Pasha, who was ably assisted by a political officer, Nuri Bey.

The first use of the armored cars was the usual case of too little, too late, since Peyton had only allocated four of the cars to the assault on the little town of Agagya. Unfortunately, bad route reconnaissance had gotten every one of them stuck and the most they could do was dismount their guns, lug them forward on foot, and fire from tripods. The battle was won, however, and then Sidi Barrâni fell on 28 February, and then the march toward Sollum and its large garrison was resumed.

All this time, there had been absolutely no word of the fate of the crew of the *Tara*. Not one of the captured Sennusi or Turks seemed to know of their existence. Even Ja'far Pasha, who had been captured, seemed not to know where the captives had been taken—or was not telling. After interrogation, Pasha was marched off to Cairo to an officers' prison. Nuri Bey, according to one of the armormen, S. C. "Sammy" Rolls, whose journal has survived, rode off on a beautiful piebald mare, vanishing into rough country.

When the march on Sollum began, the infantry and cavalry moved out along the coast, but it was considered that the enemy might hold the high plain and General Peyton decided to send the armored car squadron up through a barely negotiable pass to clear out any resistance and approach Sollum from the south After digging themselves out from the evening sandstorm, the armormen tackled the steep, sandy pass. One officer was heard to comment that "the last wheels through here must have been Roman." The first wheels up that slope probably had belonged to the charioteers of Ramses II, many of whom were a mixture of Philistine, Cananite and Ethiopian mercenaries. Like the chariot mercenaries before them, the armormen would fight first in Libya and then in Palestine, almost in the same wheel tracks as the chariots.

Fortunately, the cargo trucks or tenders for the force were a lot lighter than the armored cars. They were the classic Ford model T trucks and were light enough to be manhandled. There was enough manpower available, and by actually lifting and pulling the first trucks over the pass, enough horsepower was gotten on top to pull the rest through. The drill was for a dozen or so men to manhandle a Ford up the escarpment, trailing a rope behind it. Then they would all get into the cargo box to give the "Tin Lizzie" traction and it would pull the next vehicle up. One suspects that chariots were gotten up the slope in about the same way, with the same exertion and the taking of the names of the local gods in vain.

The men were digging wheels out of the sand and prying rocks out of the way all day long. They spent long hours rigging tow ropes, changing flat tires, and feeding boiling, thirsty radiators, for pressurized radiators hadn't been invented yet. That effort took one whole day—for just fifteen miles of travel—but that night they camped on top of the escarpment, the first armored combat machines in the high desert.

At that time, Erwin Rommel was leading an infantry company in Europe. In his spare time, Captain Rommel was reading Heros Von Borcke's book and had taken a great fancy to the tactics of one J.E.B. Stuart. Those slashing cavalry tactics would be seen again, in the high desert of Africa. The genius of the Afrika Korps had its antecedents in the Civil War of America, whose generals had studied ancient history.

The next day, the British armored force was slowly probing along the edge of the high cliffs, surveying and mapping as they went. Sammy Rolls records:

Before dawn, we were all astir, and as the first light came into the sky, the column, still led by *Blast*, proceeded on its way. I drove as close as possible to edge of the precipice, picking my way between the great stones, and stopping frequently when further movement was made impossible by the obstructions. The men from the other cars would run forward and remove some of the stones until a passage had been opened large enough to drive through. For mile after mile we carried on in this manner, sometimes being forced to turn away from the cliff for a distance in order to avoid a deep gully. Many of these gaps were so steep that they might have been cut with a huge axe in the side of the mountain.

When we had gone fourteen miles on this nerve-wracking journey, a halt was called and I received the order to drive as close as possible to the edge of a ravine so that the signaller whom I carried might set up his equipment, and get into communications with the troops advancing across the plain below.

The news brought by the flashing light was not particularly encouraging: "LEFT BUQ BUQ EARLY THIS MORNING, WELLS HERE ALMOST DRY, SEARCHING FOR WATER, SITUATION SERIOUS," was the report from General Sir Henry Lufkin, commanding the forces on that plain. Later on in the day, infantry from a South African regiment began scrambling up over the cliffs, desperate for water, but all that was left was what was in the guns' cooling jackets or in the vehicles' radiators. Carefully, what little was available was doled out of the crew's canteens and the desperate search for water went on. One South African officer, a bank manager in Capetown, even went so far as to offer Sammy Rolls 50 British pounds for a drink of water, but Rolls refused the money and found a few drops for him in a canteen.

Finally, by draining water from several cars to keep one's radiator full, a scouting Ford truck was able to find a native well at Siwiat and start ferrying water back to the dehydrated troops. The Rolls armored cars were the fighting ma-

chines of this troop, but all the scouting and carrying was
done by the unstoppable Fords. On 14 March, they finally
got through Halfaya Pass (known to two generations of soldiers as "Hellfire Pass") and into Sollum—which the Senussi
and Turks had abandoned. Here, however, they got their
first word of the plight of the crew of the *Tara*.

A squad of soldiers, going through the town on a house-
to-house search for holdouts, found a letter by the captain
of the *Tara*, Captain Gwatkin-Williams, which had been addressed to the commander of the British garrison before the
original Senussi attack. Apparently it had simply lain on a
table, or in a drawer, unread, all this time. Supposedly, the
prisoner's location was El Hakkim, or maybe Bir Hachiem,
depending on the dialect used—nobody had ever heard of
the place. In the meantime, scouting aircraft had finally
found the Senussi main camp, at a place called Bir Wair,
inside what was technically Italian territory.

Peyton, fed up with all this search and fumble, ordered
his fastest, most mobile force into action. Specifically, he
ordered the Duke of Westminster to take his armored cars
and act with such aggression as the situation demanded. Generic orders of this type are not given to infantry or artillery.
Only the iron cavalry can carry out such an instruction, and
carry it out they did.

A Rolls, which T. E. Lawrence had praised as "valued
above rubies in the desert," could do 70 miles per hour on
a hard surface, and that was just what was found west of
Sollum. At Bir Wair, the Senussi had again decamped, but
camel- and horse-conveyed troops are not about to outrun
a Rolls-Royce, and at a rocky well called Bir Aziz, they and
their Turkish technicians and advisers were finally brought
to bay.

The Senussi had set up in the rocks and crags with machine guns and four-inch mountain cannons, which could
blow a Rolls apart. This was their main host, and just 34
men in ten armored cars went for them with the Vickers
guns yammering and the throttles wide open. This was the
first armored charge ever made, 14 March 1916, and those
men knew they were making history. Behind each gray-
painted armored car a rolling plume of dust and a shimmer

of heated exhaust lifted into the desert air. They lurched and swayed and streams of cartridge casings poured from them as they fought against overwhelming odds—as usual.

Life in an iron combat machine is never comfortable and the guns and radiators were both boiling steam from their caps, bullets were flickering off the hoods and turrets, spalling metal into the crews' bodies from impacts. The heat was terrible as the fumes and steam from the chattering Vickers guns were added to the exhaust and the spraying hot oil from the engines. The men were bleeding from dozens of tiny cuts made by spalling metal, and only the aviator's goggles that they wore saved their eyes.

By common consent, the machine gunners in the turrets concentrated on those mountain cannons and quickly killed off the crews. Those guns alone could have saved that army, but neither their Turkish crews nor their sights were capable of handling a moving target, most especially not a moving armored target that was filing the air around them with lethal metal. When those guns, upon which the sole surviving Turkish officer, Nuri Bey, was depending, went out of action, the heart went out of the Senussi army. They broke into tribal bands and ran—right into the machine gun fire of the armored cars, which by that time had circled around the rocky well and caught them in the open, slaughtering hundreds of them. This is the way Sammy Rolls remembers the day:

My duties were to drive the car somehow, anyhow, as long as I got her forward, dodging the larger stones, which were difficult to see through the narrow slits, to find suitable targets for the gunner, bring the car into a position which would allow him to fire at them without sitting on my head, keep a keen eye on the enemy's gun positions so as to try to approach them without being hit, and frequently to drive with one hand while I fed a belt into the Maxim." [Note: The job description has not changed one whit in eighty years.] The third man of us, an officer, acted as an observer, peering out of the various apertures in turn and shouting orders at intervals, to turn right or turn left and make for such and such an objective. At the same time the gunner shouted to me to turn here or turn towards something he had seen. Altogether I was very busy indeed and in a state of mind between cursing and laughing.

A bullet found its way into our little fortress somehow and hit the lieutenant's arm, but he went on urgently requesting me to turn left and turn right. So engrossed were we in our own affairs that we forgot about the other fighting cars. They were in the same condition, and before long, we were widely separated. The enemy had scattered and their fire seemed to have ceased. Suddenly I shouted, "THERE GOES NURI." Again he'd been cornered, and again he was slipping away.

The Turk was galloping away to the southwest like a streak of light on his beautiful piebald mare. Her long mane flew in his face as he bent low in his saddle and her tail streamed out like a white plume. There was something fairylike about their figures, as they flew across the plain together, and for the moment, they seemed unreal apparitions flitting in the grim desert. Suddenly I thought, "now for it!" and swinging the nose of my car towards the fast-receding rider, I gave chase, but what a run he gave us.

He plunged at once into even more difficult ground, strewn thick with rocks. The excitement became intense as I strained every nerve to keep the car at the highest possible speed, and at the same time to avoid colliding with dangerous rocks. The other two continually urged me to greater speed. Yes, we were surely gaining on the wily Turk, and I could see him now and then turn his head to mark our progress. All the while I twisted and snatched the wheel this way and that, often missing the boulders by an inch or two.

Suddenly, Nuri swerved more to the westward and all but the top of his head disappeared behind a large rock. "Get the gun ready," I gasped, "we'll have him yet." For the moment, we could no longer see anything of him, but in a minute or two we came abreast of the rock and then saw why he had turned off to his right.

He had plunged into a belt of small dunes of shifting sand and was rising and dipping in that heavy going but making good speed. . . . Slower and slower became our progress as the yielding sand sucked the life out of my engine and gradually Nuri drew away. My radiator was boiling dangerously and I began to feel that the time had come to give up the chase. However, I kept on grimly and at last we struggled on to harder ground, but Nuri was now no more than a dot on the horizon. Suddenly there was a loud bang and *"Blast,"* lurched clumsily. "Burst tire!" gasped in response to the explanations of the others, and we had to give Nuri the Palm. This was the second time he had escaped after the defeat of his troops and I had to admire the skill of his getaway.

After changing the tire, refilling the radiator, and dressing the lieutenant's wounded arm, Rolls and *Blast* circled back to the scene of the day's action, where they found the rest of the squadron pulling maintenance and collecting prisoners and loot. Rolls's share of the loot was a German automatic pistol. Wounded prisoners were loaded into ambulances and the dead were left to the vultures, which were already circling overhead—just as they had for thousands of years of human conflict.

Just 34 men with armor, guns, and engines—and above all, courage—had broken a small army, with only two slight wounds themselves. There'd been a few flat tires, of course, but those old, high wheels could run on the rims for a while, and they did, long enough to do the job. Nuri Bey escaped capture, barely, and the duke took possession of all of his heavy weaponry. Guns that had been built in Germany by Krupp and shipped across an ocean by submarine were now captive prizes, towed behind the new iron cavalry. The rules had been changed—forever.

The next day the armored cars and their Ford tenders towed three cannons into Sollum and marched in an impressive collection of captives, along with nine Maxim machine guns and a quarter million rounds of ammunition. The Senussi had had their fangs pulled. There remained the matter

of the crew of the *Tara,* and some progress was being made
on that matter too—and high time, as over four months had
gone by since the sinking of the *Tara* and the *Moorina*

In Arabic, the word *Bir* means "well" or "cistern," and
inquiries were being made all over Sollum as to the where-
abouts of a Bir Hacheim, with no result. It wasn't until the
prisoners from the battle at Bir Aziz were questioned that
one weather-wizened, almost toothless ancient Senussi warrior admitted that he had tended cattle there as a youth,
and said that he would act as a guide.

Immediately the Duke of Westminister offered his armored cars to escort the rescue mission. Since the crew of
the *Tara* had been prisoners at the mercy of the Senussi for
some months now, no time was wasted and at 0100 hours
on 17th March, a column of some 45 vehicles left Sollum.
The original dozen armored cars were in the lead, followed
by the Ford tenders and a string of ambulances.

The distance, the old Senussi warrior had said, was five
days by camel. Motorcars he didn't know about. When they
passed Bir Wair, through which a barely marked track led
to Tobruk, they dropped off a pair of cars to hold the junction, just in case the Senussi rallied. By dawn the column
was far into the unmapped desert, totally dependent on the
eyesight and memory of one old man.

After a halt for breakfast and maintenance, they pushed
on, making good time but still wondering about the accuracy
of their guide. Some reassurance was made when they ran
across a camel caravan carrying supplies from the coast to
the tribesmen in the interior. The camels were loaded with
grain, but the British armormen, by now suspicious of anything Arabic, ordered the caravan to stop and began probing
around in the grain sacks. Suddenly a soldier's probing bayonet clinked against metal and he reached into a grain pan-
nier and pulled out a fistful of cartridges—8mm Mauser,
exactly the caliber the Senussi's German-manufactured rifles
used! Sam Rolls recorded his share of the loot as being a
cake of soap and a pair of Turkish slippers.

In order to throttle any more raids by the tribesmen, the
supplies were confiscated, the camels shot, and the drivers
taken prisoner and loaded up in the Ford tenders. The Brit-

ish soldiers hoped this meant they were on the right track, because their fuel supplies were limited. Those old Rolls-Royces and the Model Ts wouldn't get more than about eight to ten miles per gallon in that kind of rough going and the duke was watching his fuel supplies drop alarmingly. Most of the Ford trucks were carrying extra fuel in the kind of two-gallon tins used to ship vegetable oil for restaurant kitchens. That was all that was available to carry spare fuel for the Brits, even up into the next war a quarter century later. No one had ever thought to make sturdy extra fuel cans until the Germans invented them, which is why they are called jerry cans.

At 1500 hours, the old Senussi, who'd been sitting in the lead car silently watching the miles slip by, suddenly pointed south and said that that was the way to Bir Hacheim, he was sure. The internal compass that sailors and desert dwellers have had just given the old man the final bearing that they needed—but would they believe him? There was some intense discussion right then, because they were just about at the point of no return as far as their fuel supplies went. They were 120 miles out when suddenly the old man shouted that he could see Bir Hacheim.

The wells proved to be beneath two unremarkable humps in a mud-walled village on the horizon, and there was a swarm of activity as the inhabitants spotted the onrushing column. Completely panicked, the Senussi garrison, with its women and children, went running into the desert mounted on a motley herd of camels and donkeys—almost as if the knew what the British would most likely do when they found how their countrymen had been treated.

Then horribly starved, half-naked, filthy figures began to come out of the hovels around the well. Wretched white men, starved almost beyond recognition, tears in their eyes, welcomed their liberators. Most were half dead from dysentery and lack of nutrition, some could merely stand, incapable of even the effort of walking. Already four of them had died of malnutrition, and the rest were only just hanging on.

As the column of ambulances pulled to a halt, the armormen went mad, roaring off into the desert after the departing guards. There was a very short, sharp massacre,

and that entire tribe—men, women, and older children—
died, save for two children who were brought back to Sollum. That was the only stain on a perfect long-range desert
operation, the first of its kind. At that, though, one can
understand the attitude of the armormen, as the crew of the
Tara had been deliberately starved so that they could not
run as the Sennusi had. Brutality breeds more brutality.

Blast and Sam Rolls were first into the encampment, and
later in the day, Captain Gwatkin-Williams showed Rolls's
crew how they had survived:

> See here," he said, stopping in his walk and pointing to
> the barren ground. I looked, but could see nothing but
> sand and rock anywhere. "Watch this," he said again,
> stooping down with an old penknife in his hand. "Look.
> This little weed!" yes there was a little weed growing
> there. He scraped away the sand and pulled it up. Then
> from the root, he extracted a small kernel. "Eat this,"
> said he, handing it to me. A wan smile lit up his face
> as he watched my expression change, for I found the
> kernel sweet and told him so.
>
> Then he led me a little further and presently kicked
> away a loose stone. I saw some snails under it. As he
> cracked one of these with a stone and took out the
> slimy contents and offered it to me, I shuddered with
> disgust. But he smiled again and put it in his mouth.
> "What, eat that?" I exclaimed. "Why yes," said he.
> "Just as good as a small oyster. . . . We've lived on
> little else but these little morsels for weeks. I've kept
> my boys alive with them, at least the majority of them,
> but dysentery was gradually getting us down. . . . We
> kept on hoping that something would be done to rescue
> us but it seemed as though that hope was never going
> to be realized."

After giving immediate first aid and getting some real
food into the rescued men, and rather than camp in the
desert with sick and wounded patients, the column did what
no animal-borne force could have done. They switched gun-

ners to the driving position, relieving the exhausted drivers. Then, putting the last of their stored fuel in the driving tanks, they turned on the headlights and headed back to Sollum, 120 miles away, a week's travel by camel caravan. At 2300 hours that same day, they passed into safety at Bir Wair just ahead of a sandstorm. They got the ambulances through to Sollum, though, and the crew of the *Tara* into a hospital ship.

Then the armored cars and their tenders holed up for two days to wait out the sandstorm. Even modern machinery is no match for the high desert. The crewmen and the mechanics spread tarps over their vehicles, plugged the carburetors, crankcase vents, and exhausts to keep the sand out of the engines, and then hunkered down beside their mounts under the tarps to wait out the storm.

This time, when they got through to Sollum, it was to the cheers of the infantry and a salute fired by the guns of the garrison. A new era of war had begun, and the work of the duke's men was just beginning, for these were the ones who surveyed that desert in Rolls armored cars and T-model Fords with machine guns. These were the men who made the maps that would guide the Desert Rats of the Eighth Army twenty-five years later, when they went head to head with the Afrika Korps.

Their desert war wasn't over yet, by far. Some of these men would finish their war in Palestine, Mesopotamia, and Arabia, fighting for the legendary T. E. Lawrence. The series of events that got them to the Holy Land was bizarre, and involved the captured Turkish officer, Ja'far Pasha, who had received his military education in Germany. Ja'far was not a Turk at all, he was a Baghdadi, or what one would now call an Iraqi, and his inner loyalties were to the people of the land, not the lordly Turk. When he found out from an article in a Cairo newspaper that the Turkish army was making war on his people, he gave his parole to the English and offered his services to the sharif of Mecca, who would have none of him, distrusting Baghdadis on general principle. Eventually, Sam Rolls would finish out his war as personal driver for T. E. Lawrence and his new military assistants,

Nuri Bey and Ja'far Pasha. This was in mid-1917, however, and in Europe, the tanks were rolling into battle.

REFERENCE SOURCES

Desert Warfare, Bryan Perrett, Patrick Stephens, Ltd.
Steel Chariots in the Desert, S. C. Rolls, Jonathan Cape.
Small Wars, C. E., Callwell, Bison Books.

CHAPTER 10

Gaza Strip, Spring 1917

HIS MAJESTY'S LANDSHIP DETACHMENT

DRY, HOT, AND SANDY, THE MIDDLE EAST SEEMS A LAND made especially for war and not much else—except producing the fuel for war. Where chariot horses once grazed in Mesopotamia, oil wells now produce fuel for, among other things, the tanks that have replaced the ancient war machines. Thirty-five hundred years ago, at the end of the Bronze Age, Egyptian and Hittite, Canaanite and Philistine, Hebrew and Assyrian, all contested the land that is now Israel. Down the long centuries, there has been much more war than peace in those tortured lands. Where mercenary charioteers once battled over the fate of city-states like Kadesh and Gaza, armored war came again in 1917, clanking on the steel treads of a British naval invention, the Mk-I tanks, or as they were called then, landships.

Invented by a committee composed of naval experts, mechanical engineers, and military theoreticians, the first tank was a compromise and a mechanical nightmare. Designed to support walking infantry, span trenches, and crush barbed-wire entanglements, the Mk-I was a very specialized weapon—and a very clumsy one. Of the crew of eight men, three were drivers and shifters. The driver had the brakes and the throttle. There was a gearsman for each tread, and each time the vehicle needed to turn, it had to be stopped, the differential locked, and pivoted for the new direction. For small corrections en route, there was a tail wheel that acted just like a ship's rudder, when not wrapped into uselessness with barbed wire and debris.

The engine, of just 105 horsepower, was cranky, hard to start, and drove the 28-ton beast up to 5 miles per hour. Its armor was only half an inch thick and tended to leak bullets, pop rivets, and spall off steel fragments if hit hard enough. Due to the heat generated by the engines and weapons, the crews would have stripped to the waist, if not continually peppered by small bits of metal, which required heavy uniform jackets—in a Middle Eastern desert in the summer! Heat prostration was a major cause of crew injury and the log of "His Majesty's Land Ship Detachment" records more men sent to hospital for heat and sickness than were injured in combat.

With four of eight men trying to steer and shift and the other four trying to fire as many as six guns in the general direction of an enemy, it is a wonder that they were effective at all. Especially as they had a range of just 26 miles, after which they needed not only another hundred gallons of fuel, but possibly extensive repairs. It was considered remarkable if the tracks lasted 20 miles before requiring major work.

When first used in combat, they tended to drastically alter the course of action, and soon after their advent in the Battle of the Somme, on 15 September 1916, commanders on all fronts were clamoring for a few of the new war machines. There was a problem, though: those commanders simply didn't understand the new ways of war. General Sir Archibald Murray, who'd already been exposed to tanks, naturally wanted a few when he was sent to Egypt to oversee the war against the Turks, who were determined to hang on to their fast-shrinking empire. He thought of them as roving machine gun nests, however, not as a new weapon entirely.

The British, operating out of Egypt, were equally determined that the Turks and their German allies *not* complete the Baghdad railroad and gain access to the newly discovered oil fields in the Middle East. When the light armored cars proved their worth in North Africa, in Mesopotamia and with the legendary Lawrence of Arabia, the decision was made to send Major Norman Nutt and his tank detachment to the Holy Land.

At 1100 hours, 9 January 1917, the landships, officially the heavy section of the Mideast Machine Gun Corps, disembarked from His Majesty's Transport *Euripides* at the port of Alexandria in the delta of the Nile River. Their strength was just eight decrepit tanks, 15 officers, and 123 other ranks. Naturally, the first thing that happened was an inspection by the general commanding officer and then they were allowed to get their act together and load up on flatcars for the train and ferry trip across the Nile Delta. By a strange coincidence, the railroad follows the path of the *original* Suez Canal, built by the Egyptians and Persians, around 600 B.C. After crossing the canal on a railroad ferry, the tankers detrained and set up camp near a town named Gilbana.

Roughly 2,000 years before, an Israelite refugee from King Herod's persecution had stopped at this same place. The man's name was Joseph and his wife's name was Mary, who was nursing a boy-child named Jesus. Their home city was called Nazareth and they were living on the proceeds of the sale of the gifts of frankincense and myrrh, given them by three travelers. The tankers were following an ancient path indeed, for 1,275 years before Joseph and Mary, Pharaoh Ramses II had made the same trip to Gaza with a chariot-mounted army. Ramses made his trip to Gaza in two weeks, at 15 miles per day. When the tankers finally left the canal, their train made the distance, over the same chariot and camel route, in 21 hours, arriving at a place called Khan Yunus, which was one of Ramses' old Forts, at 2300 hours, 28 March 1917. Slowly, in stages, they were working their way toward the war.

Due to the fact that the original tanks were not capable of sharp turns, they had to be driven onto the flatcars at the end of the train, one at a time, and then driven down the length of the train. To off-load, they had to be driven down a ramp specially made of railroad ties. The next morning, the little detachment of fighting machines traveled cross-country to their new base south of Gaza, a village named

Der el Belah. Finally, they had gotten within driving distance of the city and environs of Gaza, which the Turkish army had fully garrisoned and fortified in the current European style. The Germans were the Turkish army's mentors at the time, and they had set up exactly the same trench and wire fortifications in Gaza that had worked so well in France and Belgium—until the tanks arrived.

The British had already tried once, unsuccessfully, to bounce the Turks out of Gaza and had gotten hung up on the Flanders-style defenses. On the 26 March 1917, they'd mounted a conventional assault, which worked about as well as would be expected. The British casualties were 509 killed, 2,932 wounded, and 412 missing. Turkish losses were 301 killed, 1,085 wounded, and 1,061 missing.

Now they would try again, on 14 April, this time with heavy tanks. But as usual, the tanks were sent in small packets and their very unreliability proved to be a problem. At 1800 hours, the tanks worked their way to an assault position in a shallow, rocky ravine named Wadi el Ghuzzi. They would be assaulting the defenses of Gaza at a position named Sheikh Neban. The following is adapted from information in Major Nutt's war diary:

163rd Infantry Infantry Brigade; Operations Report No 7.

Two tanks proceeded into action at 0430 hours, from point 300 on Dumbell Hill, proceeding around Sheikh Abbas Ridge. HMLS *Sir Archibald*, with the port two-pounder firing into the enemy positions, was hit on the left track by an enemy shell that knocked the track off, putting the tank out of action. The officer commanding, second Lieutenant Irving, was wounded in the eyes by bullet fragments that came through his vision slit. The Turks continued to shell the tank and it eventually caught fire.

Gunners Fergeson and Janes were severely wounded and eventually died of wounds. Gunner Janes was wounded in the forearm. The driver and two other crewmen escaped with a severe shaking.

The unit commander, Major Nutt, who was out there in his own tank, has this to say: "Lance Corporal Hathnell and gunner Janes acted in a very gallant manner in assisting me to get the wounded from the tank under heavy shell fire."

The other tank, HMLS *Nutty,* traveled northwest around Sheikh Abbas and Mansura Ridges but reported that no enemy was encountered. It eventually returned via Mansura Ridge to Wadi Huckabin. At this point, there is a divergence between the official combat diary and most of the formal histories of this battle. This tank belonged to the detachment commander, Major Norman Nutt, and while he doesn't claim to have been in combat, a lone tank was observed to have done considerable damage to the Turks, right at the place and time that Nutt's own diary places his tank. This is due to Nutt's having turned his vehicle over to a subordinate.

For the rest of that day and well into the next, the tankers worked desperately on their primitive machines, getting ready for what they knew was coming, as they were being sent in what the British call "penny packets" instead of a mass formation, which would have been their choice. Several months later, at Cambrai in eastern France, the tanks would have a chance to show what a mass assault could do, but the loners in Palestine were still working for the infantry.

On the night of the 18–19 April, one tank, HMLS *Nutty* (Second Lieutenant Carr was now using the command tank, as Nutt was too busy with administrative work) moved from Wadi Nukhabari behind Sheikh Abbas Ridge and then received orders to advance over the ridge and attack enemy positions northeast of Sheikh Abbas Ridge, on the Beersheba road. The tank reached the Kirbet Sihan redoubt, coming under fire as it clattered over the ridge. Using its six-pounders, the tank broke open the redoubt and its infantry, following in, and occupied the hilltop

This done, on moving forward to its next planned objective, one track broke, rendering the tank immobile. The enemy then shelled this position and the tank heavily. The tank was hit, bursting into flames. It is supposed that Carr and the crew escaped the tank and got back into the Kirbet

Sihan redoubt, which was recaptured by the Turks later on
in the afternoon. It is presumed that Carr and his crew were
made prisoners. They were so listed on the daily report.

Four tanks in support of the 155th Brigade moved from
Wadi Nukhabari into position behind El Sineh Ridge.
At 0600 on the morning of the 19th they moved into
position North of Kurd Hill. At 0730, tank HMLS *Otazel* (commanded by Second Lieutenant Blakeway)
moved forward in front of the infantry, taking much
rifle fire and raking the trenches with its machine guns.
After a short advance, the tank was ditched, owing to
the ground giving way as it passed over a shallow gully,
and had to be dug out. This was the last action of that
tank for that day.

Also at 0730, tank HMLS *War Baby* (commanded
by Second Lieutenant Braime) led its infantry into the
assault, the objective being Green Hill. After they'd
gone a short distance uphill, an officer of the infantry
requested that Lieutenant Braime go to Outpost Hill
instead, owing to HMLS *Otazel* being out of action.
This Braime did, taking the hill and inflicting many casualties on the Turkish infantry. Owing to the heavy
shelling at this point, the infantry were unable to
proceed.

What was being found out both in Palestine and in Flanders at this time was that tanks could travel and fight in
conditions where infantry couldn't even live—*if* they could
be kept running.

After destroying the wire defenses of the hill with his
tracks, Braime and his crew roamed over the top of the
position, still under artillery fire but finding no hostiles. Returning down the hill to the infantry position, he informed
the infantry officer of this and the infantrymen decided that
they would be unable to hold the position due to the heavy
and accurate shell fire. The decision was made to then attack
a large machine gun nest, but in the midst of the assault, a
track broke and the tank was hit by a shell, which further
disabled it—in the middle of a hostile machine gun emplace-

ment. Tank casualties and vehicles knocked out for this battle eventually added up to 50 percent of the tank unit strength.

Braime then led his men in a rush out of the crippled tank, through the Turkish positions, and eventually brought them to safety with their own infantry. Major Nutt was quite complimentary to Lieutenant's Braime in the unit's war diary, saying,

The inventive pluck shown by this officer in attacking these positions with no support was highly commendable. His action undoubtedly saved a great many casualties among the infantry."

At 1130 on the 19th, HMLS *Kia-Ora* (commanded by Lieutenant Winder) also advanced under orders to Outpost Hill to assist the infantry. On arrival at the objective he reported to LTC (Lieutenant Colonel) Thompson, who said that they could not hold the position owing to shell fire. What was necessary was for the tank to cover the withdrawal of the infantrymen, and this Winder then proceeded to do. Finding a good overlooking position, he had his gunners deliver machine gun fire on the Turks, who were forted up in a clump of cactus bushes. Then, owing to mechanical trouble with his brakes, he had to return to base. Stopping off at Lieutenant Braime's tank, he sought to offer assistance but found the vehicle evacuated and continued his return to base.

At 1400 hours, HMLS *Pincher* (commanded by Second Lieutenant Patrick), which had been held in reserve, proceeded under orders to a point where it was proposed to attack up the valley. The attack, however, was called off.

Earlier, at 0730 hours, HMLS *Tiger* (commanded by Second Lieutenant Shore), supporting the 160th Brigade, attempted an assault on Samson's Ridge, but at a point 700 yards east of the ridge the track came off the shoes, temporarily halting the vehicle. Shore and his crew, however, using six-foot crowbars and sledgehammers, were able to effect repairs and to continue on with their mission.

On arrival at Samson's Ridge, HMLS *Tiger* took the defenders under machine gun fire and the enemy started to retreat toward the El Arish redoubt. The Royal West Kent Regiment took the opportunity to charge with the bayonet, and took the ridge. Shore and *Tiger* then proceeded down the back of the ridge to the redoubt, under heavy shell fire that drove the infantry from him. For six hours, Shore and *Tiger* held the redoubt, expending 27,000 rounds of machine gun ammunition and denying its use to the Turks. Owing to the fact that his tank, a female armed only with machine guns, was under intense shell fire, with all his gunners, himself, and his driver wounded, Shore was forced to take shelter behind Samson's Ridge. His commanding officer, Major Norman Nutt, commented, "I consider that the initiative and pluck of this officer in holding the redoubt until it became clear that the infantry couldn't live up there was highly praiseworthy. How he managed to get his tank back to safety is a mystery as all his crew were knocked out.

Later on, another report partially cleared the mystery. Lieutenant C. L. Dunkerly of the 2/4 Royal West Kents, who accompanied Shore into action, acting as guide, bandaged up the gunners as they fell back wounded, and also passed up ammunition to the surviving gunners until they were all knocked out by heat exhaustion, wounds, and disablement of their guns. Then, although knowing nothing about machine guns himself, he undertook to get one back into service, under the instructions of one of the wounded crewman. Dunkerly kept the gun going while the tank was gotten back to safety. Reading between the austere lines of the official report, one can figure out that with the engine shut down, the crew gradually recovered from heat exhaustion, to the point where they were able to function again.

The remaining tank of the detachment, HMLS *Ole-Luk-One* (commanded by Lieutenant Farquhar-Thompson), lost its magneto in the initial assault and was unable to travel farther.

Thus ended the second battle of Gaza and the first use of heavy tanks in a desert. Although they had mechanical problems, their battle-worthiness boded well for a later time and many other scattered battles. After this second, half-successful battle for the city of Gaza, the tankers pulled back to their base, licked their wounds, both physical and mechanical, and got ready for the final push.

The final casualty list for this debacle were: British, 509 killed, 4,539 wounded, and 1,576 missing. The Turks: 402 killed, 1,364 wounded, and 245 missing. At this time, General Archibald Murray blamed the tactical commander, General Sir Charles Dobell, and dismissed him. Then Murray was himself relieved by General Sir Edmund Allenby and things began to change for the better. Allenby, a cavalryman, had already seen tanks working at Arras, and knew how to handle them. He also had the leverage to get new tanks shipped direct from the factory, and this made a radical difference.

While the Gaza detachment had, because of a bureaucratic foul-up, been equipped with the original, outmoded Mk-I tanks, the War Department, due to continuing pressure from General Allenby, Major Nutt, and Prime Minister David Lloyd George, finally got them some state-of-the-art Mk-IV tanks, which they would need very badly when the third and final battle for Gaza began. And Prime Minister Lloyd George had told General Allenby that he would appreciate the city of Jerusalem for a Christmas present.

On the night of 1–2 November 1917, it happened. The heavy guns of the British army dropped more than 500 tons of explosives on the Turkish lines that wound through Gaza and its outlying districts. The tank detachment, now fully up to strength under its own commander and with brand-new tanks, rolled forward in one tight group instead of in tiny packets—and into history. Before Rommel, before Montgomery and the rest, there were His Majesty's landships in Gaza, Palestine.

The general battle plan depended on the capture of the wells around Beersheba, due to the need for water for the horse cavalry, which back then provided the element of maneuver. A sudden night charge by New Zealand and Australian cavalry coming out of the desert completely unhinged the defenders of Beersheba, and the Turks began to fall back on Gaza. At the same time, an attack on Gaza by the British 54th Division, which was supposed to have been only a feint, broke through the Turkish position and the retreat turned into a route. What had happened was that the tanks had finally been used as a cohesive unit instead of as individual portable machine gun nests. They had smashed a huge hole in the Turkish lines and were on an armored rampage. Also, for the first time in history, a tank assault was being supported by naval gunfire. Their area of operations was within sight of the sea, and part of the artillery bombardment came from two cruisers and a seagoing monitor.

At 0300 hours, 2 November, the battle smoke and dust was so heavy that the tanks couldn't navigate by vision or stars—they had to rumble forward on compass headings, always a bit dicey inside a mass of steel. Two tanks broke into a redoubt in the wire known as El Arish, routed the defenders, but got trapped in the maze of trenches—temporarily. They could shoot and fight, but couldn't drive out of the maze. At least their presence denied the use of the fortifications to the defenders, and more and more British infantry streamed in on the discomfited Turks. Eventually, by dismounting a few men on foot and following their own track prints, the tankers found their entrance point, worked their way back out, remounted and went back to assassinating machine gun nests. The tankers were earning their nickname as "battlefield bullies."

Two more tanks broke into a nearby redoubt known as the Rafah, got lost in the dawn mist, and had to circle back on an escape azimuth to a rally point. Then, staying within sight of each other, they began to beat up the Rafah, Yunis, and Belah trenchworks, pushing down the wire for the infantry, taking out bunkers with their 57mm guns, and raking the trenches with machine gun fire. Due to these tanks being state-of-the-art Mk-IVS, there were no unexpected mechanical breakdowns, one tank making a full 40 miles before needing serious work, which was something of a miracle in those days. There were now four fully operational tanks in one small area of the Turkish works and the Turks were departing in large numbers.

The fifth tank of the group, its way prepared by the two who'd beaten up the trenchworks, went on a rampage. In quick succession, it broke the defenses of a coastal works called the Sea Post, smashed a built-up area known as The Cricket redoubt, and then, as soon as the infantry had consolidated behind it, swung its armored prow north, up the coast. Coming over Turtle Hill, the tankers tore up a position known as Sheikh Hassan and, having outrun their own infantry, linked up with scouting, probing elements of the 53rd Infantry Division. The infantry were short of ammunition, having cut behind Gaza, so the tankers dropped off extra ammo and some rations for them and moved on, still looking for something to beat up. Suddenly they discovered that they were out in open country, *behind* the Turks.

Five tanks, allowed to work as a tight unit, had turned the enemy's flank, gotten behind him, and opened up the coast road for Allenby's army. The total casualties to the tankers were one man killed, one wounded. On 7 November, the tanks, almost unopposed, growled over Ali el Muntar Ridge and the third battle for Gaza was over. The Turks were on the run and the tanks couldn't even keep up with the retreating enemy. On 14 November, armored cars were probing toward Jerusalem. Lloyd George would get his Christmas present a bit early in 1917.

Just six days later, at Cambrai in Europe, General Sir Hugh Elles would be riding a tank named *Hilda,* and would be leading 474 tanks into battle, massed as a unit for the first time in "formal" history. The accomplishments of the big battalions would overshadow the efforts of the Palestine detachment, but they paved the way for the desert tankers and a surprising number of them stayed in the desert, experimenting and surveying for the next war, which even then was looming on the horizon.

The adventures of the armored warriors in Palestine were far from over, however, for Ja'far Pasha had switched his allegiance from Germany to England, and this had brought a strange series of events into existence. Eventually, Sam

Rolls, most of the Duke of Westminister's car crews, Nuri
Bey, and Ja'far Pasha would wind up working for T. E.
Lawrence.

REFERENCE SOURCES

Desert Warfare, Bryan Perrett, Patrick Stephens, Ltd.
Seven Pillars of Wisdom, T. E. Lawrence, Anchor Books.
Steel Chariots in the Desert, S. C. Rolls, H. Shanley, Printers.
Daily Log of the Gaza Tank Detachment, Tank Museum,
    Bovington, England. David Fletcher, Librarian.

CHAPTER 11

Cambrai, 20 November 1917

BEFORE THERE COULD BE A CAMBRAI, LESSONS WOULD HAVE to be assimilated and newer models of tanks built. While the Germans went into high gear on their own tank project, coded A7V, Britain was having its difficulties with the new concept. The Mk-1 had proved that the concept was workable, but there were still a few bugs in the design. The first thing that went by the board were the tail wheels. Many crews disconnected these steering links and used them as supply trailers. Next the internal 60-gallon fuel tank was removed from right next to the driver and given its own armored box, outside the hull proper.

These few modifications resulted in the Mk-II and Mk-III, some of which saw combat at Arras in early April 1917 The tank designers were still on the short end of the learning curve, and it was only with the Mk-IV in mid-1917 that things began to get really good. The tracks, rollers, and links were all larger and heavier, and now the tracks could be expected to last more than about 20 miles. This made it possible for the tank to cruise about the landscape looking for trouble, instead of clattering two dozen miles and breaking a track.

Also, at this time, the Germans had developed an armor-piercing rifle and machine gun bullet, which could get through a Mk-I with frightening ease. This projectile was a machined, hardened steel needle of 6.5mm diameter inside a conventional 8mm copper bullet jacket. When it hit something, the jacket was stripped off and the core went on through, even through a half-inch of steel plate. Supposedly, the Mk-IV was proof against this projectile, due to heavier, hardened armor plate. It was in the acquisition of the plate that the supply system broke down and creative politics had to be used.

In his book *The World Crisis,* Winston Churchill wrote, "The one great blot upon the high economy of the British war effort in the last year of the struggle was the undue and unwarrantable inroads upon the common fund made by the Admiralty." Plainly put, Sir Eric Geddes, head of the Admiralty Board, dug his heels in and demanded so much of the nation's output of steel plate that there wouldn't be enough left for anything, let alone armored landships.

Possibly the British government should have installed a senility clause in its war charter. At any rate, Churchill became quite devious. "Since we were unable to overcome Sir Eric Geddes by reason, it became necessary to engorge him with ship plates. This the munitions council and Sir John Hunter's steel department soon succeeded in doing. . . . We watched with unsleeping attention the accumulations which soon began in every shipyard. Not until the moment was ripe did we unmask the guilty fact. . . . The proud department condescended to parley and eventually the modest requirements of the tank programme were satisfied."

Since there is a considerable difference in quarter-inch ship plate and half- to three-quarters-inch armor plate, it is distinctly possible that Churchill, who carried deviousness to Machiavellian levels, already had the plate stashed away, waiting for a go-ahead. At any rate, new tanks began to appear with suspicious alacrity.

While the British were planning the spring campaigns of 1917, the Germans were trying to figure a way out of the impasse of trench warfare. During March 1917, they pulled off a strategic withdrawal to the Hindenburg Line and began to dig furiously and string barbed wire like madmen. Slowly, laboriously, the Allies followed through an area made almost impassable by billions of water- and gas-filled shell craters. Even today, eighty years later, there are occasional stories of one of those old shells or mines going off and killing someone.

There was a supposed weak point in the German lines at Arras, where the Hindenburg fortifications ended and normal trenches extended farther south. Here, it was thought, an assault would break through, and the decision was made to try the tanks. Again, it would be a case of too little, spread out too far. The usual three-day artillery prepping dropped about ten kilotons of explosives into already damp ground and turned it into a morass—and the 60 tanks that were available were already obsolete Mk-Is and IIs. On 9 April, the attack began. Most of the tanks either ditched, bogged, or simply broke down.

The British were learning, though, and ever-improving models of heavy tanks, gun carriers, supply tanks and light tanks, and armored cars were coming off the assembly lines in England. Flers, Arras, and Ypres all taught their lessons in a harsh way, even as the Mk-IVs were assembling. Finally, the British were ready for the critical assault of the year, at Cambrai. The British tank general, Sir Hugh Elles, and the area commanding general, Sir Julian Byng, had finally convinced the powers that be to try it their way. No three-week prepping to muddy the ground. Only a morning barrage out of which the tanks would appear, hopefully as a total surprise.

Among those most surprised would surely be the British high command of the day. After the war, Britain's premier armored theoretician, J. F. C. Fuller, referring to the seemingly endless battles of World War I, wrote of General Haig and his cohort, General Sir Lancelot Kiggle:

They considered that their doctrine of war was infallible, that the wearing battle must succeed if sufficient reinforcements were forthcoming and that as ultimately this doctrine demands on onslaught of cavalrymen, without cavalry the battle could not be won. The truth

is, I believe, that long before the outbreak of war their
brains had become ossified and even the terrible circumstances of this battle would not penetrate the historic
concrete in which they were encased. If this is not the
true explanation, then Haig and Kiggle must be two
of the greatest knaves in the history of war, which I
cannot believe.

Unfortunately, the series of battles that had caused the
great loss of life to which Fuller referred had also included
the first use of tanks, disastrously. As a result, not only the
cavalry, but the infantry commanders were distrustful of this
new engine of destruction. As one army commander wrote,
"One, tanks are unable to negotiate bad ground. Two, the
ground on a battlefield will always be bad. Three, therefore,
tanks are no good on a battlefield." These comments pretty
well summarized the attitude of the senior Allied commanders, with a few exceptions, notably Elles and Byng. At this
point in history, Haig was so desperate for a victory of any
kind that he was ready to try anything, even tanks, and to
do it the tankers' way.

On 3 August 1917, J. F. C. Fuller, now promoted to lieutenant colonel and in the position of chief staff officer of
the Tank Corps, reported to General Elles at Bermicourt.
Most of the tankers were already in Flanders being frittered
away, and Fuller had just returned from the appalling
slaughter at Ypres. One suspects that he poured something
rather stiff from a bottle on the sideboard of the large, stone
flagged conference room before he sat down and reported
to General Elles.

"They're just throwing the tanks away," he growled.
"First they shell the area until the ground is a swamp, then
they send the tanks in. How can they be expected to work
in such conditions? They just sink in the mud and become
sitting targets for German artillery."

"That's what we've been telling GHQ since the campaign
started," Elles replied. "But what about morale?"

"It's not good. The infantry think tanks are a failure and
even the tank crews feel they're being wasted."

Fuller had risen and walked to a tall window outside of

which the late summer rain of France beat an incessant downpour. Perhaps sight of the mud of the courtyard congealed his thoughts. "General Mud" has always been the enemy of the soldier. At no place or time on earth had this ever been more true than in Flanders in World War I.

"What we need," he said at least, "is a surprise attack by tanks—on good ground."

Elles looked up at the standing Fuller and smiled somewhat wryly. "You know what happened the last time we put up that idea to GHQ."

What had happened was that Haig's and Kiggle's petrified mental processes couldn't separate themselves from artillery barrages and masses of corpses, so the idea had been pigeonholed for the duration; indeed, their paper had barely escaped the circular file. A year earlier, Swinton whose genius had invented the tank had also suggested such a raid, by a large number of tanks, but Haig and Kiggle had not been quite so desperate then. For some time the two generals batted the idea about. Then Elles said, somewhat doubtfully, "Well, we can suggest it. Put it down on paper and I'll see what can be done." From such dubious beginnings came the great tank raid on Cambrai. While Elles went out to test the waters, Fuller sat down and began to cook up what he hoped was a convincing memorandum.

This time, things clicked. Third Army commander, Sir Julian Byng, already had something in the works for Cambrai and saw the tanks as a valuable contribution to his own plan. He'd originally planned a deep penetration to destroy German communications in the area and the use of tanks appealed to him. What Fuller and Elles had seen as a raid, Byng saw as a full-scale battle. He agreed to their proposition and together the three officers took their half-hatched plan to Generals Haig and Kiggle.

At first Haig was inclined to go along, but Kiggle, the staff officer, wanted every man available shoveled into the slaughterhouse in the Ypres battles to "force an eventual victory." One thing must be remembered about this unimaginative traditionalist. He had not yet actually seen the battlefront with his own eyes, even after four years of butchery. That war was being run by absentee commanders in perfumed palaces far from the stench of rotting men and destroyed farms.

August passed, then September, and still young men walked willingly into the jaws of death for their generals and politicians. Finally, the pressure from England was unbearable. No one could hide or explain away 2 million casualties from England alone, and 4 million from France—and 3.25 million Germans. It took that many deaths to shock what can only be called evil old men out of their mental ruts. Casting about for an inspiration, Haig finally remembered the plan Byng and his tankers had put forward in August—three-and-a-half months ago. Finally, what would be known to history as "Operation GY" was scheduled for 20 November 1917. Unfortunately, the army that was to execute the plan was now understrength and bone-weary. The war of attrition had worn them down to a mere shell of a field army. Men were tired and battle fatigued, and many regiments were at 75 percent of rated strength. This was the broken tool they would use in an attempt to execute the first armored breakthrough in history.

Cambrai, a city on the Scheldt River, like much of northern France, has a long history of battle. Celts fought Neolitic tribesmen for the land, and then lost it to Roman legions. Northmen raided and settled and became Normans. From here they raided England, and were raided in turn. Not far from Cambrai, in 1346 and 1415 the armor of French chivalry fell before the English longbow, and now English armor was to grind down Krupp steel and Prussian flesh.

The city takes its name from three historic cathedrals and has given the name to a fine linen fabric that we know as "cambric." In 1917, Cambrai was a valid military target, as it was a major center of communications. Four railways met at its marshaling yards, several motorways intersected in the city, and two large canals passed under its bridges. Since August 1914, it had been occupied by the Germans, and the population was very much ready to be liberated. The Germans would fight for it because it was the pivot of the supply lines that fed a large segment of the front.

Fuller and Elles, however, were having qualms. They had envisioned a tank raid with a reserve striking force, and

Byng had taken their vision and converted it to a full-scale assault—with no reserves. As eventually planned, the attack would be undertaken by six infantry divisions, five cavalry divisions, all three tank brigades, and 1,003 field guns of various calibers. What would make Cambrai different from all other tank engagements to date was this: There would be no massive month-long barrage of artillery to muddy the going. The land in front of Cambrai was hard, gently rolling ground covered with a strong mat of grass.

The area of the attack, running from the outskirts of Cambrai to the south, was six miles wide and seven miles long. Running from Cambrai south were a string of rural villages; Ribécourt, Marcoing, Masnières, Flesquieres, Graincourt, Cantaing, Bourlon and Fontaine. On November 20, heavy armor would roll into them.

The plan was to use tanks to smash the wire, fill in the trenches with fascines, and generally destroy and demoralize the Germans while the horse cavalry charged through and developed the situation. The hope was that they would be able to secure the bridges over the canals and rivers before the Germans had a chance to destroy them. The first rule of battle, however, is, "No battle plan survives contact with the enemy"—or one's own ossified general staff. Fortunately, the tank brigade had an excellent staff itself, and on 25 October Elles called a meeting of his officers in the ex-nunnery at Chateau Bermicourt. Regardless of what Third Army planned, Elles wanted his Tank Corps to succeed.

After much discussion, three main objectives were set out for the tankers, no matter how they were subsequently dispersed. First was to break through the main Hindenburg Line from where it crossed an unfinished French shipping canal called the Canal du Nord, to an isolated chateau called Bleak House, and capture the village of Ribécourt. Second, they were to penetrate far enough to break up the Hindenburg support network, and do as much damage as possible. Third, they were to exploit the breakthrough northward to the city of Cambrai and, if possible, to drive the Germans out of the area.

What was to make all this possible was that, for the first time since the beginning of trench warfare, there was to be no long bombardment. The official estimate, due to the intensive German trenchworks and wire, was that it would have taken five weeks of artillery work at a cost of 20 million British pounds to break up the defenses. The reason that Generals Haig and Kiggle were willing to go along with the experiment was that Elles and Byng had had the Royal Engineers build an exact duplicate of a section of the Hindenburg line in the British rear area, and then reduced it with tanks in half an hour! Granted, nobody was shooting at them at the time.

They had a go, but the administrative problems were gigantic. A total of 1,003 artillery pieces and 374 tanks had to be smuggled in the Boise du Havrincourt—and the tanks weren't even in France yet. Many were on their way by ship and by rail from the new tank school in Bovington, or direct from the factories in England. The crews were still being assembled and trained, but at least they would all be trained and led by veterans, and this would make a difference. There would be no more blind stumbles like those in Flers and Arras.

More importantly, the infantry for the first time were actually being trained with the tanks with which they would work. The basic plan was for the tanks, in groups of three, to simply flatten the wire for the closely following infantry. Each tank was carrying a two-ton bundle of brushwood on its bow, and these were designed to fill in the trenches. The lead tank was to penetrate the wire, smash it flat, and turn sharply to the left, waiting and working the defenders over with its guns while the other two came on with the infantry. Tank number two would come straight on and drop its fascine, filling in trench number one. Tank number three would fill in trench number two, adding its firepower to that of number one. Then the lead tank would leave its position inside the outer wire, cross both trenches, and drop its fascine in the third and, they hoped, last trench.

At this point, the trenches were to have been cleared and a way made for the infantry. The infantry, except for the special platoons designated to follow and assist the tanks, were to fill in and garrison the trenches against the evicted Germans. Then they were to be followed by two specially equipped wire-pulling tanks, which were to drop anchors into the wire and pull it out of the way so that the cavalry could advance for the exploitation stage.

The story of the fascines is fascinating in itself, as it illustrates the inventiveness of the tankers. Bundles of brushwood, like those used for hasty road repairs in lieu of corduroying, were brought in from the surrounding countryside and dropped on heavy chains that had been laid in threes on the ground. Then men pulled the loose ends of the chains over the bundles and attached them to tow chains that had been bolted to a pair of tanks. Then the tankers put their mounts into gear and pulled until the bundles were compressed and the engineers bolted the chains in place. When they ran out of small anchor chains, Fuller sent back to England and they stripped the chains off the park railings of half of England and shipped them to the tank depots.

Since the fascines now weighed about two tons, it took twenty men to roll them across the muddy ground and up a ramp. A tank had already nosed up to the ramp and the fascine was bolted to a specially made pivot, which could be released from inside the vehicle. The next time it left the hull would be inside German lines. Between tank/infantry cooperation, timed artillery, and the trench-crossing methods, it seemed that nothing could go wrong. There were, however, a couple of high-ranking flies still in the lubricant.

One was Major General G. M. Harper of the 51st Highland Division, who wanted nothing to do with the twentieth century. He had originally been opposed to the development of machine guns earlier in the decade. He called the tanks "fantastic and unmilitary." Now he got on his high horse and insisted that his Highlanders stay at least one hundred yards behind the tanks. Then he rearranged the organization of the tanks assigned to him into fours instead of threes, hampering Fuller's well-thought-out trench-breaching methods. Fuller, naturally, complained about this, but the authority had been "delegated," and that was that. Fortunately, there was no radio in most of the tanks and when combat began, Harper simply could not get out there to interfere.

The other knighted nitwit was Lieutenant General Sir C. T. McM. Kavenaugh, the commander of the British Cavalry

Corps at Byng's Third Army HQ. It is directly at this gentle-man's feet that the blame for the absence of modern horsed cavalry must be laid. The British mounted force has taken much unearned criticism down the decades for their alleged failure at Cambrai. It was not for lack of courage or willingness that they failed. It was for lack of imaginative leadership.

The cavalry was locked down by specific orders to hold in place and wait for orders from Kavenaugh, who was miles in the rear of the battle—shades of Raglan in the Crimea, who had won his spurs against Napoleon, and had not seen action since the battle of Waterloo. This was a classic case of "fighting the last war."

Kavenaugh had laid out orders that all battlefield intelli-gence of interest to the cavalry should come to his HQ at Fins, 12 miles behind the lines. There were several ways that information could move on that battlefield, none of them fast. There were a few—very few—telegraph lines across the combat area. An aircraft could drop a message streamer attached to a rock. A tank could release one of its few carrier pigeons. Or a man on horseback could hand-carry a message 12 miles back to Kavenaugh. Then he would dis-seminate it to his divisional, brigade, and regimental com-manders. The gentleman was very insistent that none of them were to move by themselves. In effect, he locked his cavalrymen down and, by so doing, removed them from his-tory. The mind-set of the cavalry officers, of course, did not help. Charges into automatic weapons are suicide, and saber charges had been useless since Bedford Forrest.

By 9 November, a week and a half before the battle, Elles had moved his field HQ out of its nunnery and into a shot-out cabaret named the Des Hommes Du Mort in the town of Albert. In order to maintain some bit of secrecy, it was still called the Tank Training Office. The walls were still covered with posters of long-legged French dancing girls and Fuller writes of the period:

> My original staff had been increased by the appoint-ment of Major H. Boyd-Rochfort and Captain the Hon. Evan Charteris, who Elles had got out from Tank Corps Command in London to compile our records and write

up our history. Charteris was older than the rest of us. He was somewhat of a sybarite, an eclectic and an epicurean. In London he lived in an exquisite maisonette in Mount street, surrounded by exquisite pictures and exquisite furniture and all in exquisite taste. He was so obviously fashioned by his creator to rule our mess that his presidency over it was one of those gravitational processes which have no fixed origin. No sooner was he one of us when strange little packets began to arrive from Paris and London, containing Beechnut bacon, roseleaf honey and rare, exotic condiments.

Work went on in these surroundings, however, and a string of directives issued from Fuller and his staffers that showed a grasp of mechanized warfare far ahead of its day. Those early armor officers were geniuses of the first rank, who, strangely, would be more appreciated by their enemies than by their commanders. They were building a method of warfare that would not see fruition for 20 years, but the groundwork would be laid at Cambrai.

The Achilles' heel of armored warfare was also being discovered. A cavalry horse in an emergency can graze sustenance off the land. An infantryman or cavalry trooper can subsist on beans and horsemeat. Tanks, however, need support. An armored vehicle is not an independent entity. The supplies for three brigades of tanks for Cambrai were: 165,000 gallons of gasoline, 75,000 pounds of grease, 500,000 rounds of 57mm shells, and 5 million rounds of .303-caliber machine gun ammunition. Basically, the Boise Du Havrincourt was filling to bursting with tanks and tankers.

Major Watson, commander of a company of D Battalion, gives this description of the delivery of this company of tanks to Havrincourt woods:

I watched the trains pull out from the ramps. The lorries had already started for our next halting place. We were clear of Wailly. I motored down to the neighborhood of Albert, and at dusk my car was feeling its way through a bank of fog along the road from Bray to the great railhead at Le Plateau, at the edge of the old Somme battlefield. It was a vast, confusing place, and one felt insignificant among the mulitudinous rails, the slow dark trains, the sudden lights.

Tanks which had just detrained came rumbling round the corners of odd huts. Lorries bumped through the mist with food and kit. Quiet railwaymen—mostly American—went steadily about their business. Just after midnight, word came that our train was expected. We walked up to the ramp and at last, after an abominable wait, our train glided out of the darkness. There was a slight miscalculation and the train hit the ramp with a bump, carrying away the lower timbers so that it could not bear the weight of tanks. Wearily, we tramped another mile or so to another ramp. This time the train behaved with more discretion. The tanks were driven off into a wood, where they were carefully camouflaged. The cooks set to work and produced steaming tea.

Two miles south of Havrincourt, the Boise du Dessart was also full of tanks, the Second Brigade of the Tank Corps. Near the village of Gouzeucourt yet another brigade of tanks sat in the open under camouflage, hoping that their secret would not leak out—but it did. Some resourceful German commander had invented commandos.

Their name was "Stosstrupps," and their mission was to raid and probe into Allied positions and find out whether there were any attacks planned. A Lieutenant Hegermann led one of these parties on the night of 18 November, and soon nabbed a couple of unwary Tommies from the 1st Battalion, Royal Irish Fusileers. They were not overly security conscious and soon began to reveal details of the buildup. One even divulged the date of the planned attack, two days hence, and this threw the Germans completely off. If the British were going to attack, they reasoned, the guns should have been firing for over a month by now. The presence of tanks was dismissed out of hand, since they were considered to be no more than a mechanical novelty, of no real combat use. The German high command was not worried, but the local field commanders were getting distinctly nervous—as well they should.

On the evening of 19 November, General Elles began to close down his office in the cabaret in the town of Albert. His last official act was to sit down and write the field order that launched the tank force:

SPECIAL ORDER NO. 6

1. Tomorrow the Tank Corps will have the chance for which it has been waiting for many months—to operate on good going in the van of the battle.
2. All that hard work and ingenuity can achieve has been done in the way of preparation.
3. It remains for unit commanders and for tank crews to complete the work by judgement and pluck in the battle itself.
4. In the light of experience, I leave the good name of the Corps with great confidence in their hands.
5. I propose leading the attack in the centre division.

Hugh Elles, Brig. Gen.
Commanding Tank Corps

Blitzkrieg, the combination of artillery, airpower, and tanks, was not born full-blown in the fertile mind of Heinz Guderian—it was born at Cambrai, at Villers Bretonneux, on Salisbury plain, in the minds of J. F. C. Fuller, Charles de Gaulle, and others. Guderian was the one who put it all together, and one of the major keys was air support. The Allies invented it, and then went to sleep for about 20 years, while the Germans studied.

The first example of planned air-armor assault was Cambrai. On the side of the Bapaume-Cambrai road, the pilots of the Third Brigade, Royal Flying Corps were getting a novel briefing. None of them had ever worked with a roving armored fortress before, nor had they ever been timed to come in behind a thunderous timed artillery barrage before. The brigade was overstrength for this mission. There were 14 squadrons comprising bombers, fighters, and scouts, 275 aircraft in all, with 376 tanks beneath them and over a thousand guns behind them—the Kaiser was about to have a bad day.

CHAPTER 12

Tank Battle for Cambrai

THE GERMAN HIGH COMMAND, SPECIFICALLY GENERAL MAR-
WITZ, had taken Lt. Hegermann's report, examined it, and
dismissed even the mention of tanks out of hand. After all,
they reasoned, if the British were going to attack, they would
have been shelling for at least a month, wouldn't they? And
wasn't the Hindenburg line the heaviest fortification on the
whole frontier? Tanks? What had they done since that
stroke of luck at Flers? Get lost in the mud, that's what.
Forget an attack. Just to be sure, though, Marwitz ordered
the reserves around the German end of the Havricourt
Wood increased. He did not, however, order up any more
of the special SK armor-piercing bullets.

According to Captain D. E. Hickey, Dessart Woods, H
Battalion, 3rd Tank Brigade, at 0500 hours on 19 November 1917:

> Darkness fell at about five o'clock, we left Dessart
> Woods on our approach march to Beaucamp. A white
> tape about two-inches wide with a black line along the
> center had been laid over the whole distance. The offi-
> cer walked in front of the tank, able to see the driver

and guided him by the glow of a cigarette. . . . Then the tape ended abruptly. It was quite impossible to direct the tanks by the lay of the country for the night was pitch black and no landmarks were visible. . . . On these occasions I walked ahead trying to pick out the trackmarks of a preceding tank by the light of a cigarette. . . . About midnight we reached our jumping off place taking up a position behind a hedge. The four miles of approach march had taken seven hours—The rollers of the tanks were greased up, and the men turned in to snatch a few hours of sleep inside the tank.

Another group of tankers had gotten lost on a scrounging expedition, and were trying to find their tank:

The wind had dropped and the stillness was very little disturbed, with only the distant sputter of a machine gun or the occasional roar of a heavy gun. Very lights [flares] cast a pale unnatural light over wide tracts of country and illuminated the clouds, which were lying low and heavy over our heads. It seemed quite hopeless to try and find any particular tank, but Mansfield, with his earthenware keg of rum tucked under his arm, plunged into the darkness like a sprite. Soon he picked up a strip of white tape and we followed across what seemed moorland, taking heavy falls and getting tangled up in the wire.

We could hear tanks moving, purring very mildly on their second speed and one could see pinpoints of light, no bigger than fireflies, behind their portholes—Another half-mile brought us to a group of four, drawn up in a line under some trees. They were filling up with petrol. Some of the men were trying to sleep on tarpaulins spread on the ground. Behind them were sledges laden with drums of telegraph wire and reserves of petrol. We found our tank and tried to sleep—without success.

Suddenly, at 1500, there was a barrage from the German side that set them all jittering. Had the enemy discovered something or just gotten their wind up? The German artillery was probing, accompanied by the usual display of rockets and flares. For half an hour the tankers had to just sit and take it. Among them, the British artillerymen sat in their hastily built bunkers and gritted their teeth. They knew from aerial photographs just where their tormentors were and could easily calculate deflection and elevation, but they had to wait for the tanks to move. At 0530 the barrage ceased. To those who remembered other battles, the silence was uncanny and menacing.

Slowly the light grew, color became visible to night-accustomed eyes, and before them could be seen the gray-green of the gently sloping fields before Cambrai. Partridges, larks, and crows began to stir about and forage in the few brownish patches of weeds brush and thistles. No sign of motion was seen in the German lines. Had they found out and set some horrible surprise? Had the guns last night been covering a registration in no-man's-land? Were their gunners even now loading up with gas shells?

The ground slopes first down to the village of Ribécourt, then rises gently to a ridge on which sits the town of Flesquieres. To the northern end of the attack area, the land seems to rise endlessly and in the far distance the picturesque outline of the ancient city of Cambrai became visible through the mist, almost like a fairy city out of some medieval tale, with its cathedral spires pointing heavenward. German, Irish, British, and Canadian soldiers would die this day.

At 0600 hours, men began to climb into their tanks and warm their engines. The heat from the rumbling Ricardo motors quickly dissipated the chill of the misty night and the crews began to don their padded leather helmets and chain-mail facemasks, which protected their faces from splinters of steel. Gun breeches were checked, machine guns were given a last greasing, and belts of ammunition fed into them. Carefully the inhabitants of this mechanical world found their places, some involuntarily. The normal crew of a Mk-IV was a driver, a lieutenant, two gearsmen, and four gunners, three to six carrier pigeons in a basket, maybe a cat or dog, and assorted rodents who'd taken up residence in the landship's bilges. Everybody would soon be rudely jolted into full awareness and many of the four-footed tenants would abandon ship.

A Lieutenant Leach sat nervously in his tank, *Hilda,* of H Battalion. A sharp rap on his hull door startled him and he reached over to unlatch it. His commander, Major Huntbach, stood there, along with a tall, spare individual with a salt-and-pepper mustache, who was holding an ash walking stick. There was a cloth wrapped around the stick and the man, whom the tankers recognized as General Hugh Elles, shook it out.

The cloth was the new flag of the British Armored Corps which the general's wife had sewn for them. The colors were brown for the mud they lived in, red for the courageous blood they shed, green for the fields they crossed—or, just possibly, for the fiddler's green that is the tanker's waystation between heaven and hell, where valiant souls pass tales while waiting for another call. "Five minutes to go," Elles said. "I'm going over in this tank, Lieutenant." And with that he stepped through the sponson door and soon popped out of a hatch in the tank's roof, holding his battle flag aloft. . . . Would that General Kavenaugh had been made of the same stern material. History would have been written differently that day.

At 0610, as if pushed by a single hand, 474 throttles went wide open and exhaust smoke belched into the dawn. With an awful clatter, as of a hundred scrap piles being dumped, 948 Caterpillar treads began to roll. Surely at this time the Germans must have realized that the tanks were coming for them. How do you hide almost half a thousand tanks on an open plain? With guns and aircraft. When the tanks began to roll, Third Brigade RFC was already in the air, coming up behind them. The first bullets into the Hindenburg line came not from tanks but from the air. Sopwith Camels came shrieking out of the sky, wind in their wires, twin Vickers guns winking through their props—hundreds of them. DeHaviland bombers came low on bombing runs and Bristol fighters circled overhead, waiting for the German Albatross fighter/scouts to challenge them.

At 0620 hours, a thousand British guns, already targeted by surveyors transit and slide rule opened up, firing on geographic coordinates. A rain of a thousand tons of explosive iron was falling on the hapless Germans while cloth-and-wire airplanes shot and bombed them. The Germans, however, were safe behind wire and under concrete, weren't they? This, they reasoned, must be the beginning of the *real* assault bombardment, and it would be at least a whole month before the British arrived. . . . Right, Fritz.

The tanks all this time were rumbling forward and could see the massive, bubbling, flaming continuous explosion before them. Black, red, yellow, orange, even some green explosions rocked the lines as the tankers with their companion infantry rolled steadily forward. A large percentage of those shells were smoke shells, intended to lessen the visibility of the defenders. There was no return fire, none at all. The Germans had gone into their deep bunkers to wait out the bombardment and were calmly cooking their breakfasts. Only the sentries were aloft, and they were expecting nothing special. This had been tried before and their wire was impenetrable. They would wait, and then, as usual, they would kill the attackers.

Private Hans Pomgratz of the German 84th Infantry Regiment was nineteen-years-old and new to battle. He was to look out for the first wave of fanatic Englishmen to throw themselves to die on the wire. At 0700 hours, the shelling stopped, and Pomgratz peeped out of his sandbagged observation bunker. Nothing! Only an airplane engine, but sounding impossibly close. *Hell, If it is this close, why can't I see it?* he must have thought. He stepped out of his bunker to look and froze, unable to move. His worst nightmares could not have prepared him for this. A huge gray shape with Caterpillar treads was thundering at him with cannons and machine guns exploding from its sides. Like two evil eyes, a pair of hatches, half open and with men behind them, were in the center of the beast. Under the right "eye" a machine gun was mounted, and the yellow flicker of its muzzle was the last thing that Hans ever saw. He died wondering how this thing had gotten here.

Three separate courses of wire, so thick that one could not see through them, had stood in front of the tanks. Even with their practice on the engineer-made dummy fortification, they approached this fabled barrier with more than a little trepidation. The wire didn't even slow them down. At a stately two miles per hour, they ground it flat, as if running through a cactus patch. The first tanks, females and grotesque with the fascines on their bows, ground through the wire and, as per plan, turned left along the first trench line and filled it with machine gun fire. This was not a battle, it was raw slaughter. The floors of the trenches were spattered with blood and the Germans were running in panic when the second wave of tanks came through and dropped their fascines. Suddenly there were 32 eight-foot-wide holes in the impassable wire and the Tommies were trotting through, bayonets gleaming on their Enfield rifles.

Hilda's bow dipped into a trench, the driver aiming at the fascine he'd just dropped. Down, down, the bow dipped, *crash,* she hit bottom and the jolt came up the unsprung rollers and jarred the crew's very teeth. *Pray to the war gods that the engine doesn't stall. No, it was still roaring in low gear.* Now, up, up, treads ripping the sandbagged walls and she climbs like a clawing bear. The stout ash stick doesn't snap, and the battle flag still snaps from the general's tank. Now the bow begins to drop again, but more slowly. The driver has figured out a new trick: back off on the throttle and the beast will come down slower. *Hilda* pulls aside, shielding her precious passenger while other tanks, still bearing fascines, come growling through the gap, heading for the next trench line. The impossible has happened, the Hindenburg line is breaking and Jerry is on the run everywhere. Satisfying himself that the assault was going in good order, General Elles reluctantly debarked from his tank, lit his battered briar pipe and *walked* back to his temporary field HQ at Beauchamps. Several parties of German prisoners, guarded by lightly wounded Tommies, followed him at a distance. Meanwhile, during a short consolidation period, the British had a chance to examine the trenchworks, and they were impressed.

A William Dawson, who had ridden with a C Battalion tank describes one of the bunkers:

It was very deep, possibly in the region of 20 feet, and consisted of a number of rooms off a long, wide passage

with an entrance downstairs at each end. The roof and
sides were all covered with heavy timber and the rooms
made comfortable with beds and furniture taken from
houses in the vicinity. It must have taken a long time
to construct. In the trench outside there was even a
kind of summerhouse where the officers could sit.

The surprise had been complete and shocking. Blankets,
boots, rifles, even letters from home were scattered everywhere. Like all soldiers everywhere, if there was no instant
danger, the tankers took time for a bit of looting. For a few
minutes, most of the tanks must have been almost
unmanned . . . One tank commander walked ahead to check
out his proposed route and found that his crew, save for the
driver, had vanished into the underground works. In minutes
they came trickling back with "the most amazing collection
of loot I have ever seen, chiefly consisting of field-glasses,
greatcoats, cigars, spirits, and water bottles. A tough little
Scots lance corporal had come back with a frying pan of
sausage he had found in an officer's dugout, still cooking on
the fire."

A Major Watson, commanding a company of G Battalion,
went over with the 51st Highland Division and followed the
trenchworks to a point where one of the peculiarly French
sunken roads cut across it. Being tankers, they decided to
do a little exploring and turned east on the road, which led
to a French village:

We walked up the road which in a few yards widened
out. On either side were dugouts, stores and cook-
houses. This regimental headquarters the enemy had
defended desperately. The trench boards were slippery
with blood and fifteen to twenty corpses, all German
and bayonetted lay strewn about the road like
drunken men.

A Highland sergeant who with a handful of men was
now in charge of the place, came out to greet us, puffing
at a long cigar. All his men were smoking cigars and it
was indeed difficult that morning to find a Highlander
without one. He invited us into a large chamber cut out

of the rock, from which a wide staircase descended into an enormous dugout. The chamber was panelled deliciously with coloured woods and decorated with choice prints. Our host produced a bottle of claret, and we drank to the health of the 51st Division.

At 0800 hours, more tanks were coming through the original gaps in the wire. The specially equipped wire-pulling tanks came through in pairs and dropped their grapnels in the flattened wire. Then, turning right and left, they ground along in low gear, pulled the stakes out of the ground, and rolled the wire up in vast bundles. Now the gaps were a hundred-yards wide and the way was clear for the artillery and cavalry to come through and take advantage of this military miracle. Word was sent back to the guns situated in Havrincourt Woods. One after another, the horsedrawn batteries limbered up and came galloping through the gaps to set up in the middle of the captured works—ready for what might come. . . . But where were the all-important cavalry?

The messages were going back, by runner, by carrier pigeon, and by wire. They were going to third Army HQ to Allied HQ in Paris, and by cable to London. Church bells were ordered rung in London, but where was the bloody cavalry? In Tank Corps HQ in London, Colonel Earnest Swinton had already figured that out. He'd been given the glad tidings by Lord Maurice Hankey, his immediate superior in the Committee of Imperial Defense. After a few moments of almost delirious delight, he suddenly lost his smile, and looked almost pensively out of this office in Whitehall.

"What's the matter?" Hankey asked, somewhat nonplussed. "You don't seem too pleased."

"I'm pleased all right," replied Swinton, "but I'm wondering. I bet that GHQ [General Head Quarters] are just as much surprised by our success as the Germans and are quite unready to exploit it." Swinton was right, dead right, for the breaching of the wire at Cambrai was one of history's turning points and the fossilized brains in command simply couldn't see it. Julian Byng, in spite of his enthusiasm, had never envisioned a total success and Kavenaugh still thought

of grand charges with drawn saber. Twelve miles behind his
own cavalry, he was still trying to figure out where to throw
five thousand mounted men in a consolidated charge. At
that point in time "eastward" would have been enough.

They weren't needed en masse, they were needed all over
the place, alongside the tanks. The charge has been made
for 80 years now that the cavalry couldn't keep up with the
tanks, and that is simply not true. The Mk-IV tanks could
only make five miles per hour and had a combat radius of
about 12 miles on 60 gallons of fuel. A plowhorse could
have kept up with them. The holes were torn in the wire
and horsedrawn artillery was already through and setting
up. The cavalry, however, were bound by strict orders not
to try anything gallant, like actually fighting. *They were not
shot out of history, they were ordered out of it by an
ignoramus.*

Twenty-two years later, the Germans would face an
enemy who knew how to use tanks and horse cavalry. When
the Germans went into Russia, Cossacks rode against them
beside Russian tanks. Georgi Zhukov used his cavalry not
mounted, but as scouts and extremely mobile riflemen. And
it worked. It could have worked at Cambrai and shortened
that war by almost a whole year. What happened, in fact,
was that the cavalry did not get orders to advance until 1230
hours. By that time the Germans were starting to regroup.
They had been given a precious few hours by British command indecision, and the British seem never to have learned
about German reaction time. As the leaders dithered, however, the tankers fought, and in one case, the tank went
on alone.

On the extreme south end of the assault, at Bleak House
on the British right flank, the Germans had a battery of field
guns, including a 5.9-inch howitzer camouflaged in the La-
teau Woods, and it was killing tanks right and left. One tank
of C Battalion took a hit directly in the nose, which must
have killed the driver and officer instantly. The crew bailed
out and dove into the woods. The tank, however, hadn't
been told that it was dead—the engine was still in gear with
its steering locked. Like something out of a nightmare, it
kept rumbling forward as the horrified German gun crew

worked frantically to reload their cannon. They gave up and ran when the unmanned monster climbed their gunshield and crushed its own assassin into the ground.

At 1130 hours, the attack had been a rousing success—except at one point. There had been a 4,000-yard advance, over 2.25 miles, with very few British casualties. Two thousand Germans and most of their guns had been captured. Two German divisions and their reserves had been eliminated as fighting units. The tanks had regrouped, reorganized their units to take care of losses, and were being refueled and re-ammoed by supply tanks and lorries. The Germans had not only been routed, the whole German Second Army was getting orders to pull out of Cambrai—and it did. The citizens recount that, for just a few hours, on 20 November, the city of Cambrai was free, the Germans had left. There was, however, one slight problem in the center of the line, one holdup without which the advance could not continue, even if it did have cavalry.

One Scottish general had made an incredibly stupid error: he simply did not like those "rude mechanicals" and had *ordered* his Highlanders to stay away from them. The result was chaos in the center of the attack. Unfortunately, because he commanded Highlanders, he had been given one of the most important objectives in the entire attack, the village and high ground of Flesquieres. Once this was taken, artillery could command the land all the way to Cambrai and cavalry could spread out in a classic pursuit-exploitation operation.

General Sir Harper, unfortunately, had refused to have anything to do with the newfangled clanking, smelly monsters; as a result, when the tanks assigned to him opened up the wire in front of Flesquieres, his troops were 100 yards behind the tanks and couldn't even *see* the holes in the wire. Worse, far worse, was to come.

Seventy tanks (C and E Battalions of the 2d Tank Brigade) had punched holes in the German wire, exactly on schedule. Behind them were the Gordon Highlanders, the Black Watch, the Seaforth Highlanders, and the Argyle and Sutherland Highlanders. Those four regiments of Scots, with the aid of 70 tanks, should have hit the Germans so hard

that they wouldn't have stopped short of Berlin. The sound
of bagpipes and tank engines alone would have caused
havoc. Harper, however, not only kept his men back from
the tanks, he kept to the original timetable instead of taking
advantage of the German rout. The Hindenburg Line was
history by 0800, and the tanks were on a rampage, except
for those assigned to Harper. His timetable said consolidate
and advance at 0930, and by God that's exactly what he
would do.

For one hour, his Scotsmen and tankers were allowed to
rest and loot while the enemy had time to figure out what
to do. You don't *do* that when you are fighting Germans.
Initially panicked, the 84th German Infantry had bugged
out. Its commander, a Major Hoffmeister, after he came
out of shock, managed to rally his men and sent off for
reinforcements. What he eventually got was part of the 27th
Reserve Infantry Regiment, including its organic artillery—
several batteries of 77mm dual-purpose guns, the predecessor of the 88 antiaircraft guns, which could break armor.

Hoffmeister ordered the guns of the Second Company,
108th Artillery, commanded by a Lieutenant Ruppell, to be
set up on the slope behind the ridge, in a classic reverse-
slope defense. Anybody or anything coming over that ridge
would be skylined for as long as it took them to get over
the crest. At an average speed of 2.6 miles per hour, a tank
would be vulnerable for long enough. The German artillery
would be shooting at an extremely close range, only 400
years or so, and almost couldn't miss. Their only vulnerability was the lack of shielding infantry. They had no canister
shells and a few Highlanders could have wiped them up in
short order. Ruppell managed to get his guns in place while
the British were taking a rest on the other side of the ridge.
The rest of the 108th Artillery Regiment's batteries were
set up farther east and camouflaged into place. Due to the
camouflage, they were not spotted by the RFC and when
the Highlanders finally gave their tanks orders to move, they
rolled right into the German's sights.

At 0930 the Highlanders began to move. As per General
Harper's orders, the tanks were sent on ahead, unsupported;
as per General Kavenaugh's orders, the desperately needed

cavalry was still cooling their heels at Fins. When the tankers began crushing the secondary wire on top of Flesquieres ridge, north of the village, the Highlanders were 400 yards, almost one-third of a *mile* behind them. When the infantry finally found the gaps and began to stream through, they were machine-gunned from the village, where the Germans had reinfiltrated and set up a strong point. Meanwhile, the tanks chugged blissfully into a trap.

When they reached the top of Flesquieres ridge, the tanks were now skylined and looking down the muzzles of guns so close that they could have been charged by infantry, let alone cavalry. Gleefully, the German gunners opened up, and the tanks could not even dodge, they had to chug on at five miles-per-hour downhill into murderous fire. To change directions in a Mk-IV, the tank had to stop and throw one track out of gear and then apply the brakes to it, a cumbrous job requiring at least three men. One does not do too much zigzagging with that kind of machine. All one can do is charge on and die.

But come on they did. Tank after tank took a shell in the bow that killed its commander and driver. Tank after tank slewed sideways, burning fiercely while machine gunners and six-pounder gunners tried to answer the deadly fire. Oddly, it was the dying tanks that were most effective because it was almost impossible to shoot accurately from a dodging tank. All they could do was to smother the German battery with tanks, and that is what they did. In just a few minutes 16 tanks lay burning on the reverse slope of Flesquieres Ridge—and still the tanks came on. With no radio communication, most crews could not even know their mates were dying in packaged droves. All told, 27 tanks drove to an unnecessary death because of a lack of leadership.

To those who study history, ask yourself this: What could even one troop of cavalry have done to those four lone, undefended 77mm field guns? If one company of infantry, or a troop of cavalry had been alongside the half-blind tanks, the attack would not have lost momentum and the war would have been months closer to a conclusion. Twenty-seven tanks . . . and no survivors. Two hundred and sixteen tankers died in flames that November morning, but they did not die alone. Not one of that gun battery survived, and one of them died a hero, venerated by even his enemies.

When an English observer named Captain Dugale of the British 6th Division came upon the ghastly scene, he walked slowly past hulk after hulk—all still burning, some still exploding—until he came to one group frozen in time and facing one German cannon. Five tanks, hit from several directions, but each having obviously been attacking this last gun, lay burning, dead men lying around them. Behind the gun lay a single German soldier, dead, alone. We, today, think he may have been Lieutenant Karl Müller of the 108th Artillery. What a bloody waste.

Slowly, painfully, the battle of Cambrai sputtered to a halt. The delay at Flesquieres had completely unhinged the assault. The rest of the commanders, knowing that they would have an unprotected flank if they advanced, were forced to wait, consolidate, and send out scouting patrols until the debacle on the ridge behind them resolved itself. General Braithwaite, commanding the 62nd Division on Harper's flank, found himself stopped by Harper's inaction and sent an offer of help, which the Highland officer peremptorily refused, further delaying the day's action. By now, the English line was beginning to bow in the center and the indecision at Flesquieres had stopped the flanking units, the 62nd Division, and the 186th Brigade.

Meanwhile, the Germans were marching reinforcements into the area and remanning positions from which shocked soldiers had fled only a few hours earlier. By now, word had gotten back to Fins and General Kavenaugh had released a few token squadrons of cavalry to move forward but only tentatively. Apparently he still had delusions of one grand stroke of glory. By midafternoon, the momentum had definitely been lost. The tanks had rallied and been resupplied and were ready for more, but the infantrymen were, predictably, about out of steam, having marched and fought from 0600 till several hours after noon . . . all the time carrying 72-pound "battle-necessity" packs. The cavalry, who could easily have trotted up and if nothing else, dismounted and fought as dragoons, arrived in dribs and drabs with no orders to go any farther than the Forward Edge of the Battle Area (FEBA). By 1530, the mist had turned to rain.

The Fort Gary Horse, a squadron of Canadian cavalry, became a bit impatient, took the bit in their teeth, and ignoring several dithering high-rankers, found a footbridge across the Canal de Escaut, near Masnieres, and went adventuring while awaiting the arrival of the main body of cavalry. B Squadron, commanded by Captain Duncan Campbell, got the farthest, running into a German artillery battery and several parties of infantry. They engaged, believing that the rest of the cavalry couldn't be far behind. They were wrong. All that was behind them was a string of galloping messengers bearing orders of recall.

By nightfall, the gallant Canadians, only 150 strong to begin with, were down to 50 men and fewer horses. They'd lost 100 men, including Captain Campbell. Near nightfall, at the village of Rumilly (on the road to Cambrai), they finally gave up, drove their horses into the advancing Germans, and began to filter back to British lines. One hundred and fifty "Colonials" had made the only noteworthy cavalry advance of the day, and that by ignoring orders. Though fighting went on for several more days, the battle of Cambrai was effectively over. . . . But blitzkrieg had been invented, not by Germany, but by General Sir Hugh Elles and Colonel J.F.C. Fuller.

The example would not be lost on the Germans. At that point in time, they were the only army in the world to have been subjected to "tank terror." Stubborn old Erick Ludendorff was beginning to come around, at least to the point of authorizing 20 German tanks built. These would eventually meet their natural opponents at another little French village not far from a pair of ancient battlefields—Crécy and Agincourt.

A Few Numbers

The British tanks were committed on 20 November 1917, and fought for 11 days, until 1 December, although the battle went on until 7 December. They fought until exhausted and took the heaviest casualties of any force committed, because they were sent where no one else dared to tread. Of the 474 tanks sent, less than one-third survived in condition to be repaired. Of the 4,000 officers and men of the Tank Corps, 1,153 became casualties: killed, wounded, or missing. Even then, with casualties that would have totaled out any other type of unit, the armormen were still fighting when withdrawn.

They had cost the Germans around 50,000 men—killed, missing, or prisoners—as well as 142 guns, 350 machine guns, and 70 mortars. Several German divisions had been destroyed as fighting units and would have to be rebuilt. One division was so broken that its colors were retired.

REFERENCE SOURCES

The Battle of Cambrai, Bryan Cooper, Stein & Day.

Tanks and Trenches, Edited by David Fletcher, Alan Sutton, Ltd.

Tank, Macksey and Batchelor, Ballantine Books.

Tank vs. Tank, Kenneth Macksey, Salem House.

Famous Tank Battles, Robert J. Icks, U.S. Government Printing Office.

Tank Warfare, Kenneth Macksey, Stein & Day.

Achtung-Panzer!, Major General Heinz Guderian, trans. Christofer Duffy, Arms and Armor Press.

Tank Commanders, George Forty, Firebird Books.

"Cambrai," November 20, 1917, by Captain Robert Galusha, *Armor* magazine, January–February 1965.

CHAPTER 13

Armored Cars with Lawrence in Arabia

COLONEL JA'FAR, AFTER HIS CAPTURE BY THE ARMORED-CAR force (with which he was quite impressed), was lodged in the military citadel at Cairo. Reading in an Arabic newspaper of the Sharif of Arbia's revolt from the old Ottoman Empire, he discovered that the Turks were executing Arab nationalists. Not only that, they had also been proven to have slaughtered hundreds of women and children, and Ja'far Pasha considered these people his friends. He had given his military parole not to act against the British, and now he joined them against the Ottoman Turks and offered his not inconsiderable military skills to the sharif of Arabia, who was now King Hussein of most of Arabia.

The king, however, was old, stubborn, and disliked Mesopotamians and Syrians on general principles. He would have nothing to do with Ja'far, who then offered himself to Prince Faisal, the principal employer of T. E. Lawrence. This convoluted path got Ja'far's opinions of armored cars in general, and the Rolls-Royce in particular, to the ear of Lawrence, who promptly badgered the British high command for a few cars of his own. Eventually, General Murray, Lawrence's immediate superior, managed to find a few and got them

diverted to Arabia. The result, after some tragicomic experimentation, became the little-known mechanized core of
Lawrence's desert army. There were free-running armored
raiders inside the legendary Arabic war for independence,
and they rolled over chariot tracks that were millennia old.

Some of the cars had come from the British colonial war
in German East Africa, Tanganyika, now known as Tanza-
nia. Others, including Roll's famous *Blast*, were picked from
the original North African force and overhauled by R-R's
field mechanical detachment. Many of the crews were recruited from the Duke of Westminster's Armored Car
Squadron, which at the time, was a bit underutilized. The
gunners came from the British Machine Gun Corps, which
at that time was a separate army unit. The tenders, or cargo
vehicles, were, as usual, Model-T Fords.

Several of the cars and their crews were lightered ashore
at Wejh on the Red Sea coast, roughly 400 miles northwest
of the port of Jidda. The village was a collection of mud
huts in a mud-walled compound, and at the time was the
encampment of a Bedouin army and a few British naval
ratings, along with the famed Lawrence. The Arabs themselves were distinctly nonmechanical and regarded machinery as being half-alive. Motor bicycles were called devil
horses and were considered to be the children of the cars
and trucks that, in turn, were the sons and daughters of
trains.

The land is desolate, rocky, and inhospitable. The insects
beastly, the climate hot, dry and brassy. The food and drink
had been medically condemned, and the water had to be
trucked in from a briny desert well several miles inland.
Due to factional fighting among the various tribes, personal
arguments and plain joy-shooting, stray bullets tended to fly
at odd times, keeping the armormen a bit tense. Not long
after they'd landed, a few children, playing with a "dud"
aircraft bomb—left over from the town's capture—set it off
and splattered themselves all over the nearest tents.

All in all, Wejh was not a comfortable place for an armor
base, nor was it centrally located for raiding. What was
needed was a place farther north and inland, a good hideout
with access to supplies and a defendable perimeter. That

would have to wait a bit for more progress in the formal war. At the time, the small port on the Red Sea was the point where the various armored cars and their tenders and, most important, their truck-borne long-range radio began to assemble and train. Finally, in mid-1917, the time became ripe and the armored cars and their crews were shipped north to Aqaba, the port on the eastern arm of the Red Sea.

Aqaba, still a bone of contention between Egypt and Israel, is the city captured by Lawrence at the end of his famous desert march in May of 1917. Lawrence's advance from Wejh resulted from a brilliant strategy for getting a desert army across an impassable stretch. He took several camel loads of gold with him and simply bought his army out of the tribesmen near Aqaba. After the battles around Aqaba, Lawrence took what was left of the city once British and French warships had soundly trashed it.

He then found that he'd painted himself into a corner, for he had not only his tribesmen to feed, but several hundred newly captured Turks. At this point, Lawrence was at one arm of the Red Sea and his only source of supplies was 150 miles away at Suez. What this meant was that the indomitable Englishman would have to take a small party of followers and cross the Sinai. They were already tired when they pushed their camels up the Sinai escarpment behind Aqaba, carrying only their weapons, water, a few lumps of broiled camel meat, and bags of dates. They moved at a steady walk and got through Mitla Pass and then to the docks at Shatt, across the canal from Suez—49 hours out of Aqaba, which the Arabs told Lawrence was "fair time for a raiding party."

In Cairo, he seems to have made a thoroughly good impression on Sir Edmund Allenby who had replaced the unfortunate Murray, who'd been blamed for the failed second battle of Gaza. So, not long after the armored landship detachment finished the battle of Gaza, its baptism of fire, Lawrence was in the process of getting his own armored force together. It is quite possible that the success of the tanks aided Lawrence's requests to the general. Allenby gave Lawrence 200,000 British pounds in credit, all the supplies he could have asked for, and his own armored force.

There was, however, one small problem. The only way up to the interior was through the old pilgrim road, the pass through the Wadi Itm and through the gorge of Rumm, but it was fit only for feet, not wheels. Fortunately, the British Quartermaster Corps was generous with gelignite (gelatin dynamite), which is an excellent quarrying explosive.

By now, the full squadron of eight turreted armored cars and two newly modified tenders for Very Important Person transport were in place, with their usual complement of "Rude Mechanicals," including Sam Rolls, whose car, *Blast*, would go into history as Lawrence's personal chariot. Day after day, Rolls and his mates (with some of their officers working beside them) dug, hammered, and blasted rock out of the way, working in brain-blasting heat until midday and then taking a forced siesta until 1700 hours. Then they'd be back at it until sunset. Every three or four days, they moved their camp—tarps strung between armored vehicles—a bit further up the gorge. Sam Rolls had some pity for the few regular officers around the unit, "they were finding it difficult to organize rocks and sand and a truculent lot of scallywags who were here today and gone tomorrow."

Three weeks and ten miles into the pass, they had visitors. Hassan, the foreman of the hired Egyptian laborers pointed to a group of scruffy Arabs on richly harnessed camels who were riding down from the top of the pass, working their way through the still unblasted rocks. "Arab no good," he said, "thief!"

"Yalla! Imshi! Clear off" Rolls shouted to the first of the Arabs, who was now walking toward him, and then he stopped cold, looking into not liquid brown eyes but steel gray eyes. "Is your captain with you?" Colonel Lawrence asked Rolls who, dumbfounded, stood in silence for most of a minute and then led Lawrence over to his officer's tent. Their future had just arrived.

Two weeks later, they had finally blasted their way to the top of Wadi Itm, and justifiably proud of their efforts, considered themselves to be the equal of the Royal Engineers. Once again it seemed that armormen and engineers were natural partners—not everywhere is the land smooth enough for wheels and even tracks and roads must be built out of whatever is available. Sam Rolls, too, turned out to have been most inventive. During *Blast*'s conversion back to touring configuration in Egypt, he'd had the running boards made detachable for use as temporary bridging and had invented a unique sand channel.

The dual rear wheels of the cars were designed to give added traction and flotation in sand and Rolls had had a V-shaped wooden ramp made that would set on the sand with the top of the ramp riding between the tires, thus providing enough traction to get out of soft sand. Rolls describes the day they decided to see if the combat cars could take their new road.

Our officers, swelling visibly with zeal to report to some noble brass hat what had been done, went off to find one at Akaba. . . . The time came when the silence of the pass was shattered by a metallic clanging. The noise grew louder and louder, suddenly, round the last bend, charged the first of our armored cars, roaring in low gear and hissing steam like a railway engine. Another appeared, and then another and soon the narrow gorge seemed filled with the stream of them, rocking and pitching in great style. We gave them a cheer and then ran to point out to the drivers suitable places in which to pull up. . . .

When they came to a standstill, I saw Lawrence sitting on the rifle-box of the first of them, with Major Marshal, our doctor, opposite him. There were other officers in the cars too. Our captain had found a good supply of brass hats. Colonels and majors were there in plenty and all told, I believe there were as many officers as rank and file in the British details of the Arab expedition at this time. . . . We refilled the hot and thirsty radiators and the officers gathered about Lawrence. While their discussion went on, we straightened out the column and I drew up my tender at its head while the other was stationed at the rear. At last our captain came towards me, accompanied by Lawrence. "You will take Colonel Lawrence," he said.

Of such simple things, fate is made, for Rolls and that car made much of the Lawrence miracle possible, because desert Arabs do not take to paper or electronic orders. The desert Bedouin likes to look into the eyes of the man who is sending him to his fate, and Rolls and *Blast* moved the guerrilla leader where he needed to go, ran his messages, and delivered the gold with which the loyalty of Bedouin patriots was bought.

From the head of the gorge of Itm the group motored over barely distinguishable tan-gray flint-and-sand roads to the junction known as Guwiera. Now formally organized as a cohesive unit, they entered history as the Hejaz Armored Car Company. Based in a remote valley, shielded with impassable cliffs like the fabled "Hole in the wall" of the wild bunch, they began a series of slashing raids . . . teaming up with camel cavalry.

The armormen's operational constraints were: the Rolls could range a bit over 300 miles on "good going" and could average something around 100 or so miles per day, crosscountry. They would cruise around 20 miles per hour and could top out at something over 60 miles per hour. Their main armament was a Vickers water-cooled machine gun that could fire about 500 rounds per minute. They could carry about a half ton of supplies, demolitions, and ammunition per car.

On the other hand, Lawrence's camel cavalry operated in a slightly different world. With a top, or racing, speed of around 30 miles per hour, a battle speed of about 18, and a traveling speed of less than ten, they would have to start much earlier than the cars to reach a given objective. Under expert handling, they could be independent of a base for as much as six weeks, provided that each man carried about 50 pounds of a coarse cracked wheat known as bulgur, dried meat, and condiments. The camels could go as much as 250 miles after watering, and that in high summer. In cooler weather, their range between "refuelings" equaled that of the armored cars, nor was their average speed, per day, that much less. "Ship of the desert" is no exaggeration when speaking of the camel.

Lawrence states that 50 miles per day was an average

march and 80 an exceptional one. In an emergency, the camels could do as much as 110 miles in 24 hours, with their riders sleeping in the saddles. Twice, a female racing camel named Gazala, carried Lawrence 140 miles in 24 hours. Granted that is only 6 miles per hour, but what other animal could keep that pace in those conditions? And what machine, with the driver asleep?

The other secret of their freedom of operations was that they knew the desert and the location of the wells, which were seldom more than 100 miles apart. This means that, with a Bedouin guide attached to each armored car detachment to show them the wells, the mechanized unit could top off their radiators at will. Those tribesmen had grown up traveling that network of desert wells and could recognize them as easily as a modern American locates himself in his city. Knowing the well at which they were located, they also knew the course to set and the landmarks to look for in any given direction.

The desert dweller, like the sailor, gets his directions from the sun in the daytime and the stars at night. The sky is his map, the moon his calendar. For each direction, a star is selected and the course set, only switching stars as they fall below the horizon or get too high for use. For the latitude of each destination, a star will be found that just touches the horizon when directly below the North Star. The Bedouin travels north or south until his latitude is correct and then, having deliberately aimed a bit east or west in his travels, simply turns into his destination for the last few miles. By this method desert travelers have been navigating for millennia, and by this method, ships have been crossing oceans since the Bronze Age.

Guided by Bedouins, and with due synchronization, the armormen could strike a target supported by camel cavalry. Not only could the cars carry extra fuel and lubricants, small camel caravans could install fuel dumps at selected wells. Now the armored car had become another ship of the desert, albeit a somewhat short-ranged vessel. Lawrence estimated that with the camel carrying the rifle-armed Bedouin, 50 pounds of food, and some personal gear, a camel force could make good 1,500 miles in six weeks, with no resupply whatsoever. . . . Modern machinery, to this day, has never equaled this. An Abrams tank would require 2,621 gallons of fuel for that distance.

At Guwiera, Sam Rolls and his mates went into advanced culture shock when they found an army already camped there. There were desert Bedouins from several tribes, Iraqi mercenaries, Syrians, giant black Sudanese, and a few renegade Turks who hired out as weapons instructors (large numbers of Turkish soldiers "went missing" after Gaza). The armored cars were greeted by a swirling swarm of horsemen riding bareback, brandishing their swords and rifles and yelling "Ya Aurens, Ya Aurens." As Lawrence went into conference with Prince Faisal and old Auda, the war chief, the armored cars went into their night laager and the men were free to wander about a camp that seemed to have fallen out of a storybook.

The camp fires and star-filled ebony sky were reflected in the dark eyes of the warriors who sat on robes around the fires. Some of the Arabs were baking coarse bread in the embers while others sat smoking pipes with clay stems and stone bowls. Although the Koran forbids the imbibing of alcohol, it is not unknown for a bit of wild yeast to get into the apricot or date juice. Thus an occasional argument broke out, generally ending with laughter all around. Most of the men, however, were drinking small cups of sweet, strong eastern coffee. Rolls, for his part, found a comfortable bed on the front seat of *Blast* and began to prepare for the morrow. . . . That bed would be his home for a year and a half and 20,000 miles of desert travel.

It has been said that he who commands the sea is at great liberty, for he can take as little or as much of war as he wishes. The same reasoning applies to the armored desert raider. The raiding parties can cruise unhindered across the sand seas and strike at will at the enemy's unguarded rear or cut his vital transportation links—and then vanish into the trackless desert. In no way could the general staffs of the various armies have taken the motorized, armored, desert raider into their prewar plans, for he did not exist. The high desert was his home and his birthplace.

The next morning, as Lawrence and a few men were getting ready to put the cars into instant use, Rolls got other shocks. A group of officers in khaki uniforms rode out to inspect the Arab mounted force that was assembling, and Rolls did a double take when he saw one officer.

" 'Look,' I exclaimed, gripping a man's arm, 'That's Ja'far Pasha. I know him, we captured him near Sollum and sent him to Cairo. He was leading the Senussi against us.' Then my eye fell on another of them and I cried. 'Good God, there's another of them. That's Nuri Bey, the cunning dodger. . . . Now what's the game here?' "

The game as we have seen, was that Ja'far Pasha had switched sides, and Lawrence had met Nuri Bey in a Cairo hospital while getting treated for boils, and one thing had led to another. With a sense of unreality, Rolls watched Lawrence and Nuri Bey approach his car and helped them get ready for a raid on the Turkish railway.

They loaded a week's rations, a good supply of gun-cotton explosive, detonators and blasting wire, and a case of 5,000 British gold sovereigns from the Commonwealth Bank of Australia, among other items. A machine gun on a tripod was mounted in the pickup bed and then Nuri and Lawrence climbed in beside Rolls—the other tender, *Grey Knight,* was alongside them and they were off on Lawrence's first armored raid. Rolls, still somewhat mystified, stole quick glances at the Turk, who did not speak English, remembering their encounters in Cyrenaica.

Lawrence, ever alert, spotted Rolls' nervousness and inquired about the cause. In a few quick sentences, Rolls brought Lawrence up to date on his North African adventures, after which Lawrence spoke a few sentences to Nuri in Arabic.

Nuri began to babble excitedly and Rolls told Lawrence, "Ask him if he remembers Bir Wair, where he only just managed to escape our armored cars on his piebald horse." This set off a round of excited, "I was here and you were there" type of conversation until Rolls patted the dash of *Blast* and said, "Tell him that this is the very car in which I chased him." This set off roars of laughter, and suddenly the English driver, the English colonel, and the Turkish renegade were the best of friends, united in a common cause.

Lawrence, while not professionally trained, had instinctively hit on the tradition of the commander's reconnaissance. His basic mission at that time was not to destroy the railway, which he could have done at any time. It was to keep the Turkish army as busy and spread out as possible. This particular recon was to find out just how much damage could be done by motor as opposed to camel transport. After getting down out of the hills and onto flat land, they were agreeably surprised to find that the cars could still do 65 miles per hour on the mud flats. They had quite a bit of probing to do and had to put down brushwood corduroy roads across invasive sand dunes. But after only one day, they were within striking distance of the railway, with a fully pioneered assault trail behind them. Unfortunately, they would find that they were too little, too soon.

They camped that night, under the open stars, in enemy territory, sleeping between the cars around a small sparky fire of brushwood, and made their plans. The next day they set off back to Guwiera to pick up a section of armored cars and a pair of light ten-pounder guns (about 65mm) mounted on Talbot trucks. These guns and their crews had been found drifting at loose ends in Egypt and were snapped up by one of Lawrence's protectors within the establishment, a General Clayton. The gun crews were Scottish and were commanded by a Lieutenant Brodie, a rangy, quiet man who would not tolerate adversity. Any problem that got in his way was simply ground down until it did not exist.

There were eight cars on that raid. Four armored cars, two Talbots with their guns, and a pair of Rolls tenders, *Blast* (with Rolls driving, for Lawrence, who for a change was only an observer), and the *Grey Knight,* for an officer named Joyce—who was in command of the actual attack. By evening of their first day, they were in their old camp behind the low hill range that shielded the village of Mudowara. The next day was spent by Lawrence and Joyce finding the final assault route and firing positions above a railroad way station and watering stop named Tel Shahm, two stations north of Mudowara. That night they camped and made their final plans. The next day would be New Year's Day, 1918.

Their initial objective was a small entrenched work that protected the way station. The Talbot Battery opened the affair, dropping a series of ten-pounder shells into the trench-works while the cars advanced to the flanks of the position, dusting up the defenders with machine gun fire. No damage was done on either side, Lawrence's main objective being to prove that the railway could, in fact, be broken at will from the armored car base at Guwiera. All this time, Lawrence's raids on the Hejaz railway had been calculated to draw Turkish strength out of Palestine, away from the formal war, and to starve the garrison at Medina of enough supplies to march. Now the time for fooling around was ending and the time for an end to the war was coming.

Arcing south a bit, they again took up firing positions and the two-gun Talbot battery began sniping at the Shahm station, sending shells all over the area—just to stir up the Turks. The defenders promptly scampered off into a block-house, which the gun battery proceeded to shell while the cars prowled around the helpless station, putting a few bursts of machine gun fire into windows and doors. They had proved their point. To quote Lawrence, "All the Turks in Arabia could not fight a single armored car in the open." The railway would get a few months to forget its humiliation; then the cars would be back, this time under command of a professional, and it would not be pretty for the Turks.

Ja'far Pasha had by then created a regular Arab army out of a rabble of tribesmen; Lawrence had created his mobile Bedouin force with its armored core; and the British Army under General Allenby stood ready to strike—it all hinged on one armored car raid. For this, it is worth quoting Lawrence again, from *Seven Pillars of Wisdom*.

"With Joyce, we laid our triple plan to support Allenby's first stroke. In our center, the Arab regulars under Ja'far, would occupy the line a march north of Maan. Joyce with our armored cars would slip down to Mudowara, and destroy the railway—permanently this time, for now we were ready to cut off Medina." For this operation, the armored detachment got for a time, its own field officer, Colonel Alan Dawnay, of whom Lawrence was a bit dubious, at first.

Forthwith, I took a car to join Dawnay. I was uneasy at a regular fighting his first guerrilla war with that most involved and intricate weapon, the armored car. Also, Dawnay was no Arabist, and neither Peake, his camel expert, nor Marshal, his doctor was fluent [in Arabic]. His troops were mixed, British, Egyptian, and Bedouin. The last two were antipathetic. So I drove into his camp above Tel Shahm after midnight and offered myself, delicately, as an interpreter.

Fortunately, he received me well, and took me round his lines. A wonderful show. The cars were parked geometrically here; armored cars there; sentries and picket were out, with machine guns ready. Even the Arabs were in a tactical place behind a hill, in support, but out of sight and hearing. By some magic, Sherif Hazaa and himself had kept them where they were put. My tongue coiled into my cheek with the wish to say that the only thing lacking was an enemy.

Lawrence's doubts stemmed from the problems he had had in the past, convincing orthodox officers of the facts of guerrilla war and of the fractious nature of the lordly Bedouin tribes. Dawnay, however, seemed to have all in hand, and was quite familiar with the "intricacies of armored cars,"—and would Lawrence please synchronize his watch.

The next morning, the column rolled at dawn, three Rolls tenders, all eight turreted armored cars, the Talbot Battery, and an indetermine number of Model-T Ford tenders, themselves armed with Lewis machine guns. Soon the dust became so heavy that the cars could not travel in column and had to spread out in line, this procedure soon generated a race between the drivers as they approached the great level-floored gorge named Rumm.

Soon they were in the great natural amphitheater and parked in military precision as military stores were unloaded for the airplanes that would be operating from the level floor of Rumm. While the men worked, the officers planned, finalizing their operations for the morrow. Then, aircraft fuel and bombs unloaded, they left the Gorge of Rumm and headed east across a level dried swamp, still in line abreast with the drivers vying for fastest vehicle. Sam Rolls tells it best.

Lawrence and Dawnay mounted to their seats and I let in my clutch and flew after the racing battery. Soon we were in the thick of the race, and keeping pace with them, we were able to observe their antics. A Rolls Royce armored car drew ahead, passing a fussy little Ford tender loaded with all kinds of gear. Then a Rolls tender came to the fore, screaming past us at seventy miles per hour. Having shown the mettle of his car, the driver slowed her a little so as to give somebody else a chance of tasting glory.

Lawrence pointed out to me another Ford which was straining to get to the fore, panting visibly. For some distance it skimmed along, bonnet and bonnet with a great Rolls armored car, its driver obviously putting every grain of power into the effort. Then, very suddenly, there was a loud report and the Ford whirled round like a firework on a stick, turning two complete circles and narrowly missing the armored car. Then it rolled over in a double somersault, throwing off its load in all directions.

I turned my wheel and drove straight to the scene, fearing for the fate of the driver. The Ford was standing squarely and quietly on all four wheels as though it had just been pulled up to allow the driver to look for his cigarettes or something equally simple. Only the driver was ruefully rubbing a bump on his head. This driver was afterwards nicknamed "Lucky Eddie.

From this little episode, the officers drew the obvious conclusion that a bit of march discipline was in order and a speed limit was imposed in order to keep down the wear and tear on government property. They were learning. That night they were in a quiet camp behind the ridge that overlooked their objective, the station at Tel Shahm and there was considerable less boisterousness as they prepared for battle.

The Rolls armored car was equipped with both a muffler

and an exhaust cutout that could produce a few extra horsepower, at the cost of silence. At dawn then, with the cutouts
closed, the cars rolled silently over the low ridge and down
upon the sleeping garrison around Tell Shahm.

First the armored cars opened up, then the Talbot Battery
let loose and the camel cavalry came swarming out of the
desert in a classic mounted assault. Then, just to add to
the confusion, a couple of light bombers came up from the
Gorge of Rumm and dropped their bombloads on the garrison encampment. At 1120 hours, the Turks, astonished beyond comprehension, walked out with their hands up,
completely trashing Colonel Dawnay's schedule, which
called for the surrender at 1130.

A Lieutenant Hornby, who was riding the *Gray Knight*
and had a third tender, *Blue Mist,* drove up to the bridges
and began loading them with over a hundred pounds of
explosives, which was a bit of overkill. The resulting blast
almost lifted Rolls, Lawrence, and Dawnay out of their own
car. Hornby was quickly shown the more economical
method of tamping a few pounds of explosive into the drain-
age holes, and the rest of the bridges in the section came
down much more peacefully.

In the meantime, the rest of the garrison had holed up in
a place called the Rock Post, a circle of stones of unknown
ancient origin. The cars, unable to make the steep slope,
circled slowly, peppering the position with machine gun fire.
With the defenders' heads kept down, an Arab infantry assault plucked the position like a ripe peach. Then the combat troops could rest a bit, while Lawrence, now acting as
a demolitions expert for Hornby, took 2 tons of explosives
and proceeded to demolish several miles of track, bridges,
and switches with his famed tulip charges. They were covered by a pair of armored cars that also served as refuges
from falling flint rock; they were working in a hurry and
several times the rocks landed on the turrets of their cars.

Then came the reduction of the southern breastworks,
which fell to a wild camel charge. Next, the station itself,
already under airplane bombardment, was subject to long-
range fire from the mobile Talbot battery. Shortly thereafter,
the war-weary Turks began leaving the trenches waving "all

manner of white things." Then it became simply a rush for loot, and even Lawrence joined in, getting for his prize the station bell. He records that the Turks became quite indignant that their surrender became secondary to looting.

The next day the armored column—now almost totally bereft of Bedouin auxiliaries who, loot-loaded had gone home to celebrate—swooped down on Mudowara, to find a long train in the station. Unfortunately, there was an artillery battery on that train and when the armored cars opened up at long distance, so did a pair of extremely accurate Austrian mountain howitzers. After several very close misses, the armored car detachment wisely stayed out of the 7,000-yard range of those guns and contented itself with blowing up and making unusable over 80 miles of track and seven stations. Thus, the entire Arabian Peninsula was cut off from the Turkish army, by one small armored cavalry unit, which had learned to live in the desert and to work with a variety of camel and horse cavalry.

With Medina now cut off and in the process of being starved out, Lawrence and his Arabs and armormen were free to start chewing up the rest of the railroad, and for this they began working with the Royal Flying Service. Thus they got into even more wild action. Word came that the Turks, besieged in their great railyard at Maan, were either about to sortie or, conversely, were about to be reinforced by the Turkish garrison at Amman (in what is now Jordan). One morning, the armored car squadron had worked its way up a dry wadi and, right on schedule, the light bombing aircraft came up from Aqaba, and, flying low and slow, they began to bomb the railyards.

The planes drew quite a bit of antiaircraft fire, but the Rolls cars took this distraction to slip over the last crest and open fire. First, the ten-pounder battery—now assigned to Nuri Bey and his camel cavalry—opened up. This was the signal for the cars to begin machine gunning the AA batteries to keep them from downing the planes bombing the railyards. The guns, being water-cooled, needed to be fired alternately, so that they would not all boil dry at once. As the cars were running out of targets, a scouting plane dropped a message streamer—Turkish infantry was coming up the rail line to reinforce the defenders, and they were off again.

Naturally, all this violent activity began to take its toll on even the rugged Rolls-Royce cars, and the drivers began to cannibalize the crippled vehicles. Eventually, this wore their members down to exactly three running cars. *Blast*, and two armored cars, and some Fords, of course. Lawrence, finding that without the armor to support his camel and horse-mounted troops, his effectiveness was falling off, typically cut straight through the whole chain of command. "If you will make out a detailed indent," he told Rolls, "I will see what can be done." Rolls apparently had inherited the thankless job of squadron motor sergeant.

Among other things, the link between air and armor was becoming more and more apparent. Allenby had taken a string of cities: Nablus, Beisän, Afula, Semakh, and Haifa, and suddenly the Arabs were demanding an advance on Damascus. The cars, however, were still crippled, most of them sitting on "deadline row." One morning, very early, a tremendous roar came out of the clear, bright desert dawn, and Rolls and his mates woke up to see the largest airplane that anyone could imagine circling overhead. Quickly, working like fiends, they cleared an extra section of runway so that the big ship could land.

It was a Handley Page bomber, with wings a full 100 feet in span. Between the upper and lower wings, a pair of 250-horsepower Rolls engines were suspended. There was an open machine gun pit in the nose of the fuselage, with a pilot and copilot sitting side by side behind the gunner. The big plane took to the ground with a smooth roll, and as the men looked her over, Lawrence appeared, having come in a smaller plane that had almost been overlooked. "Got the stuff?" Sam Rolls asked anxiously, and Lawrence answered enigmatically. "It *should* be in the Handly-Page." He'd obviously been talking to Allenby and had given Rolls's indent to one of the general's staffers and hoped for the best.

The armormen rushed up to the great fuselage and when their eyes became accustomed to the gloom, they widened in astonishment. Everything they had asked for was there, and 40 cases of petrol as well. In a few weeks of work by the crews and mechanics, every vehicle was again battle worthy, and they finished out the war with all cars running. This is the example they set, and this is the example we follow to this day.

REFERENCE SOURCES

Seven Pillars of Wisdom, T. E. Lawrence, Anchor Books.
Revolt in the Desert, T. E. Lawrence, George Oran Inc.
Steel Chariots in the Desert, S. C. Rolls, Jonathan Cape.
Desert Warfare, Bryan Perrett, Patrick Stephens, Ltd.

CHAPTER 14

The First Tank vs. Tank Battle
VILLERS-BRETONNEUX, FRANCE, APRIL 24, 1918

THE BRITISH, CLOSELY FOLLOWED BY THE FRENCH, INVENTED the tank, and as we have seen, it was an awful shock to the world's military minds. While General Erich Ludendorff, like many of his Allied contemporaries initially dismissed the tank as a mechanical novelty, he was not too stubborn to authorize some research and development. While the British tank stemmed from the American Holt artillery tractor that had been bought from Holt/London, the German tank basic model stemmed from Holt/Budapest. Both machines had an American ancestor, but from there on national differences dictated the designs. The British needed to be able to cross wide and deep trench works. The Germans simply had to kill large numbers of infantrymen. No one had really thought about tank fighting tank.

All through 1917, a German development program coded A7V, after the German automotive committee, worked on the design of a German tank. Meanwhile, since so many Allied tanks had been left on the battlefield, due to mechanical casualties and mud, the Germans had recovered and repaired them and put the vehicles to good use. Like the Allies, though, their only concept for the tank was as an infantry support weapon, to free the riflemen from the trap of trenches, barbed wire, and machine guns.

As far as any writings of the period show, the concept of tank fighting tank wasn't even thought of. Most "experts" considered the concept of a fighting machine to be ludicrous and the tank valuable only to get the trench warfare phase of military evolution out of the way. Then men could go back to the more "honorable" methods of killing each other—such as bayonet duels, rifle fire, and artillery barrages that has shredded a whole generation of European youth. As a result of this mentality, even the new tanks coming off the drawing boards were slow-motion monsters.

The Tanks

The 29-ton British Mk-IV was powered by a 105-horsepower engine, but geared to only five miles per hour. It had a cruising range of about 60 miles, by which time the tracks also might be worn out due to their unlubricated slides. German field guns having proven fatal to the machine-gun-only "female" tanks, most new construction by 1918 was either cannon-armed "males" or "hermaphrodites," which had both cannon and machine guns. There were, however, substantial numbers of female tanks still in the inventory. As a result, sections and platoons were made up or at least one male tank, shepherding a few females. Steering in the Mk-IV still took up to four men, since to make major course changes, one track had to be declutched manually and brakes put on from a different position. This made sudden moves impossible and even slowed down shooting. The cannon loaders were also the gearsmen, and it takes a good man to do two things at once.

Things were getting seriously modern in the newer tanks though. Not only was the cooling system better, easing the heat load on the crews, there was now something that could almost be called an intercommunication device: the commander only needed to push a button that would turn on a light to tell the steersman which way to go, like a turn signal in reverse. Some tanks were now equipped with crude spark-gap Morse Code radios that let commanders communicate with HQ at something faster than pigeon speed—all it takes is one hungry hawk to terminate communications, permanently.

There was now another style of British tank, called the Whippet, due to its speed of almost double that of the older Mk-IV. The 14-ton Whippet was armed with four machine guns in a rear mounted tower, which were handled by a commander and a gunner. This meant that the Whippet was a female and would suffer badly in a tank versus tank duel. Of course it could always depend on its speed of almost 9 miles per hour to extract it from danger. The third member of the crew was the driver; instead of steering with brakes and gears, he had a steering wheel that was hooked directly to the throttles of the two 45-horsepower engines.

Each engine drove one track, and steering was a function of separate engine speed. If an engine broke down, the crew had to install a cross shaft and steer with the brakes. This may sound a bit flaky, but it worked surprisingly well, and the system was used in World War II in several models of the famed Amtrack. Later, in the mid 1950s, the M-59 Armored Personnel Carrier (APC) used the same arrangement, and that machine is still in service in some nations.

To complete the set of vehicles that fought at Villers-Bretonneux, we must now look at the German response to the Allied invention. The A7V tank was basically a square box that weighted 32 tons. It was powered by a pair of 100-horsepower engines that drove it at speeds of up to eight miles per hour on roads. Once it left the pavement, though, it was limited to four or five miles per hour. Further, its tracks were underhung, or shorter than the hull, which meant that it could get hung up rather easily.

Like the Mk-IV male, it had a 57mm cannon, and mounted six machine guns. The gun was originally a Norwegian Nordenfeldt that had been sold to both the Russians and the Belgians. The Germans had no gun in that caliber, so they used captured stocks. It fired a canister shell as well as high-explosive and solid shot. The A7V's frontal armor, at 30mm was more than double that of the Allied tanks, but a six-pounder shell could still penetrate the hull. While the Mk-IV had a crew of 8, and the Whippet used only 3 men, the A7V carried anywhere from 18 to 22 men on board! In modern parlance, it would have been called an infantry fighting vehicle.

There was a driver and one or two mechanics to guide the tank and maintain the machinery, two or three artillerymen to operate the 57mm cannon in the bow, and a pair of infantrymen for each of the six machine guns, plus an officer to command the vehicle. Each was drawn from a separate segment of the German army; this alone generated a bit of crew friction. Then, for training and combat operations, the new Tank Korps—comprising just 20 new A7Vs and a dozen captured Mk-1s, IIIs, and IVs—was assigned to the German Combat Engineers.

The experimental pioneer unit that took responsibility was commanded by a Captain Willie Rohr, who was known as *Sturm bataillion Rohr.* As in all competent armies, the combat engineers were responsible for "breaking and entering," and in addition, the engineer force had the shops necessary to maintain the new machines. So, in the German Army as in the British and American, the engineers, not the cavalry or infantry, gave birth to the tanks.

The Situation

The first tank vs. tank encounter might not have happened at all if it hadn't been for General Ludendorff's last-gasp offensive in the spring of 1918. His objective, it would seem, was to knock the Allies about just enough to be able to negotiate a peace before the fresh American Army came in and "disrupted" the war. He also thought that if he could capture the critical rail and road juncture at Amiens, it might be possible to split the British from the French, and drive them into the sea at Dunkirk. Twenty-two years later, Heinz Guderian and Erwin Rommel did just that. World War II was merely unfinished business—and it may not be over yet.

What General Ludendorff hadn't counted on, though, was that President Wilson's 14-point propaganda campaign would help to trigger the revolution in Germany, forcing the Kaiser to abdicate and leave the German nation in the hands of a demoralized military and the artificial Weimar Republic.

As has been said before, history is a long record of dishonest politicians getting honest soldiers in trouble. While Germany starved and seethed behind him, Ludendorff launched a series of offensives by blowing the Allied barbwire with intensive artillery bombardments, and then rushing special troopers through the temporary gaps—back in World War I, the combined arms team of infantry, artillery, and armor was already being born.

The British, of course, knew where their own weak points were, and backed them up with tanks. A cannon-armed male would be assigned to protect several females, or Whippets. This small tank unit, usually from three to eight vehicles, was sent with supplies and mechanics to selected villages and remote farms and told to go to ground until needed. The code name for these little groups, in typical British understatement, was "Savage Rabbits."

The system worked, after a fashion, but it also diluted the effect of their armor. As a result, there were more gun-equipped German tanks at Villers-Bretonneux than British. Thirteen of them to be exact, almost three-quarters of the entire A7V force. In a misty, foggy, French dawn on 24 April 1918, they bumbled into each other and into history. For the first time in roughly 300 years, armored men again faced each other across a battlefield.

Northeastern France is historic ground and armored men have been fighting there since medieval days. Villers-Bretonneux is east of the city of Amiens, less than an hour's drive south of the historic battlefield of Crécy and about 60 miles south of Agincourt, where the English longbow broke the armor plate of French chivalry in the year 1415. Now, 503 years later, the contest began again, over the same land that Henry V had traversed on his way to that battle. As a matter of fact, several British tank units had been stationed at Agincourt, prior to the battle of Arras, in mid-1917.

The town lies in what is called "good tank country," open rolling plains dotted with villages. The land is hard enough to support armored vehicles, but there are no steep hills or unsmashable obstacles. European farmers do not usually live on their land like Americans. Instead, they live in small villages and follow paths out to the fields they have worked since their ancestors were the serfs of armor-plated aristocrats. The only exceptions are the compounds of wealthier families, and these are usually not too far from the villages.

In the spring of 1918, the Allied frontline had been pushed back by Ludendorff's attacks to less than a mile east of Villers-Bretonneux, and there had been some hasty fortifying going on. The initial momentum of the "Kaiserschlact" assault had petered out due to troop exhaustion, and both sides were regrouping. There was a crude trench line to the east of the village, a fortified farm to its south, and a hastily built airdrome, also to the east. In the eastern outskirts of the village, a tile factory/brickworks had been turned into a hard point, staffed with a company of infantry and large numbers of machine guns. There were dozens of machine gun nests, fortified with sandbags, all around the town. Several lines of communication connected it with the rest of the world. A narrow country road on a Roman foundation entered the village at its eastern edge and a railroad just grazed its southern edge.

That railway ran eastwards toward the town of Guillaucourt, and on the evening of 21 April at the Guillaucourt siding 15 A7V German tanks had been unloaded from their flatcars. The detraining procedure was interrupted by Allied bombing, and two tanks broke down due to engine problems. reducing the total number of available A7Vs to 13. The air attack caused no damage, and the tanks used the cover of night to move several kilometers westward, to the town of Wiencourt. The next night, they moved again, and set up shop in the warehouse of a sugar beet refinery in the hamlet of Marcelcave. Apparently the aviators did not recognize the boxy shapes of the A7Vs as threatening, for they made no report to the Allied command. . . . From the air, the German tanks would have looked like boxcars. With typical Teutonic thoroughness, the tankers used rakes and brooms to erase the tread marks from the loading dock to the staging point.

The defenders were a heterogeneous lot, representing the colonial empires of both England and France. There were Australians, French cavalry, Moroccans, and a detachment

of the Legion of Frontiersmen riding Arab ponies. There
was horsedrawn artillery, pulled by massive Percherons that
dwarfed the Arab ponies, and hidden in lying-up points, the
"Savage Rabbits." The majority of the defenders, though,
were British and Australian line infantry. The overall British
units were the 14th and 18th Divisions with the Australian
9th Brigade in the center, its 35th Battalion direction in
front of the town of Villers-Bretonneux.

In the air above the area, savage combat went on with
gaily painted biplanes and triplanes circling and darting like
the knights of old. A Canadian pilot named Roy Brown
got behind a red Fokker triplane, and Baron Manfred von
Richthofen was finally brought to earth on the morning of
21 April, just a little north of the scene of the first tank vs.
tank encounter. Two nights later, a prowling German fighter
dropped a flare, just to see what the British might be up to,
and caught a group of tanks in the open, probably moving
from one wooded area to another.

As soon as he landed, the pilot telephoned his report to
his HQ and the local commander added a mustard gas com-
ponent to his scheduled dawn artillery barrage. The assault
plan the Germans were using began with a short, extremely
dense artillery bombardment designed by a Major George
"Breakthrough" Brückmueller, that would hide the A7Vs
until they had almost reached the Allied lines. What they
were depending on was surprise, aided by a natural fog and
the added smoke shelling, which would blind the defenders
until the German assault troops struck.

Of the Allied tanks allocated to defend this sector, which
protected the vital rail center of Amiens, seven were Whippets with machine gun armament, commanded by a Captain
T. R. Price. They were in reserve and had no radio communication. When the battle began, a patrolling aircraft observed the assault and circled back over Price's headquarters
in the Boise d' Blangy. The message he dropped among the
tanks somehow failed to mention the German tanks involved in the new assault, and as a result, Price was ordered
out, unwarned that his enemy was approaching.

Captain F. C. Brown commanded the "Savage Rabbit"
detachment from British A Company, First Tank Battalion.

Two of the tanks were female Mk-IVS, again armed only with automatic weapons. Only the cannon-armed Mk-IV commanded by Second Lieutenant Frank Mitchell stood a chance of going gun to gun against the Germans. Effectively, he would be outnumbered thirteen to one. His crew of eight had already taken two casualties because the Germans had added gas and smoke to the dawn artillery attack. He was missing two loaders and both his gunners were crippled by blistered arms and faces.

On the cool, foggy morning of 24 April, 13 German tanks clattered into history. The tank force had been divided into three separate units, each attached to a different infantry division. Group One, commanded by a Lieutenant Skopnik, was working for the 228th Division. It consisted of 3 tanks— each commanded by a lieutenant. Skopnik's tank was named *Hagen,* Vietze's tank was named *Lotti* and Ernst Volckheim's tank was named *Alter Fritz* (although there is some confusion as to just whose tank it was). *Hagen,* for instance, isn't listed in the German official report, but it was photographed in the town of Villers-Bretonneux. One suspects that there was some serious mechanical work going on in the sugar beet factory and that there may have been some engine swapping going on as well as crew shuffling. These machines were new and still being debugged.

Group Two was attached to the 4th Guards Division and consisted of six tanks. Tank *Baden-1* was commanded by Lieutenant Hennecke. Tank *Cyclop* belonged to Burmann. *Mephisto* was Theunissen's tank. *Gretchen* was Lappe's tank. Tank *No. 541* belonged to Block, and Tank *Herkules* was bossed by Wolfgang Barton. Group Three, supporting the 77th Reserve Division, was the one that rolled into history. It was commanded by Stein from his tank *Elfriede.* Second was Biltz in *Nixe.* Albert Müller had *Schnuck* and Friedrich Bitter in Tank *Siegfried* completed this section.

At precisely 0445 hours, that extremely heavy preliminary barrage fell on the Allied defenses, partly to numb the troops and partly to mask the engine and track noises of the approaching tanks. . . . It worked to perfection and the surprise was complete.

At 0650, the German armor began to roll through fog that

had now become dense and dirty with smoke shells. Skopnik, commanding Group One from his own tank, was the first to engage. When Skopnik's *Hagen* loomed up out of the fog, everybody who could see it opened fire, and a perfect hail of ricocheting bullets enveloped the tank, deafening the crew and knocking rivets loose from the armor. Skopnik's tank spanned the hastily dug trenches and when his 57mm cannon began shooting up other machine gun nests, his machine gunners raked the British trenches, causing so many casualties that the defenders surrendered to the German infantry that was trotting along behind the tanks. Driving parallel to the railroad embankment, *Hagen* came within 100 yards of the eastern edge of the town, under heavy rifle and machine gun fire all the way.

By 0800, the British commanding general, G. W. Grogan, had sent for his tank officer and Captain Brown had accomplished his initial recon. By 0845, he'd gotten back to the Bois d'Aquenne and ordered Mitchell's tanks underway—at 3.7 miles per hour.

By this time Skopnik's tanks, even at 5 miles per hour, had outdistanced their infantry and he had to go back through the fog and pick them up. Then, accompanied by the riflemen, Skopnik worked his way through the town to a point where the railroad crossed the old Roman road. Noticing that he was mixed up with the wrong infantry—the 4th Guards instead of the 228th Jaegers—he retraced his route, hashing up the British who were just recovering from his first pass. On the eastern boundary of the town, the fortified brickworks was still holding out, so Skopnick parked in front of it and began heavy shelling.

By this time, tanks *Lotti* (Vietze) and *Alter Fritz* (Volckheim) had come through he village, after thoroughly beating up the defenders, and joined Skopnik in front of the fortified building. This also was at 0845 and the fog and smoke had finally thinned enough for the tanks to see each other. After a period of intense 57mm cannon fire, the British had had enough and surrendered . . . after sending a runner off to the Bois D'Aquenne which was the lying-up point of the British tank unit.

We have available a German report from a Sergeant Eggert who was Volckheim's cannon gunner, and we can now see the battle through German eyes, which had not been possible earlier. On the morning of 24 April, Eggert wrote later:

I was the senior gunner in an A7V named *Baden I* (?) *Alter Fritz* (?) . . . reports differ, commanded by Lt. Volckheim. We were part of group one and were about 50m behind the line of departure. After a night of work in the Marcelcave sugar beet factory, which was our tank shed, we were fueled up, ammoed, and ready.

We had a group of combat engineers from Sturm bataillon Rohr attached to us for the assault. Our group of tanks and engineers was assigned to the right flank of the attack force of the Fourth Guards division. To our left was group two, of six tanks, and beyond them was group three, of another four tanks. Our group had the mission of supporting the infantry attacks on the enemy trenches at Villers-Bretonneux.

A few minutes before the attack command came, our tank rolled forward across the fallow ground toward the enemy. We were moving through very thick fog and smoke and soon lost our connection with our infantry. . . . Soon even our engineers were not to be seen. Then we began to receive our first enemy fire and came on the first trench lines. Great was our astonishment when we found the trenches empty, except for a few M.G. nests. This did not square with our experience of British and French soldiers. The appearance of our German tanks must have unnerved them.

When we recovered from our first fright, we stopped the tank and I began to shoot through the small sights of my cannon. As soon as the Englanders received some of our case shot and began to take casualties they became smart ones and surrendered.

After turning the prisoners over to their own infantry, Veitze and Volckheim took their tanks back through the village, breaking up more pockets of resistance, and then attacked the airdrome, shooting the place up and setting the hangars on fire. . . . They also took time out to have themselves photographed. Sergeant Eggert's report now continues.

Then our tank drove through the second and third enemy lines and our morale was growing as we moved quickly. We were first in that place but unfortunately the birds had already flown. Driving further, we met a lone German infantry officer who waved us over to him. He told us that the English had abandoned line two but had regrouped at line three. We again moved forward quickly and had some good shooting with our artillery and machine guns, driving the whole of them back. Unfortunately, they were getting used to us and no longer surrendered so readily.

Now also our connection with our infantry had improved. Again our tank went forward and beside the brickworks we sat, its garrison of machine gunners and one of our tanks fighting this fortress and its outlying trench complexes. We came on line beside the other tank and took our share of the fighting. Soon our infantry stormed the building, and then out of trenches and holes streamed the enemy into the destroying fire of our tanks. They ran cross-country and all around until they were tired and then they surrendered.

We next parked our tank by a haystack, shut it down and began disarming the English prisoners, which was an imposing number (170). After our infantry had taken them over, we restarted the tank and a spark from our engine set the haystack on fire. Suddenly, there was a large commotion and out of the haystack jumped and dove about fifteen Englanders with four machine rifles. We had just had our latest updating on where the English were supposed to be, and were naturally greatly surprised when they showed up with four machine guns still in action. After we had terminated this situation, we left in an orderly fashion.

By noon, low on fuel and ammunition but feeling pretty satisfied with themselves, Skopnik, Vietze, and Volckheim returned to their starting point in the town of Marcelcave just a bit east of Villers-Bretonneux.

Group Two, under a Lieutenant Uihlein, had moved out at 0700, parallel to Skopnik's route, but some hundred yards south of the railroad track. Working as "battlefield bullies," the tank group went south around the town, taking the railroad station and many prisoners, whom they handed over to the advancing infantry. The Tank named *Baden-1*, under Hennecke, began to lose efficiency due to several supports breaking in its gunmount, but he still joined his assigned partner, Burmann, and began shooting up the Bois D'Aquenne, where the Allied reserves were just arriving. Like several others, Burmann's *Cyclop* sported a large white skull and crossbones on its bow.

The time was about 0800 and the fog was still thick when *Gretchen* blundered into concentrated British fire; its driver, mounted in a cupola on top of the hull, was severely wounded as bullets came through his vision slits. Screaming with agony, he convulsively pulled back on both brake levers, jamming the tracks and stalling both engines. Hennecke immediately dismounted most of his crew, while the on-board mechanic worked frantically on the brakes and one of the men attended to the wounded driver.

Tank *Mephisto*, under Theunissen, attacked on schedule, first reducing a large trench works south of the village and causing the surrender of 45 survivors. Then Theunissen turned his attention to the fortified railroad station south of the village. Just at that time, one of his engines broke down because of a faulty intake valve. Those Daimler engines used sleeve values that were prone to stick if overheated. While Theunissen put his crew in a defensive perimeter, his mechanic got the valve unstuck and then, back in action, his gunners began to shell and machine gun the railroad station, causing many British casualties and taking the surrender of about 175 troops.

Then joining another tank, *Mephisto* began to advance on a fortified farm south of Villers-Bretonneux, but it began to have more mechanical problems. This time it was the jets in the primitive carburetor. In the garden of the farm, with an infantry firefight swirling around them, Theunissen's machine gunners dismounted and fought as infantry while the driver and mechanic worked feverishly on the engine. After a short time, which seemed like hours, the engines were again running smoothly. Theunissen and the crew then reboarded the vehicle, advanced for a few minutes, and then the tank tipped down into a shell crater and became hopelessly trapped.

Theunissen couldn't remove his weapons due to heavy pressure from the British, so he rigged *Mephisto* for demolition and retreated with his crew. The explosion didn't seriously damage the tank, though, and several days later, the advancing Australian 13th Division recovered the tank with the help of a British tank crew and shipped it off as a battle trophy. *Mephisto* now sits in front of the Queensland Military Museum, the only surviving original A7V in the world.

Things were now moving at a rapid pace. The last two tanks of the second tank group, commanded by Bartens and Lappe, were attacking the British reserve trenches south of the fortified farm, where the second Devons, under Colonel Anderson Morslead, were holding out. This area was still fogged in. Morslead first heard the rumbling of tracks and then behind a hail of machine gun fire and 57mm canister fire, the ominous shape of an A7V with the name *Herkules* painted on its bow came through the fog and easily spanned the trench. Morslead later said the tracks were only feet from his face as the sandbagged walls came down.

As the tank cleared the trench, he drew his Webley .455 revolver and shot at the only vulnerable point on the tank, the water jackets of the machine guns. Then there was a shout and a huge German with a rifle and bayonet plunged into the trench. Somebody shot him, and then several more Germans jumped into the trench just as an immense ball of flame licked at the parapet. The German Storm Troopers had also brought along a flame thrower. Morslead led his men in a mad dash down the railroad tracks that cut through his position.

Eventually a counterattack was organized, but it only ran straight into the A7Vs and was broken up. This time Morslead was wounded and when his group retreated, it ran into just what was needed. Three British tanks commanded by

Captain J. C. Brown. The tanks were two females and one male, whose commander. Lieutenant Frank Mitchell was the only tanker who knew the area, the other two TCs being green men, right out of the tank school at Bovington.

Running up to the male tank, one of Morslead's men said, "Look out, there's Jerry tanks out there." Brown immediately jumped from the male tank and ran to warn the two females of their danger. This left Mitchell to go hunting his opponent, as he was the only tank in the British force with any chance at all of stopping the Germans. At that point in time, he was outnumbered thirteen guns to two, as all A7Vs were still in the area.

Even as the captain passed his warning, the nearest A7V, commanded by Wilhelm Biltz, and named *Nixe*, opened fire at a range of 400 yards and put a shell into one of the females. The Mk-IV wasn't immobilized and both females turned from the fight and tried to get out of Biltz's line of fire. The time was just 1000 hours. Historians have wondered why Biltz put his shots into the female tanks, which couldn't harm him, but the answer is fairly simple. The females were armed with Lewis-type machine guns that have a cooling jacket the same diameter as a six-pounder's barrel. From 400 yards he could not have seen the difference.

Mitchell, now coming on as fast as his Mk-IV could waddle, was handicapped by his smaller crew because his gearsmen, who had to help steer the tank, were also his six-pounder loaders. Both were in the hospital from crippling gas burns. Both of his gunners had puffed-up faces from the morning's mustard gassing and one had to aim with his left eye, because his right was swollen closed. When Captain Brown jumped out of Mitchell's tank a squarish gray lump came into range, it was Biltz's tank *Nixe* coming to do battle. Later Mitchell wrote,

I informed the crew and a great thrill ran through us all. Opening a loophole, I looked out. There, some 300 yards away, a round, squat looking monster was advancing. Behind it came waves of infantry, and farther away, to the left and right crawled two more of these armed tortoises. So we had met our rivals at last. For the first time in history, tank was encountering tank.

Mitchell was taking no chances with that 57mm gun, and kept the tank moving. His lefthand gunner, Carter, tried for *Nixe* with his 6-pounder, but the rocking of the tank threw him off and he missed. All the while, *Nixe* was just sitting there, shooting holes in the hapless female tanks with his 57mm gun. Neither tank was completely knocked out, but each drove off with wounded crews and great holes blasted in them. Mitchell ordered a sharp turn to cover them and "suddenly there was a sound like a storm of hail beating against our right wall and the tank became alive with splinters. Something rattled against the steel helmet of the driver sitting next to me and my face was stung with minute fragments of steel."

Biltz (or someone) was using belt after belt of German armor-piercing machine gun ammunition, and the British crew was driven to the floor with multiple splinter wounds. The bullets weren't penetrating but were knocking sharp-edged chips off the steel walls. Mitchell later wrote;

The crew flung themselves flat on the floor. The driver ducked his head and drove straight on.

Nearing the village of Cachy, I noticed to my astonishment that the two females were limping away to the rear. . . . Now the battle was left to us, with our infantry in their trenches tensely watching the duel like spectators in a theatre. As we turned and twisted to dodge the enemy's shells, I looked down to find that we were going straight into a trench full of British soldiers who were yelling at the tops of their voices to get our attention. A quick signal to the gearsman seated at the rear of the tank, and we turned swiftly, (180°), avoiding catastrophe by a second.

Then came our first casualty. Another raking broadside from the German tank and the rear Lewis gunner was wounded in both legs by an armor-piercing bullet. . . . We had no time to put on more than a temporary dressing, and he lay on the floor, bleeding and groaning while the six-pounder boomed over his head and shell casings clattered all around him.

Finally, traveling to the north toward Villers-Bretonneux, Mitchell's big Mk-IV got out of range of the machine gun fire and turned to engage with his righthand sponson gun. Again the rocking and jolting of the tank made accurate shooting impossible and the righthand gunner, Sergeant J. R. MacKenzie missed also. Both gunners were hampered by not only having to load their own weapons, but by having to aid with the gear shifting that made turning possible. It was time to take a chance. They all had a sense of history and weren't going to let this moment slip by.

Mitchell ordered another sharp 180-degree turn to throw the German gunner off, and then a complete stop, giving Carter another chance. One was all he needed. Carefully he lined up his sights on the blocky gray hull and pulled the six-pounder's trigger. The time was exactly 1020 hours. Two armored fighting machines sat on opposite sides of a shallow valley, north of a village named Cachy, and sighted on each other. Carter shot first, and accurately. With his eye to the telescope sight, and his puffed, blistered, face against the gun breech, he set the crosshairs on the center front of the German hull and fired. McKenzie, who'd come over from his gun, reloaded for Carter.

WHAM, a cannon shell went completely through Biltz's armor, giving off a white spark as it struck. The second shell also struck true, and a third hit *Nixe's* reserve oil tank. The artillery gunner was killed, two more men were dying, and there were serious injuries in the rest of the crew. By some miracle Biltz managed to get his crippled tank, with a wounded crew, back to the safety of the nearest German position. The British were now in hot pursuit, and after his crew were evacuated, the tank had to be rigged for demolition. The German report of this action, in Biltz's words:

Around noon, we were steering toward Cachy, navigating by the steeple on the church when we were surprised by seeing several British tanks of the usual type coming out of the south point of the Aquenne Woods in a convoy formation. The lead tank fired on us with his cannon (a Lewis gun), I then turned my tank directly into the enemy tanks, but I wasn't hurrying. I could see level going and trenches and shot slowly, not missing. Then we took a direct hit and were on the short stick. Immediately after that hit, we took one in the right entrance hatch. Now as a result of one man's hesitation, we had two fatalities and two lightly wounded men.

This action had not quite broken the German attack; there were still two more A7Vs in the area, and the Storm Troopers were coming on with Bergmann submachine guns and flamethrowers. Flame and grenades could knock his tank out, so Mitchells again did the only thing possible, he attacked. Ordering his gunners to switch to newly issued case shot, he began to mow the men of the elite unit down. He literally cut them to pieces with what were, in effect, giant man-killing shotguns. (Case shot for that gun was iron balls strung together on steel wire; when fired from a rifled gun, they would have broken into sections and gone through the air like giant propellors.) These A7Vs were from Group Three, and at that time there were still three German tanks left on the field, *Siegfried, Nixe,* and *Schnuck.*

German Group Three, under Stein, had reached its line of departure in the Bois d'Hangard (almost due south of Villers-Bretonneux) at 0640 and proceeded to clean up several hundred yards of British trenchworks. The tanks were *Elfriede, Nixe, Siegfried,* and *Schnuck.* At 0945, however, Stein's tank, *Elfriede,* got a little too close to a sand pit owned by the brickworks, and the ground began to give under its right track. The driver tried frantically to avoid the sand trap, but slowly, almost majestically, *Elfriede* went over on its side, exposing its unarmored belly. With no hope of extracting the hull from the sand pit, Stein and his crew set demolition charges, took their machine guns, and joined the infantry for the rest of the day. Stein was later killed in action.

At about 1000 hours, a scouting airplane dropped a message to the "Savage Rabbit" HQ. Orders were sent to Captain T. R. Price. The crews had had breakfast and were warming their engines when the message streamer dropped. The report stated that an estimated two enemy battalions were forming up for an attack about one thousand yards east of Cachy. By 1030 the tanks were moving. While his tanks were running flat out for the town, Captain Price mounted a horse he'd pilfered and rode for the battle. Unfortunately, the pilot hadn't seen the German tanks and Price was about to face enemy heavy guns in female tanks with no supporting infantry.

Arriving at a point south of Cachy, Price was given a quick battle report from the local commander, a Captain Sheppard, who was from Price's old regiment, the Northamptons. The two captains were more or less on their own: Sheppard was commanding a pick-up group of infantry known as "Sheppard's Force"; and Price's unit known as "X Company" was made up of orphans from other units decimated by breakdowns and battle damage. Many times in military history, such a pick-up force has done more damage than a formal unit.

Price quickly ascertained that the land was excellent for tanks and that the first German attack had petered out. The two officers suspected that there would be another attack wave and were determined to disrupt that assault. Their basic plan of battle was to attack with the Whippets and catch the Germans before they got their assault lines shaken out. What they aimed to do was catch the next wave of infantry massed in their assembly point and destroy them. The plan the two hatched out between them was for the infantry to run alongside the attacking Whippets to protect them from grenadiers while the British tanks attacked the Germans in their assembly area. With the rough details worked out, Price remounted his horse and galloped back to where the Whippets should be.

Meeting his oncoming tanks, he stopped to brief his two section leaders, lieutenants Hore and Ellsbury. They were to form on line, 50 yards between tanks, then cross the Cachy switch trench and charge at full speed southwards toward the Bois d' Hangard where the next attack wave was suspected to be getting ready. Then, provided the enemy was actually in the target area, they were to reverse direction, sweep back, and finish the job.

Unfortunately, just at this time, the general officer commanding the battle, Brigadier G. W. Grogan, got wind of the plan and tried to stop the unauthorized and impromptu attack. The result was that the infantry were called off just as Price was beginning his charge.

Price's calculations were absolutely correct, and his charging tanks caught the Germans at lunch, some with their rifles stacked as they took their midday meal of hard bread and sausage. They were two battalions of the German 77th Reserve Division, some one thousand strong. The seven Whippets carried 28 machine guns and the surprised German infantrymen were cut down in droves and then run over by the clanking monsters. Passing the assembly area, the Whippets wheeled and cut back through, totally destroying that German unit as a military force. Over 400 casualties were later counted in those battalions. Several of the tanks, however, inadvertently skylined themselves. . . . Right in front of the guns of *Siegfried,* and Lieutenant Friedric Bitter. The time was roughly an hour after the battle between Mitchell and Biltz, and Mitchell had watched the sweep of the Whippets from his hilltop, not knowing exactly what was going on.

For some time, *Siegfried,* the fourth tank of Group Three, had been crushing machine gun nests, clearing infantry out of trenches, and Bitter had used his cannon to beat up the hamlet of Cachy. About noon, though, he spotted German infantry running toward him in full retreat. He'd been tasked to support the 77th Division, which was supposed to be taking the little village of Cachy, but there had obviously been problems. Lieutenant Bitter reports:

> I drove flat out for Cachy, understanding the situation and to back up the infantry. I was to be their rock in the stream. The infantry rallied but was hesitant and abruptly, the squadron of seven enemy tanks burst out again, from the direction of Cachy. The first tanks drove northward on our right flank. The others minutes later, developed a frontal attack, and so with great speed I

turned my tank half right to face the fire of the first tank. The one closest to the infantry. One shot, one direct hit on his right Caterpillar track. They [the Whippets] continued to fire the machine guns; we shot twice more, two hits making white flashes, high up on their casemates.

We were now nervous as the enemy tanks were beginning to circle us toward the infantry. We shot once more and hit high up on an enemy tank, there was flame but then our cannon failed due to the breaking of a replacement firing pin. Now we were two German tanks firing against four British tanks, and only four of my six machine guns would work as two of them required ordnance mechanical work. Then the enemy broke and left.

At this point, Price and his four remaining tanks decided to leave the field. Here, the accounts begin to vary. Price's account of battle damage doesn't quite match up with German or even other British accounts, as he says he brought five tanks back, while the Germans claim to have killed three out of seven. Bitter and *Siegfreid* had become tank killers. There are, however a few battlefield mysteries.

That the two female Mk-IVs were shot up everybody agrees, but sometime later in the morning than stated, Mitchell's tank took a hit from an "unknown artillery piece," and was crippled. The point of curiosity is that the smallest German artillery piece was the 77mm gun, and that would have completely destroyed the Mk-IV. There is also one A7V unaccounted for. . . . Did the Germans get in one more shot? In this last report, Lieutenant Müeller and *Schnuck* are unaccounted for, but they were in the area with a fully active A7V.

Later on that forenoon, lieutenants Müeller and Biltz again attacked Cachy, but their infantry was by now exhausted and couldn't follow the tanks. As a result, *Schnuck* and *Nixe* returned to their rendezvous point minus their infantry, but after a battle well fought. North of Cachy, through the Bois d'Aquenne, another of the First Battalion's sections of Mk-IVs—led by a Lieutenant Holton—came out of the woods in support of the Australian infantry. They were observed by the German tankers of Section Two but apparently no shots were exchanged. North of the woods, another tank detachment, led by a Captain Groves, rolled into battle along the railroad track leading into the eastern edge of Villers-Bretonneux. Again, the tanks were seen in the distance by the Germans, but they were too far off for an engagement.

By this time the "Savage Rabbits," with three Mk-IVs shot to mobile scrap and three Whippets destroyed as well, resembled *hasenpfeffer* (rabbit stew) more than a tank force. The Germans had lost *Elfriede* and *Mephisto;* later on *Nixe* had to be towed off but was unsalvable and had to be used for spare parts. At this point in time, both groups of tankers declared victory and left the field of battle.

For the completeness of this chapter, the author would like to thank LTC Rolf Meyer, German Army Liaison Officer to Fort Knox, KY, who contributed important German-based information that has never been translated until now. Most important, I would like to thank LTC Günther Guderian, German Army Liaison Officer to Fort Bragg, NC, who approved this version of the battle and who sent it to his father Heinz Günter Guderian, a German historian, who gave of his time to check the manuscript for overall accuracy. My good friend, Major William Schneck, U.S. Army Engineers, currently our mining and breaching authority, also gave of his time and enthusiasm, and found (apparently) every English language report of the battle. Without the efforts of these men, this account would not have been possible.

REFERENCE SOURCES

Tanks and Trenches, Edited by David Fletcher, Alan Sutton, Ltd.
Tank vs. Tank, Kenneth Macksey, Salem House.
Sturmpanzerwagon (German Army publication) loaned by LTC Meyer, German Liaison Officer, Ft. Knox, trans. by Ralph Zumbro.

Armored Duel, Ronald McGlothlen, *Military History* magazine, December, 1989.

General Pershing's Report, Encyclopedia Americana, 1940.

Tanks and Weapons of World War I, Beekman House.

German Tanks in World War I, Schneider & Strasheim, Schiffer Publishing.

A7V Sturmpanzerwagon, John Foley, Great Booban.

The German A7V and Captured British Tanks of World War I, Maxwell Hundley and Rainer Strasheim, Haynes/Foulis.

Iron Fist, Bryan Perrett, Arms and Armor Press.

"German Tanks," R. Kruger, *Ordnance* magazine, 1924.

The Fighting Tanks, since 1916, Jones, Rarey & Icks, U.S. Government.

Achtung-Panzer!, Major General Heinz Guderian, Arms and Armor Press.

CHAPTER 15

The French Tankers, Spring 1918

THE RENAULT'S BAPTISM OF FIRE

GENERAL ERICH LUDENDORFF'S SPRING 1918 OFFENSIVE HAS been called several things, the *Kaiserschlact* (Emperor's Battle), for one. Another was the "Peace Offensive," which in Ludendorff's plan really applies only to his fifth and final try in July. This was his last attempt to obtain a negotiated peace with honor, and he has been quoted as having said that Germany was beaten not by General Ferdinand Foch, but by "General tank." He was also beaten by the fact that the Allies were beginning to use more mechanized transport than Germany could employ at that time.

Specifically, France had a better rail transport system and a more developed road system. Probably, due to the fact that France was an old nation, consolidated for hundreds of years, whereas Germany and, more lately, Italy, were only recently assembled out of dozens of competing princedoms. It was not until the Treaty of Frankfurt on 10 May 1871 that Count Otto von Bismarck was able to say, "Germany is now complete." . . . He also is quoted as saying, "If there is ever another war in Europe, it will probably be over some stupid eruption in the Balkans."

The French rail system made possible the quick movement of supplies and fresh American troops into battle. It also had made possible the quick reinforcement of the Cambrai battle line after the British lost momentum. While the English dithered, the Germans were using that part of the French rail system, which they controlled, to move in enough troops to retake, for a while, lost ground. Germany, however, was suffering from not only a lack of material but from a lack of seasoned officers and noncommissioned officers. Verdun had cost the German army 300,000 men, a large proportion of the professional leadership of the army. The Peace Offensive took the remainder of the heart of the German army. A further 300,000 irreplaceable men—NCOs and officers—were lost, including the last of the Stosstrups from Captain Rohr's school.

The purpose of Sturm Battalion Rohr had been to test new methods and equipment under combat conditions, but there was only the one unit. While the Storm Troop tactics and the use of the A7V tanks proved that Germany had finally found a way to free its soldiers from "the grip of Hiram Maxim"—they were too few and too late. There were also several hundred thousand fresh American troops in Europe, and tanks were beginning to show up in the thousands, while Germany had just 45 operational armored combat vehicles, most of them captured. The French got both the Schneider and the St. Chamond tank into battle, but they were less effective than the British Mk-I, let alone a Whippet or an Mk-IV. At the same time, Renault was cranking out literally hundreds of the little six-tonners, which the Germans had yet to meet. At the end of May 1918, it happened.

While the large battles of history, such as Cambrai and Soissons, are studied to death by conventional historians and budding general officers, it is in the little actions where lieutenants and captains learn their trade. While the large French tank action at Soissons on 18 July is in most history books, its predecessor at Vertefeuille Farm is almost forgotten, and this was where the little Renault got its combat initiation on 31 May, deep in a French woods and out of the limelight. It is also from this woods that the main French counteroffensive was launched later in the year. General

Guderian in *Achtung-Panzer!* also has something to say about these actions and the actions of the German General Staff at the time. . . . He should know, as he was on the staff in those days and read the disaster messages as they came in.

At Chaudun, south of Soissons, a battalion of 30 Renaults and a division of Moroccan colonial troops temporarily halted the Germans, but there were too few of them to go back on the offensive. The momentary check did, however, give the American Second and Third Divisions time to get into place in Belleau Wood and that hard-fought battle has gone into history as well. It is the little wars that teach the young commanders, though, and now we're going to take a look at a classic small unit action, possibly the first of its kind.

North of Belleau Wood is a little town named Villers-Cotterêts, which is only 45 miles northeast of Paris, and the Germans were moving straight in on it. The French infantry were spread out thin in the area. Only one full regiment was nearby when the Germans were detected, and that one quite tired. But there were two battalions, 35 tanks each, of shiny new Renaults available, along with the steam-driven ten-ton trucks that were necessary to move them.

This is something else absent from most histories, the fact that the early tanks couldn't make more than twenty-odd miles on a load of fuel and that their tracks wore out very quickly, which is why they required the tank transporter— these also carried extra fuel, ammunition, crews, and so on. A company of Renaults in an area also meant the existence of a small fleet of trucks and other supporting needs, including a shop, a mess hall, and an HQ. Even pigeon lofts were carried along in the days before radio. The problem with pigeons, of course, is that they have to be in an area for almost a week before they will home reliably to the loft truck where the rest of the flock is kept.

One of the two battalions of the French 501st Tank Regiment was placed at the disposal of the 8th Infantry Regiment, and the combination was told to hold those woods. The wooded area, known as the Forêt du Retz, was between Villers-Cotterêts to the southwest and Soissons to the northeast. There was a small farm known as the Le Translon Farm directly in front of the forest and a larger one called Vertefeuille Farm on the southeast corner of the forest. When the Germans began filtering into the forest, one company of tanks was at Furneaux crossroads, a charcoal burner's home, deep in the western half of the area. They had already detrucked and were available. Their infantry had never been trained to work with them; they were that new. The French commander, however, seems to have been a canny individual, for he used them just right. Probably, he'd been studying the British and earlier French experiences.

By 1730 hours on 3 June, the Germans had taken Vertefeuille farm, which was a considerable compound, set up a HQ, and were digging in. German infantry patrols were going out into the forest; the Germans seemed to have only trench mortars and machine guns for support. . . . No heavy artillery or tanks just yet. *It should be possible*, the French commander must have thought, *to bounce them back out before they get their position hardened.* He put two platoons of Renaults from the tank battalion's Number One Company and two platoons from Number Four Company at the disposal of the infantry regimental commander. . . . And the Germans didn't know that tanks were anyplace near them. One would have liked to have seen the reaction of the first German patrol that walked into those woods.

The French commander's plan seems to have been to work his regiment forward, more or less on line, through the woods. Two tank platoons were to work forward from Furneaux crossing headed due east. Halfway through the woods, one platoon was to peel off with its infantry company and strike south along a diagonal road, while the first was to continue straight toward the captured farm. At the same time, two more platoons of Renaults were to engage the Germans in the woods and attempt to drive them out into the open. At 1800 hours, they moved out.

The normal mix of Renaults in a five-tank platoon is two with 37mm cannons and three with machine guns. At 1830, the Third Platoon, Number One Company, 501st Tank Battalion came growling out of the woods, following a narrow road named Laie du Fond d'Argent. Dropping back into an echelon formation, they stopped and the gun tanks began to shell the farm just a few hundred yards south of them, while the machine gun tanks took on unarmored machine gun nests along the road. Then the two righthand tanks curved down behind the farm to join with their own First Platoon, which had followed a different lane, the Lai du Jardin, and come out just west of the farm.

After rousting out the few Germans in the area, the five tanks crossed the main road from Soissons to Villers-Cotterêts in a short column, on signal they then faced left into an assault line and tore into the Germans, each tank followed by two squads of French infantry. Another heavy blast of machine gun fire came from the farm and with aid from the three tanks still in the northern tree line, this was terminated by 37mm fire from one of the gun tanks and, at that point, the Germans began to leave—Very hastily. They had no idea that there were iron dragons in those woods. French infantry retook the farm while the tanks patrolled some five hundred yards east and then returned, vastly satisfied with themselves.

The entire action, which would have taken an infantry battalion most of a day and cost hundreds of casualties, had taken the tanks just half an hour, with two French casualties, both tank drivers who had facial wounds. The vision slots in those early tanks were open to the air and it was required that the driver put his head against a spring-loaded rubber pad just over the slot, in order to have a decent field of vision. Occasionally some splinters got through and the driver could easily get wounded, blinded, or killed. . . . Some drivers even got bayonetted or stabbed by a cavalryman's sword.

By 1930, the tanks were back at Furneaux crossroad, probably drinking cheap wine and bragging, as well they should. They had just pulled off a double envelopment with the proper tank/infantry combination for the first time in history. There had been just one company of infantry with four platoons of Renaults, exactly enough to escort the tanks and act as their eyes and ears and to keep grenadiers from getting close enough to shoot into their vision slits or wedge grenades into their tracks. The Renault FT-17 had been blooded and was beginning its long career. This was 1918, and they would be still fighting in 1940.

The Germans were running out of steam, but they tried to keep up the pressure. On 2 June, elements of the 28th Reserve Division again tried to capture Villers-Cotterêts, were stopped by a platoon of tanks, and had to use artillery to get clear, suffering heavy casualties. The Germans reinforced and the next day tried it again, but even more tanks came out of those woods, and the Renaults were considerably more reliable and harder to hit than the larger fighting machines. Once engaged, they could usually stay the day.

The expected morning mist and covering fighter flights helped the Germans for a while and then, when the mist burned off, the tanks began their drumroll of death. Then French fighter planes arrived and, as usual, the opposing airforces canceled each other out. The 28th Division was in the center, flanked by the 111th and 110th Reserve Regiments, and from all accounts they were still facing that lone battalion of the 501st Tank Regiment. Five tanks attacked the 111th, penetrated two of its lines . . . and then suddenly two tanks were immobilized by minethrowers, but continued to fire as the other three tanks turned north and tore into another battalion.

Now two other German infantry battalions broke off from their missions and attacked the tanks. Then the First and Third Battalions, 109th Jager Reserve Regiment, diverted and attacked the tanks. Eventually, there were five full German battalions attacking just ten Frenchmen in five tanks, two of which were already crippled. Eventually, the firepower of five infantry battalions overpowered the tanks and forced them to surrender. . . . Or did they just run out of ammo? At that, those 10 men had cost the Germans 19 officers and 514 men killed, wounded, or just plain missing. On the same day, another unit, the Augusta Regiment, lost 12 officers and almost six hundred men. Not bad for a bunch of green troops fresh out of tank school and untried machines that had never seen combat. . . . . For the emphasis that Guderian places on this incident, it may have impressed him more than the larger battles.

There was a lot of this sparring for the next few weeks

as the French learned the hard way that it wouldn't always be so easy. At Chaudun on 31 May, six platoons of Renaults and several battalions of the Moroccan division attacked a known German division across open ground with no artillery prepping, no reconnaissance, and no air support. They got too cocky! The German machine guns kept the Moroccans pinned down, and Minenwerfer and armor-piercing bullets drove the tanks back. Time after time the action was repeated, until the tankers gave up in exhaustion. The Germans were tiring, however, and the French kept pouring platoon after platoon out of that forest. . . . What the Germans saw as part of an overall assault, the French saw as a thrust aimed directly at Paris.

The little Renaults were coming off the assembly lines at ever-increasing speed and first battalions, then regiments, and finally brigades of armor were being formed and the lessons of battle taught. Infantry were learning their role in the combined arms team, and the commanders were learning to use the new radio tanks—Renaults with command boxes instead of turrets coordinated HQ with their artillery. Orders would come down by radio, and be communicated to the line tanks by flag signal.

Most important, they were now beyond most of the entrenchments of the previous years, and the Allies could move their infantry around with trucks, of which the Germans were desperately short. Guderian's book specifically mentions their lack of motorized transport and the Allied superiority in mobility. This, obviously, made a deep impression on the future inventor of the Panzer Force.

At that time, the French, British, Americans, and Germans were still teaching each other valuable lessons—lessons only the Germans would remember. At 0535, 18 July 1918, the wild battle of Soissons opened with a French preparatory barrage on a line between Soissons and Château-Thierry. Almost five hundred tanks came swarming out of, among other places, Villers-Cotterêts. At first, all the German positions were pushed back, many of their infantry became casualties or prisoners, and almost all their guns were captured. By 0840, however, the French seemed to have run out of steam and were no longer in pursuit. What had happened? German units that had been on the verge of annihilation by tanks suddenly found themselves depressurized and given the time to pull clear. Why did the French artillery, which had been pounding them with rolling, timed advancing barrages simply cease firing? The French had obviously done something wrong, but it took some time for the Germans to figure out what had happened.

First, the French had split up their tank force and attached it to the infantry, some of which was sent over ground unsuitable for tanks. For instance, there had been 132 tanks available for the assault on the 10th Bavarian Jäger (Hunter) Division, which was to be hit by two French divisions, the 2nd and 47th, with the 63rd in reserve. The 63rd already had its 30 tanks, leaving only 102 for the assault. Then, when the assault line reached the limit of its artillery coverage, two things were discovered. First, that *all* the artillery had been assigned to that initial barrage; there was none limbered up ready to leapfrog forward. Second, the artillery was still mostly horsedrawn and could not keep up with an advancing assault, especially over roads already clogged with trucks. . . . There was a lot more to this mechanized, mobile war than anyone had thought about.

For instance, no one had thought to keep back a mobile reserve with tanks and truck-mounted infantry, in order to throw a hook around the German rear while they were bringing reserves forward and digging in. Also, since this was going to be a grand battle, the senior "experts" took over—all the tank commanders were brought back to HQ to be used as advisors and generally kept out from underfoot. The horsed cavalry, doodling about with their outdated lances, did no more good here than at Cambrai, although they were armed with Lebel carbines, and could have been sent off cross-country and used as dragoons. . . . Each could also have been given a saddle bag full of hand grenades. There were also some *very* interesting episodes in which the very maneuverable horse-drawn *light* artillery got into place to do quite a lot of damage, but that lesson also was lost, for the time being.

Also, no one on the Allied side had figured out that trucks or no trucks, German response speed is extremely quick—

even with one set of guns captured, they got more into place and began to take potshots at the Renaults over open sights. Timed air attacks could have prevented that, but the idea never seems to have occurred to anyone. There was, of course, one officer watching and taking notes, Captain Heinz Guderian.

Guderian is also quite bitter that two years after tanks were first used and eight months after Cambrai, the German soldier still had no adequate antitank defense at the squad or platoon level. His comment is worth quoting:

> At Soissons on 18 July, the infantry never came to terms with the armored attack at all, and it was only in the afternoon that the artillery began to hit back at the tanks from new and more intelligently chosen sites. This episode (and it would not be the last) should have shattered the dream world of the people who had dismissed the surprise attack by tanks as a "one off" weapon.

Things were to get worse for the General Staff, much worse. So far they had twice been utterly surprised by hordes of loud, smelly, clanking, noisy machines. Could it happen again?

On 8 August, west of the city of Amiens, the firestorm hit yet again. To the usual fog of battle were added the smoke and mirrors of a tank force that had learned quite well the use of deceit, camouflage, and misdirection. The Allies used elaborate trickery, such as convoys of empty trucks going in the wrong direction, the movement of tanks at night, and strict control over communications. They also had the newest models of tank, the Whippet and the Mk-V, which was much more reliable and maneuverable than the older Marks. It was the first heavy tank that could be handled by only one driver and some had radio communication with HQ. There was also one indication of original thinking—for the first time, tanks, in this case Whippets, were assigned to the cavalry.

At 0500 hours, the artillery began a creeping barrage under which 500 tanks rolled and over which 500 fighters and bombers swept. The Canadians and French tore a 32-

kilometer-wide hole in the German lines and, horror of horrors, achieved complete surprise. For the third time in a year, just like Cambrai and Soissons, the Germans had not prepared for a tank assault. The only thing that could have saved them, direct-fire artillery, was sited far back in the rear, ready for a counterbattery of defensive fire, not anti-tank duties.

First the all-important infantry and the machine gun posts were destroyed, then the phonelines were torn up by gunfire and the churning treads. All it takes is a pivot steer on top of the switchboard truck to destroy land communication lines. Human messengers simply never came back. Smoke and HE shells were falling impossibly close to the advancing Allies because the armored monsters were shielding the infantry with their hulls.

Around 0800, the creeping barrage ceased as the Allies reached their preplanned phase line and stopped—Right under the muzzles of the German artillery, which had figured out what was happening and were rapidly getting set up for direct fire. Because of this hesitation, several of the German gun batteries were able not only to hold off the assault for a while, but to deliver flanking fire into the Australians, who, like the Canadians, were moving steadily.

The colonials, it seems had somewhat more verve and vigor than the Brits or the French, and they kept on going into the fog and smoke to shoot up and capture the German's gun batteries. One after another, the German positions fell silent, even the batteries around Villers-Bretonneux and Marcelcave were captured, in this last of the seesaw battles. From now on the tanks would move forward like an implacable wave—when they were allowed to.

There is a place on the old Roman road, east of Villers-Bretonneux, where the land goes through a cut, called the Roman Gorge, and a German force with a few artillery pieces attempted to set up a defense there. To quote General Guderian:

It was literally smashed to pieces. . . . The armored cars of the 17th Tank Battalion appeared on the Roman road. They were moving so fast that the German gunners were unable to take a bead on them, and they played havoc among the columns of German vehicles seeking to escape. The British aircraft dropped smoke bombs on the Roman gorge which blinded the defenders further east and helped the British armour to approach unobserved. The enemy took Harbonnières and reached their third objective at noon.

Ten days later, the Imperial Council decided to open peace negotiations at a suitable opportunity. As General Erich Ludendorff has said, "It was a black day for the German army."

CHAPTER 16

The Rif Wars

NORTH AFRICA, 1922–1927

As HAS BEEN MENTIONED IN THE CHAPTERS ON ARMORED CARS, the new mechanized force was used between the wars for colonial policing. Oddly enough, the preferred tank was the little French FT-17, and Renault sold several thousand of them during the interwar period. The Spanish used them in Morocco during the Rif Rebellion, the French themselves used them in Morocco and Syria. A license-built copy, the M-1917, was the first American light tank, and a Major Serano Brett took a detachment of them to Panama in 1923. The Marines also took a company of tanks to Shanghai in 1927.

In Abyssinia, the Italians, who were then having dreams of empire, used their CV-33 "Tankette" against the Ethiopian tribesmen of Haile Selassie. This eventually provoked an armored-car expedition from South Africa and an expeditionary force from Great Britain. As the interwar period advanced, the colonial wars began to have an influence on the Great Powers as the experience of long-range armored actions accumulated and the knowledge was applied to newer models of tanks. The Spanish civil war, for instance, was a proving ground for the armored vehicles of Germany,

Russia, and Italy. Like vivisectionists turned loose in a slaughterhouse, the squabbling nations of Europe tried out their new toys on a helpless population—while America dozed away in isolationist bliss.

The basic reasons for the popularity of the FT-17 and its derivatives were cost, simplicity, and weight. The little Renault weighed only 6.5 tons and, while it was short-ranged itself, it could be loaded on a commercial ten-ton truck and driven any place the truck itself could go. The truck and the tank were an operational pair: when the desert roads became impassable for the truck, the tank would unload and tow the truck through the bad going. If rail transport was available, two tanks could be loaded on a standard flatcar. This created the intriguing possibility of an instant armored train that could defend itself from raiders.

The FT series needed external transport, for with its internal tankage, it could only travel 20 miles (34 for the American version). It was armed with either a machine gun or a low velocity 37mm cannon. The turret was muscle powered, being swung by the gunner's shoulders and clamped in place for shooting. Once the turret clamp had been engaged, the gunner again used muscle power to swing the gun in its ball joint to a target. Against horse- and camel-mounted tribesmen, they were fairly effective. Against modern tanks, they were suicide.

The colonial wars, however, formed one of the laboratories from which the tactics of World War II sprang. While theorists like Charles de Gaulle, J. F. C. Fuller, Basil Lidell-Hart (later Sir Basil), and Heinz Guderian theorized and practiced, the colonial wars and civil wars were the proving ground. The great maneuvers on Salisbury Plain and in the Southern United States owed much to one of Fuller's books. The First of the League wars was a study of the Rif and Ethiopian wars and should have taught several lessons, but it was not well received at the time.

All over the world, the 1920s and 1930s were a time of adventure and experimentation. The race between armor protection, firepower, and horsepower was on, and some weird and wonderful designs were being transferred from the minds of inventors like Walter Christie to the shop floors ... with varying degrees of success. As the developing power of engines went up, so did the weight of armor that they would push. The British Cruiser tanks, for instance, were powered by modified fighter aircraft engines. While Germany, Britain, and America were building tanks with gasoline engines, the Russians and Japanese were experimenting with diesel engines that gave, at some expense, improved range and that were less prone to go up in flames. One hundred-ton monsters were designed, as well as tanks intended to jump trenches with the aid of rocket engines. Meanwhile out in the real world, the tank was meeting the barbarian warrior. Sometimes they triumphed, sometimes they went down to humiliating defeats.

Morocco, 1922

The first example of the use of colonial armor is in the battle of Ambar in Morocco, 18 March 1922. In order to understand the reasons for the battle, a bit of history is necessary. Basically, the natives of the area were not capable of the concept of civilization. Since before the fall of the Roman Empire and the waves of Islamic conquest, the port cities of North Africa were nests of pirates who captured cargo ships, sold their goods in north Mediterranean ports, and sold their crews and passengers as slaves to other Islamic nations.

For over a thousand years, the nations of Europe had been paying protection monies to these seagoing bandits, until a brash young nation called America put a stop to it with its warships and marines. After America withdrew its forces, the Moroccans and Algerians began to raid again, and this time France, followed by Spain, simply moved in and colonized them by force. . . . Civilization at gunpoint.

The problem was that in order to open up trade routes across the Sahara to the more fertile lands and colonies of Central Africa, one had to deal with the even less-civilized denizens of the desert. Even today, in much of North Africa, it is usually not safe to travel alone (particularly for a woman) without an armed escort. Barbarians have always

existed and probably always will: Mu'ammar Qaddafi being
a case in point.

In 1921, the Spanish Army was pushing into the heart of
the Rif country. The Rif, however, weren't going quietly and
they knew their land, whereas the Spanish were interlopers.
Two brothers, Mohammed and Mhamed ben Abd el-Krim,
had proven to be very effective war leaders, while the Spanish commandant, Manual Fernandez Silvestre, was an arrogant, strutting cavalryman with no experience of guerrilla
warfare.

The Spanish base was at Mellila, near the Moroccan border with French Algeria. The Spanish forces were spreading
out from that port city deep into Rif territory, trying to
bring the tribesmen under control. Unfortunately, the Spanish Army was going through a recruit and train phase and
most of the troops, including the cavalry, were raw, un-
trained conscripts with no battle experience.

Silvestre was in the process of leading 20,000 half-trained
recruits across Rif territory, heading for Alhucemas Bay,
near modern Al Hoceima. His method of advance was to
pick defensible sites for forts and then throw up a breast-
work of local rock and leave a small garrison—usually too
small. Then he would move his steadily shrinking column
on, looking for both another site and a fight with the tribesmen. Like many cavalrymen, he gave no thought to his
flanks, rear, or supply columns.

In late July 1921, the Krim brothers struck one fort after
another with war parties drawn from a host that exceeded
3,000 men. In rapid succession, the recently captured forts
fell, usually to the last man, and Silvestre's conscript army
began to bolt. With no leavening of experienced veterans,
company after company simply turned and ran from the
tribesmen. Finally, at a large fort named Annual, Silvestre
managed to catch up with the Rif main host, and promptly
got himself and his army slaughtered.

The total Spanish casualty list topped 12,000 with about
six hundred more captured in good enough condition to be
kept alive for ransom. This was the worst defeat suffered by
a European colonial army in the twentieth century and,
aside from the casualty list, it had two extremely negative

results. First, of course, was the fact that an army of 20,000 men had been rendered militarily ineffective. Second, the Rif could now afford to give up their ancient flintlock muskets, lances, and swords. They now had all the trappings of a modern army, including artillery. Whether they got their instructions on modern machine guns and artillery from captives, turncoats, or mercenaries is not known, but learn they did.

After the Spanish government came out of shock, they did what they should have done the first time, given the military abilities of the Rif—they sent in the Spanish Foreign Legion *Tercio de Extranjeros*. These excellent troops and the *Regulares* (Moroccan troops with Spanish officers) quick marched from western Morocco and began fighting their way through the Rif. The problem was now much larger than before Silvestre's July debacle. First, not only because of the captured weaponry, but because many wavering tribes had flocked to the cause of the Rif. Twelve thousand casualties, remember, means 12,000 captured weapons, more or less.

The Legion was commanded by its revered founder, Lieutenant Colonel José Millan-Astray. His three most promising majors were Francisco Franco Bahamonde, Rodriguez Fontanies, and Alberto Bayo. While the Legion chewed on the rapidly swelling native horde, the military commissioners in Madrid went shopping. Realizing that something would have to be done to balance out the suddenly modernized followers of the brothers Krim, they wanted tanks.

They first looked at the latest version of the British Whippet, but the Brits wanted more money than a financially strapped Spain could afford. The French, however, were in the war-surplus business and in August 1921, the French prime minister gave the go-ahead to sell tanks, airplanes, and artillery to the Spanish government. The tanks, known as *"carros de combate/asalto"* arrived at the Spanish national testing ground in January 1922. There were just a dozen of them, and they were quickly formed into a company and put into intensive training.

Eleven of the 6.5-ton Renaults were armed with 7mm Hotchkiss machine guns and one, the command tank, had its turret replaced with a sheetmetal box containing a radio. The company was also equipped with 12 specially built tank-transport trucks, two fuel tankers, and several auxiliary vehicles, including a repair truck. The TO&E listed a captain, two lieutenants, one sergeant major, eight sergeants, and 40 enlisted men, including truck drivers, cooks, and mechanics. All in all a nicely balanced modern force.

After training and a review by King Alfonso XIII, the new armored force was shipped by rail to the port of Malaga and then by sea to Melilla, arriving on 9 March 1922. By 18 March, just two months after they had first seen their tanks, the crews were in action.

The Beni Said tribe, allies of the Rif and still partly armed with muskets and swords, held the towns of Tugunz and Ambar and the plan was for the Legion infantry, supported by the tanks, to evict them. Traveling by truck, the tank company reached the outpost city of Ichtiuen on the afternoon of 17 March, detrucked and began mounting the weapons (World War I surplus) in their turrets. The guns were stored in hard grease and had to be cleaned with hot water and gasoline and then bolted into the turrets by hand.

This was not going to be an auspicious day. The crews were half-trained, the weapons were not installed and tested, and there had been *NO* practice with the infantry. Also, it was winter in Morocco, which meant rain, and the tanks leaked like sieves. As a result, their ignition systems were unreliable. Mechanical problems notwithstanding, they advanced on the enemy at 0600 on 18 March.

On level ground, even at 4 miles per hour, the tanks soon outdistanced their infantry and when they got in among the tribesmen, the legionnaires were about a thousand yards behind them. The Beni Said were not impressed; they shot muskets at the tanks, jumped on board and stuck daggers through the vision slits, wounding some of the gunners. Then the brand new Hotchkiss guns began to jam. The tribesmen even began to throw large rocks at the tanks. Unable to do any harm, the tanks began to withdraw but now their engines failed and those tanks had to be abandoned. There was no armored recovery vehicle, thus the two Renaults had to be left on the field of battle. Four days later, a group of Rif and Beni Said blew them up with captured dynamite.

This event terminated the mass use of tanks. Although for the next few years, they were used as small units, never larger than a platoon, and they trained with their infantry, learned their weapons and tactics, and became the professional core of the Spanish Armor Corps. Finally, in 1925 the tanks got another chance and in an amphibious landing at Alhucemas Bay in September of that year, they helped protect the open Spanish left flank and took the heights of the three overlooking hills, Malmusi Alto, Malmusi Bajo, and Malmusi Viejo. Although the war would sputter on for two more years, the "Rif Republic" was effectively doomed, especially after they managed to irritate the French.

The Krim brothers simply got too big too fast and decided that not only would they take on the Spanish, they would also kick the French out of North Africa. France and Spain, with the memory of some thousand years of Berber piracy, weren't going to accept that attempt, and in 1925, French tanks began to arrive in French Morocco. Again, they were Renault FT-17s and the French were on the short end of their learning curve.

The French First Moroccan Tank Battalion was created from one company each of the 504th, 511th, and 61st Tank Battalions of the regular French Army. Most of the tankers were veterans of World War I—they just didn't have any desert experience. First Moroccan Battalion Headquarters consisted of only three officers and 14 men with four vehicles. This was because the companies were almost independent and the colonel and his adjutants were basically a communications relay.

The tank companies were comparatively large, consisting of four officers and 106 men. The unit was equipped with 13 tanks and 15 carrying trucks. A line platoon had 3 tanks—a single tank armed with a 37mm gun and 2 with machine guns. There was also a radio tank and a reserve platoon of 3 additional tanks. The company had a mess section, a shop truck, and 11 mechanics. This TO&E pretty well matches the author's experience in the Republic of Vietnam (RVN)

over four decades later. As will be seen, they had enough
maintenance people to keep the tracks turning.

In June 1925, the Battalion debarked at Casablanca and
set up for operations. There is, however, a vast difference
between policing wild hill country and running a modern
war with good roads, a tight supply base, and the conve-
nience of railroads. The French had been studying the Spanish experience and had had some of their own in Syria. What
they had learned is that the large tanks of the time were
too cumbersome to operate in the wilds and that an armored
force has to have *both* cannons and machine guns.

Also the problem of a short range and tank tracks that
wore out very quickly in rough going meant that the trucks
were more necessary than ever. The problem was that the
infantry commanders kept commandeering the vehicles to
move their own sometimes luxurious HQs. The result was
that many times, their own greed for transportation deprived
them of the tanks they needed for combat. Slowly though,
they learned. A tank could be transported by truck along a
barely passable road to a dry stream bed and then use that
bed to climb into the mountains and flush out tribesmen.

By the time France had 150,000 men, two battalions of
tanks, and 20 assorted air squadrons in Morocco, the Rif
were on the run. But they did not go quietly. Nor were they
terrorized by tanks. Before the French figured out that the
infantry was part of the team, the Rifs would simply lie by
a tank track with a few iron bars and wait for a prowling
FT-17. As the almost blind, deaf tank clattered by, they
would rise up and drive the bars into the sprockets, thus
peeling the track off and leaving the tank helpless. Crippled
or stuck tanks were invariably abandoned at night, and the
next morning the crews might find them burned, blownup,
or booby-trapped. Finally the French and Spanish both resorted to a method that had worked against German grenadiers. They protected the vulnerable tracks with wire netting
and then had to put up with trapping rocks and sticks in the
netting. Because the Rif were very good snipers, they had
to keep the tanks together so that three tanks could fight as
a team. When the sniping started, the tanks armed with
machine guns would form up to keep local fanatics down

while the cannon tank bounced the sniper out of his rock hole. The following accounts are adapted from various journals of the times, mainly the *Revue Militaire Française.*

The 504th company was sent into the Quezzan region on account of the threat made by the presence of Abd ell-Krim's regular troops, now combat experienced to a level of competence equal to European troops. It made the trip from Quezzan to the Bab el Moroundj saddle on 5 September 1925. The trucks managed to get the tanks within 12 miles of their objective and then the Renaults detrucked and began their night approach march over rugged terrain, arriving at 0400. Then the crews transferred gasoline from the spare drums carried on their unditching rails and set off for the Issoul Bast legion post. Climbing torturous mountain trails the company arrived at the post at 0745.

Their mission was to provide armored support to the Legion infantry as the latter spread out from the post onto the plain to the east. Then one platoon was detached back to the post to help defend it from the ever-present snipers. The other two platoons after traveling for 18 hours straight, refueled and began to patrol between the infantry and the Rif guerrillas.

During this period the tank platoons protecting the infantry were used as mobile blockhouses. They continually came under sniper fire from the artillery the Rif had captured. The tanks had learned not to stay stationary too long, however, and sustained no losses. Company 504 took part in the attack on Fort de bab Haouceine on 11–12 September. During this action the tanks seemed to be everywhere, fighting and even evacuating dead and wounded legionaires. One tank under the platoon leader even had to pull out of the assault line and go back to collect a machine gun whose crew had been killed while acting as the infantry rear guard.

The link between infantry, cavalry and tanks, and artillery was an experiment—however something was proved here and then lost. Infantry, time after time was outrun by the tanks when traveling (even at only 4 to 5 miles per hour), but the Legion Spahis (light mounted dragoon-horsemen) who could dismount and fight on foot had no problem keeping up. At first they were skittish around the noisy little monsters, but after a few months, the cooperation was good enough to put the Rif out of business. Once the prowling Spahis spotted a group of Rif, a messenger would be sent off to the nearest tank platoon, and the Renaults would come up and back up the cavalry assault.

Company 61 at this time was used to resupply Fort Tiffilassenne; their Commanding officer (C.O.) appears to have been a highly creative officer. He had his mechanics build wooden sledges with steel runners so that the tanks could tow the sledges cross-country with supplies for the Legion post that was surrounded by small parties of Rifs. The only problem was that the chains were continually breaking and had to be repaired with replacement links while under sniper fire.

During this period, the tanks were continually in action, sometimes camping out *with the tanks* in a circle, guns facing outward. The tankers stayed inside, bedding down, cooking rations, pulling maintenance duty, and so on. Only the extensive knowledge and experience of dedicated mechanics and supply people could have accounted for the reliability and availability of the full 13-tank company most of the time. The wear and tear on the running gear of the supply trucks must have been incredible.

On 7 October, Company 61 was sent on reconnaissance to the village of Quizert where a group of the locals had asked to talk to French officials. They were not all friendly though, as the gun tank that was taking the intelligence officer to the village came under fire. The company commander then rolled his whole unit forward and used his 37mm cannons to destroy several houses in the village, which promptly put up a white flag. The rebels came forward, were interviewed by the intelligence officer, and asked their own questions in turn. Satisfied with the officer's answers, they sacrificed a ram in his presence as a sign of submission. For the next few days the company was used as infantry support, mopping up various small bands in the valleys of this region.

The French also figured out a unique method of surveillance that overcame the short endurance of 1920s aircraft. They parked an observation balloon over the top of a suspect area of Rif operations manned by soldiers with binoculars as well as telephone or radio communication.

A balloon 2,000-feet straight up is effectively out of rifle range, and the Rif had neither antiaircraft or antitank weapons. As an example, at a little place named Bou Ganous north of the city of Quezzan, the Rif cut off a blockhouse and blew up its road, intending to kill the platoon that garrisoned the area. They infiltrated ravines, dug trenches, and began to act like a formal army—a miscalculation on the part of guerrillas facing a *real* army. The French hung an observation balloon over Bou Ganous and then sent a team of one tank platoon and a group of automatic rifle teams to back them up. Another full tank company covered the egress/access routes with a tank platoon as mobile reserve and HQ security.

When the Rif realized they were outnumbered and outsmarted they pulled their usual trick of taking access in caves and crannies in the rocks that had sheltered them from invaders for centuries. This time though, the tankers set their fuzes on delay and sat there for a day, bouncing 37mm HE into those caves and listening to the screams. When the tanks quit firing, the caves were an abatoir, all the infantry had to do was mop up. There had been no French casualties.

One of the officers commanding a column of the Spanish forces wrote:

> Armored cars and tanks are greatly suitable for this kind of war. We shall see if time proves me right.
>
> Major Francisco Franco,
> Cdr. 1st Bandero,
> Tiercio de Extranjeros

We will be meeting Major Franco later, as Generalissimo of Spain. One of his compatriots, known to history as Alberto Bayo, was Che Guevara's mentor

REFERENCE SOURCES

"Tank Warfare During the Rif Rebellion," José E Alvarez, *Armor* Magazine, Jan.–Feb., 1997.
The Fighting Tanks since 1917, Jones, Rarey & Icks.

CHAPTER 17

The Chaco War, 1932–1933
PARAGUAY VS. BOLIVIA

IT SEEMS TO BE A HISTORICAL TOSS-UP WHETHER HUMAN GREED or a need for more real estate causes more wars. Paraguay, in the 1860s, not too many years after winning its freedom from Spain, developed delusions of empire. The cause seems to have been one Carlos Antonio López, one of South America's first generalissimos. With good relations with all of his neighbors, López began to build his army into the largest military establishment in South America. His neighbors of course got nervous and started an arms race.

Next, in order to terminate López's interference in Uruguay's affairs, Brazil, which had a common defense treaty with that small nation, invaded to remove López's unwanted presence. From that point things escalated until small Paraguay was fighting an allied army consisting of Brazil, Uruguay, and—eventually—Argentina. This little-known war stems from the greed of just one man, who caused as much damage to his nation as Hitler did to Germany.

By the end of the fighting, Paraguay's population had fallen from half a million, to only 221,000, of which only 28,000 were adult males. The nation was occupied by the victorious armies until 1876, and those troops are considered to be the fathers of most of the present-day family lines of that country. It wasn't until the early 1900s that Paraguay was back in the military business—and they had another real estate problem. Bolivia, it seemed, wanted a piece of their northern jungles, swamps, plains, and rivers . . . mostly the rivers. Their plan was to simply annex the area known as the Gran Chaco, which is essentially the northern quarter of their unfortunate neighbor

The problem stemmed from an earlier war between Bolivia and Peru on one side and Chile on the other. Peru and Bolivia, envious of the wealth that Chile was gaining from honest trade, signed a secret treaty of self-defense, then Bolivia suddenly increased taxes on Chilean mining interests in its Antofagasta province. When the dust settled from that bit of human greed, Boliva had lost its sole port on the Pacific and Peru was licking its wounds. After the war, which ended in 1881, Bolivia was out of the military business for a time, its economy being unable to support soldiers until the early 1900s. Then they began to covet part of little Paraguay's real estate, which might give them access to the Atlantic—if grabbed quickly enough.

The Paraguay–Panay River runs from southern Brazil down the eastern border of Paraguay, then through central Paraguay and out to the sea at Buenos Aires. Bolivia, now landlocked and with no port on the Pacific seems to have thought that it would be no trick to annex the whole of Chaco province, 100,000 square miles of northern Paraguay. They had a good but small army, German instructors, and a few British-made light tanks. Trouble was, the Gran Chaco was called a Green hell. There were few roads, and the jungle trails had been hacked out with machetes—that kind of cutting leaves little stakes poking up to shred tires and cripple horses. There were no bridges, no electric power, and few radio sets. This was raw, undeveloped land and the climate was extremely humid.

The Bolivian Army was German-trained. This was during the period when Adolf Hitler was taking power: the Reichstag fire had not happened, and according to the Treaty of Versailles, Germany was limited to a 100,000-man army—all of which were considered to be officer or noncommissioned officer (NCO) grade. In effect, the Wehrmacht was being run as a giant officer/NCO Academy. In addition, the Germans were actively encouraging their men to seek experience in foreign armies. Some universities were even awarding degrees in military science to men who wrote acceptable treatises on foreign combat. In effect, they were harvesting the experiences of soldiers of fortune. There had also been a German military mission in Bolivia since 1911, operated by a Major Hans Kundt.

This gentleman trained the Bolivian army until 1914, then fought in World War I and returned as a Brigadier General, serving as the Bolivian army's chief of staff until 1926. At just about that time, a French military training mission was arriving in Paraguay and both nations were putting up forts in the Chaco. The pressures and clashes built up until an open war evolved. In May 1933, Paraguay declared it to be an official war, but Bolivia never seems to have gone formal. The kind of war was a regular 1917-style trench/artillery war and, as would be expected, it was eating up another whole generation.

Since the tactical use of tanks was still in its infancy, it is instructive to look at this little war. Only the Bolivians had tanks, and even though it was the South American winter, the jungle was the real enemy—a hot humid hell. There were just five tanks, three Vickers' six-tonners, and two Carden-Lloyds, which were the forerunners of the Universal Carrier of World War II. Of the Vickers, one was armed with a single 47mm cannon in a muscle-powered turret; the other two each had a pair of one-man machine gun turrets mounted side by side. They were about the same class of tank as the Renault FT series, but their suspension and engines made them capable of about 20 miles per hour.

The Carden-Lloyds were little three-tonners with an air-cooled engine in the back and an open cockpit with a pair of flaps that could be used to cover the crew compartment. The normal crew was a driver and machine gunner. Due to the heat and the constant bullet battering, the Bolivians developed the practice of assigning two or three crews to each vehicle, one to rest while the others fought.

The tactical situation at the village of Ayala was this: two lines of trenches backed up by the usual artillery parks faced each other just west of the town, and there had been desultory patroling, artillery exchanges, and attacks for some time.

On 4 July 1933, the Paraguayans were defending, the Bolivians attacking from the west through heavy brush into a line of trenches heavily held with infantry and machine guns. This was the first tank attack in South America, and it was also the first intensive use of submachine guns instead of infantry rifles. The SMGs were mostly Bergmanns with a few Schmiessers.

The Bolivian disposition was a two-winged attack, each wing with three infantry battalions of 450 riflemen and 25 machine gunners, plus a dismounted cavalry regiment with flamethrowers, short 65mm cannons, and trench mortars. There were a further five infantry battalions in reserve behind the assault wave. After a 15-minute barrage from 25 guns and a dozen howitzers, the infantry trotted forward and the tanks rolled with them. With the left wing was the gun-armed six-tonner and the two Carden-Lloyds. The armor support for the right wing was the other two six-tonners.

Unfortunately for the Bolivians, their artillery had fallen short, leaving the enemy practically unhurt. On the left, the Bolivians were stopped cold, and the lone gun-armed six-tonner tank roamed along the line of stalled infantry, potting machine gun nests with its cannon. Of the two Carden-Lloyds, one was knocked out by armor-piercing ammunition and the other one was ditched. Two hours after the attack began, something large and lethal, probably a small artillery piece, knocked out the six-tonner permanently.

On the right, the two Vickers machine gun tanks worked well until the turret of one was jammed by an armor-piercing bullet and the other began to break down. The commander pulled both of them back for repairs and then sent them back in. There were other problems too. The crews had to be replaced several times, the radios quit working due to heat and humidity, and the tanks had to revert to siren signals. Then, due to corrosion of the ammunition, rounds began to swell on firing and thus jam the machine guns. In late afternoon a Paraguayan counterattack ejected the invaders with great loss.

The next day the Bolivians attacked again, with just the two running six-tonners, but the Paraguayans reverted to form and poured in a prodigal number of infantry reserves, stalling the attack. Shortly after this, the Paraguayans, now fully mobilized and on the offensive, began to eject the invaders, tanks or no tanks. The Bolivians began to resist what they now considered an invasion of their territory and the war ground down to a stalemate. The war was ended by mediation by Argentina, Brazil, Chile, Peru, and the United States. In other far-flung corners of the world, the preliminary bouts of the World War II were beginning. The next would be Ethiopia, then Spain, and a small town in Asia, Nomonham in Mongolia.

CHAPTER 18

Ethiopia, 1934

THE LAND THAT IS NOW ETHIOPIA IS A LAND OF HISTORY AND legend. The nation is the first recognizable national name listed in the Bible of Christianity and the Pentateuch of Israel. It is the biblical land of Cush and there are many Old Testament references to the Ethiopian practice of renting out mercenary warriors to empire builders. Herodotus lists them in the mercenary regiments of Darius and Xerxes. Like many another ancient land, there are many fragmented peoples embedded in the cultural makeup of the clans that inhabit Abyssinia: the name given to the Horn of Africa by Portuguese explorers—a corruption of an Arabic word meaning fragmented.

That the biblical Ethiopians were black has never been in doubt. The biblical quote is "Can the Ethiopian change his skin or the leopard his spots (Jeremiah 13:23). . . . or for that matter" (Numbers 12:1). Their original animist, pagan religion was mostly replaced by Coptic Christianity in the fourth century, but there are still pockets of animist tribesmen in those hills. In later times there came small colonies of Jewish traders who set up in the towns. In the seventh century, the waves of Islam swept through the hapless land

and again the flames of religious war burned bright. In the sixteenth century, the king of Ethiopia asked the Portuguese for help against the Muslims who were pressing him. The Portuguese gave him aid but pressed him to convert from Coptic Christianity to Roman Catholicism . . . and were in turn asked to leave. When the Ethiopians ask someone to leave, the process can get messy.

South of Ethiopia is the land of the Somali. Between the two peoples, men of the same basic stock, the border province of the Ogaden peoples has always been the bone of contention. For the few thousands of years of history that we know, the peoples of Abyssinia have been contesting that border, first on foot with spears and clubs, later on horse and camel with bows, swords, and muskets.

Then came the Portuguese, the British, the French, and the Italians with cavalry, tanks, and even mustard gas. World War II was followed by decolonization, a Marxist "protectorate," and more tanks carried by helicopters into the *new* Ogaden war.

The Ethiopians have a description of the Somali that bears repeating: "Where there are two Somali, you will have a fistfight. Three of them will create a riot, four a war." Like many areas around the Mideast and North Africa, the land has known no peace since the sons of man have walked its hills and valleys.

The modern involvement with Ethiopia/Somalia begins with the Age of Exploration and a mad king who liked to kidnap exploring Europeans. The practice cost him his crown and that headpiece did not return to Ethiopia until World War II.

In January 1864, Emperor Theodore I, King of Kings, Chosen of God, etc., etc., of Ethiopia, had a misunderstanding with HM Victoria, Empress of the British Empire. Young Theodore had started off as an educated scribe in the hinterlands, serving some tribal chieftain. Graduating to banditry, he became so successful that the rest of the tribes crowned him emperor, at the age of thirty-seven. Unfortunately, young Theodore would have been diagnosed as a manic-depressive today.

Having some problems with his Arabic neighbors, he

wrote a letter to Victoria, complaining that his Muslim adversaries were oppressing good Christians and that he wanted to send a delegation to explain the situation. The letter was duly given to the British consul, Captain Charles Cameron, and posted to England . . . where it disappeared into the bureaucracy. Theodore, after losing patience, had Cameron arrested, tortured on the rack, and flogged with a hippopotamus hide whip. When word of this reached Victoria, she immediately sent a letter demanding her consul's release. The letter, given to a Turkish Assyriologist named Hormuzd Rassam, took until 1866 to arrive due to Rassam's private affairs. When Rassam handed the letter to Theodore, he and all his retainers promptly joined Cameron in Theodore's dungeon. This kind of behavior was simply not safe in the Victorian era. In July 1867, the secretary of state for India telegraphed the governor of Bombay to ask how long it would take to mount an expedition to extract the prisoners by force. The bumblings of bureaucrats had caused an expedition that would involve 62,000 men before it was over.

Theodore I had just stepped on the toes of the largest military power of the day, and Great Britain felt duty bound to protect its world-roving citizens. In 1850, Lord Henry Palmerston had said in debate: "As the Roman of old could say 'civis Romanis sum,' so also a British subject in whatever land he may be, shall feel confident that the watchful eye and strong arm of England will protect him from injustice and wrong." One could wish that American citizens today were so valued that their government would extract them from unearned peril.

The extraction in this case was not done by the British Army, but by the Bombay Army of the British East India Company, under one Robert Cornelis Napier. This gentleman was one of the "military Napiers," and was a veteran of the first Sikh War and the Sepoy Mutiny, saw considerable border combat in the northwestern India, and served in the China War of 1860. In 1867, Napier was commanding general of the Bombay Army and was to earn a knighthood for two military traits, dogged persistence and preparedness.

Early in his career, he'd learned that while generals are only mildly criticized for overspending, they are *never* forgiven for losing battles. The terrain of Ethiopia not being suited for flying columns and lightning raids, Napier set up for the long haul. What Great Britain had forgotten as a whole, after the Crimean War, was that logistics is as important as the combat troops. Napier, on active service in the hinterlands, knew it well.

By the time he was done moving into Ethiopia, he had an army of 16,000 British and Indian troops; scads of servants, porters, and support personnel; and 36,000 horses, camels, donkeys, and even elephants for transport. Napier had gone thoroughly modern and had steam-driven saltwater condensers and pumps from America, and he even had a field photography unit to record his campaign. He was also accompanied by a young American war correspondent, Henry M. Stanley, whose description is worth repeating:

> The encampment was a most extraordinary and novel sight. It was as if a whole nation had immigrated here and were about to plant a great city on the fervid beach. Napier had been saddled with such a heterogeneous lot of mixed troops that he had British and Indian soldiers, African units, Turks, Arabs and even Germans from the British Foreign legion. The only way to handle troops this disparate is to keep them in their national groups. So, keeping his British and Indian troops as a 5000-man striking force, Napier used the rest for route security to protect his lines from local bandits.

By 8 April 1868, Theodore must have been a bit apprehensive, sitting in his mountain retreat, a stone fortress named Magdala, watching a modern army building roads toward him and pulling cannons into his hills with elephants. On 9 April, the Ethiopians thought they saw a weakness as one of the British supply columns got a bit too close to their hill. Picking up their double-barreled, muzzle loading muskets, they plunged screaming down the slope . . . right into the breech-loading Snider-Enfield rifles of the 23rd Punjabi Pioneers. Then into the confused, swirling horde of Ethiopians, the Naval Rocket Brigade launched their weapons and the battle began to unravel as little parties of Ethiopians sought to escape. By nightfall there were around 700 Ethiopian dead and 1,200 wounded on the field. As Henry Stanley sat, rolled in his buffalo robe around a campfire, he wrote, "The night was filled with the screeching of animals. In ravenous packs, the jackals and hyenas had come to devour the abundant feast spread out by the ruthless hand of war."

By morning, Theodore had had enough and after trying to negotiate, eventually sent down all 49 of his prisoners— among them was a pregnant lady named Mrs. Moritz who gave birth next day to a son whom she named Theodore— one does wonder. Napier then began to assault the fortress, and Emperor Theodore retaliated by throwing his own native prisoners from the cliffs of his fortress. Magdala, held by a professional military force, could have held out for years, but by now Theodore was coming unglued. With only 200 half-demoralized followers, he couldn't hold out long, even when it was discovered that the British sappers had forgotten their scaling ladders and blasting charges.

At this point, the bravery and resourcefulness of the British infantryman came to the fore and saved the day. A strong, tall private named Bergin threw a drummer boy named Magner to the top of the 12-foot-high wall by launching him from the butt of his rifle. Then Magner reached down, took the rifle and helped Bergin climb up. Bergin, still, it must be remembered, armed only with a single-shot rifle, began to shoot down "every black face in sight." Magner helped up more men of his regiment (the 33rd) over the wall. Then they reached down and pulled up Ensign Walter Wynter who carried the regimental colors. The records have it that this was the last occasion on which that regiment carried its colors at the forefront, things like Gatling guns and rifled muskets made that ancient practice a bit too hazardous.

Theodore was then treated to the sight of the battle flag of a British Regiment coming over his walls and shot himself with a pistol that had been a present from Queen Victoria. The British losses, surprisingly, were only two officers and 13 other ranks wounded, no deaths—against what should have been an impregnable fortress. Napier then ordered the works of Magdala destroyed, looted the castle thoroughly, and left the Ethiopians to stew in their own juices. Among the loot was Theodore's gold crown, which 68 years later, King George V of England returned to Ethiopia's new Emperor, Haile Selassie.

The expedition had cost the English 8 million pounds. But, as Benjamin Disraeli said, "Money is not to be thought of in such matters: success only is to be thought of."

While the inhabitants of Abyssinia stewed in their juices, the British colonial wars went on, World War I flamed on the world scene, and the League of Nations was born. Most of the world had been parceled out as colonies or protectorates of the major European powers, who were busily dragging the benighted Third World into the twentieth century, and getting quite rich at the job. The Abyssinians, now approaching nationhood, wished to find an European trading partner and protector, and chose Italy as their mentor into the modern world. They could not have made a worse choice for two reasons: the secret treaties of Europe, after World War I, had guaranteed economic control of Abyssinia to Italy; and Italy had been taken over by Benito Mussolini, a bombastic blowhard militarist with delusions of empire.

By 1928, one of the ever-feuding warlords of Ethiopia, Ras Tafari, managed to overcome his competition and was crowned negus or king. On 2 November 1930, he proclaimed himself Emperor Haile Selassie the First. Unfortunately for him, the Italians, commanded by the Duke of Amadeo Aosta, were steadily building an invasion force in Italian Somaliland, just south of his empire. Haile Selassie brought his ancient land into the League of Nations, and that toothless debating body discussed, declaimed, and dithered to no good effect—except that Great Britain considered an oil embargo against Italy, with about the same effect as the current embargo against Iraq. . . . On 3 October 1935, the Italians moved their army into the Ogaden province and began to march on Selassie's capital, Addis Ababa, with a modern army. They had artillery, cavalry, airplanes and tanks—of a sort.

The Carro Veloce model 1933, or CV 33(s), was what one would call a tankette. At 10-feet-long and 4.5-feet-wide, it

A platoon of Renaults, with their crews ready to mount. *(Armor* magazine)

Training aids. The job of the man behind the dummy tank: Rock it to rattle the gunner. *(Armor)*

A French St. Chamond tank, with most of the crew riding on top, in 1918. *(Armor)*

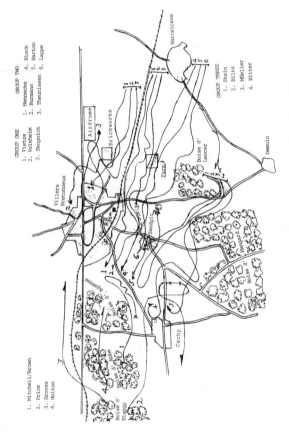

GROUP ONE
1. Vietze
2. Volkheim
3. Skopnick

GROUP TWO
1. Hennecke
2. Burmann
3. Theunissen
4. Block
5. Barton
6. Lappe

GROUP THREE
1. Stein
2. Blitz
3. Müeller
4. Bitter

1. Mitchell/Brown
2. Price
3. Groves
4. Holton

Villers Bretonneux: the first tank vs. tank battle in history.
(Ralph Zumbro)

German A7V
tanks rumbling
through a French
village in 1918.
(Armor)

A British
Whippet tank
escorting horse
cavalry in
eastern France
near the town of
Busigny.
(Armor)

French radio
tank as
used in the
Rif wars.
(Armor)

Japanese Type 97 tank in World War II— probably the best one they ever built. But not good enough. *(Armor)*

A shot-up German assault gun in 1942 Russia. (Jody Harmon)

A shot-up, captured assault gun, which can be cannibalized into another vehicle. (Jody Harmon)

German tanks in Russia—captured and being cannibalized into Russian service against their former owners. (Jody Harmon)

A pair of demolished T-34s. The Russian drill was to drag them home, hose them out, and drop another engine and crew into them. *(Armor)*

A Russian Sherman tank—the first one into Vienna. *(Armor)*

Russian Sherman in Eastern Europe—note welded-on extra armor plates. *(Armor)*

Sherman tanks under Russian management in western Asia. *(Armor)*

Shermans in British service—one is named *Bourbon.* Is the other *Brandy?* *(Armor)*

Tank retriever in Korea. The winches in these vehicles made mountain climbing possible.
(Armor)

Armored cavalry assault vehicle (ACAV) in central highlands, Vietnam, 1968. The canvas is for crew privacy, because the security provided by the vehicle created an instant business point, with villagers trading.
(Ralph Zumbro)

Viet Cong undergoing "field debriefing."
(Ralph Zumbro)

An ACAV, a Vietnamese invention created out of an
American armored personnel carrier, in 1966.
(Ralph Zumbro)

was about the size of a modern sedan. With 43 horsepower moving a weight of 7,574 pounds, its combat agility was considerably less than that of a horse. The CV's top speed was just 26 miles per hour, and its main armament was a pair of 8mm machine guns in a nonrotating square box in the center of the hull. Its armor would—just barely—keep out rifle bullets. The CV was considered to be good enough for "colonial work" and soldiered on through the Ethiopian conflict, the Spanish civil war, and on into the invasion of Russia. Their first battle debut, however, was less than impressive.

When the war in Ethiopia became a reality, one of the first events was the accumulation of an international press corps in a country that was not equipped to receive them. By the time actual hostilities began, there were 120-odd reporters in a ramshackle town with one palace, one hotel, a railway station, and a post office. There were two movie houses, one radio-transmitting station, a few Indian shops, and a straggle of mud huts with corrugated tin roofs. This was Selassie's Imperial capital, not much improved from Emperor Theodore's day.

The Italian Army base in Asmara, Eretria, was more accessible, and this attracted even more people, up to 150 assorted would-be war correspondents. On 5 October, the Ethiopian forces clashed at a road construction site on the border with Italian Somaliland, costing the Ethiopians 100 casualties and the Italians some 30 killed and wounded. Haile Selassie immediately complained to the League of Nations, which found itself unable to apportion blame for the incident.

Eventually, the League imposed sanctions on Il Duce. These covered the delivery of arms and raw materials as well as the extension of credit to the Fascists, but critical items, such as the delivery of oil or the closing of the Suez Canal to the Italians, were not mentioned. During the rest of the fall of 1935, there was a lot of small unit action, raiding, and bombing, but then the winter shut operations down until April 1936—it didn't take long after that.

All during November and December 1935, the Italians were on the march. They came in two columns, one from

Eretria in the northwest, and one from Italian Somaliland.
The Italian army was mostly modern and the Ethiopians
mostly primitive, but there were a *lot* of them and they had
been getting training from the Russians and Belgians. Haile
Selassie was also proving himself to be no tyro at international propaganda and made full use of any Italian political incorrectness.

The segment of the press that crowded into Addis Ababa
was fully censored by the emperor and was further crippled
by the fact that there was exactly one radio-telegraph link
to the outer world. As a result, the press began to manufacture news to justify their existence. One reporter even went
so far as to photograph a group of Italian tanks on practice
maneuvers and foist the picture off as an "Italian armored
assault on Ethiopian troops." Estimates have been made
that as much as ninety percent of "news" issuing from all
those reporters was manufactured out of thin air. Meanwhile, without usable military intelligence, several armies
were trying to find each other.

On the morning of 15 December 1935, it happened. A
small, scattered, inept tank force ran into a barbarian host
in the valley of the Tekeze River in eastern Ethiopia. Marshal Pietro Badoglio, the Italian field commander, had concentrated his troops, guns, and tanks at Mekele in Tigre
province, in northeastern Ethiopia. The senior Ethiopian
leader, Ras Imru, had been based in the southern province
of Gojam and had just force-marched 25,000 native levies
and a small core of professional warriors some 400 miles.
Just a few days before the battle, they were north of
Gonder, approaching Dabat. Each one of these little provinces and territories was the responsibility of its local Ras
(chief). Ras Imru was now in the territory of one Dejaz
(chieftain) Ayalew Birru, a rather stout individual in his
mid-fifties. Birru, long experienced in the ways of Ethiopian
war, was not exactly vacillating, he just wasn't pushing the
Italians too hard. His orders from the emperor were to raid
into Eretria and keep the Italians off balance. He was, however, not stupid, and the times were changing. He had been
in the battle of Adowa, 40 years before, when the Ethiopians
had given an earlier generation of Italians a resounding de-

feat, but that was before airplanes and tanks. He had 10,000 men, but Ras Imru could not count on them.

On the good side, the local Italian forces were supposed to be only small contingents of native mercenaries. There were good roads between them and Mekele—and there was an airfield at Aksum. At this stage, a messenger from Haile Selassie flew in with new orders. Ayalew Birru was to cease his petty raiding operations into Eretria and join with Ras Imru to take the fords to the Takkazze river. Imru immediately sent a column off in the opposite direction of his main thrust as a diversion, which the patroling Italian Air Force spotted and bombed. Then Birru and Imru each sent a 2,000-man advance guard into the Takkazze valley at night. The Italians were facing cagey, seasoned fighters, not wildmen.

The northern group under Imru found their ford unguarded and began to filter across the river after sending runners back to their main force. Nine miles upstream, the main ford on the Gonder/Adowa mule track was guarded and the Italian commander had a small stone fort, a radio, and a squadron of tanks. The leader of Ayalew Birru's scouting force, one Fitaurari Shifferaw, took his men silently across the low, dry-season river, wiped out the Italian guard post, and began to work his way up the pass toward the main garrison.

Part way up the mountain, they ran into an Italian mounted patrol, fired too soon, and the Italian horsemen rode away to warn their commander, a Major Critini. The major immediately called for air support and sent one lone tank . . . out of a full squadron, to reconnoiter. The CV 33, it should be remembered, was a little box on tracks and its guns only had a 15-degree traverse. At the tanklets first appearance, the warriors began to try to shoot it "through the heart," but long bursts from its twin machine guns terrified them and a general rout began. One Ethiopian, however, had more courage than sense.

A man named Balambaras Tashemma dismounted from his horse, crept around the tank, dodging from rock to rock. Armed only with a sword and pistol, he crept aboard the clattering, bullet-streaming monster. Getting a good place for his feet and a good grip for his left hand, he took the

long, slightly curved horseman's saber in his right hand.
Hammering on the machine gun casemate with the sword
hilt, he yelled *"Open up"* in Italian. The dumbfounded pair
inside opened the hatches, stuck their heads out, and with
two sweeping slashes, one left and then a return to the right,
Balambaras beheaded the two tankers.

Major Critini now saw that his little *gruppo banda altopi-
ani* was badly outnumbered and tried to break out, using
the other nine tanks of the troop. Quickly forming his men
and loading their baggage animals, the Italians came down
the pass, tanks in the lead, 18 machine guns streaming copper-jacketed lead—it almost worked. Faced by 9 of the bul-
let-spitting little monsters, Shifferaw's 2,000 men turned and
ran. But by main force of personality, he rallied them, "Are
you women?" he yelled and blew his war horn. "Can't you
see that I am here?" This worked, and they charged into
the machine guns again, wounding many Italians, including
Major Critini.

These were not fast, agile Rolls armored cars in an open
desert, these were little tanklets without turrets in steep
mountain passes. Unable to press forward, the Italians crept
back to the base of the pass, with the mountain behind them.
Totally encircled, they drove their baggage train of mules
out of the laager in an attempt to distract the Ethiopians
with loot. It didn't work. Shifferaw ordered his men to drive
the mules back into the Italian position, but in the process
was himself killed. Now some of the Italians, their officers
dead, tried to surrender, and came out with their hands up.

Unfortunately, the gesture was unknown to the Ethiopians
who kept killing them. Now the survivors rallied around
their almost immobilized tanks. Shifferaw was dead and his
eighty-year-old father Nagash stood over him, rifle in hand,
crying, "my son, my son." At this point, Nagash's religious
confessor, who (like a chaplain) had followed the family into
battle said, "I will take care of your son, but you are damned
if you don't avenge his death." The old man shook off his
tears, drew his sword, and yelled, "Youngsters, Shifferaw is
not dead, he orders you. 'do not let the enemy escape.'
Follow me."

Now enraged beyond fear, warriors on horseback surrounded the tanks, which could not shoot to their sides, rear, or even very high to the front. Dismounting, leaving five horses each to a horse-holder, the Ethiopians would rush the helpless side of those little 3.5-ton tanklets and grab hold of them, heaving with all their strength. The tanks weighed over 3 tons, granted, but they were not trying to pick them up bodily, just tip them on their side—and they did! A dozen men, each lifting 200 pounds, can do the job. Slowly at first, the tanks began to lift under the terrified Italians. . . . If they had only thought to roll the tracks, they could have torn the hands and arms off their attackers, but they didn't. Then as more men could get their shoulders under the hull, the tanklet lifted and went over on its side—now helpless. As gasoline began to leak from the now-tilted fuel tanks, the attackers set them alight, forcing the crews out one by one to be killed. Only one crew survived, by coming out yelling, "Christos, Christos." By 1600 it was over, 10 tanks and an Italian garrison with modern weapons and air support had been taken by warriors on horseback—and they weren't through!

The few survivors refuged out across the pass to the town of Enda Selassie, just 5 miles away. Right after they got there, the Ethiopians, now led by Ras Imru and Fituarari Tshegger, came thundering into the town and cleared it with sword, rifle, and lance. Help for the Italians was on the way. Only 30 miles away, at Aksum, there was an airport, and a garrison of Blackshirts, not soldiers, with more tanks. Driving little tanks through a land of big stones, however, gives the enemy the advantage. Just a few miles out of Enda Selassie, the men of Ras Imru had built a surprise. Huge stones bounded down off the hills to block the road and jam the tanks, which couldn't turn on the narrow mule trails.

With the lead tanks blocked and more tanks, trucks, and troops coming on behind, the rest of the troop were dead meat. Some tanks were overturned, some riddled through the vision slits, and some just set on fire by being lit off with gasoline bombs. Some, Rif-style, were boarded and their machine guns beaten into uselessness with nothing more sophisticated than large rocks in the hands of angry men.

By 23 December, Ras Imru was on a rampage. Although

he could not directly take the Italian complex at Aksum/
Adowa, since it had 30 battalions and 193 guns, he swung
out across the Adi Abo desert, heading for the Italian main
supply dump at Adi Quala in Eretria, which had almost no
garrison. When this was discovered, Baodoglio panicked and
ordered two countermeasures—one of them drastic.

Ras Imru had gone out into that waterless rock desert
with 8,000 men and supplies for a week. If he could be
forced to battle, he could be forced back to the Takkazze.
Baodoglio now snapped out of his customary lethargy, ordered a full attack by 12,000 men on the Ethiopian van. The
resultant battle lasted for 24 hours, but it was indecisive as
the Ethiopians now were almost as well-equipped as the
Italians—save for air power.

On the morning of 23 December, a flight of planes came
low over Ras Imru's men, who immediately scattered for
cover and began to set up machine guns on rocks and hill-
ocks. They had become used to daily bombings and strafings
and could live with them. This morning was different. Long
metal cylinders with fins dropped from the airplanes and
broke almost silently as they hit the ground. From them
issued clouds of colorless gas that burned with hideous fury,
blinding men, causing instant pneumonia, and raising blisters
the size of whole arms; in seconds men began to look like
blistered sausages. Ras Imru's brilliant campaign was over,
ended by weapons the rest of the world had outlawed in
horror years before. Mustard gas, dropped from airplanes
was what eventually drove Haile Selassie to exile in Jerusalem. The exile would only last until 1940, though, when the
British and the South Africans would drive the Italians from
their Abyssinian possessions and reseat the emperor . . .
although it is questionable if they would have bothered if
the Italians had not threatened Egypt.

Mussolini, in allying with the Axis powers, had decided
to have a few casualties so that he could "sit at a bargaining
table as one who has fought a war." Unfortunately, most of
his soldiers weren't too keen on the subject, and his large,
impressive navy wasn't up to modern air attacks. He got his
casualties, lost his empire, and eventually his life by getting
too greedy. When he jumped the British in the western de-

sert and then sent a column north out of Ethiopia under the Duke of Aosta, he sealed the doom of his empire. Although the Brits were not yet equipped to handle the Germans, a long-range colonial war was something they had been doing for 300 years.

Whether the Italians could have ever pulled off an effective invasion of Egypt through the Sudan, no one will ever know, but the British Commanding Officer, General Sir William Platt, wasn't taking chances.

The principal British objective, at that time, was simply to neutralize any threat from the south, and they pulled in allies from all over Africa and the Italian colony was doomed. There were the tribesmen whom the Brits were stirring up, the French Foreign legion from Chad, the South Africans, and even a Belgian unit that had marched from the Congo all the way across Africa. By the middle of 1940, the emperor was back on his throne and the Italians were desperately begging for German help. In the meantime, however, the Spanish Foreign Legion, which had first used tanks in Morocco, had revolted under its commander, General Francisco Franco, and the Spanish civil war was under way.

REFERENCE SOURCES

Small Wars, Callwell, University of Nebraska Press.
The First Casualty, Phillip Knightly, Quartet Press.
Haile Selassie's War, Anthony Mockler, Random House.
The First of the League Wars, J.F.C. Fuller, Gordon Press.

CHAPTER 19

The Spanish Civil War, 1936–1939

THE SPANISH CIVIL WAR CAME AS NO REAL SURPRISE TO MOST observers of history. That it was so long and bloody shocked the world. Just three men are responsible for the awful carnage, Adolf Hitler, Joseph Stalin, and Benito Mussolini. When the revolt in Spain began, like vivisectionists turned loose in a slaughterhouse these men sent weapons and experts to the contestants for "field testing." Tanks, airplanes, cannon, even submarines were to be used before the Republicans had had enough. A half million Spaniards would die and almost as many would be driven into exile.

Ever since Napoléon Bonaparte destabilized Spain by placing his brother Joseph Napoléon on the throne in 1808, after deposing *both* hereditary claimants, Spanish politics had been a seething cauldron—and by the 1930s, history was catching up with the remaining European monarchs. The flame of revolution was unseating them one after another, and replacing them with prime ministers, secretaries, chancellors, and other bureaucratic riffraff. Spain's problem was not unique. It was, however, exceedingly complex and had much more outside interference than even our own Revolutionary War.

First, King Alphonso III was an able politician but what was needed was a statesman of the first quality. His problem was that he faced a full two-dozen political parties, each with an axe to grind and a program to foist off on the proletariat. There were socialists, communists, anarchists, syndacalists, Republicans, democrats, Trotskyites, separatists, and new industrialists—to name just a few. The people had just cause for complaint as the land was owned by several great power blocks: the government, the aristocracy, and the church. All realized the injustice of this, the arguments were on how to correct the problem without bloodshed. Finally, after literally decades of bickering, it was decided to hold a plebiscite.

On 11 April 1931, a national election was held and when the votes were counted, the nation went into shock. The Republicans had won by such a landslide that the monarchy was abolished. In just 24 hours, a nation that had been believed to be firmly monarchist, had voted itself into a republic. By 14 April, Alphonso III had boarded a cruiser of the Spanish Navy and gone into voluntary exile at Marseilles ... without abdicating. A provisional government was formed and a constitutional convention planned, but the nation was going mad. Like the Russian Revolution before it, Republican Spain had a communist core that soon took over the nation . . . "Now we have the Republic," went the battle cry, "now let us have our revolution."

There were soon riots against the government, the church, even the rightist newspaper, *ABC*. Churches were invaded and burned, the cardinal primate of Spain was expelled from the country, and the Pope refused to see the new Spanish ambassador to the Vatican. The problem was that the Republican Party, in order to win its landslide, had to make temporary peace with the rest of the radicals, who now wanted their separate agendas to be put into place. Catalonia wanted autonomy, as did the Basque people. The syndicalists, anarchists and communists seemed to be doing most of the striking and rioting, but they were not alone. In desperation, the provisional government used force to stop the worst of the violence, further exacerbating the situation. For 57 months, this situation went from bad to worse,

until on 31 December 1935, the newspaper *ABC* reported
"[The] last crisis of the year, for we can hardly have another
before nightfall." In those months, there had been 28 minis-
tries, each with an average life of two months before some
political contretemps brought it down in ruins.

The Republican Party, shot throughout with radicals, tried
one more time and during the recriminations on 12 July
1936, one Calvo Sotelo, the leader of the Conservative Party,
began reciting a list of the crimes and atrocities of the
anarcho-socialists, who had a long record of illegal violence
and coercion. When he finished his address, the spokesper-
son for the communists, Delores Ibarruri, who was known
as the *Passionaria*, rose and shrieked, "This man has spoken
for the last time."

That night, Sotelo was arrested by an agent of the Guardia
Civil, on communist orders, driven out to a dark, quiet spot,
and executed Chicago style by a man named Fernando Cor-
tes. That would be roughly equivalent, in an American setting, for someone to take the speaker of the house out for
assassination. At this point in time, the external machina-
tions of other nations began to take effect.

General Francisco Franco, by now the commander of the
Spanish Foreign Legion, had been sent to the Canary Islands
by the "loyalist" government in power, because he was an
effective military commander and the fanatics in power did
not trust him. Adolph Hitler, however, by now in power in
Germany, had put several aircraft at his service, and he had
been flown to his old base in Spanish Morocco and set up
"Radio Melilla." Immediately, the government, now dominated by leftists, sent ships of the Spanish Navy to blockade
him in port, so that he could not use the Spanish Legion
and his loyal Moroccan troops. Unfortunately for the leftist
"Republicans," Hitler had already, on 1 July, authorized the
use of as many Ju-52 transport aircraft as the general
might need.

Franco, it should be remembered, had been fighting the
Rif rebels for over a decade and was *very* good at this kind
of war. His radio broadcast from Melilla on 17 July was a
declaration of war on the leftist-dominated government and
he immediately began sending his army across the Strait of

Gibraltar in Hitler's airplanes. . . . One does wonder what the British garrison at Gibraltar thought of this activity. The armed forces of Spain immediately took sides, and by late 1936 Franco had all his legionaries, 35,000 men including a division of cavalry, in Spain. Of the continental army, 117,000 had gone over to him as well as 35,000 of the federal police. This should have been enough to restore order, but now the international meddling reached monumental proportions.

The leftist "Republican" government had the balance of the armed forces, some of the police, and 30,000 assault guards, or "red militia." The problem seems to have been the reinforcement of the government forces by outside agents. The international brigades were on the government side (having been hoodwinked by internationalists) and Stalin was sending in thousands of tons of military supplies, including some very good (for the times) tanks. He was also sending in thousands of so-called volunteers, including some of the Soviet Army officers who had worked with the Germans in hidden military bases in Russia in the early 1930s. In addition to the Abraham Lincoln Brigade of Americans, there was also the Russian Karl Marx Division, and many others fighting for a "Republican" cause, which was being operated straight out of Moscow by Joseph Stalin. The Russians were still expanding, and German and Italy wanted control of Gibraltar and access to the Mediterranean. Spain was on the sacrificial block of Axis ambitions.

By mid-1937, the international situation was this: England and France were supposedly neutral, Russia was allied with the leftist Republican government, and Hitler and Mussolini were aiding Franco's rebels. Effectively, the larger nations had hijacked Spain's revolution for experimental purposes. Russia had shipped 800 tanks, 300 aircraft, 800 artillery pieces, 3,000 machine guns, and 2,000 officer technical advisors. They had also shipped in an unknown but huge number of "volunteers." According to the 1938 German statistical report, in 1937 the insurgents under Franco had killed or wounded 300,000 reds and captured 220,000 prisoners of war (POWs). There were more people fighting in Spain than

America had in its Army, National Guard, and organized reserves at the time.

In one month, August 1937, 161 ships had docked in Spain's Mediterranean ports. Thirty-three carried war material, 32 coal, 18 gasoline, two were loaded with assorted vehicles, and the balance was general freight. The Germans and Italians were equally generous to Franco, even sending full divisions of professional soldiers. Politics aside, though, there was a commercial side to the assistance, and that was gold, possibly very old gold. From Luis Araquistain, former Russian ambassador to France, comes this report, "There was on deposit in Russia, from Spain, 552.3 TONS of gold ingots." If you convert that to ounces at modern values, you'll find that the Spanish communists in Spain's government had pawned Montezuma's hoard to the Russians. At the same time, according to the *New York Herald Tribune,* 19 June 1939, communists and fellow travelers had children out begging dimes for Spain on the streets of New York City. Apparently, General Franco was left out in the cold for he had no access to gold, only the wooing of his Axis friends, who were looking covetously at the fortress of Gibraltar.

From Germany came the Condor Legion with He-111 bombers, Ju-52 cargo aircraft, and Ju-87 dive bombers. Hitler also sent the 88th Panzer Division, equipped with Pzk-I and Pzk-II light tanks. From Italy came two full divisions of infantry, each with a battalion or so of the little tanklets that had been used in Ethiopia. For three years, these nations would be rotating their armies through hapless Spain, testing equipment and gaining experienced soldiers and airmen. The Condor Legion, for instance, cycled 18,000 men through Spain in two years. The troops who invaded Poland had that much combat experience, whereas the Poles had only outdated equipment, horse cavalry, and patriotism. History records that it was not enough.

In 1937, though, the units that would later be the feared Panzer divisions were undergoing a rather traumatic series of lessons. Franco, of course, had a small number of his original, slow, French six-tonners (Renaults), to this the Germans added their six-tonners (PzKw-I), which was only a slight improvement. It was armed with only two machine guns in a hand-powered turret and had only 1.6 inches of frontal armor—but it would do 24 miles per hour. Later in the war, a few of the latest Panzers, the PzKw-IIs, were added. That tank had been originally designed as a training vehicle, but this was a training war, so in they went. The Pzk-II weighed ten tons, was armed with a 20mm cannon, and had basically the same armor protection as the PzKw-I and the same speed. As can be easily seen, neither of these was much of a tank.

What the Russians shipped, however, was a horse of another color entirely. The T-26 was a copy of a good British Vickers design. It weighed ten tons, would do 18 miles per hour, and was armed with a 45mm cannon that would pierce any of the German or Italian tanks. Although it had excellent mobility, it was not heavily armored, having only one-inch on the front slope. The Russian BT-5 though, was even better. That tank was a modification of the American design by Walter Christie, and would do 40 miles per hour on tracks. It was also a convertible, in that the tracks could be removed and then it would make up to 60 miles per hour as a wheeled vehicle. It weighed 12 tons and was armed with the good Russian 45mm gun. The BT-5 was also lightly armored like most tanks of that era . . . and the Germans were already testing the 88mm antiaircraft gun as a tank destroyer.

The following tank action has been adapted from the July-August 1939 issue of the *U.S. Cavalry Journal,* whose reporters were following the action in Spain about as closely as the Germans. It is a translation from the French magazine *L'Illustration,* and refers to the T-26 tank used by the Republican forces. There were, apparently, also some armored cars in the mix. (It was translated by Lieutenant T. L. Crystal, U.S. Artillery.)

The Spanish Civil War has lasted two and a half years. The Italians and Germans have tried out many types of tanks and calibers of antitank guns, while the great majority of armored cars and antitank weapons used by the government forces were of Russian manufacture.

The two adversaries have made a complete trial of these
Russian tanks because the Nationalists have captured
many of them and even used them against their former owners.

The more the war in Spain drags out, the more the
combatants, the high command, and even the infantrymen tend toward the adoption of tanks armed solely
with a cannon, in this case, of 45mm. General Monasterio, Commander in Chief of Nationalist Cavalry told
me [the French reporter] one day, while speaking of
armaments and military tactics, "The war would have
been terminated already were it not for the power of
our enemy being made so great by the possession of
many armored vehicles equipped with cannons."

The battle of Fuentes de Ebro on 13 November 1937,
definitely established, at least for this war, the role
evolved for the tank. Before this battle, opinions dif-
fered, mainly with respect to one point. This was relative to light cars armed only with machine guns. In
combat it was definitely established that these cars were
unable to overcome either the difficulties of the terrain
or the fire of the enemy. Confronted with a tank armed
with a cannon, they were on a par with the foot soldier
of the Middle Ages clothed in his leathern jacket, opposed to a knight in armor.

Ever since the battle of Fuentes de Ebro, neither the
government troops nor the nationalists have had the
slightest doubt as to the role to be played by the various
types of combat cars. [Note: The observer, a French
civilian reporter, tends to use the term *cars* interchange-
ably with *tanks,* and the confusion seems to have been
caused by the running of BT-5s with their treads removed for greater speed.]

In this attic, the government army relied on the strategic
success of a breach in the Franco line formed by the valley
of the Ebro River, and on the tactical success of an assault
of armored vehicles against Nationalist infantry holding an
entrenched position at that point.

Approximately ninety to a hundred tanks attacked seven

Nationalist companies entrenched on both sides of the national highway between Tarragona and Saragossa at a point 27 kilometers from the latter. For an exact account, I can do no better than to give the exact words of one of the men who was there, second Lieutenant Antonio Quarte Alfarez:

> The attack took us by surprise. . . . Suddenly we heard the noise of the approaching tanks. It got louder, coming from the other side of the crest occupied by the enemy some 500 or 700 meters from our front. Then a column of tanks which seemed endless began to form, coming out of a breach in the enemy trenches, and headed for the spot which I held with my platoon.
>
> After going about 100 meters on the slope in front of us, the car which formed the head of the column obliqued towards the right and travelled thus parallel to our line of trenches in the direction of the national highway. At the instant that the end of the column executed that movement, a red flag was waved from the leading car and at this signal, every ninth or tenth car made a half turn toward the left, toward our position. These were followed by five or six others, thus making nine or ten columns of about six vehicles headed for us. The other tanks, of the number of about thirty, ranged themselves in a single line and fired on us with their cannons. The enemy artillery batteries did not open up, those thirty vehicles armed with cannon, and the cannon carried by most of the others constituted the only artillery supporting the attack.
>
> We had no artillery, only three antitank guns of 37mm caliber, one on a small hill on the right of the enemy company, and to the left of mine, another on the Saragossa national highway and the third on the extreme left, on the bank of the Ebro. My company, the 51st of the Thirtieth Division, was on the right of the highway, the 19th was on our right. On the left of the road were two companies of Phalangists [militia] and two companies of regulars. These four held the line between the highway and the Ebro River. The tank attack to which they were subject was less intense than

ours due to the roughness of the terrain. The land in front of our position was close to perfect for tanks and here came the main attack.

About half of those which attacked carried sandbags on them, behind which crouched soldiers. Those men behind the barriers who were not knocked off by our machine guns were effectively dislodged by hand grenades when the tanks got within good throwing distance. Very few of the tanks reached our trench. Their crews were rapidly killed or taken prisoner. Many attackers jumped out of their wheeled coffins as soon as they were within range of our hand grenades and fled. The closer the tanks got the more they lost their beautiful formation.

They avoided the places where our resistance was greatest or where the trenches were on a slight rise and headed always towards the least cut up sections of our line. We stopped several by throwing glass canteens of sulphur and gasoline in their caterpillar treads and ventilators and by hurling hand grenades at them. When the first tanks had broken through the several openings in our line, the thirty others which had with their cannons, supported the movement, began to advance. The enemy infantry had also come out of their trenches and seemed ready to charge.

We left the tanks which had succeeded in getting through our lines to the attentions of the companies in reserve who were holding the ravines behind our trenches. Soon we could hear the din of a violent struggle behind us, principally in the hollow separating our little crest from the village. Soon we saw two tanks in flames emerge from the village, come down the highway, and retire toward the enemy line. Then others, which had not been disabled, tried to return through the breaches and the more level portions of our defenses. Several escaped but the others were burned while returning and destroyed without having obtained their objective. On the right of the 19th company, an AA gun annihilated one tank which stopped to fire on that side, and stopped those which formed the left flank of the thirty others, all enfiladed in their support formation.

As soon as the retreat of the first assault was definitely under way, these reinforcing tanks retired and the infantry returned to their trenches. We then led about half our men to the rear to complete the destruction of those vehicles which were trying to make good their retreat. We captured sixteen. Two had reached the village but the stone houses and winding streets had not proven a favorable place for maneuvering. The colonel, the command post personnel, and the cooks set them on fire.

So ends the lieutenant's probably somewhat embroidered report. An American officer, B. G. Reilly, who was also an observer, comments:

Ever since, except for minor sorties, and those attacks well supported by infantry and artillery, the tanks stayed out of the range of those 37mm guns and carefully avoided close contact with nationalist infantry. They have taken advantage of the longer range of their cannons to put the 37mm guns out of action, and of their great mobility to avoid becoming targets for the mountain artillery.

The Nationalists themselves always use their tanks to assist the assault of the infantry. First comes the artillery preparation, and then aviation gets a crack. Then in several lines, but well spaced, come the combat cars, followed by the infantry. If there is a sufficiency of tanks mounting cannon only they are used, or the numbers are split half in half with the light tanks, but these are usually used only to cover the flanks of the attack formation. The infantry follows immediately after the tanks.

This episode, of course, refers to the Republican use of Russian tanks. The German expert, Colonel Ritter von Thoma, was having problems. Ernest Hemingway in his book *For Whom the Bell Tolls* has his Spanish protagonists

refer scornfully to the Panzers I as "toy tanks." Everytime
the PzKw-I went up against a cannon-armed tank, it died
spectacularly. Things got so bad that von Thoma, who was
then seriously depressed, even questioned the validity of the
whole Panzer concept.

Heinz Guderian, who had originally been inspired by the
World War I exploits of Lieutenant Volkheim at Villers-
Bretonneux to invent the Panzer concept, was then inspired
to write his book *Achtung-Panzer!* in defense of the concept.
This, however, was no help to von Thoma, who then took
extraordinary steps. Franco had been fighting Rif banditry
in Morocco for many years and his General of Cavalry,
Monasterio, had an excellent cavalry corps, which is usually
described as "counting 2,000 sabres." What is an anachro-
nism like sabre cavalry doing in a tank and dive bomber
war? For an answer, we'll have to dig, and a quick look at
their record will give us our clues.

In 1937, this cavalry corps covered Franco's advance on
Madrid. On 6 November, they seized an infantry position
outside and held it until reinforced. That is not done with
cold steel in the face of a determined defense.

In 1937, they operated on the Jarama river at Bilbao,
Santander, and Gijón. They were also operating in the Sierra
Palomera mountains. Again, they were working against partisans and apparently with tanks. These men, it should be
remembered, had Spanish officers and were a mixed Moorish and Spanish force, with excellent North African Barb
horses . . . although finding excellent riding stock has never
been a serious problem in Spain.

On 9 March 1938, the cavalry went through a gap opened
up by the Navarro Division in the Republican lines and
executed a deep raid in the enemy rear areas, causing complete havoc. Again, we can consult Hemingway, who if not
actually in the action, had talked to men who were there.
He consistently refers to "cavalry carbines." By looking at
the lists of equipment shipped by Germany and Italy, we
find both Bergmann and Beretta submachine guns that with
wooden stocks and bayonets would have looked like carbines, thus the problem is solved. Even with cavalry screen-

ing for him, though, von Thoma's tanks simply were too little for the job.

In desperation, he put a reward of 500 pesetas on the Russian tanks, especially the BT-5. With this incentive, Monesterio's Moorish raiders began to steal the Republican armor. The Russian crews were not well trained because by now Stalin's military purges had exterminated most of his experienced armor officers. The ones who were left were mostly politically reliable commissars who, without experience, had an almost suicidal propensity for frontal attacks against antitank guns. They also had not learned about night security and the need to keep the infantry close to the tanks or to keep the turrets manned at all times. After von Thoma's bounty policy had been in place for several months, the Germans had several battalions of modern Russian tanks.

The mind conjures up images of quiet horsemen dismounting near an encampment of tanks parked at one side of a small village while the Russian crews swig vodka, sport with Spanish village girls, and pull a little maintenance on their tracks. Perhaps only one man is awake by 0200 hours and the watchers know by now which of the vehicles is running. A man goes out to relieve himself and a hulking shadow rises silently from the bushes. The Russian tanker stands urinating when a hand covers his mouth and a blade enters his throat. With a whine and a hiss, he drops in a puddle of his own making, urine mixing with blood.

Now more shadows glide forward and one slips off to the waiting horsemen. Muffled clinks arouse no one as men slide into two of the tanks. One of the three tanks was obviously being cannibalized and is ignored. In the other two, chokes are pulled out, ignition timers retarded, and with a prayerful impulse the starter switches are hit . . . *Errr-unh, pftt*—and one engine sputters and dies. The second roars into smooth life, smoking a bit as the driver fiddles with the choke in an unfamiliar vehicle.

That was the signal. With a thunder of hooves the cavalrymen—who have been doing this to Rif tribesmen for a decade—clatter into the encampment with machine pistols raking sleeping bags and grenades being lobbed into already

half-destroyed houses and crude tents. A second man leaps
into the turret of the BT-5, and it suddenly adds fury to the
night as its machine gun begins to yammer. For good measure its cannon barks an HE shell into an open doorway
and an orange flame belches bodies out of a window. Then
they are gone into the night, perhaps a dozen Moroccan
Moors trotting alongside Colonel von Thoma's newest tank,
chuckling nervously in battle relief. This is a hard way to
build a tank battalion.

The Axis and Franco still had the problem of the constant
stream of Russian supplies to their Russian puppets. Now
the waters get very murky, indeed, for the ships coming
through the Dardanelles out of Russia's Black Sea ports
began to be sunk as they neared Spain. There were com-
plains of "pirate submarines" and mysterious attacks. Both
Great Britain and France signed nonintervention pacts and
began to patrol Spanish waters to prevent the importation
of more arms. At the same time a Spanish customs officer
in the Pyrenees estimated that about 2,000 tons a week of
supplies were crossing into Spain from France.

About this time Lord Halifax pointed out in the British
Parliament that, since this was technically a civil war, the
conflict was outside the jurisdiction of the League of Nations. The submarine attacks continued as did commerce
attacks from Franco's navy, now able to base in Spanish
ports. Finally, in late 1937, Russia gave up trying to supply
the "Republicans" by sea, and the war began to turn in
Franco's favor. By March 1938, he was able to launch an
all-out offensive on a 125-mile-wide front and by 15 April,
he had reached the sea of Vinaroz. The Red Republic had
been cut in two, and from then to 10 February 1939, the
action was more police operation than combat.

One would have thought that with all the help from Germany and Italy, Spain, with a newly rebuilt modern army,
would have automatically been at least a tacit partner in the
Axis of Germany, Italy, and Japan. Hitler, however, made
one crucial blunder. He signed a nonaggression treaty with
the one man Franco hated most in the world: Joseph Stalin.
Franco considered him to be the author of Spain's agony.

Long cured of the dream of empire, Spain would sit this one out.

The Axis was not through making aggressive blunders, though, and it is possible that the war was already lost in 1939. Half a world away, Japan's dream of an Asian mainland empire was about to run into Georgi Zhukov and 500 Russian tanks. The result would shape the whole war. As a result of that battle, the Japanese would be forced to leave Russia alone . . . But that gave them leave to turn their attentions south.

REFERENCE SOURCES
Maneuver in War, U.S. Marine Corps field manual, 1939.
For Whom the Bell Tolls, Ernest Hemingway, Macmillan.
Tank Attack in Spain, *U.S. Cavalry Journal*, July–August, 1939.
Encyclopedia Americana, 1940.
Military History, Cowley and Parker, Houghton Mifflin.
Panzer, Roger Edwards, Arms and Armor Press.
Tank War, James Piekalkiewicz, Blandford Press.
Achtung-Panzer!, Heinz Guderian, trans. Christopher Duffy, Arms and Armor Press.
Atlas of Russian History, Martin Gilbert, Dorset Press.

CHAPTER 20

Nomonhan, Mongolia, 1939

JAPAN VS. RUSSIA . . . ROUND ONE

WHILE THE 1 SEPTEMBER 1939, GERMAN INVASION OF Poland is generally considered to be the beginning of World War II, students of history know that Japan had been fighting in China since late in 1934. Japan and Russia, long at odds over the domination of the Asian mainland, had fought a violent, bloody war in 1903–1905, and that issue wasn't yet resolved to anyone's satisfaction. At that point in time, Japan completely dominated Korea and had, in 1931, set up a puppet regime in Manchuria, which they called Manchukuo. At its head as a Japanese puppet was Henry Pu Yi, the boy emperor of China, who had been forced to abdicate in 1917.

Without a strong central authority, China, as usual, had reverted to its historic warlord state. After Pu Yi abdicated, a so-called nationalist government had been established under doctor Sun Yat-Sen and his military chief, Chiang Kai-shek. In 1921, with the aid of Russian agitators, the Chinese Communist Party was set up and promptly started a war with the Nationalists.

When this war began, Japan next door in Manchukuo, smelled an opportunity and sent first advisors into Inner

Mongolia, then armed troops into China proper—thus the Asian side of World War II was launched. The Chinese communists under a librarian named Mao Tse-tung were supported by the Russians against the Japanese. The Nationalists under Chiang Kai-shek, were supported by both the United States and Russia. As the temporary object was the eviction of the Japanese, a nervous alliance was formed. The communists quickly broke faith and went out into the provinces proselytizing, leaving the Nationalists to do most of the fighting and dying.

This allowed the invading Japanese to take over great chunks of China proper and soon got them into conflict with Russia, which considered greater Mongolia to be a province of the then Soviet Union. The resulting battle of Nomonhan would have far-reaching effects, as it created a decision that freed both Russian and Japanese troops for "other endeavors." The pitched tank battle that took place across the Halhaiin River on 20 August, 1939, actually preceded the German invasion of Poland, but there were few news reporters that far out in the hinterlands.

Nomonhan was nearly 500 miles by tank from the nearest railhead of the Trans-Siberian Railway, which probably accounts for the lack of coverage. Even today, it is almost impossible to find it on a large-scale map, so we have to use reference points. West of Lake Baikal in Russia, you will find Chita, an industrial city on the Trans-Siberian Railroad. Three hundred and twenty-five miles southeast of Chita is the Inner Mongolian City of Hailaern. One hundred thirty miles south of Hailaern is the Halhaiin River and the site of the battle of Nomonhan. A more remote and desolate place would be hard to imagine . . . except perhaps the Sahara.

Japan and Russia had come a long way to fight a war, but both of them wanted to rule the whole world. "In the middle of the Twentieth Century," a Japanese aristocrat had once said, "Japan will meet Europe on the plains of Asia and wrest from them the mastery of the world." Unfortunately for the Japanese, their tank-design efforts had left something to be desired. Russia, on the other hand, was right in the forefront of combat-vehicle development and was just about to build what many consider to be the war's best tank design, the T-34, whose direct ancestor dominated the field at Nomonhan. At this point it is instructive to look at the equipment of the opposing sides.

What has to be understood, though, is that neither Russia nor Japan had originated the Industrial Revolution, the internal combustion engine, the radio, nor any of the technology that they were using. Japan was semiforceably opened to the Western World by Commodore Matthew Perry in 1853 due to trade and ocean-navigation problems. Russia's modernization began somewhat earlier when Czar Peter the Great began to force technology on his stodgy aristocracy at what amounts to gunpoint. After the 1917 revolution, the communists undertook rapid modernization, but without Western aid it would not have happened. Henry Ford, for instance, built them a modern truck factory in 1924 and all through the 1920s and 1930s purblind Western foundations poured money and technology into the "World of the Future." That money built 10,000 fairly modern tanks.

When Japan began to modernize its army, it was actually crippled by its ancient Bushido code of the warrior. Its navy, without those cast-iron traditions, was free to emulate Western ways, but the army was trapped by their own samurai past. Close combat with foot soldiers was deemed the only honorable way to fight a war, with armor and artillery only adjuncts to the infantry and horse cavalry. . . . Shades of the French knights at Agincourt.

When the army reluctantly began to modernize, they bought several versions of Western tanks and simply copied the models that suited their needs of infantry support. What they eventually wound up with was a copy of a British Vickers design that was a spin-off from World War I. While there were several Japanese models involved at Nomonhan, the 13-ton Type 89 series was their main tank.

The 89-OTSU was powered by a diesel engine, the 89-KO, by a gasoline engine. Horsepower was 120 for both engines. Both models used the Vickers spring suspension, with many small roadwheels, which limited them to a road speed of 15 miles per hour. They were armed with a 57mm gun that dated back to World War I, and 6.5mm machine gun that burned rifle ammunition. One machine gun was mounted for the use of a bow gunner, the other was coaxial with the main armament. These tanks could keep up with a running man (barely), and their guns could destroy buildings and bunkers but not other tanks. Their thickest armor was about six-tenths of an inch. This was not something you'd want to take to a modern war.

How different on the Russian side. All through the 1920s and 1930s they had been buying and experimenting with various experimental models and they had settled on a type invented by an American named Walter Christie. Their 12-ton, BT-5 series could run on either wheels or tracks and could move like the devil. Instead of using a sprocket to drive the track, the engine drove the rear two pairs of road-wheels, which were large, auto-tire size, and with the tracks run off and stored on the fenders, the tanks could make almost 70 miles per hour. With the tracks mounted, they could still do 45 miles per hour on roads, less going cross-country—but still fast. The steering method on wheels was brutally simple. In addition to a pair of steerable road wheels, a hand lever applied the brakes for each side, skid-steering the whole vehicle just as if it were on tracks.

The basic BT-5 was gasoline powered with a 45mm high-velocity gun. The BT-7M was powered by a diesel and carried a 76mm gun that would break most armor of the time. Its own armor was up to almost a half-inch in thickness on the front slope and was proof against the low-velocity 57mm gun at even point-blank range. The BT carried only one machine gun, of 7.62mm, that fired the Russian rimmed rifle cartridge. While both sides had an assortment of smaller tanks for scouting purposes, the Russians had one vicious surprise, a battalion of obsolescent OT-130 Vickers models that mounted flame throwers as main armament.

While the Japanese, admitted aggressors and conquerors, had a competent, brave little army running loose in disorganized China, they weren't set up for the big leagues nor was General Ueda Kenkichi, the commander of the Kwangtung army, anything but a traditional infantryman. The Russian commander, on the other hand, was 43-year-old Georgi Zhukov, who earned his cavalry spurs in the Russian civil war and had survived all of Stalin's purges in the 1930s. He was in modern military parlance, crude, rude and ruthless. He is described as ill-mannered and indifferent to casualties, either his own or his opponents. Zhukov was one of Stalin's favorites and was going to stay that way, no matter what it took. . . . He was also a classic Russian cavalryman, which influenced his tactics.

The land around the primitive village of Nomonhan was classic empty steppe, rolling grasslands that had vibrated to the hoofbeats of conquering horsemen since time began. The river that flows northeast into Lake Buyr Nuur and then to Lake Hulun Ch'ih is wide enough to require bridges and to support a small river fishing industry. The border, as in many parts of Asia, is vague and unmarked, being adjusted periodically when some remote military commander feels the need to exercise his troops in order to prevent them from getting stale. In the late 1930s, the land and village of Nomonhan were claimed by both the People's Democratic Republic of Mongolia and by the Japanese-backed nation of Manchukuo. Both sides had patrolling horse-cavalry units that tested each other whenever they met. So far, it was business as usual, but the stakes were just about to be raised another whole order of magnitude.

This land is classic war-fighting land and Genghis Khan had swept through here, as had his almost legendary predecessors, the H'siung-Nu who drove the ancient Chinese south—out of their original lands—to the China Sea. Manchuria had once ruled China across these plains, forming the Manchu dynasty out of Jurchen horse raiders. Now the new Iron Cavalry would fight out one of history's hidden pivot points. The tank battle fought here would influence Japanese expansion in the Pacific and aid in the defense of Moscow. It would also help to facilitate American lend-lease shipments.

The Japanese commander of the force around Nomonhan, (Lieutenant General Komatsubara Michitaro, 23rd Division), ordered his cavalry patrols to "destroy completely" the enemy forces in the ill-defined area around Nomonhan. On 28 May 1939, the Manchukuoans were pushed back across the border by the 6th Mongolian Cavalry Division, supported by Russian armored cars. The Japanese response was several small-scale attacks to keep the Mongolians and Russians busy while they brought up reinforcements. Now both sides were upping the ante and bringing in tanks. As the months wore on toward the cruel Asian winter, platoons were replaced by companies, companies by battalions. By mid June, full regiments supported by tanks, artillery, and aircraft were conducting classic small-unit actions on the grassy, mosquito-infested plains.

Initially, the Japanese seemed to have the upper hand, as they had an efficient railway system in place, and their nearest railhead was at Halun Arshan only 50 miles from the Nomonhan area. The nearest Russian railhead was several hundred miles away at Chita. The Imperial Japanese Army (IJA), however, was primarily an infantry army and wasted its energy in small-scale actions against Russians who were dug in and building strength steadily. Worse, the Japanese tanks were being steadily attrited by camouflaged artillery and hidden Russian tanks that fired from ambush. By the end of July, the IJA was about out of tanks and was faced with the superior Russian BTs.

Faced with superior tanks, the Japanese resorted to "human bullet units." These desperados fought with the classic gasoline bomb, later to be known as the Molotov cocktail, and antitank mines on ten-foot poles. They would rush on a lone tank, try to break its tracks with the mines, and then throw gasoline on the vehicle. Once it had been stopped, swords and bayonets would be pushed into the vision slits in an attempt to kill the crewmen.

The BT series tank had only three men on board, a commander who also fired the gun, a loader, and a driver. There were no periscopes and vision was through slits in the armor. Knowing from their own tankers that the crew had to keep their faces close to the slits in order to have a decent field of view, it made sense that a long blade shoved suddenly through should do some damage. In addition, a weapon barrel could get into the slit and a few dozen pistol bullets ricochetting around the interior usually killed off whichever crewmembers survived the mine, bayonet, and gasoline attack.

The Russian methods were somewhat similar, but due to

the Vickers-type suspension of the OT series tanks, wire could be used against them. The Russians drove short pegs into the ground and then nailed piano wire to the tops of them. Infantry could dance around the wire with impunity, but the small roadwheels of the Japanese tanks sucked the wire in, where it wound up the tracks, wheels, and sprockets and cut the seals that protected the bearings. Once the tanks were immobilized, they were easy prey, unless they were protected by supporting infantry.

Many battles were determined by tank-infantry teams, the opposing infantry preventing their enemies from killing the tank, while the armored weapons drove the attackers to cover. One can easily imagine a wounded crew cooped up in an immobilized tank watching its infantry die one by one, knowing that when the last friendly soldier died, a gasoline bomb would land on the deck or a rifle muzzle would come through a vision slit. Man by man, tank by tank, the Japanese were losing. In the first few days of August 1939, after shipping in more tanks, they risked all on a push against the Russian positions. The Russians, however, had been busy and devious. They didn't have positions, they just had more tanks.

When General Zhukov drew the Nomonhan assignment, he'd proceeded to the Russian command center of Tamsag Bulag, roughly a hundred miles east of Nomonhan, and began a giant build up of men and equipment. Surprisingly, one of his first imports were record players, giant loudspeakers, and amplifiers. While tanks were being shipped and driven in from the railroad at Chita, over 400 miles away, the sounds of jackhammers and other construction equipment were played, giving the impression that the Russians were digging in for a determined defense!

What was actually happening was that construction equipment was upgrading the road to Chita, and tanks were coming down it at highway speeds with their tracks curled up on the back decks. Zhukov had commandeered everything that had an engine and was moving supplies for a huge force into place. Eventually he had 3,500 cargo trucks and 1,400 fuel tankers moving up and down that road.

On the actual battle line, Russian forces to the east of the river were very light, only enough to contain the Japanese probing attacks and to shield their engineers, who were preparing a typical Asian subterfuge. What the Japanese apparently had no knowledge of were the works of Sun Tsu and six other Chinese military authors. Their books were regarded as so dangerous by the Chinese emperors that their mere possession by unauthorized individuals was an automatic death sentence.

There were about two thousand years of military knowledge condensed in those books, and they are dangerous to this day. Genghis Khan went into a corrupt China almost by invitation and emerged as the greatest conqueror of his age, with Chinese advisors and Chinese engineers in his train. Zhukov had that knowledge, and it should be remembered that Mao Tse-tung was originally a Chinese librarian. Mao's book on guerrilla war is pure Sun-Tsu. Ho Chi Minh and Vo Nguyen Giap have also been exposed to that knowledge, and it is now taught at West Point. The Japanese were just about to be outgeneraled, outtanked, and outnumbered.

What Zhukov's engineers had been doing under cover of night and the loudspeakers was building bridges . . . underwater, where they could not be seen. That was one of the old tricks, of course, but the Russians could have picked it up from the British, who crossed rivers by building tank bridges out of drums of cement in World War I. The Japanese were expecting an attack to come from the only possible place, the bridges across the Halhaiin River. They had laid their defenses accordingly and had brought in 300 horse-drawn artillery pieces and a major force (for them) of 180 tanks. What actually happened was so bad that to this day it is absent from their public history books. Nomonhan is, however, studied very intently at the Japanese Officer's Academy, as an object lesson.

At dawn on 20 August 1939, ten days before the German attack on Poland, an army began to die. One hundred and fifty obsolete but still deadly Red Army fighters and bombers swept the Japanese airforce out of the sky by sheer numbers and bombed their supply dumps. Then 500 heavy artillery pieces, of which the Japanese had no knowledge, let go with everything they had, for an hour and a half.

When the planes had left, when the guns were silent, the land was full of tanks . . . 500 of them.

Against the unsuspecting 23rd Division, Zhukov had brought two infantry divisions, two motorized armored brigades, seven artillery regiments, and three cavalry divisions. Here at Nomonhan, was where Zhukov began to experiment with using horse cavalry instead of infantry alongside his tanks. Simply put, horses are faster than infantry in battle and can keep up with the tanks . . . for just long enough to flank an infantry formation.

Japanese intelligence was also slower than it should have been. A roving pilot had spotted a large concentration of tanks on 19 August, but this information was still being "evaluated." There was *no* battalion intelligence officer in their TO and any reports had to go up to regimental or even division headquarters for analysis. This was to prove fatal. The reason why the light screening, raiding cavalry force the Soviets had kept on the eastern bank of the Halhaiin River now became apparent. It had been to deny the Japanese knowledge of the bridge construction.

There had been eight of those underwater bridges, and during the night the BT-5 tanks had come cross-country at high speed on their wheels. Then, across the bridges, but still behind their own lines, they paired up and used their tow cables to pull the treads off their fenders and roll the tanks onto the steel tracks. Now they were ready for business, and with their infantry companions aboard, they rushed straight into the Japanese defenses. Russian-Mongol horse cavalry had also crossed the river the old-fashioned way, by swimming, and were trotting rapidly ahead, pacing the tanks and scouting the flanks. In rough country most tanks have to slow down to horse speed anyway, and the Russians had figured this out long before the battle. By the evening of the 21 August, the Japanese southern flank had been turned and the regiment that had anchored their northern flank was in serious trouble.

The code of Bushido had finally let the Japanese down, for time after time, they had broken both Communist Chinese and Nationalist Chinese with bayonet charges and cold steel. Bayonets, however, won't work on infantry who are riding on tanks and won't dismount and play fair. Worse, their own artillery was suddenly immobilized because it was horse drawn and the horses were dead. The Japanese had thought they were facing just another semimedieval Asian army, but they were being rudely jerked into the modern age.

Three-and-one-half hours of artillery "prepping" shattered the Japanese field fortifications and buried many of the soldiers in their own bunkers. The few field phonelines were cut by shell fire and the defenders couldn't even talk to their HQ or artillery. Effectively, the battle had become a series of small unit actions.

0900, hill 742, Japanese northern flank, Japanese Border Guard Regiment: Russian infantry progress was stopped by a Sergeant Matsushia's heavy machine gun fire, under direction of his Lieutenant, Takashima, and an unknown sergeant in a tree using a 50mm grenade thrower. Suddenly a Russian tank appeared and 47mm explosive shells terminated the little engagement. These light attacks were intended to force the Japanese to hold position while the tanks swept around them, and they worked. By 1600 Hasebe Riei, commander of the border guards, knew he was in trouble; his scouts had spotted up to 500 tanks streaming past his northern flank.

On 21 August, the guns opened up at 0800, firing at targets the previous day's probes had discovered. Further, the Russian tanks had radios and could call in their own artillery as needed. Japanese and Russians closed in the trenches with grenade and bayonet and the wiry Nipponese infantrymen proved more than a match for the larger Russians. By the end of the day though, more than half the border guards were casualties. During the afternoon of 22 August, men were beginning to go hysterical for lack of water.

By the 23rd, the border guards near Hill 742 at the little town of Fui, had been broken by tanks and flamethrowers. Gallant Haseve Riei had committed suicide rather than allow himself to be captured. Second Battalion, 28th Infantry Regiment, under Major Kajikawa Tomiji, would be next. And morale was falling. A medical officer asked, "What are our tanks and aircraft doing? I can't see the shape of a single friendly tank or plane."

By 1500 hours on the 24 August, 2/28 was out of ammunition, fighting hand to hand, and surrounded by "hundreds
of tanks." Then the Soviets pulled back to the security of
their tanks and the Russian artillery began to decimate the
surviving Japanese. Wounded men were bandaged, given
grenades, and told to hold their ground. Companies had
been ground down to platoon size but still they held. Their
field phones were out, of course, and runners were sent out,
but few returned. A messenger on foot in a land full of
prowler cavalry is no more than a target.

By 26 August, small parties of Japanese survivors were
exfiltrating their trapped units, only to find that those to
whom they had looked to for refuge were also trapped. Then
there was nothing but open steppe between the Russians
and the Japanese 23rd HQ Division at Nomonhan, and they
were quickly surrounded, trapped with no place to go, and
all their combat assets dead along the line of the Halhaiin
River. "Hold on," they were told by their next higher command the 6th (Kwangtung) Army, "a counteroffensive is
being planned."

Right . . . on 24 August, a foot infantry division, the 7th,
marched out to meet a tank force and died by battalions.
Cavalry scouts with radios on pack horses spotted them and
began to vector aircraft and tanks on to them. By 26 August,
the offensive was over and the slaughter began. Georgi Zhukov began to systematically dismantle the Japanese 23rd Division. First their remaining artillery assets were shot up and
ground down by tank tracks. By then, most Japanese units
were either low on food and water or completely out. They
were also running low on ammunition, and their central
command had no way of resupplying or reinforcing them.

Russian mobile units would seal off frantic Japanese battalions and then their artillery, drawn into place by tractors,
would drop a "column of fire" on the embattled unit until
it ceased to exist. By 31 August, the day before Hitler's
invasion of Poland, the Japanese 23rd Division and large
parts of their 7th Division had ceased to exist, not only as
military units, but as lives. Out of 60,000 Japanese soldiers
known to have been involved, over 45,000 were dead, not
just casualties, *dead.*

When a military unit suffers 10-percent casualties, it is considered badly hurt. At 15 percent it is withdrawn from the line. At Nomonhan, some IJA battalions were at 90 percent killed in action (KIA). Survivors were not sent to Japan, lest the word get out, and investigating officers were forbidden to speak of the debacle except to the highest level of government. The war diary of the 28th infantry reports on 16 September 1939, "We terminated our combat operations and are awaiting orders." . . . They were shipped to Guadalcanal to face American Marines.

Japan had finally been convinced that it could not win a land war against Russia, and this had a direct bearing on the conduct of the rest of the war. When Japanese Foreign Minister Yosuke Matsuoka went to Berlin to sign the Tripartite Act with Germany and Italy, he made a special trip to Moscow to sign a Neutrality Act with Stalin. On signing, Stalin gave the minister a large bear hug and said, "We are both Asiatics, Japan can now turn south." That was in March 1941, and it freed Japanese forces to focus on Burma, Malaysia, and the Philippines, among other places. Worse, that treaty also guaranteed the sanctity of Russia's Pacific deep-water ports, including Vladivostok.

The defeat at Nomonhan had another effect, this time on the Germans. With the signing of the mutual nonaggression pact, Zhukov could transfer 1,700 tanks, comprising eight full brigades, 1,500 aircraft, 15 rifle divisions, and three cavalry divisions out of Asia and apply them to the defense of Moscow. These were the seasoned troops that saved Moscow in November 1941, and Nomonhan was where General Zhukov learned how to handle the vast tank forces that wrecked Germany's plans for *Lebensraum.*

World War II could be said to have started at Nomonhan and came very close to ending there too. When the United States entered the conflict, we began to ship material to Russia on the lend-lease basis and that eventually included about 7,500 tanks. Some of them were M4A2 Shermans, and they were shipped to Tamsag—Zhukov's old base—and crewed up with Russians for the trip south to Korea. They faced everything from desert to kamikaze bombs.

A final irony of the Nomonhan situation is this. Fully half

the war supplies shipped to Russia under the lend-lease treaties, came up the Trans-Siberian Railway, whose eastern ter-
minus, Vladivostok, is *inside* the Sea of Japan. The U.S.
Fleet list for 1945 records fully one hundred cargo and warships as having been transferred to Russia before 7 December 1941. Those American ships were transferred to the
Russian flag with Russo-American crews, and they delivered
millions of tons of supplies, weaponry, and experts through
Japan's inner sea, with full Japanese knowledge. The Japanese were helpless to stop the traffic that was helping America's ally fight Japan's ally.

Why? The treaty guaranteed Russia full use of its only
warm-water Pacific port. And, if Japan had closed that port,
a Russian tank army with American Sherman tanks could
easily have knocked them out of China. . . . And if Russia
had jumped Japan before 1945, the closing of the port would
have cut the American supply line that was, for a time, all
that kept them in the war. This was one of history's classic
standoffs.

REFERENCE SOURCES

"Nomonhan, Prelude to World War II," Gregory L. Sam-
son, *Armor* magazine, May–June 1993.
Russia's Fighting Forces, Sergi N. Kournakof, International
Publishers.
Nomonhan, Japanese/Soviet Combat, Edward J. Drea, U.S.
Army Command & Staff College, Ft. Leavenworth,
Kansas.
Zhukov, William Spahr, Presidio Press.
The Red Army, Edited by B. H. Liddel Hart, Harcourt,
Brace.

CHAPTER 21

Matilda Goes to War

THE FOLLOWING STORIES COME FROM A VARIETY OF SOURCES, including a 1942 book, *Tanks Advance,* by Gordon Beckles Wilson as well as the *British Tank Journal* published by the Armor Museum at Bovington, England—they serve to focus the attention of history on a neglected period of World War II, the period between the invasion of Poland that was so quiet it was called the Sitzkrieg. In reality, Hitler was extremely busy, moving his tanks from his eastern to his western front. The success of the Panzers had intoxicated the German General Staff with the heady drink of victory and they were now ready to take on the whole world.

On the dawn of 13 May 1940, the "phony war" came to an end for the heavy tankers of the British Expeditionary Force (B.E.F.). Kevin O'Reilly sat anxiously in the driver's seat of a 26-ton Matilda tank waiting for orders to move out. Behind him and to his right sat his friend Ginger Jones in the gunner's box. They'd received the word three days previously, after weeks of being posted around a French farm, where they worked on their tanks and in spare hours helped the French get their crops planted. The Germans were attacking and the British heavy tanks were going into Belgium . . . all 15 of them.

The Matilda was what was called an infantry tank, designed to chug sedately along with the Tommies and blast out machine gun nests and other hard points. The tank was powered by a pair of 87 horsepower diesel engines coupled to a bull gear that fed the manual transmission. They were steered by a pair of brake levers that slowed the tracks when pulled. Top speed was just 15 miles per hour.

Their frontal armor was 80mm or just over three-inches thick, rather heavy for the times. There were four in the crew, a driver, gunner, tank commander, and a loader who also operated the radio. They were armed with a two-pounder (40mm) quick firing gun and a coaxial machine gun. Most crews had found a way to acquire, through fair means or foul, at least one more machine gun. In armor and armament they were better tanks than the Germans had at the time, but woefully slow. The German tanks sent against them could all reach 20 or 25 miles per hour, and the speed would tell. Oddly enough, both the French and British tanks were as good as the German vehicles, except in two critical factors, command and communications—this would lose the war for them.

Every German tank had a radio that connected it with HQ whereas only French company commanders had radios. While most of the British tanks had radios, their battle doctrine tied them to the speed of the infantry and that was fatal against the Panzers, whose infantry either rode aboard or in armored carriers alongside the tanks.

In the manner of all wars, the advance of the heavy tankers was hurry up and wait. First they were led through the nearest town like a herd of circus elephants and, like elephants, loaded on a train and sent to Belgium to be placed in front of the rapidly advancing Germans. The first combat order they received was to retreat to the southwest, back into France, to try and get past the German advance, which was in the process of encircling the immovable Maginot Line. Then came that fateful, gray, morbid dawn. Battles never seem to start on bright sunshiny days. The tank commander's voice sounded in his headset.

"Driver advance, speed ten, half left, direction 80 degrees," O'Reilly dutifully advanced his throttle, held back on the left lateral bar, and kept his eye on the compass until 80 degrees came under the guideline. The tank felt its way off the hard paved road out into a plowed field through a farmyard, breaking the fence and scattering geese and pigs to the winds, and then out into another freshly planted field. Ahead O'Reilly could see a woodline and wondered would there be Hornets or Ants ahead.

The British tanker's vocabulary calls enemy tanks "Hornets," antitank guns "Ants," and machine guns "Maggies." Enemy soldiers, as in all armies, usually acquire assorted unprintable generic names. O'Reilly got his answer very quickly. The ground ahead was full of Ants and the distant woodline flickered with muzzle flashes. In the turret, Jones held a pistol-grip-shaped lever in his right hand, controlling the power-operated turret as the TC's voice came into his headseat: "Two-pounder traverse right . . . steady . . . on . . . five hundred . . . Hornet! . . . *FIRE!*"

The 40mm cannon bucked in recoil and a shell casing clattered noisily out into the turret. Suddenly the tank shuddered and rang as if someone had given the hull a whopping great blow with a giant hammer. O'Reilly saw the steel plating in front of him suddenly glow like a car's cigarette lighter and then begin to fade down through orange to a dull purple. A wash of heat struck him, but he was too busy to feel it. His head was pressed to a rubber pad on the periscope and his hands were on the steering levers. He was alone in the hull, separated from the turret crew, and his job was to steer the tank clear of obstacles while looking for mines and enemy tanks. In the back of his mind though, one fact registered clearly. The Matilda's stout armor had been hit and shrugged off the blow. He suddenly felt a lot more confident in his mount. Through his periscope he could see British infantry coming, retreating stubbornly before the iron horde of German tanks. The questions in all the tankers' minds were: *Would they rally and hold a line? Would only fifteen Matilda's be enough?"*

More hits; solid steel 20mm projectiles hit and glanced off the armor as the turret rotated above him and the two-

pounder bucked out its shells as the gun found more hard
targets. The tank was killing enemy tanks and the design
called Matilda was well on its way to earning the nickname,
"Queen of the battlefield." The noise and clamor of the
battlefield began to slack off and the tankers could now see
that the Tommies, almost exhausted from days of retreating
alongside the French, had no more fight left in them. With
only a wave of thanks, the infantry kept on retreating.

The tankers, however, were still fresh, and having just
given the famed Panzers a good thrashing, went on alone
looking for trouble. They plunged into deserted country,
having gotten past the German vanguard. With the two diesels rumbling in the rear of the hull, the Matilda came out
of a wood, crossed yet another field, and approached a row
of houses. Breaking down the walls around a garden, it came
round a corner and out into a town's central square, which
was full of Germans, dozens of them . . . Jerry had been
caught with his pants down.

In a small village west of the French city of Arras, almost
on the same ground where tank first met tank, 22 years
earlier, the latest invader was taking his ease. Germans were
writing letters, eating plundered food, and drinking stolen
wine. Some were napping, some were pulling their boots off
and massaging tired feet. There were several Panzer Pzk-IIs
in the courtyard, and the tank crews were checking track
link pins, cleaning the 20mm guns, and checking lube levels.
They had heard another tank arriving, but so what? They
were a conquering army, were they not? The nearest enemy
tanks were . . . ?

Wham! Wham! Rrrrripp! The nosy Matilda suddenly became a marauder as Jones and the turret crew got off a fast
pair of 40mm armor-piercing shells and then turned to the
coaxial machine gun and began to rip up the town square.
Germans fell by the dozen even as two of the vaunted Panzers flamed up, gasoline fuel set on fire and ammo going off.
Down in the Matilda's hull, O'Reilly had the transmission in
reverse and his left lateral bar pulled back to his belt buckle.
The tank was turning under the turret, which Jones kept
turned to the square, raking it with belt after belt to keep
the German's heads down while the tank pulled the time-

honored maneuver known as "Getting the hell outa here!" With the gun tube facing over its back deck, the Matilda made its best speed back to the rallying point.

The stories of the few tank groups that wandered like lost knights-errant across the fields of northern France may never be completely told, but fragmentary accounts exist. They carried extra ammunition, lived off the land, and "requisitioned" fuel supplies from French civilians. A Captain Cary-Thomas had collected three cruiser tanks out of what was left of a company and put himself at the disposal of the local military commander east of Rouen, near the town of Courcelles on the Seine River. He had a cruiser MK-I, two cruiser MK-IIs, and General Heinz Guderian was coming straight at him with two Panzer divisions.

As may be inferred from the designation, "Cruiser," these tanks were designed to be quite fast in order to respond to panic calls on the battlefield. At 15 tons, they weighed 10 tons less than the Matilda and had double the horsepower. Their 340 horsepower engines were modified American liberty aircraft engines which could trace their mechanical lineage back to the previous war. They carried the same firepower as the Matilda, the 40mm gun and one machine gun, so what had been sacrificed to gain the speed? Armor protection. The cruisers had only 30mm, just over one inch of frontal armor, and the sides were just about thick enough to keep out rifle bullets.

At midnight on 8 June, Captain Cary-Thomas and his little troop were ordered to proceed to Courcelles and hold the bridge at all costs as the Germans were expected to force a crossing the next day. He got there at 0300, and the road was jammed with refugees fleeing the Germans—Farm carts, bicycles, trucks, French Army transportation. People on foot and people pushing handcarts, all fleeing ahead of the Panzers. Here is an account from one who was there, 2nd Lieutenant V.C.D. York, whose story appears in *Tanks Advance* by Gordon Wilson, who got it from a British military report.

We arrived at the bridgehead at about 2:45 A.M. and, after getting the tanks under cover from the air, Captain Cary-Thomas and myself went forward to see the

French officer in charge of the demolition party and
bridge defense. This officer was a lieutenant in the artillery who had under his command one 75mm field gun,
(later reinforced by another one of the same calibre),
one 47mm antitank gun and a battery of dual-purpose
light antiaircraft and antitank guns. The 75mm was dug
in extremely well on the bridge itself, covering the approaches to it from the northern bank, while the antitank gun enfiladed the bridge and its approaches from
an excellent position on the right of the bridge. The
A.A. battery was split in half, three guns being mounted
immediately to the right of the bridge and three more
situated about three-quarters of a mile back towards
Faillon in a field on the left of the road.

The French officer asked Captain Cary-Thomas to get
into a position from which he could cover the bridgehead and support the detachment there. We made our
way back to the tanks through the mass of refugees still
pouring over the river, and I took my tank forward to
a line of trees some 500 yards behind the bridge on the
right of the road, to cover and support the French
position.

The road from Gaillon to Courcelles was almost dead
straight, and there was little or no cover on either side,
with the exception of the two belts of trees in which we
had our positions. Some 400 yards in front of the forward belt of trees, a railway line ran parallel to the
river, and in front of this, a row of houses flanked the
road almost up to the river and on either side of the
bridge. It was in the last of these houses on the right
that the French officer had his H.Q.—

At 3:05 P.M. an enemy armored car pushed its way
boldly up to the bridgehead and was promptly put out
of action by the 75 on the bridge. A volunteer picket
of six artillerymen armed with rifles who had been
posted on the northern side of the bridge sent back a
message to say that they had seen some enemy tanks
advancing towards them. At 3:15 P.M. the bridge was
blown up and this group (their numbers now reduced
to four), volunteered to remain on the German side

until they could hold out no longer, when they would attempt to swim back to us across the Seine. This gallant little band was not seen again.

As soon as the bridge was blown up, the French officer in charge told us that, as far as he knew, the Germans had established some machine gun posts on the left and right of the bridge itself, both in Courcelles and on the wooded ridge above it. He told us that some infantry had swum across the river and were endeavoring to work round his flanks under cover of the factory buildings. This very gallant officer, armed only with his revolver, directed operations from a most exposed position on the riverbank throughout the action.

What had happened was that their one decrepit cruiser Mk-I, also known as an A-9, had broken down and converted itself into a stationary pillbox. The little taskforce now consisted of just two tanks, each of which took one side of the position, north and south of the bridge, under its protection. The bridge had been blown only in the spans and it would not take much engineer work to make it trafficable to the light tanks of the period. A Pz Kpfw II (Panzer Kampfwagen), for instance, weighed ten tons, and a Panzer III, only seven tons more. Lieutenant York continues:

The enemy infantry that got across to our side were by now around on each flank. They apparently did not expect us, for they were not making a great attempt to conceal themselves. Machine gun fire from the other tank quickly mopped them up. While this was going on, the tank had been moving off the road to the right and getting into a position by the French H.Q. As the nose of the tank swung to face the bridge, an enemy light tank was seen on the bridge. Its crew were dismounted and apparently making an inspection of the damage done to the culverts, etc., of the bridge. This tank was put out of action with one round of the 2-pounder. Immediately after dealing with this tank, we spotted another one (either medium or heavy), approaching the bridge from among the trees which lined the road.

Three 2-pounder shells hit it like a machine gun and the crew tried but failed to get out.

In the meantime, my tank had advanced up the road towards the edge of the break in the bridge and having got within fifty feet of it, been fired on by a heavy machine gun, which appeared to be in a position in a house on the left of the road across the break. The gunner silenced this with three bursts from his co-ax gun, and almost immediately afterwards another heavy machine gun opened up on Captain Cary-Thomas from the region of the flagpole of the ridge above. He replied to this with all three machine guns, and my tank reversed until it could also bring fire to bear on this target and supported him until the machine gun sheared a recoil pin and jammed. While the loader tried to repair this and improvise a pin, I ran into a field on the left of the bridge and endeavored to find a target. It was not long before we found one.

Moving from left to right across our front and apparently seeking cover in the trees that flanked the shore there appeared what was probably the other half of the enemy section of tanks—a medium, or heavy, and a light. The gunner took the big one first and hit it with five 2-pounder shells—no one got out of it. One more 2-pounder stopped the light tank and two more finished the job completely.

Again we were fired on by a machine gun from among the trees. As my co-ax was still out of action, I could only use the Q.F. gun and the first shell fell slightly left and minus. An anxious few minutes followed, for we got three shells in quick succession, which were too bulged to allow the breech to close. As the loader was getting rid of these, machine gun fire from our right rear made me look sharply round, and I saw that our scout car had come up from the rear and was supporting us with its Bren Gun. The gunner, who was a trooper in a cavalry regiment, was one of the worn-out men we had gathered around us that morning. Despite his condition, he kept the gun going all the time—raking the factory building in front and mopping up the remaining Germans on our side. A good round was now in the breech of the 2-pounder and this time the gunner was dead on. Three shells silenced the machine gun nest and three more demolished one side of the factory wall.

The enemy had now opened up on Captain Cary-Thomas with an H.E. mortar, but he put it out of action with a round of 2-pounder and then his hull guns settled the matter. We on the left were suddenly subjected to this kind of fire as well, but in addition, the Germans had got either a field gun or an infantry gun somewhere on the heights above us and were searching for us with that also. Running to and from the bridge to the far side of the field, we plastered the mortar and put it out of action. But during this shoot, the boggy ground caused the nearside track to run half off the sprocket so that it was travelling around a portion of the final drive box. The driver, by fine driving kept the tank going throughout the whole of the rest of the action.

The infantry gun was still shelling us, and so moving very slowly and cautiously, we went back towards the road. I told the gunner to put maximum range on his drum and to rake the top of the ridge with his 2-pounder. This he did, and with the seventh shot, that gun stopped firing, so we put another five shells into the same place, and as he did not open fire again, we ran straight back to the road in time to see Captain Cary-Thomas completely smothering another heavy machine gun nest, which had opened up on him. While he was doing this, I demolished the wall of a suspicious looking house in Courcelles which the French said held an antitank rifle. After this salvo, quite reigned and, down to the last of our ammunition, we withdrew.

This is classic tank small unit action, the tank acting as "battlefield bully" and pounding the stuffing out of the enemy. What is proved here is that man for man and tank for tank, the Allies were neither outgunned nor outclassed, nor were they outnumbered. The French alone, had more, and better tanks than the Germans. What they lacked was farsighted, electrified leaders to match the likes of Guderian and Rommel. While the tankers fought, a desperate retreat was being planned that would end at Dunkirk, but history has almost lost the other Dunkirk, where the last of the British tankers got their tanks out to fight another day. That story takes place at the battered port of Cherbourg. The iron cavalry had fought for almost three weeks after Dunkirk, delayed the Germans, and got quite a few of their tanks out.

REFERENCE SOURCES

Tanks Advance, Gordon Beckles, Wilson, Cassell, & Co. London.

Tank vs. Tank, Kenneth Macksey, Salem House.

Achtung-Panzer!, Guderian, Ballantine War Books.

Panzer Leader, Guderian, Ballantine War Books.

Papers in hand from the British Tank Museum, Bovington, England.

CHAPTER 22

Escape From Cherbourg

HISTORY SEEMS TO RECORD THAT THE EVACUATION OF DUN-kirk, during the last week of May 1940, was the end of the Allied expeditionary forces in France. However, an examination of several sources—including: *Panzer Leader* by Heinz Guderian, the Rommel Papers, and mentions in several British reports from the time—reveal an adventure. For almost three weeks, from the period of Dunkirk to the French surrender, there were varied British tank units darting desperately across northern France seeking to escape with their tanks. . . . Some of them made it.

As is well known, the period between the wars was filled with false starts, political infighting, and general malfeasance in most of what would later become the Allied armies. The British were no exception, and the blitzkrieg across Poland and France found them grossly unprepared but gallantly willing to go to war. The war preparations of their First (and only) Armored Division can serve as an example. The division consisted of two brigades, each supposed to be made up of three regiments, that had only recently been converted from horse to armored operations. Their horse-man's mind-set was to cost them dearly later on. Taking off

in a wild charge for adventure does no good if you are
running a prewar antique and your opponent has a Mk-
IV Panzer.

In the First Armored Division (AD), the Second Brigade
consisted of three regular cavalry regiments, the Queen's
Bays, the Ninth Royal Lancers, and the Tenth Royal Hussars. The Third Brigade consisted of three Royal Tank Regiments (RTRs), these were the Second, Third, and Fifth
Regiments. It was the so-called heavy brigade and operated
cruiser tanks, as opposed to the light machine gun armed
tanks of the cavalrymen.

The division's support group consisted of two infantry regiments, the Second Kings Royal Rifle Corps and the First
Rifle Brigade, both of battalion strength of around five hundred men. Due to interwar funding rollbacks, they had been
cut down to cadre size. There was also the 101st antiaircraft
and antitank artillery regiment. On paper it looked good,
reality was something else again. Each tank regiment held
ten scout cars and 52 tanks, or about the size of a later
American armored battalion. At the last minute before shipping, some bureaucratic genius decided that there should
not be heavy and light regiments, and it was decided to
"equalize" all the units.

The plan was for each of the heavy regiments to give up
half their cruiser tanks for light tanks of little fighting but
some reconnaissance value. As would be expected, each regiment immediately loaded up all its mechanical cripples to
foist off on another unsuspecting unit. No sooner would they
ship off their rambling wrecks when another convoy of tank
carriers would arrive with the sister units' junkers. This
meant that a lot of light tankers would have to suddenly
learn new tasks—with the Germans already on the march.
Worse, not all of the tanks had even been delivered. This
was the state of affairs on 10 May, when the Germans burst
out of the Ardennes—not supposed to be good tank country.

Tank country is *not* what some manual or staff officer says
is tank country. It is where a competent crew can force a
tank to go, and that means mountains, swamps, rice paddies,
and deserts as well as jungles, forests, and open fields. The
Germans had thoroughly learned this while the Allies had

not. Later on, though, the Germans would forget their own tricks, only to have American Shermans come out of impassable swamps and British Churchills climb tank-proof mountains right in their faces.

What happened was this: on 21 May, the British 3rd Royal Tank Regiment (RTR) had been sent to France, landing at Calais. On that same day, two British mobile columns had torn into the flank of the rapidly advancing 7th Panzer and SS Totenkopf divisions, giving General Erwin Rommel a good shaking up. The intent of 3rd RTR had been to eliminate the German bridgeheads over the Somme. They were placed under command of the French, who were somewhat deficient in leaders who understood armored warfare. As a result, mismanaged and sent in as rolling pillboxes, they were slaughtered and forced to join the general retreat to the sea. When the time for Dunkirk came however, the southernmost units, who had had some successes and attracted Rommel's unwelcome attention, were cut off from the beaches.

Hitler's mystifying "hold in place" order has never been satisfactorily explained, but there is one possibility, that he was trying to figure out just what to do about the remains of the British First Armored Division, which was still running around loose in northern France, and thoroughly destabilizing his invasion. From the point of view of military intelligence, all those engagements might have indicated many more tanks than were actually involved. A three-tank section *should* indicate the existence of a company in the area, which means at least a battalion.

Third Armored Brigade, under General Sir John Crocker, had been seriously mauled; out of its original 150 tanks, now had just 43 cruisers, 42 light tanks, and 7 Matildas which had been assembled from running wreckage. Crocker on 7 June had been ordered to halt German progress to the east of the Andelle River, south of the town of Sigy. Coming straight for him was Rommel, who had recently been given a shaking up by the British First Tank Brigade near Arras. He seemed to have recovered though, and Crocker's stand on the Andelle didn't last long.

Rommel, a keen student of our Civil War, was using Phil

Sheridan's "hit 'em and flank 'em" tactics. He simply pierced the British front and began to tear up their supply and control areas, forcing an immediate retreat. On the morning of 8 June, Crocker was forced to cut *behind* Rommel's lead Panzers in order to get across the Andelle. Crocker was almost captured when he led his last units into Elbeuf. Blowing the bridges slowed the Germans down but couldn't stop them. In the opinion of Lieutenant Colonel Raymond Briggs, a staffer in the British Expeditionary Force, the British commanders in northern France lacked "sufficient flair" to deal with the likes of Guderian and Rommel. In situations like this, things tend to come unglued rather easily.

One of the little bits of information that got lost in the shuffle—(remember this was the chaotic period *after* Dunkirk)—was that many of the German scouts were *horse* cavalry and could swim rivers without bridging. The German 6th Infantry Regiment was one of Rommel's Panzer Grenadier units, and its horse-mounted scouts were simply invisible to the British and French who thought they were fighting a fully mechanized war. That scouting squadron was commanded by Lieutenant von Boeselager, who would later show up in Russia . . . on horseback in the middle of a Panzer war. In France the horse scouts were skulking cross-country and easily keeping up with the speed of advance while the tanks stopped to fight.

A letter written by Crocker on 13 June reveals the British state of mind:

> Bro Bosche is having it all his own way. . . . One of the most ghastly sidelines on the business which I see a lot here is the miserable refugees. The whole population is on the move, roads crammed with every kind and condition of person and vehicle. I came up a long main road the other day, and for forty miles it was just packed. Lord knows where they are going—they don't—just like a herd of sheep.

Two days later, the 3rd Tank Brigade itself had been converted to mechanized refugees by the rumor that French capitulation was imminent. With just 29 tanks, 60 trucks, and 409 men remaining, Crocker and his tank crews drove like madmen for the sea—up the Cherbourg Peninsula, with Rommel on an almost parallel course trying to cut him off. This was one of the most exciting chases of the war.

The situation was, to use a modern term, fluid. On 25 May, with the Dunkirk evacuation well underway, 11 tanks were located—still in storage grease—at an Ordnance Depot at Rouen. They were all Matildas, five Mk-I infantry versions and six M-II's, but without guns; these had been shipped earlier and stored separately. Thus there ensued a frantic search for the armament. Finally, armed and ready, they were designated the Composite Army Tank Company and put under the command of a Captain Colan. There were, however, to be problems.

5 June 1940, 3:30 A.M.

Dearest Lu,

Today the second stage of the offensive begins, we shall be crossing the canal [the Somme is canalized at this point]. We've had plenty of time and so everything, as far as can be foreseen, is well prepared. I shall be observing the attack from well back in the rear. A fortnight, I hope, will see the war over on the mainland. Masses of post coming in every day. The whole world sending its congratulations. I've opened nowhere near all the letters yet. There hasn't been time.

Erwin [Rommel]

With Bock's Army Group led by Guderian and Rommel, there wasn't a lot of time left for the British Expeditionary Force. At this point, Guderian's force turned south and raced for the Swiss frontier to cut off that retreat for the remains of the French Army. Rommel continued his hectic pace westward, sometimes making up to 30 miles of conquest per day. By 7 June he was past Rouen, and it is worth noting that his horsemen, under von Boeslager were first across the Seine. On the afternoon of the following day, he pierced the Andelle line and split the segments of the Third Armored Brigade in two. German practice at that time was for the senior commander to take a given unit under his personal control to, as Rommel later stated, "force the pace."

What he did near the Andelle was to personally reconnoiter a crossing, after the British had blown the bridge at Argeuil. About 400 yards south of the little hamlet of Sigy, he found one and sent a half-company of panzers across. Very quickly it was found out that while the larger Panzer IIIs could take 3 feet of water, the small Panzer IIs would "drown" and had to be towed out of deep water and restarted. By then he received the welcome word that his scouts had caught the British rear elements and prevented the demolition of the bridges at Normanville. When von Boeslager brought the word to Rommel, he found the general up to his waist in water, personally rigging a tow rope to a drowned Tank.

At 20:00 hours on 8 June, the Germans came into contact with a British scratch-up force, probably Colan's Matildas, as nothing else was known to be in the area. Brushing aside that unit, the Germans went on through the night and were met by cheering villagers who thought they were the returning British. By now Rommel was in the historic valley of the Seine heading for a triumph; if he could reach Ebuelf and capture its two bridges, he'd be in Paris that day.

Their route was now as much cross-country as by road and when Rommel followed his lead battalion into Ebuelf, he must have just known that he'd made it. Unfortunately, it was 0100 hours, everybody was exhausted, and the Brits and a few French had filled the town with barricades—broken down tanks and antitank guns. Around 0330, the Brits had their most important assets across the Seine and one can almost hear a historic raspberry as the two bridges were blown right in the attackers' faces.

9 June, 1940

Dearest Lu:

Two glorious days in pursuit, first south, and then southwest. A roaring success, 45 miles yesterday.

10 June, 1940, 5 A.M.

We'll soon be at the sea between the Somme and the
Seine. I'm on the go the whole time. Our successes are
tremendous and it looks to me inevitable that the other
side will soon collapse.

We never imagined war in the west would be like
this. There's been no post from you for several days.

Erwin

After being thwarted at Elbuef, Rommel had to reverse
course and pull out of that long bend of the Seine River.
Reaching the coast at Les Petites Dalles, the Germans set
about consolidating the ground they had overrun and then
continued on down the coast: Fécamp, St. Leonard, Le
Havre—all fell to the Panzers like ripe plums. Their 88mm
and 100mm gun batteries, temporarily short of targets, began
to engage freighters and even small warships off the coast.
At every minor port, it seemed that there were roadblocks
and that the British were embarking small units of survivors.
What has generally escaped the history books is that there
were over 150,000 Brits left after Dunkirk—all fighting for
survival.

At this point Rommel began to suspect that there would
be a massive breakout at some major port, probably Cherbourg, and he began to make plans to thwart the escape.
By 12 June, he was taking the surrender of massive amounts
of troops and weaponry, mostly French, but quite a few
British also. The number of prisoners bagged at St. Valéry,
for instance, was 46,000 . . . including a round dozen French
and English generals.

By 16 June, the ruin of France was almost complete, and
Marshal Pétain was about to give up. When he did, the
British still in France would automatically be turned over to
the tender mercies of the Germans. Now there was to be
little of combat, only a motor race over a land full of refugees. The British, it should be remembered, were fleeing
across a foreign land with few or no parts and supplies,
whereas Rommel had a solid line of supply going straight
back to Germany along undamaged railroads. That the Brits

could keep going at all speaks well for their maintenance skills and for their tanks.

Fortunately, we have an eyewitness to the escape, an un-named British tank officer's diary. At the time we join him at Montigny, his squadron consisted of 12 scout cars, 18 light tanks, 5 Cruiser Is, and 14 Cruiser IIs—plus, of course, the usual attendant fitters and supply vehicles. They had apparently been quartered on the grounds of a French chateau for administrative purposes.

Sunday, June 16, 1940: The Brigade moved off at 11:00 hours and by 13:00 was harboured in the Chateau grounds. Here, late in the afternoon, four lorries, which had been fetched from Vire, brought us 1000 gallons of petrol and 1 & ½ days rations.

At about 20:00 hours, a warning order was received verbally from General Pétain that we should be required to withdraw a further fifty kilometers in a south-westerly direction, starting before dawn next day. Our situation was thus becoming serious. We knew our eventual march to, and reembarkation from Cherbourg was intended, and that French resistance was disintegrating. We were now faced with a further march, which would take us still further from Cherbourg, already 175 miles away. Our tanks were almost on their last legs, mechanically; all we had in the way of petrol, ammunition and supplies was what there was in our own transport column—enough to carry us 225 miles and feed us for 2 & ½ days. After that, no further supplies of any sort could be procured from British sources, as all other British troops were already embarked or well on their way.

With radio communications, the Brigade would have *had* to know about Dunkirk. That port, of course, did not have the crane facilities to load the tanks that would be needed in the desert—very soon. . . . Actually, most of the rescued tanks were used as trainers and this released the newly man-ufactured vehicles to the desert.

Our condition was, therefore, represented to General Marshal-Cornwall, who had established his H.Q. in Alençon, pointing out that, while we were prepared to carry out any orders we were given, our future action must be considered in the light of an administrative situation, and unless some proper arrangements were made for our maintenance, we should quickly become noneffective. At 22:00 hours, a reply was received from General Marshal-Cornwall: "You will proceed forthwith to Cherbourg via Domfront-Vire-St. Lo. My H.Q. moves to Avaranches. 10th French Army is withdrawing tonight, southwestwards.

At the same time, a liaison officer arrived from General Péteit, informing us that we were no longer under his command.

Monday, June 17: We commenced to move at midnight, halting near Domfront for two hours for breakfast. Here we met General Marshal-Cornwall, who was on his way to Avaranches, who said that the French Twelfth Corps, which had been up on the River Dives, east of Caen, was retiring southwest through Vire and Mortain and, in view of this, we must change our route to avoid being hopelessly blocked. Orders were given accordingly, and the march continued.

From now on, we began to meet heavy refugee and French military traffic. Mortain was blocked solid and it took over an hour to get through. Once we turned north at Bracey, conditions improved. We moved at wide intervals, at a steady pace, observing regular maintenance halts. Fitter's lorries brought up the rear of each squadron, and any tank which broke down was repaired and came on. Squadron commanders also traveled in the rear of their squadrons to make the decision whether a tank was beyond repair and must be abandoned.

The column halted under cover off the road, halfway between Villedieu and St. Leo. It was intended to have a good long halt there—for three hours—but news came through (on the wireless in a farmhouse where we happened to be getting some food and a wash) that the

French Government had asked for peace terms. In view
of this it was thought better to get on to Cherbourg
with the least possible delay. Since leaving Lovigny on
June 12, those squadrons had covered by road about
some 400 miles. . . . We marched into Cherbourg with
eleven scout cars, twelve light tanks and thirteen
Cruiser IIs. The rest, including the solitary cruiser I, had
succumbed to enemy action or mechanical breakdown.

And Rommel was right behind them, having covered 250
miles in one day, the longest single-day advance in military
history. He was burning a new trail against an enemy who
only wanted to escape to fight another day. And they were
both riding iron horses, not animals of flesh and blood. The
pace of war had picked up to an almost inhuman rate of
advance, and the old leaders would have to get out of the
way—their minds worked at 2.5 miles per hour, not 30.
Rommel's Panzers had arrived on the outskirts of Cherbourg on Tuesday, 18 June. Our British officer's log now
finishes this tale:

Tuesday, June 18: At embarkation H.Q. at the Casino,
it was learned that the tanks would be loaded during
the night or early in the morning. Also, only "key"
transport vehicles would be loaded. For example, special vehicles like machinery lorries, wireless trucks, etc.
All other transport was to be destroyed. The tanks were
therefore marched down to the docks at once and
parked ready for embarkation. All valuable stores were
loaded into two or three lorries and these, together with
the wireless van and ambulance were marched down
just after dawn. During the morning, amid scenes of
considerable confusion, embarkation started, the bulk
of the 52nd Division had already left. All tanks and
"key" vehicles were put on board and we sailed.
    Earlier, there were reports of the approach of the
enemy. An air raid occurred during the night but no
damage on shore was caused; a ship was sunk in the
harbour. The quayside and town presented a miserable
sight. Lorries were being burnt all over the place, am-

munition was exploding continuously and the area was covered by a pall of smoke. At 16:30 hours, we finally got on board the last ship to leave and cast off. Just before leaving, a German aircraft came over and dropped some bombs harmlessly in the harbour.

As we sailed through the harbour entrance, we saw the great cranes and docks being systematically blown up by naval parties landed from a destroyer. And as we sailed out to sea, German artillery (that was Rommel himself) was seen in action, apparently firing into the town from the high ground west of Cherbourg. . . . We arrived at Southampton about midnight.

The escape of the last of the British was covered by a barrage of naval fire from outside Rommel's reach, even had his artillery been able to keep up, which it had not. Much of the artillery of the German Army, even at that late date, was still horse drawn and even his truck-hauled guns were miles behind, not having been able to maintain the pace of a 200-mile pursuit.

These men, and some of the tanks, would meet again, in improbable places. When the Italian military adventure in Africa fizzled out, Rommel would be sent to shore them up. Some of the tanks lifted into ships at Cherbourg would be used as training tanks in England; some would make the long trip down the coast of Africa and round the Cape of Good Hope to be unloaded in Egypt. Some British tankers would form the core of the famed "Desert Rats" of the Eighth Army; some would go on to man American tanks in Burma against the Japanese.

It was to be a long war. So long that some of the tanks Rommel captured would eventually be shipped to Russia to be manned by Spanish volunteers. . . . And many of the budding petro-nations of Mesopotamia would start out with German hardware and German instructors. By this time, of course, France had surrendered and that caused worldwide shock effects due to the transfer of France's colonial empire to the Axis.

French Indochina, which includes Vietnam, was turned over to the Japanese, who used it as a springboard for the

conquest of Malaysia. They also allowed the Germans to
build a U-boat base at Penang, which made possible much
technological transfer from Germany to Japan. In North Africa, with the French forces in Algeria and Tunis neutralized,
Mussolini now felt emboldened to attack British Egypt.

REFERENCE SOURCES

Tanks Advance, Gordon Beckles, Wilson, Cassell, & Co.,
London.

The Rommel Papers, edited by J.F.C. Fuller, Ballantine
War Books.

Panzer Leader, Guderian, Ballantine War Books.

Papers in hand from the Tank Museum, Bovington,
England.

Tank vs. Tank, Kenneth Macksey, Salem House.

Tank War, Janus Piekalkiewicz, Blandford Press.

The Cavalry of World War II, Piekalkiewicz, Stein & Day.

CHAPTER 23

The Western Desert, 1940

THE LEAST STUDIED AND MOST MISUNDERSTOOD SEGMENT OF the war in the western desert in 1940 is its beginnings. These events go back to the last few months of World War I in Mesopotamia. There a group of Rolls Royce armored cars were influencing history and almost accidentally saving the lives of two British officers, one of whom would later become instrumental in the formation of a valuable desert tool.

Link by link, the chain that leads from the first armored cars to modern mechanized special operations was being forged. The crews of the Rolls armored cars and their Ford tenders learned to navigate like sailors; to always keep track of combustibles, such as fuel, food, and water; and to cross-train many of their men as mechanics. They learned to deal with aircraft, both friendly and hostile. Also, they learned some of the skills of combining mechanized with animal transport. . . . Skills that are valuable for small wars but are now in danger of being completely lost.

At Khan Baghdadi in Mesopotamia on 26 March 1918, an armored car unit, called a Light Armored Motor Battery (LAMB), directly assaulted Turkish positions while horsed cavalry cut around cross-country and ambushed the retreating Turks. Then the cavalry set off down the Aleppo road in pursuit, the cars traveling slowly to conserve fuel while the cavalry took the cross-country routes. In combat, many of the cavalry dismounted and fought as foot soldiers, keeping their mounts out of harm's way. At a town named Ānah, the commander of the 8th LAMB, a Captain Tod, was told that the fleeing Turks were holding two captured British officers.

The two were Major Percy Hobart of the British Sappers and his pilot, Colonel Tennant, who was commander of the Royal Flying Corps in Mesopotamia. They had been shot down during the battle for Khan Baghdadi and had been thought to have perished. Captain Tod was ordered to pursue to a distance of 100 miles if need be and was also promised aerial resupply if necessary. If he could hold a straight stretch of road, a bomber converted to carry cargo could bring him fuel and water.

The cars set off in hot pursuit and after only 32 miles caught up with Hobart, Tennant, and their "escort," which was just about to murder them. With the two officers rescued, Captain Tod took advantage of the leeway in his orders and made another 40-mile raid into the disorganized fleeing army. He bagged several high-ranking Turkish and German officers, along with their maps and documents. This episode had several far-reaching results. First the war in Mesopotamia came to a close a month earlier than in Europe, and the treaties that resulted secured Western access to gulf oil supplies. Second, Major Hobart transferred to the new armored corps and began surveying the desert. He would be the one who, 20 years later, would build the 7th Armored Division into the force that could battle Rommel. He would also be the genius behind the British special tanks, "Hobart's funnies," that so eased the storming of Hitler's *Festung Europa* in 1944. There were, however, lean times in between, and the desert warriors were on their own for two long, dry decades . . . just like special operations units today. When wars end, the bureaucrats take over and regulations rule—until it hits the fan again.

The time was not wasted though. A new era of war had begun, and the work of the desert rovers was just beginning, for these were the ones who surveyed that desert in Rolls armored cars and Model-T Fords with machine guns. These were the men who made the maps that would guide the "Desert Rats" of the Eighth Army, 25 years later, when they went head to head with the Afrika Korps.

While power politics turned Mesopotamia into Iraq, Persia into Iran (an ancient form of the word *Aryan*), and Trans-Jordan into the Kingdom of Jordan, expeditions were going out into the deserts, mapping and experimenting. Most of them, however, were either civilian or done on the cheap. The British Army was in an interwar period with its budget slashed to the bone. By the mid-1930s, though, desert motor trips of up to 6,000 miles were being made by a group set up by a Major Ralph Bagnold, who had been commissioned into the Royal Engineers in 1915. The cost of these expeditions averaged about one hundred British pounds per person, paid for by the men and a few women who either saw the need or were just out for adventure. This was at a time when five hundred pounds yearly was considered a good middle-class salary, although the Royal Geographical Society came through with periodic grants. Also, at this point, much of Britain's intelligence work was being funded by the family fortune of the Windsors; King George V has not received nearly his due in formal history.

Whatever their reasons, while officialdom had its head in the sand, these people were out mapping and inventing such things as the sun compass, the condensing radiator, sand channels, and variable tire pressure. They would also discover the advantages of the American 30 hundredweight (or ton-and-a-half) truck, whose light weight, ruggedness, and reliability was one of the first secret weapons of the war. When 1940 rolled around, the knowledge, the men, and the hardware would be there. During mid-1935 though, the Abyssinian crises finally convinced officialdom that there was a need for an increased military presence in Egypt, and a unit to be called the Matrûh Mobile Force was created (the troops involved immediately dubbed it the Matrûh Immobile Farce). It consisted of the 11th Hussars in World War I vintage Rolls armored cars with Crosly command cars. The light armored contingent was the Seventh Hussars in

Mk-II light tanks, and the 8th Hussars mounted in lorries (trucks). Gradually, though, it grew, under the command of Major General Percy Cleghorn Hobart, the same gentleman who was rescued by the Eighth LAMB north of Khan Baghdadi in 1918. After that adventure he was to have a long, honorable, but somewhat rocky career.

By mid-1939, the Matrûh Mobile Force had been redesginated Mobile Division Egypt and consisted of the 11th Hussars, still in their Rolls cars; the Light Armored Brigade, consisting of the Seventh and Eighth Hussars in light tanks; and a heavy armored brigade consisting of the First RTR in light tanks and the Sixth RTR in cruiser tanks. There was also a Pivot (support group) containing a battalion of infantry in trucks and the 3rd Royal Horse Artillery with both field guns and AT guns. One can also assume the usual support, medical, engineer, and transport units.

These support units were just about to become much more important in history than ever before, and most military "expert operators" were going to get caught short. . . . Even Rommel and Guderian would periodically run out of combustibles at inopportune times. What few of the initial general officers realized was that in mobile warfare one cannot simply trust to the usual civilian supply contractors. The combustibles have to be taken with the combat troops and have to be protected. Time and time again, this lesson would be taught, and time and time again ignored . . . until the tuition was charged in blood, burning tanks, and captured generals. The key to long-range operations is simplicity itself . . . *scouts* and *supplies*. Keep the feelers out and keep 'em rolling and shooting.

General Hobart worked all through 1938, constantly drilling his division into a crack unit, constantly conducting desert field exercises, and constantly experimenting with new formations. He has been called a hard taskmaster with an abrasive personality, one who did not suffer fools *at all*. The problem was that he could get away with grinding his subordinates into submission. This did not work, however, when he was disagreeable to the point of insult with his superiors when he thought they were wrong . . . which was apparently much of the time. In September 1939, with the war already started, Hobart was relieved by General Sir Archibald Wavell, Commander in Chief Middle East forces, and sent home. When the Dunkirk debacle occurred, and when the 7th RTR evacuated from Cherbourg shortly after, Winston Churchill sent out a call for the old soldier and found him serving as a lance corporal in a home guard unit!!!

On 10 June 1940, with France about to surrender, Benito Mussolini declared war on the Allies and prepared to launch an attack into Egypt's western Desert. The Brits were thoroughly outnumbered and on paper they were in serious trouble. General "Archie" Wavell had just 50,000 troops to cover the distance from Suez to Somaliland, whereas the Italians had 250,000 in Libya alone and another 200,000 in Somaliland.

The British Egyptian Division was quickly renamed the Seventh Armored Division and training was stepped up. Wavell also had the 4th Indian Division in Egypt, and a pair of independent infantry Brigades, one of which was on permanent internal police duty to deal with considerable anti-British sentiment among the populace. In Palestine, the Australian 6th Division was forming, but it would be some time until it was combat worthy. At sea, things were considerably worse.

Although Italy had only six modern battleships to England's seven, in almost every other type, they outnumbered the British Navy, which was already fighting U-boats and surface raiders. The Royal Navy, however, had an ace up its sleeve, in the form of two aircraft carriers, the *Illustrious* and the *Eagle,* which the Italians discounted because they had over 2,000 aircraft in their land bases. In theory, British forces in the Middle East were outnumbered and about to be cut off by a superior navy. Into this seeming debacle strode one of the most underrated generals of history, Lieutenant General Richard O'Connor.

General O'Connor was a slightly built sandy-haired Irishman who had fought as a light infantryman on the Italian front in World War I and won the Silver Valour Medal. He had also commanded light mobile operations against the Afghans on India's northwest frontier between the wars. He not only spoke Italian, he thoroughly understood his new enemies—their luxury-loving ways and their vulnerability to surprise actions. While the Italians were preparing for war, O'Connor launched his initial probes. Only hours after hearing Mussolini's declaration on 10 June, raiders were through the barbed wire barrier and harassing the Italian supply columns.

What had happened was that a light mechanized cavalry-style raiding unit had been born out of the interwar exploration groups. Major Ralph Bagnold quickly organized a scouting unit around the best vehicles he could find. Chevrolet one-ton open trucks, specially modified for desert work. The unit became known as the Long Range Desert Group or LRDG. Eventually the patrol forces reached a strength of 25 officers and 324 men, manning 110 vehicles, all armed with machine guns and equipped with radios and full desert gear. This unit would one day became the parent of the more famous Special Air Service or SAS.

The men were volunteers from the existing desert units, recruited into the LRDG for "unspecified but dangerous work" and selected by interview. There were New Zealand light cavalrymen ex-tankers, Australian armored car troopers, and British Yeomanry and Rhodesian volunteers. The trucks were fitted with overflow condensers for their radiators, sand channels, and two pairs of machine guns, one fore and one aft. For extra mobility they sported oversized tires, winches, and tow cables. They also carried a variety of personal automatic weapons and demolitions. The crews were four to six men per vehicle and the basic unit was the patrol, which usually consisted of two sections of five or six trucks each, totaling up to a dozen.

As might be expected, standard uniform regulations went by the board, as did shaving, in order to both live with the desert and conserve water. No military, it seems, has ever quite designed a uniform for desert comfort . . . especially when the troopers in question are constantly working on machinery that is operating in the second harshest environment in the world. Most of them on patrol looked like Arabs, and many of them spoke Arabic. The experienced men from the interwar years also had many Arabic friends among the populace. The local Arabs were mostly of the Senussi religious persuasion and hated the Italians, so the LRDG were actually mechanized guerrillas operating in a semi-friendly population.

One of the first things that they found out was that although Mussolini was eager for war, his generals and his army were not. General Italo Balboa's 250,000 troops were not moving anything but supply columns along the coast road, and the LRDG groups began to snap them up, appearing from out of the southern deserts where no military force was supposed to be. As the Italians began to feel the sting and to get a bit more ready for war, it was learned that the LRDG patrols were a bit underarmed when faced with Italian tank units, who were not quite as incompetent as conventional history paints them.

This was brought to the notice of Colonel "Jock" Campbell, who immediately proceeded to design mobile raiding columns built around a core of light tanks and "porteé cannons." While the British Mk-IVB light tank of the time wasn't much of a tank, it was relatively long ranged and fairly reliable. It had a three man crew and was armed with one .303 British light machine gun and an American .50 Browning heavy machine gun. The little tank weighed just five tons and had a front slope armor thickness of one-half inch. On one filling of gasoline, it could make 120 miles of good going. While good for patrol work and beating up supply convoys, these light tanks were not capable of taking on a *real* tank. This was why Campbell began to use porteés.

Although the Brits are usually given credit for this invention, reference to them keeps showing up in the Spanish civil war and even earlier in the Spanish Sahara against the Brothers Krim. Possibly either Franco or the French Foreign Legion built the first one. The reasoning is: an antitank cannon on its own wheels takes an awful battering when being towed across the desert, especially in rough going, but when put into combat, its sights may be off enough to cause misses. Why not, someone must have reasoned, simply lift the cannon into the bed of the towing vehicle and strap it down. The trick was an instant success, and has been used

ever since. The vehicle used was the American 15 hundredweight light lorry (Chevy three-quarters-ton pickup).

Not only does the gun save on wear and tear, but the
crew can get it into action quickly, as they are riding in the
back of the truck and the driver only has to turn away from
the intended target and stop. There is also the advantage of
being faced in the proper direction for a fast getaway. The
normal drill was for the porteés to get into an ambush position behind some means of concealment, such as a clump of
bush, a boulder field, or a low hill. The light tanks would
be completely out of sight until the 37mm cannons dealt
with the Italian tanks, and then they would swoop out of
cover and either capture or destroy the column.

More than one Italian column came back to Egypt under
new management. The high command of the Italian army
had expensive tastes and lived in comparative luxury with
mobile-traveling command vans; motorized kitchens, with
gourmet chefs; mobile wine cellars; and even busses converted into traveling bordellos. This allowed the LRDG and
the "Jock" columns to resupply with Italian fuel, gourmet
officers' rations, blankets, vintage, etc. . . . History makes
no mention of the fate of the motorized bordellos. The reason they could do this and simply appear on the Axis flanks
all during that campaign, was that they were not based in
the Nile Delta like the rest of the British Army. They were
based 200 miles south, in an isolated oasis whose place in
history goes back to the days of the Pharaohs.

Conventional military wisdom dictates that the flanks of
a defensive works should be hinged on "impassable terrain
features," like the shores of the Mediterranean Sea and the
Qattârra Depression, and that was where the Brits set their
MLR every time they retreated. Although there was a
chance of naval bombardment from the sea, there was supposedly no way that the southern Qattârra flank could be
turned. . . . Or was there?

Known to the Egyptian fellahin as Munkhafad el Qattârra,
this massive scar on the earth's surface looks like one of
the places where the gods of creation dumped their leftover
experiments. Perhaps it is a long-dried seabed from an earlier era. The land—just 60 miles from the shores of the Med-

iterranean Sea—drops off the Libyan plateau, some 866-feet high at the top down to 436-feet below sea level in some places. That is a one-quarter-mile drop into a hell of salt flats that will not support a camel's foot let alone wheels or tracks. The temperature at the bottom can reach 160 degrees Fahrenheit, and there are places where a human will slowly sink into salt quicksand.

There were, however, two barely passable routes through the depression, and the Brits knew about both of them due to the probing desert groups between the wars. They were the ancient caravan tracks through the sand-covered salt. The northern one, named the Kaneitra crossing, could just barely support the SAS's jeeps, and came out on the Nile Delta north of Cairo. The southern, Quara track, could support Bagnold's LRDG trucks, if they were careful, and it cut into the Giza/Bawîti road. The pass down into the depression near the Qâra oasis was rugged to say the least.

West of Qattârra is the tannish, rolling sand-dune sea of Calanscio, which is only marginally trafficable and which did not even show on the Italian maps, as they had never explored much to the south. Between the sand sea and the escarpment of Quattârra, though, two ancient caravan routes run south from the ports of Sollum and Matrûh, which figured in World War I and the escapades of the Duke of Westminster's Armored Car Squadron. One of these, the caravan trail south from Matrûh, was used over 2,300 years ago by Alexander of Macedon after he conquered Egypt, but before he went on his conquest of Persia.

Alexander, then at the height of his military prowess, wanted to be sure that he had a place in history equal to that of Hercules and Pericles, both of whose blood (he believed) flowed in his veins. Hearing of the fame of the Oraculary that was run by the priests of Ammon, he first went west from the Nile Delta where he had just laid the city plan of Alexandria. Turning south from Matrûh, he and his escort promptly got lost in the desert and, so legend goes, were guided to the nearest water by a pair of god-sent ravens. There, after descending a steep hillside, is the ancient oasis of Siwa. According to legend, Alexander may have received his inspiration at Siwa; there he also may have been

reburied after the sacking of his library at Alexandria. In
modern times it was the base of the LRDG and many of
the "Jock" Columns. Siwa, it turns out, can easily be
reached from Egypt. This was unknown to the Italians, and
for a long time, even to the Germans.

There is a road that leaves the Cairo/Giza area and, running southwestward, a traveler first climbs a steep track onto
the high desert until the dusty blue mountains of Baharīya
are seen. Just short of the small, mud hovels of the village
of Bawîti, the traveler can cut off straight west into the
valley of the oasis of El Bahrein. If his tires and vehicle can
take the rough gravel plain, he will eventually, after skating
the southern edge of the hell of Qattârra, come near the
first of the rolling dunes of Calanscio. A further turn to the
northwest, along the edge of a chain of low, desolate mountains will bring the traveler to Siwa, which is best described
by Sammy Rolls, who had come down from Matrūh in 1916:

As we rounded a low hill, the morning light revealed
an astonishing scene. Along a deep valley cut in the
yellow rocks, a mass of dark palm trees stretched for
mile upon mile to the eastward. This paradise of color
and shadow was the Siwa Oasis. We had not descended
far into the valley when a man dressed in a white robe
and waving a white flag was seen coming toward us. A
halt was called and the envoy beckoned to us to come
near. As he approached, he bowed continually and
placed his hand to his forehead. . . . Our new friend,
one of the notables of Siwa, had come to welcome us
to the place in the name of the local sheikhs and the
Egyptian Government.

We asked him to ride with us in one of the cars and
he mounted to a seat on a rifle box of one of them,
and there remained in motionless dignity. The road
soon entered between avenues of trees, heavily laden
with limes, figs, olives, pomegranates, oranges, lemons
and other fruits; and rows of date palms extended for
miles about us. We drove across quaint little wooden
bridges (with three ton cars) which spanned the irriga-

tion channels of cool clear water, and passed several lakes bordered by green fields and more orchards.

Presently we turned into a larger avenue which wound in curves through the groves to our right, and as we drove through the silent, peaceful scene, we began to meet a few of the peasants. These stared at our travelling forts with wide-opened eyes or turned to flee for their lives; but not one flicker of a smile or any change of expression crossed the face of our guide. His face remained like a mask as he made a sign with his hand. Right!—Left!—Straight on!—and he said nothing.

I was almost awed by the richness of the scene into which we had come. Many times on the blazing thirsty desert, I had wondered what these oases were like, and had supposed they were places where there were good wells and a few palm trees growing in the sand. But this was far beyond anything I had ever imagined. We had come in out of the wilderness into a veritable Garden of Eden.

We made another turn to the right and suddenly emerged from the trees into a wide expanse of open ground, lit by strong sunlight. And in the distance lay the queerest town I have ever seen. It resembled a very large and very ancient ruined castle of giants, in which a swarm of pygmies had made themselves dwellings in the crannies. . . . The castle like town was built of mud, and on its decayed walls, tier above tier of little wood and mud houses were stuck like swallows nests. Some of the crumbling mounds looked like huge ant-heaps, swarming with brown humans instead of ants.

Such was the oasis of Siwa, and like the 40 thieves of Ali Baba, Major Bagnold and his LRDG began to set up in the rock caves north of the lakes, fields, and groves. The Italians could not know that they were there, and from that base they began to quietly set up supply depots far out into the desert. Slowly, the desert was becoming a permeable flank whose mechanized denizens would bedevil first the Italians, then Rommel himself. The Germans, however, would take as easily to the desert as the Brits, and there would be fought one of the classic campaigns of history.

First, however, General O'Connor would have to set the stage and make up the rules under which the business of desert war would be done. What the British, Italians, and Germans were about to do was totally new to history. The battle in the western desert has been called many things, from a "sea-battle war" to "the last gentleman's war." Never again would the surgeons of both sides set up communal hospitals and take on all comers, and never again, until Desert Storm, would armored battlewagons roll to battle in naval formations. Nor would opposing generals compliment each other on promotions and exchange prisoners. Those days are gone forever.

The Italian offensive began badly, with Marshal Italo Balbo being shot down by his own antiaircraft gunners as his converted bomber came in to land at Tobruk. His replacement, Marshal Rodolfo Graziani, took his time to get set up and had to be violently prodded by Mussolini before he invaded Egypt. This gave the British time to get set for him, and the first thing they did was to send out their raiding columns. Three months into the North African War, the Brits had captured hundreds of tons of fuel, ammunition, and general supplies. They had cost the Italians over 3,000 casualties and only taken 150 of their own.

Marshal Graziani did *not* want to march until he built up "adequate supplies," which seemed to mean half of Italy. It was not until threatened with replacement that he began to move his troops. Finally, on 13 September 1940, he sent the entire Tenth Army, under General Berti, across the border into Egypt. Berti's nickname, "Sly Murderer," stemmed from his time in the Spanish civil war, and he still had his German liaison officer, Colonel Heinz Hegenreimer, with him. At dawn, 13 September, the Tenth Army rolled across the frontier at Fort Capuzzo, just north of Sollum.

The army consisted of two Italian corps, a Libyan colonial force and a motorized/armored group commanded by a General Maletti, which was intended to cover the desert flank against the probing British mechanized units. There were also several large Arab units of which both the Italians and their German advisors were suspicious. These were Senussi, whose leader was an ally of the British, having been won over during the interwar years.

Hegenreimer, having been given charge of reconnaissance, went forward to observe the battle, and inserted himself into the advancing Italio/Arab motorized force. What they found was a ruined Fort Sollum, and a skillfully conducted leapfrog withdrawal conducted by British desert troops. O'Connor's rear guard was trying to suck the Italian forces into headlong pursuit and into a trap laid on the western defenses of Matrūh. The idea was for the Italians to be stalled by the mines and wire of Matrūh and to be hit on the flanks by the Seventh Armored Division. Unfortunately, the motorized Italian advance guard was chained to its walking infantry which was coming up the coast road at 2 miles per hour.

Four days after the initial assault, the Italians were in Sidi Barâni and Maktila . . . consolidating and building a monument to the advance into Egypt. They were out of supplies and their tanks were battered due to abrasion on their tracks from the rocky terrain and sand in their unfiltered engines. From that point, the war degenerated into small-unit patrol actions that the Brits dominated. Events in the larger war, however, were now beginning to influence the situation.

The Germans had just about given up trying to beat England into submission with aerial bombardment. With no more threat of invasion, Churchill began to ship more equipment to North Africa, including a regiment of Matilda tanks whose crews were the experienced escapees from Cherbourg. The problem was that Franco in Spain was still an unknown quantity, though these reinforcements had to be shipped the long way around Africa and up the Red Sea to Egypt. Then Germany signed a treaty with Spain's hated enemy, Russia, and Franco promptly went neutral . . . with a slightly Axis tilt. Spain, for instance, was Japan's Caucasian connection to the Americas for spying.

Next, the aircraft carrier *Illustrious*, from far out in the Mediterranean—which Mussolini liked to call "*mare nostrum*"— launched all of its ancient biplane Fairey Swordfish torpedo bombers. Several hours later, around midnight 11–12 November, they came low and slow, flying just off the water into Taranto's harbor. Taranto is one of Italy's prime naval installations, right inside the instep of the bootheel that forms the south of Italy. At the time the majority of Italy's fleet was in port. The aerial torpedoes had been modified to run in shallow water and were lowered by cable from an altitude of only yards off the water. They did not plunge into the harbor bottom but ran hot and true into the battleships and cruisers of the Italian Navy, removing it from the war.

Suddenly, the whole balance of power in the Mediterranean had been altered. Now Graziani and the Germans would be starved of supplies, and North Africa would be vulnerable to British naval bombardment. There was one more consequence of this operation that normally slips through the cracks of history. The Japanese had observers there and that attack was studied—*very carefully*—by one Isoroku Yamamoto and his chief of operations Commander Minoru Genda for just over a year—until 7 December 1941. Japan, which had imperial ambitions on mainland China, had tried conclusions with the Russians and was blocked from further expansion northward by several Russian tank corps. They would have to forego Manchuria and Siberia and settle for their Greater East Asia Co-Prosperity Sphere.

This debacle, of course, gave Graziani and Mussolini even more pause, and Churchill got tired of waiting and ordered General Wavell to launch a spoiling attack to get the war underway. Wavell took the Seventh Armored Division, under General O'Moore Creagh, and the 4th Indian Division, under General Noel Beresford-Pierce, designated them the Western Desert Force and gave them to O'Connor and told him to get cracking. O'Connor, who had fought with the Italians in World War I, knew his new enemy. Having run light mechanized units in the Peshawar Brigade in India, he was fully aware of the Achilles' heel of motorized units— they burn supplies faster than anything except aircraft.

The Italians had built a small cluster of fortified camps in a staggered line running south from Sidi Barrâni, and O'Connor's plan was to stall off any planned Italian attack by taking those camps. From north to south, they were: Point 90, a triangular cluster called the Tummars, Nibeiwa,

Bir Tahr Awad, and Bir Enba. They were hinged on the desert escarpment that was supposed to be impassable—except that south of Sidi Barrâni in 1916, the Duke of Westminster's armored cars had made the traverse. Above the Italian line on the plateau were four more small forts, a triangle called the Sofafis, and a bit farther east, a lone encampment called Rabia. At the present time, a modern railroad slants upward through that gap and then across the escarpment to Sollum.

The Italians were slowly incorporating their defenses, but there were still unpatrolled gaps. Also, while the British did not know it yet, the Italian tank units were split up and parceled out with the infantry. Most of the camps were also protected by mines and wire, but as yet only on the British side. The Italians were starting to send out probes, so O'Connor knew he didn't have much time to lose. . . . He also didn't have much in the line of supplies forward yet. From the port of Alexandria, a paved road and a rail line both led westward to Mersa Matrûh. At this small port, which heretofore had been used only by sponge divers and the shippers who handled the produce from the Siwa Oasis, a giant base began to grow.

One of its most important assets was the heavy Matilda tanks of 7th RTR, which O'Connor kept under separate control from either the 7th or 4th divisions. O'Connor, a student of military history, studied both U. S. Grant and Stonewall Jackson and preferred to keep a heavy striking unit directly under his own control. Throughout this period, there were almost constant small-unit actions, and the British were learning the naked feeling that develops when the enemy has air superiority. The Regia Aeronautica had 191 modern fighters against which the Brits could loft only 48, of which 16 were colonial era biplanes and the rest Hawker Hurricanes. The Italians also had a bit over a hundred modern bombers. This imbalance caused the Brits to develop the habit of keeping their armor in small, easily hidden units. Still, they seemed to be winning most of the engagements.

The first British assault, Operation Compass, came on the night of 8–9 December 1940. One armored division, one infantry division, and a few loose brigades against an army of almost 300,000. The initial plan, accepted by Wavell, was for a five-day raid only, then for a short respite to see just what would develop. O'Connor, however, had been plotting and gathering supplies. He had figured out that once a situation broke loose, the force that had its combustibles within reach on trucks would inevitably win—it took even Rommel some time to get used to this.

O'Connor's initial plan was to cut through the gap between the Sofafis and Nibeiwa camps and fall upon the uncompleted defenses from the rear. In the meantime, a group called the Selby Force would assault the main garrison at Sidi Barrâni directly from the front. As a military plan, it was brash in the extreme. O'Connor would leave his assembly point, run his approach march through the enemy's main army, set his assault line behind enemy lines, and attack back toward his own assembly point. The reason he could do this is that like men such as Wellington and Rommel, he did his own commander's reconnaissance. One time, for instance, Brigadier A. L. Caunter, who was in command of forward forces, wrote:

> One night about three weeks after the Libyan campaign began, while I was commanding all our forward troops beyond the frontier wire, it was reported to me by the 11th Hussars that one of their forward patrols had reported that General O'Connor had, in his staff car, come on the patrol car from the west, i.e., from the enemy's direction. . . . I did *not* like this.

REFERENCE SOURCES—FOR WESTERN DESERT CHAPTERS

The Desert Generals, Correlli Barnett, Berkley Medallion.
The Foxes of the Desert, Paul Carell, Bantam Books.
Brazen Chariots, Robert Crisp, Ballantine War Series.
Panzer, Roger Edwards, Arms and Armor Press.
Tank Commanders, George Forty, Firebird Books.
Seize and Hold, Bryan Perrett, Arms and Armor Press.
Desert Warfare, Bryan Perrett, Patrick Stephens, Ltd.
Tank War, Janus Piekalkiewicz, Blandford Press.
Panzer Battles, von Mellenthin, Ballantine War Series.

CHAPTER 24

The Western Desert: O'Connor Strikes Back

GENERAL GRAZIANI, WITH ABOUT A FIVE-TO-ONE TROOP-strength advantage against the British, must have felt quite secure in his new bases at Sidi Barrâni and Mektiela. His line of forts stretched south to the almost impassable escarpment that guarded the high desert, and he had a group of camps at the top of that pass also. There were several problems with his army, and O'Connor meant to take advantage of them. Since Graziani wouldn't cooperate by falling into his trap at Mersa Matrûh, the British general took the trap to Graziani.

While the Italians were moving supplies to their new fort, the British were moving their own depots into the open desert. What O'Connor figured was that moving his entire force 60 miles in one dawn assault from Matrûh to Sidi Barrâni would have left him with some tanks broken down because of desert wear to the tracks. He would also have half-empty fuel tanks and tired crews after a long approach march in the dark. He was also short of most categories of supplies, including fuel—but his most pressing need was transport. The British simply did not have enough trucks to move everything they needed forward with the assault force, which had by now been considerably augmented.

With the Battle of Britain won, and negotiations for American equipment underway, Churchill could now release a few more regiments. Specifically, he sent the Third Hussars with light tanks, the Second RTR with A10 cruisers, and the Seventh RTR with 50 Matildas. The heavies were under a Colonel R. M. Jerram. There was a bit of troop and hardware juggling as the Second RTR and the Third Hussars swapped heavy for light battalions, giving each unit a good tactical mix of vehicles. Then the two regiments went into the Seventh Armored Division. The Seventh RTR was kept under Corps control and then handed over to O'Connor when needed.

As has been said many times, "genius makes the difficult seem easy." Graziani's mindset seems to have been formed in World War I, and he was building a line of redoubts that would eventually be connected by wire, mines, and trenches . . . if he was allowed the time to complete his projects. Warfare originally began as a two-dimensional enterprise and elevated itself into three dimensions with the advent of aircraft. But successful commanders have always known about the hidden dimension—time. O'Connor began using his few trucks to move a supply dump forward into the empty desert, into deep camouflage. Night after night, the trucks rolled into the empty desert, guided by LRDG teams in blacked-out vehicles. The race was between assault transport and defense engineering. The determining factor would be whether both sides felt the same sense of urgency.

Finally, on 2 November, General Archibald Wavell gave his OK to "a planned five-days raid," and then the British were to withdraw to Matrūh and see how the enemy reacted. That was not exactly what O'Connor wanted, but he figured that if he developed enough momentum, possibly the high command would let go of his leash. The fact that Egypt was brimming with Axis spies actually worked to O'Connor's advantage. In order to keep the secret from the spies, only a few high-ranking officers knew that "Operation Compass" was much more than a series of elaborate live-fire training exercises.

Training operation Number One would actually be a war march order. What Wavell did not know was that the tight group of officers in O'Connor's staff and in command of his two divisions were in cahoots. They wanted victory, not a reconnaissance in force, and the secrecy enforced in Cairo allowed them to plan a long-range battle like no other in history. Basically, they broke every rule in the book and pulled off an operation so audacious that even Rommel would copy it. What drove them to desperation were the supply and equipment shortages.

They had no tank transporters and the tanks had always to move on their own tracks, wearing the metal off them. O'Connor's staff solved that one by moving the repair shops on trucks and trailers to a magazine area out in the desert between the two opposing fortifications at Sidi Barrâni and Matrûh. For the first few days all his transport was devoted to establishing this base and keeping it hidden. For one day and one night, though, his striking force, just two divisions that were about to attack 200,000 men in forts, would lie out in the desert.

What O'Connor was banking on was the dearth of Italian ground patrols and the firepower of the Matildas, of which the enemy knew nothing. According to his calculations, even if discovered, all he would lose would be the element of surprise. Against air attack, he would depend on the excellent British 3.7-inch AA cannon, which would keep most aircraft at a distance while the ground forces dispersed . . . oddly enough, that gun was a larger and harder-hitting weapon than the famed German 88.

Midnight, 8/9 November, under a brilliant moon, there came a sound that the world never expected to hear again. The opening barrage of a British offensive. The ocean monitor *Terror,* with a pair of 15-inch battleship cannons and three "insect class" river gunboats, the *Aphis, Ladybird,* and *Gnat,* with 6.5-inch naval rifles opened up on Sidi Barrâni and Maktila from the sea. Based at Matrûh, they were known as "Force W." Farther inland in the desert, the naval gunfire was followed by the ancient 60-pounders of the Seventh Medium Artillery Regiment, whose guns had not fired in anger since 1918. What was happening to the garrison at

Nibeiwa could not have been found in their soldier's worst nightmares.

Two columns of tanks were rolling out of a desert assembly point between O'Connor's magazine area and the Italian line. The northern column was the 4th Indian Division with Jerram's Matildas. Their mission was to take the central and the northern camps and then swing up to Sidi Barrâni. The southern column was the Seventh Armored division, which was to screen off any interference by the southern camps and then break through to the coast and try to trap any escaping Italian units at Buq-buq.

The central Italian camp south of Sidi Barrâni was named Nibeiwa. It was roughly two square kilometers, mined and wired in front and protected by dry stone bunkers that were laid out with good fields of fire against approaching infantry. There was a dangerous gap between it and the next camp, named Enba, at the foot of the escarpment. South of Enba was yet another open door that led to the old drivable gorge through the cliffs and the camps on the high desert. O'Connor's basic tactical concepts were maneuver and surprise, and they were happening at the same time. First the artillery and naval bombardment had shocked the enemy, and then with the tanks already on the move, fighters and bombers began to fly low over Nibeiwa, masking the sound of the tank's engines and tracks with their engines, a trick that had its roots in World War I.

As the Italians were waking up in shock and their tankers were getting their engines running, the Matildas swept through the Nibeiwa/Enba gap and around to the northeast corner of the camp. Aerial photos had shown that all traffic seemed to be entering at that point and there had been no observation of any trick routes. It was a good enough gamble that the minefields were, as yet, only on the British side. The 4/7th Rajput Artillery Regiment from the Fourth Indian Division began to bombard the camp with 25 pounders as the Matildas of Seventh RTR hit the back door. Only when the rumble/clatter of approaching tanks was heard in the *middle* of the Italian camp did they realize that they had been breached.

The whole encampment began to swarm as some Italians

fought, some surrendered, and some ran wild in shock. Yet another army was facing Tank *Terror*. General Maletti, whose armored force was mixing it up with the British tanks, came out of his dugout in his pajamas with a Beretta machine pistol in his hand, shooting at anything that moved. Unfortunately, what was moving was a Matilda and at least one report has the general taking a main cannon round in the chest.

The dawn of 8 September came out of the east . . . the east gate of Hades. A Squadron, Seventh RTR, commanded by Major Henry Rew, led the attack through the suddenly opened western gate. The fact that Maletti's lone battalion of M11/39 tanks was laagered up just inside the gate only served to concentrate the targets. Tankers were caught getting out of their blankets, servicing their mounts, getting breakfast, and even in the latrines by the roaring Matildas. The surprise had been complete and a battalion died that morning while the seemingly invincible Matildas waddled through the perimeter toward the Italian artillery park. Gun crew after gun crew fought in the manner of artillerymen the world over, alongside their guns until killed. Bravery, even against hopeless odds, seems to transcend all national boundaries.

More than one attack has died among the guns, but not here, not with hand-layed guns fighting against powered turrets. As the guns, one by one, were silenced, the disheartened infantry began surrendering—and then things got worse. To the rumble of engines, the clink of tracks, the thumping of cannons, and the rattle of machine guns was added another hideous sound. The soul-searing skirl of the pipes. B Squadron, Seventh RTR was leading the Second Cameron Highlanders and the 1/6 Rajputana rifles on a sweep around the camp's inner defenses. Even against this, the Italians fought back and history records plenty of bayonet work in the trenches.

By 1000 hours it was over, Nibeiwa had produced 4,000 captives and 35 repairable medium tanks for the British. Several British tanks had broken tracks due to mines, but the tankers casualties only amounted to two killed and six wounded. Major Rew had been killed when he stuck his

head out of his cupola at the wrong time, but this is known
in the tank force as an occupational hazard. Colonel Jerram
appointed a new commander for A Squadron, reshuffled his
tanks, left nine, including the cripples at Nibeiwa, and re-
joined the attack.

A POW control force was peeled off from the 4th Indians,
and the British main force left them to garrison the fort
temporarily while the supply element from the desert base
began a systematic plundering. Italian rations would taste as
good to English palates as to Italians. It was quickly found,
however, that there was a radical difference between what
Italian officers were fed and the much simpler rations given
to the enlisted men. Much of what they gained was far more
important than food, tentage, and blankets, as O'Connor
had two overriding priorities . . . fuel and transport trucks.
After Nibeiwa was secured, the raiding force, with Seventh
RTR's heavies in the lead, swung north toward the group
of camps named the Tummars.

The Seventh Armored Division, after clearing the Enba
gap, peeled off several elements. The Third and Eighth Hus-
sars in light tanks and Rolls armored cars, along with the
First RTR in Cruisers, covered the passage down from the
Sofafis camps on top of the escarpment, while the division's
Seventh and Fourth brigades went on to Buq-buq and the
coastal road. The road and the pipeline that supplied Sidi
Barrâni were to be cut, isolating the base.

In the north, the 16th British Brigade and the Fourth
Royal House Artillery (RHA), named Selby Force after its
commander, Brigadier Selby, moved into Maktila on the
coast. Unfortunately, they were temporarily blinded by a
sandstorm that allowed much of the Italian garrison to escape to Sidi Barrâni. They would be taken care of the next
day, which in the words of one historian, Correlli Barnett,
was a "considerably more fluid situation than the morning
of the ninth."

In the litter of battle—blowing paper, crumpled corpses,
smouldering tanks, scattered weapons, circling scavengers,
drifting smoke—the victors of the first day of Operation
Compass settled down. Tracks were tightened, lube levels
were topped off, and the all-important road wheel bearings

checked and greased. Captured food was cooked and night watches set. No one knew what the morrow would bring: victory? possibly; death? probably. Late into the night, ammunition handlers stepped over grumbling tankers, restoking their "steeds" with cannon shells and machine gun belts.

From several reports at that time, this story is assembled:

A squadron of Matildas, in numbers about equivalent to an American tank company, is laagered in a rough circle about a place distinguished only by a set of coordinates on a map. They have had action and expect more. The troopers are already hard-bitten from Normandy and the first few weeks of this campaign. They work on their mounts and get what sleep they can. They have found that they have two enemies, the Italians and the sand.

With dawn only a pale streak in the eastern sky, the troopers are up and stirring about. The last of the night watch rather than trying to get a few winks begins to wake the others. Some men wake easily, springing alert, others need more attention. There is a leathery, rattling sound as boots are checked for small, stinging tenants. The platoon officer, knowing that his sergeants will attend to matters, takes a hooded flashlight and a compass and makes off toward where the HQ was last night. There are no features in the black desert, and he has to navigate by compass inside his own perimeter.

The nightwatch, having no further duties, starts up the small gasoline stove and begins to heat water for the inevitable tea. As the driver/mechanics come awake, they patiently check the oil and water levels in the Matilda's two diesel engines. Then, not trusting the gauges, they poke a stick in the fuel tanks to measure what is supposed to be in there. A Matilda's fuel equation is simplicity itself. Each gallon of fuel will carry the tank one mile. Satisfied, the drivers drop into their seats and begin to run the engines up while the rest of the crew start to check the tracks and stow gear. There is a feeling of action in the air.

By now, mugs of hot tea are passed around and grate-

ful hands are wrapped around them, as the desert night
is almighty cold. The crunch of footsteps announces the
arrival of their officer, head bent over his compass, clip-
board full of notes for the day's operations. He grabs
his cuppa, which has enough sugar and probably a tot
of something stronger, to get his heart started and ducks
under a tarp strung from his tank's fender.

He sets his acetate map case against the suspension
skirting, and by flashlight, he gives the other crews a
hurried description of the day's work. The tank commanders use grease pencils or children's crayons to
transfer his battle plans to their own map covers, while
the drivers strain their ears for the dreaded word
"minefield." Then the tarps are struck and their bedding is shaken clear of sand, rolled up, and lashed to
the turret sides or hull fenders. The little troop is ready.
Wheeling out of its part of the night laager, they take
a compass heading and roll toward a crest, toward
enemy tanks with the sunrise behind them. The sun will
be in the enemy's eyes, but the English tankers will be
silhouetted against it in Italian sights.

Stopping carefully just behind a crest of land, they
see dust trails and armored vehicles coming rapidly
toward them. The TCs pour their eyes into their
binoculars. . . . What is it, friend or foe? It is a troop
of British armored scout cars, the 11th Hussars in their
ancient Rolls Royces, coming like the very devil with
enemy tanks behind them. Suddenly the cars are here—
then through and nothing but enemy to the front. The
three Matildas roll steadily forward and over the
crest. . . . At 15 miles per hour, one cannot dash gallantly into battle. The squadron commander transmits
a quick contact report over the radio and then gets
down to the business at hand. Enemy tanks. This can
be serious because it has been learned that while the
37mm gun of an M11 cannot break the front of a Matilda, the newer Italian M13 with its 47mm gun can, if
close enough, get through, and it could easily break a
track. This tank, if well handled must be respected.

His head is half out of the turret as he orders, "Driver

steady on course. Gunner, action front tank. M11, looks like." The gunner swings his sights and the loader flips the breech safety off. They must throw enemy gunners off. "Driver right," and the tank obediently swerves. "Driver left, now steady; Gunner, *Hornet*, two-pounder, traverse right, traverse right, range five hundred." With a whine of motors, the turret swings and the gunner says, "Identified, sighting." The turret was laid by power, now he fine tunes the sights with hand controls. He cannot now afford any wild moves by the driver. The tank commander reaches for his binoculars again and commands, a bit nervously, "Driver steeaddy . . . Gunner *fire*," and a flash of fire bellows out of the muzzle into the not quite daylight.

An empty shell casing is bucked out of the 40mm and a reek of cordite powder fills the turret. "*Hit*," yells the TC. "By god, we've knocked a track off the bugger." "Loaded," shouts the loader and again the gun bucks in recoil. The first shot had sent suspension parts and tracks splaying across the desert while roadwheels roll from the Italian hull toward the horizon. The second shot plunges into the hull and black smoke begins to pour out. *Clang!!* Someone has the Matilda in its sights, sparks fly from the side of the turret as their ears ring. Automatically now, the driver does something violent, ducking the incoming shells.

"Driver, now steady, two-pounder, left, left, *Tank!!* range 200, fire," is the command and again the turret is filled with the stink of gunpowder. The shot is short and wide, incoming shots whizz past. "*Tank*, now two hundred fifty, fire!" The gunner spins his range wheel, elevating the gun, and fires again. The enemy tank is hit, staggers, rises against a slope, and another tank holes it in the belly. Smoke belches from its hatches and two of its crew jump frantically from the doomed vehicle, dragging another, to crouch in a hole. *Ka-wham!* A jolting crash and the tank begins to veer, the right track is broken by another shell, but their wingman terminates that menace.

"Driver, *stop*," yells the TC in frantic haste, and the

driver obediently pulls back both lateral bars, locking the sprockets . . . only a few feet before rolling completely off the track. Behind the tank, looking for all the world like a shed snakeskin, lies one of their tracks. Anxiously they look around, but the battle has left them. Now it is repair time. With no infantry to secure their flanks, the little four-man crew are on their own in the vastness of a desert morning. The gunner stays on watch in the turret while the other three including the sergeant tank commander, drop to the ground and dig out the tool kit. A newly captured Beretta 9mm carbine rests across the turret alongside a pair of binoculars. The men all wear Webley revolvers in shoulder holsters as they work.

One trackplate is destroyed and the pins are out of two others. Out come hammers, wrenches and files and soon another plate is fitted, two more pins installed and the crew is manhandling the heavy steel track back onto the rollers. Up in the turret, the gunner, binoculars in one hand, is relaying the actions of the rest of the section to his mates . . . They are having a high old time in the Italian camp.

The term *knocked out* means to a tanker exactly what it means to a prizefighter. Time after time, this would be repeated throughout the desert war. A tank with a turret jammed by shell splinters, a track broken, or even a hull penetrated and set on fire is *not* destroyed. Splinters can be hammered loose, tracks repaired, and fires put out. A half-crewed limping tank is still lethal, and many a tanker has played dead only to blow a too curious enemy to Fiddler's Green. More than one tank has been towed home with blood dripping from the belly hatch, only to be hosed out and sent into battle with one experienced tanker, two cooks, and a clerk as crew. . . . During TET in 1968 we even nabbed airmen to crew the tanks.

Next morning, Sidi Barrâni was to be attacked but the situation was fluid. The English translation of that time-honored military term is "We don't know just what the hell is going on around here." The attack was to be led by the

Seventh RTR and the British 16th Brigade. The latter moved out too early and was immediately pinned down by Italian artillery, losing 250 casualties. Colonel Jerram was riding his own command tank and going along with a newly created composite squadron under a Major Hawthorn: most of the Seventh RTR was spread out from the base of the escarpment to Sidi Barrâni doing guard duty, licking its wounds, and generally getting itself back together.

With his infantry pinned down, Jerram, an ex-cavalryman like so many other tankers, charged straight into the artillery fire for *4,000 yards* . . . longer than the famed charge of the Light Brigade at Balaklava. Once in among the guns, the tanks went on an hour-long rampage, destroying seven gun batteries by blowing them up with cannon fire and crushing them with the grinding tracks. By 0930 on 10 December, he had ripped a huge hole in the defenses of Sidi Barrâni. Although tanks can destroy a position, only infantry on the ground can hold it—so Jerram picked up a few prisoners and then returned to the start line to rally with his infantry.

A sandstorm promptly smothered the operation. While huddling in the lee of their tanks, the tankers replanned the attack, as the Italians had been moving around. The First Libyan Division had retreated from Maktila and was trapped on the road between it and Sidi Barrâni. Selby Force and Sixth RTR were fighting against the First Libyan, keeping them out of the latter city. Since Jerram had already made a nice open hole in the defenses of the city, he was elected to lead the 16th Brigade, now reinforced by the Highlanders and the Rajputna Rifles, back into the gap. This resulted in the capture of a further 2,500 prisoners and a hundred guns.

By the evening of the 11th, Graziani, whose base was in Cyrene, 300 miles from the frontlines, radioed a panic-stricken message to Rome, indicating a need to relocate suddenly to Tripoli. Mussolini, of course, refused permission and the debacle had to continue. O'Connor, commanding his troops from the front, had won a brilliant victory over a much larger enemy and was contemplating further advances when fate dealt him a crushing blow.

On the night of 11 December, a message was received in the headquarters of a victorious O'Connor that would have

crushed a lesser man. He was to lose the Fourth Indian
Division to General Sir Alan Cunningham in East Africa
for an attack on the Italians in Ethiopia. Wavell did, however, promise to bring the desert force back to strength by
shipping the 6th Australians from their training ground in
Palestine. This left O'Connor in a peculiar situation: There
was not enough transport in his command to move his remaining troops forward and at the same time get the 4th
Indian back to the railhead at Mersa Matrūh.

The Italian POWs knowing that survival depended on an
orderly withdrawal (transportation back to Egypt and the
necessary supplies of food and medicine) were already using
their own trucks and O'Connor simply bent the rules again.
He sent the 4th Indian Division back to Matrūh on captured
trucks with captured drivers . . . and went on with his war.
He now had only two brigades, the Seventh Armored Division and the 16th British Brigade.

O'Connor's use of forward supplies, an efficient radio net,
and his command-from-the-front style had allowed two divisions and Selby's Infantry brigade to smash two Italian
Corps, take 37,000 prisoners, capture four generals, 73 tanks,
and 237 guns—all in three days. Now, with his force almost
halved and outnumbered by his prisoners, what could he
do? On 12 November, the Seventh Division split in two.
The Fourth Armored Brigade was sent westward along the
top of the escarpment to come down on Sollum through
Halfaya Pass. The Seventh Brigade was sent up to the coast
to intercept the Italian 64th Division, which was fleeing
along the coast road with Selby snapping at their heels.
There were, however, problems. Although the Italian high
command was soft and luxury loving, its soldiers and company officers could fight.

Brigadier Caunter ordered his Seventh Brigade to launch
a hook out into the desert. The Italian 64th Division was
moving fast on the coast road, using both lanes as a west-
bound escape route. Convoy discipline, always a difficult
military operation, was bad, and the inevitable accordion
effect slowed them down to a crawl. The Seventh Brigade,
moving much faster across the open desert, came upon them,
but the hook had fallen short. The brigade's lead regiment,

the Third Hussars, struck the coast road behind the Italians, turned westward, and sent its scout cars out in a fan. When they caught up to the Italians, someone of competence had set up an artillery trap behind a row of dunes—and tanks began to die.

The Hussars immediately launched an assault with their light tanks, which broke through the thin sand covering of a salt swamp and began to get mired in. The Italians, now firing over open sights, began to blow the light tanks to scrap. Then a battery of Fourth Royal Horse Artillery's 40mm Portees swung into position on the desert flank while the Third Hussar's cruiser squadron and all of the Eighth Hussar's tanks began a wider flank. Italian motorcycle scouts spotted the maneuver and the gun crews began to swing their cannons. Then someone got a shot into their central ammo dump, which, being a cluster of hastily parked trucks, had not yet been dispersed to gun positions.

The resulting explosion apparently stunned anyone not under armor, and when the trash stopped falling out of the sky, the tanks were again in among the guns. This action took place just short of the city of Buq-buq, and before the dust properly settled, the British were off again, with a solid stream of prisoners flowing east behind them. The Italians used their own trucks and organized their own convoys under their own officers and voluntarily drove unescorted to Egypt. Meanwhile the surviving Italian combat units stretched westward along the coast road.

At sea, the ancient warships of Force W were rendering yeoman service, shelling fleeing units on the coast road and carrying hundreds of tons of supplies up from Mersa Matrūh. *Aphis,* never missing an opportunity to bug the Italians, steamed into Bardia harbor, north of the border at Salum, and sank three freighters, firing at point blank range with her six-inch naval rifles. *Ladybird* and *Gnat,* working close inshore, ferried water, replacements, and supplies forward and took prisoners back. They also acted as spotters for *Terror,* which kept her deep-draught hull farther out to sea. Whenever the fleeing enemy clumped up into a tempting target, the radios sang and those awesome 15-inch guns would each throw their ton of steel and explosives into the Italians.

Bardia, like Tobruk, was fast becoming a fortress that would be difficult to take. Inside an 18-mile belt of ditches, wire, and mines were 45,000 men with a generating station, water desalinating plant, adequate supplies, and more than adequate weaponry. There were over 100 tanks and 400 guns in there as well as two units that were fresh and had never been engaged, the First and Second Blackshirt Divisions. There were also the battered remains of the 62nd, 63rd, and 64th divisions. In command was General "Electric Whiskers" Bergonzoli whose trademark red beard was shot with gray. The old warrior was something of an anomaly among Italian officers. A veteran of both World War I and the Spanish civil war, he preferred to spend his campaigns with his men instead of in a plush headquarters. His mobile HQ (as will be seen later) was civilized enough for any taste, and his tentage was stocked like that of a desert Bedouin.

The loss of the Fourth Indian Division cost O'Connor the strength he needed for a siege. But with the arrival of the Sixth Australians, under General Iven Mackay, and with the addition of three ancient battleships—*Barham, Valiant,* and *Warspite*—and their screening destroyers, he calculated that he had enough firepower and manpower. After a week of practice, on the morning of 3 January 1941, the division went in. Outside the wire, all night long, tanks had been circling out of sight, running around with their mufflers removed, trying to make sounds like a much larger force.

This was probably done with light tanks or cruisers as the initial 50 Matildas were now down to just 23 runners. They'd only lost one in combat, the others were down for engine and track wear and tear. At 0500 hours, 123 guns opened up on selected targets in Bardia, mostly as a diversion. The actual assault was going to be done the old fashioned way . . . by hand.

On a morning so cold that the Australians were wearing their greatcoats, the infantry came out of the morning mist and rushed three machine gun posts in the wire. Once these were taken, three small groups of sappers quickly slipped through the wire and one party began throwing down the sides of the antitank ditches by hand and shovel. Another party of assault engineer specialists began to hand probe for mines, and they cut their way through some of the staked-down barbed wire with Italian wire cutters captured at Sidi Razegh. A third group carefully slid the sections of Bangalore torpedoes under the inner belt of wire. One after another the four-foot-by-four-inch sections of explosive-filled pipe were pushed into the entanglements and twistlocked together. Then the last segment was fused and the whole unit slithered quickly out of there.

The engineers had done their work to perfection and the blasts of the Bangalores were hardly noticed in the overall fury of the bombardment, which suddenly, ominously ceased. There were now six causeways right through the defenses. At 0640, four somewhat understrength troops of Jerram's Matildas went through, each leading a column of infantry. The outer two tanks turning left and right began to roll up the perimeter defenses; the inner pair struck straight for the Italian artillery batteries. As usual, the tanks attracted everything that would shoot at them and immediately became fountains of ricocheting tracers and exploding antiaircraft shells as their thick armor shrugged off incoming fire and their cannon and machine guns went to work.

By full daylight there was one hell of a firefight going on as the Italian tanks struck back. Things got so close that when one unwary Italian tanker popped his turret hatch, an Australian jumped aboard and cleaned out the interior with a captured Beretta machine pistol. The 16th Brigade was attacked by a company of M-13 tanks with a few M-11s tagging along, and it was pinned down until a few Matildas and a couple of Portees came along and broke the deadlock. By dusk, although there was still some fighting going on, the assault on the Bardia garrison was all but over. General Bergonzoli who had stayed a bit too long almost got trapped, but he escaped on foot, heading for Tobruk.

The next morning, during the mopping up of some of the still doggedly resisting garrison, the rest of the Australians began to filter into Bardia town, which they took intact along with the water distillation plant. The only serious combat came when a coast defense battery on the south harbor

headland began shooting up the town in an effort to dislodge
the Aussies. One of Jerram's officers, a Second Lieutenant
Taylor, took a troop of Matildas south around the town,
smashed open the landgates of the gun battery, and shot the
place up from the inside.

When the loot was counted, it was found that O'Connor
was making war support war. In addition to collecting another 40,000 Italian prisoners and casualties, he had suddenly solved his transport problem by capturing 706 trucks,
and most of them were in running order. The division had
also nabbed 400 guns and most of the light and medium
tanks. The Australians, intrigued with the possibilities, began
to experiment with the captured M-13s. They already had a
divisional mechanized cavalry regiment, equipped with
tracked "universal carriers" and armored cars, and the men
were experienced with engines and tracks. Several days after
the assault, three Australian tank squadrons began to pull
themselves into existence with Italian tanks, scout vehicles,
and trucks. Each ex-Italian vehicle now sported a large white
kangaroo on its turret, just in case of a misidentification in
the heat of battle. Whimsically, they were named *Dingo*,
Wombat, and *Rabbit*.

O'Connor, never one to let the momentum drop, was already on the way west. Maktila, Sidi Barrâni, and Buq-buq;
now Bardia; then Tobruk, Gazala, and Derna all fell to the
same basic assault method: maneuver, surprise, shock assault, and then a remorseless grinding battle. The western
desert force was by now redesignated the XIIIth Corps, and
O'Connor was looking hungrily across the bulge of Cyrenaica to the large and valuable port of Benghazi. . . . And
perhaps even Tripoli. The tanks, however, were wearing out
quite rapidly. No one had ever expected British tanks to
have to play hound to Italian hares across hundreds of miles
of Libyan desert.

The war was heating up with new supplies and new units.
The Babini Armored Brigade, fresh from Italy, was unloading on the quays at Benghazi, and the British 2nd Armored Division was coming ashore at Alexandria. General
Graziani decided to abandon Cyrenaica altogether in the
face of all this aggression. He therefore set a defensive line

across the entrance to the green mountain country called the Djebel el Akhdar, and he began to retreat along the coastal road. The line led from the town and wadi named Derne on the coast to the small city of Merchili that was to be the holding line for the Tenth Italian Army, now under the command of a General Tellera. Leaving most of the Babini Brigade to act as a rear guard, Tellera burned what supplies he couldn't carry and began a somewhat frantic retreat, constantly harried by the Australians . . . who were using Italian tanks with kangaroos painted on them, riding in Italian trucks, and eating canned spaghetti.

This was the beginning of a long and honorable tank and ration-swapping tradition in that war. While the Italian tanks have taken much undeserved criticism, both the British and Germans found them to be adequate. Time after time, the Germans would be attacked by the British in captured M-13s and German Mk-IIIs and IVS. On the other hand, the Brits would be surprised by Germans in Crusaders, Matildas, and Valentines. Then American Grants, Lees, Stuarts, and Shermans were added to the mix. Tank identification became a fine art and things got to the point that sometimes the only way to tell if a unit was hostile was to wait for action.

At this point of time, with a retreating, demoralized enemy getting away from him behind a rear guard, O'Connor smelled blood. While his probing Hussars in their Rolls and Morris cars reported no easy passage through those green mountains, there was a possibility of cutting under the hump of Cyrenaica and trapping a whole army. *That* was a goal worth trying for. It was also becoming strategically necessary.

CHAPTER 25

Death of an Army

IL DUCE, ANGERED BY HITLER'S UNANNOUNCED OCCUPATION of Yugoslavia, had decided to occupy Greece and was being stubbornly resisted. England, in the person of Winston Churchill, had offered aid to Greece, which could only come from Wavell's African force. Fortunately, the Greek prime minister/dictator, General Ioannis Metaxas turned him down. . . . For a time.

Hitler was now flying Luftwaffe squadrons from Sicily, attacking British shipping and the airfields on Malta. Suddenly the acquisition of Royal Air Force (RAF) bases in the Benghazi bulge became a necessity. Since the Regia Aeronautica had lost its bases at Tobruk and Gazala, it could no longer fly cover for the Italian Tenth Army. The RAF also was flying at the extreme range of its fighter bombers. Air support for the coming campaign would be a bit thin on both sides. Tanks were another matter.

Unknown to Archibald Wavell and Richard O'Connor, the Babini brigade was fully unloaded and was equipped with 150 brand new tanks, mostly M-13s with 47mm guns, but with half-trained crews. The British, on the other hand, had desert-wise experienced tank crews, but their tanks were dying. All of Jerrad's Matildas were in the shops at Tobruk with round-the-clock shifts of welders and fitters working on them. Creagh's Seventh Armored Division had been reduced to 80 light tanks armed with machine guns only and 40 assorted models of cruiser tanks armed with the two-pounder, or 40mm gun. The mechanical reliability of his tanks was, in his own words, "dubious." What this boiled down to was that Creagh, holding back a reserve just in case something broke loose, could send only 32 cruisers and 50 light tanks against 100 brand new mediums and 50 light tankettes.

Into this rather "iffy" situation, O'Connor launched one of history's master strokes. What determined his decision was that there was no defensible terrain line between Derna and Tripolitania. Once Tellera was on the move, he would have to keep going through Benghazi, down through the turn of the Gulf of Sirte, and far into Libya before he could find a line to hold. If he could be cut off some place south of Benghazi, he would be in the bag. This was, as has been said, a very "iffy" operation.

The Benghazi bulge both juts out into the blue waters of the Mediterranean Sea, and lifts above the Libyan plateau. Since time immemorial, nations have been fighting over this green, lush land, so different from the harsh desert behind it. Riding on the coastal road, not long after leaving Gazala, the traveler begins to see tall green mountains rising to the left that are dotted with whitewashed cubist towns and plantations. There are flowing streams instead of desert wells and where the land is level wheat grows. The small towns are surrounded by lush gardens and can be taken as parts of either Greece or Italy. . . . As once they were. The Greeks colonized this land back during the Bronze Age when Mycenae was fighting Troy over access to the Black Sea and Egypt was contesting Canaan with the Hittites. Indeed, some of the first colonists claimed to have been refugees from Troy.

The tankers of the Seventh Division were to see little of this land. Their track lay to the south of the Jebel al Akhdar, across some of the ruggedest land on earth. While the Australians fought out the Derna battles and the Italians made ready to escape, O'Connor began to accumulate supplies as rapidly as he could, which as things turned out, wasn't fast enough. Now ordered to take Benghazi as quickly as possible, he was headquartered at Bomba, north of Gazala, living on Italian cheese, bully beef, and Chianti—and fighting an ulcer—when the bad news came in. The Italians had broken contact with the Australians during the night of 2 February, and they were retreating along the Via Balbia around the hump toward Benghazi.

The British Quartermasters had already been busy bringing supplies up in the captured trucks and were building a desert supply magazine west of Gazala near the city of Mechili. They were still, as usual, desperately short of everything, but the old military truism, "You go with what you've got," was the driving force. O'Connor quickly changed the orders of the 7th Armored's advance force, pulling them out of the Jebel al Akhdar and sending them out into the open desert to the south. They left Mechili on the morning of 4 February at dawn's first light, probing into an unmapped rocky unknown. Their mission was to recon and secure a route southwest first to M'sus, and then to Antelat, Beda Fomm, and Sidi Saleh. At M'sus, a desert track separated from the caravan route toward the village of Sceleidima and then up to Benghazi, and this would also have to be investigated and secured. Obviously, this was a job for a fairly strong force and O'Connor proceeded to create one.

The advance guard consisted of the 11th Hussars, still mounted in their 1924 model Rolls cars, which by now were equipped with Boy's antitank rifles as well as their ancient Vickers guns. Next came C Battery of the Fourth Royal Horse Artillery with four 25-pounders and nine 37mm portees on the usual cut-down Chevrolet trucks. Interspersed with the guns were the trunks of the Second Battalion, 16th Rifles. Additional firepower was added by 106th RHA, which was a territorial unit with 40mm antiaircraft/antitank guns, and one battery of captured Italian 20mm antiaircraft guns.

Due to the efficiency of the 11th Hussars, their commander, Lieutenant John Combe, had had to loan out two of his squadrons and now O'Connor hastily replaced them with one squadron of the King's Dragoon Guards in American Marmington-Herrington armored cars, and one from Number Two Armored Car Company, just in from Palestine and riding in Fordson armored cars. This was the patch-up force that headed dubiously out along a 120-mile-long section of a seldom used caravan track with no maps. . . . And an armored division coming along behind them. The first 20 miles were a driver's nightmare—a giant boulder field of upended and tilted slab rock in loose sand and gravel beds.

Then the light tanks, the division's leading force, entered the field and, due to the short length of the little Mk-VI, they lurched wildly. The tank commanders had no seats, but sat in canvas slings and were thrown about like potato sacks as the tanks rolled and pitched like small boats at sea. Soon the TCs were beaten, battered, and burned as they bounced off hard metal and hot engines. The radiators began to boil, fuel consumption rose alarmingly, and the two-gallon "flimsies," in which their fuel and water were carried, began to break and spread their contents across the desert. In the midst of all this mechanized pandemonium, rode General Creagh, doing what a commander does . . . worrying.

After 40 miles of this torture, first the advance guard, then the tank columns emerged from the torture zone, just as more information came crackling in over the radio. Creagh first received a report that the Italians were making better progress than expected and their column was already clear of Benghazi, heading south. Then the 11th Hussars' lead cars reported better going ahead, so the force could speed up. A little map work served to convince Creagh that he might miss the interception, so he gave two quick, terse orders.

The first changed the division's main axis from due west after M'sus, to southwestward toward the town of Agadabia. The second put the 11th Hussars into history. They were to form a flying column and by using the speed of the wheeled vehicles on good going set up a roadblock at Sidi Saleh, south of a map point and a windmill called Beda Fomm, and hold it until the tanks arrived. . . . The tanks were beginning to run out of fuel and the fuel trucks were having a rough time of it too.

Colonel Combe was chosen to command this force, with Lieutenant Colonel J. C. Campbell, who was the investor of the Jock columns, as his deputy. At that point in time, Campbell was Commanding Officer of the Fourth RHA and was riding with his C Battery. The flying column was named Combeforce and the organization took most of a night, which has since been described as "deliberate chaos." By dawn on 5 February, Combeforce consisted of the 11th Hussars with their two added squadrons, plus the 106th RHA and C Battery Fourth RHA. The lead element, the 11th's A Squadron in their Rolls cars, were already out on the Via Balbia anxiously waiting the arrival of either Combeforce or the Italians, and they did not know which would be first.

At 0800 hours, the column moved out, headed down the road to Antelat and then Sidi Saleh. They were discovered and strafed without result by two Italian biplane fighters, then, not knowing whether they had been reported, they had to speed up just in case the Italians sent a reconnaissance in force. They found Antelat deserted and they cut cross-country to the as-yet unpopulated Via Balbia. By now the Rifle Brigades' tracked Universal Carriers were running out of gasoline, so the men were transferred to the truck while the carrier crews waited for the main force and the fuel trucks.

Just after noon, the 11th's new C Squadron (ex-Second Armored Car Company) under Major Payne Gallwey, hit the road in an area of gently rolling sand hills covered with scrub brush. West of them, toward the coast was an area of dunes with a native track cutting through it. Between the sea and the desert edge of the Jebel al Akhdar was a gap of three-and-one-half miles. Combeforce would have to hold this for an indefinite amount of time against an army of 30,000 with just their own weapons and 2,000 men. They were at the end of their fuel supplies, outgunned, and outnumbered about fifteen to one. Early in the afternoon of 5 February, they began digging in, feeling like Leonidas and his band at Thermopylae.

By 1400 they were dug in, just one rifle brigade, assorted armored cars, and 20 assorted small artillery pieces against a horde. A horde that stuck its head into a trap, not knowing

that they had been backdoored across "impassable terrain."
The British were only just in time with their preparations;
at 1430, the northern pickets reported a huge truck column
approaching from the direction of Benghazi. By then, the
Rifle Brigade was dug in on a line that crossed the road and
all of the 106 RHA's portees were in defilade, camouflaged
with only their guns and sights visible above the brush.

The Italian supplies and headquarters troops were leading
the column, thinking that the entire British force was behind
them. Seventy miles south of Benghazi, they came in range
of the British force and on signal, Combeforce opened up
on a defenseless column. With no warning, a line of riflemen;
heavy machine guns, man-portable antitank rifles; 40mm,
37mm, and a few 25-pounders erupted in flame and hot
screaming steel projectiles.

The result was chaos squared. Trucks blew up, took off,
or backed into each other. Some ran off the road and
promptly got stuck while men boiled from them like ants
out of a disturbed hill. This lead section of the convoy was
the whole army's administrative unit, escorted by one small
battalion of elite Bersaglieri and some motorcycle troops.
There was an adequate number of armed Italians available,
but the administrative types were quite incapable of organiz-
ing for combat. Some junior leaders got moving and tried
to get past the British left flank, west of the road. This
caused Lieutenant Colonel J. M. L. Renton, commanding
the rifle brigade, to spread his B Company's western flank
out to the coast, further thinning the British line. A group
of motorcycle riders tried to rush the British line and
promptly had their bikes shot out from under them, becoming the first prisoners of war of the action.

Creagh, listening anxiously to all this action over the radio
from his temporary HQ at M'sus, around 1630 hours, inquired of LTC Combe where General A. L. "Blood" Caunter's Fourth Armored Brigade could do the most damage.
Combe radioed back that the Brigade should cut cross-country and come out of a series of north-south ridges to the
west of Beda Fomm and attack the rapidly growing column
from that flank before Bergonzoli got his tanks up to wipe
out the roadblock, which they could easily do.

Creagh agreed, but there was a problem. All afternoon
he had been losing tanks to the desert, which at that point
in time was disabling more vehicles than enemy fire. Later
on, O'Connor was to drive the desert track to Beda Fomm
and be able to navigate by the line of disabled tanks. "My
God, do you think it's going to work?" he is reported to
have asked his liaison with Wavell, General Dorman-Smith.

Taking stock of his dwindling reserve of tanks, Caunter
did the best he could. The 7th Hussars, equipped with only
light tanks along with a squadron of the Second RTR, by
now down to just six running cruisers, were sent to harry
the truck column. These cruisers were A-15s, armed with
40mm guns and powered with the Liberty engine, which was
derived from an American World War I aircraft engine.
They could top out at almost 30 miles per hour and carried
frontal armor of 1.93 inches. . . . They would be needed
desperately.

By 1700 hours, the light tanks were coming over the hump
of Beda Fomm and savaging the convoy with the machine
guns that were their only armament. By then, Bergonzoli
had at least a platoon of M-13s down the length of the line
of trucks, and they began to engage the lighter British tanks,
until the six-tank Squadron from Second RTR arrived. By
1750, this being February, the light was beginning to fade,
but desultory combat was carried on by the light of burning
fuel tankers.

One of the A-15s, commanded by a Lieutenant Plough,
had been working up a line of burning trucks, both hiding
his hull in the smoke and looking for an opportunity, when
coming to the end of that group of vehicles, he came upon
a glorious sight. Two M-13s were sitting side by side, just
off the road, taking potshots at distant targets, probably
sighting on British muzzle flashes that would have become
visible about that time. Ordering his driver to pull up alongside the two Italian tanks, Plough simply ordered his loader,
one Eldred Hughes, to "get the crews out." Hughes jumped
from his tank and began to beat on the top hatches of the
M-13s with a pistol butt. When the crews opened up, obviously thinking that the men on their hulls were friendly,

Hughes motioned them out. A few machine gun bursts from the cruiser's turret emphasized the order.

The night of 5 February fell on the battlefield of Beda Fomm with a wet, palpable thud as there was heavy rain and high winds for most of the night. The Italian column was now 11 miles long and still growing. The British were still picking their way across country, and many small units were just lost. New morning, they would find their way to battle by homing in on the sound of guns and the sight of columns of black oily smoke. General Telera now knew that he had a heavy force to overcome and gave that job to General Bergonzoli, who ordered the Babini Armored Brigade to work its way forward and make ready to attack at dawn.

His battle plan was basic Bergonzoli: Attack the British force from the east under cover of artillery. The Brits were also working their way forward to the trapped supply and HQ trucks. After breaking through the cruisers and ignoring the light tanks, the Brigade was to roll south, flank Combeforce, and clear the road for the rest of Tenth Army. . . . Simple, right?

Creagh had also been busy. There was a road that led from M'sus to the town of Sceleidima and thence to Benghazi. The remainder of the 7th Armored Division was to take this track, then cut west cross-country and fall on the rear of the Italian force. There would, therefore, be three connected battles on 6 February, the attack on the convoy's rear, the battle at Beda Fomm, and the battle to clear Combeforce out of the way. All would be fought ferociously.

During the night, dozens of forlorn parties of Italians were rounded up and put into a POW camp. So many, in fact, were slipping past the seaward flank that Renton used his support company to fill the gap between his flank and the shore. To the south, near Agedabia, held by the Third Armored Car Troop of the Hussars, the Kings Dragoons, there was some pressure and probing from the west and they, too, were picking up escapees. Combeforce at this point was short of just about everything but resupply was not in the offing. They were told "to hold at all costs" but "make the best of what you've got."

The gray, wet dawn of 6 February was announced by a
growing thunder of gunfire as soon as there was light enough
to shoot. The Fourth Armored Brigade began chewing up
the convoy, which was now somewhat better organized; at
the same time three columns of infantry with a few tanks
began to threaten Combeforce: one column on the road, one
in the dunes, and one on a track just to seaward of the
dunes. Only the one on the road chose to accept combat;
the other two stopped to offer surrender. After a gun duel
between a 75mm artillery piece and a 37mm portee, which
the 37mm crew won, that column too gave up. This kept
up for most of the day and by evening Combeforce was
considerably outnumbered by its POWs. By now, there was
a good chance that the prisoners, under cover of darkness,
might try something..

Up north, at the Beda Fomm site, things were getting
considerably warmer. Between the paved road and the windmill site to the east, was a small hill that gained the name
"The Pimple," and it became the site of battle. The British
had developed an after-battle policy of withdrawing to night
laagers, and they sometimes moved about after dark to con-
fuse enemy artillery and possible air strikes. Bergonzoli, observing the British pulling out the previous evening, calculated that they might be moving to reinforce
Combeforce. What they were actually doing was maintenance and plotting; they would still be there in the morning.

The same dawn that saw the three columns staggering to
a halt against Combeforce saw a series of attacks on The
Pimple, which at that time was held only by the few cruisers
of the Second RTR. They were just two understrength
squadrons alone, although the First RTR had been ordered
to rendezvous with its ten cruisers and 8 light tanks. The
First RTR, coming out of Sceleidima, had been stopped by
a sandstorm that rapidly dried out the wet sand of the night
before and then lifted it into half-mile-high wall of fury. For
the time, the Second RTR would be alone.

At 0800, 6 February, the first Italian tank attack came in
a flashing wide-open charge against no more than two dozen
hull-down cruisers, low on both fuel and ammunition. The
M-13s came over open ground, firing as they came—that

was their downfall. With no gun stabilization and with the crude optics of the time, they stood little, if any, chance of hitting the turrets of the British cruisers, which were all that was showing above the hilltops. In the turrets of the cruisers, the British sat and waited, all in full radio contact with their commanders. The Italians had radios in only commanders' tanks, so once the attack was launched, they had no control except flag signals.

The Second RTR, under Colonel A. C. Harcourt, waited stationary until they couldn't miss their target. Then began a slow drumroll of controlled fire against targets coming straight at them, getting steadily larger in their sights. Wave after wave of M-13s broke against the cruisers. Between 6 and 10 Italian tanks were knocked out with each attack, and since they were used as soon as they came in, company by company, they never mounted a battalion-sized attack that would have easily overwhelmed the cruisers. As Erwin Rommel later asked a captured British officer, "What does it matter if you have more tanks than I, if you send them in driblets?"

When one attack eventually used enough M-13s to force the cruisers back, the Regiment's C Squadron under Major James Richardson pulled a fast fadeback and counterattacked to the Italian right flank. They were covered by the guns of A Squadron, Major G. S. Strong, firing from the next terrain feature back, which was a ridge known as "the Mosque" due to a small tomb on its crest. That effort cost Bergonzoli 18 more tanks.

Then part of the trapped column broke loose and began to work its way south toward Combeforce, resulting in Harcourt's sending A Squadron with a group of light tanks from the Third Hussars in pursuit. This resulted in a 10-mile running fight that cost 10 more M-13s. It *is* possible to fire on the move, but one thing has to be considered as a trick of gunnery. If both you and your opponent are moving parallel to each other, you must *not* lead your target, as you are stationary in relation to it. . . . A certain amount of experience is necessary to learn this bit of gunnery. The mind conjures up the mental image of two lines of armored vehicles running south across the open scrubland banging away

at each other like ships at sea, with the unarmored supply
trucks, shop, and radio vehicles as the prizes. This is a good
comparison for desert war, for like the sea, there is no place
to hide and the tanks have to slug it out in open formation.

By the time the two squadrons got back to The Pimple,
several changes were evident. First, Italian artillery was
ranging on the feature and beginning to hit the defending
tanks. Second, they were by now just about out of ammunition. Harcourt had already arranged for fuel and ammunition trucks to be waiting in the fire-lee of the Mosque ridge
and with the loss of three cruisers in the movement, pulled
back for replenishing. What he had done was divert *all* of
his Hussars with their light tanks to cause as much pain at
the north end of the Italian column as possible.

Since Bergonzoli had not left back an M-13 reserve, he
then had to take pressure off The Pimple to chase the Hussars off. He managed to find enough armored mass and send
it to the right place. The Third Hussars in Mk-VI light tanks
got a rude shock when two dozen Mk-13s burst out of the
middle of the burning trucks and took them in the flank. By
this time, B Squadron Two RTR was back in the fight and,
taking the Italians in their flank, rescued most of the Hussars. By now the battle was a hopeless mess, and then D
battery, Three RHA, backed its 40mm portees into the battle and began to snipe tanks, accounting for two more
M-13s.

By 1400, The Pimple was in Italian hands and their artillery was firing from the little hillock. Between 1415 and
1600 a raging artillery duel between defiladed cannons and
armored tanks raged, finally ending with the Italians retiring
reluctantly. By now, the rest of Bergonzoli's M-13s were
causing serious damage to Caunter's Fourth Brigade, and
the 1st RTR had broken out from under its sandstorm west
of Antelat and, refueled and ammoed up, were headed for
the battle. Unfortunately they had for one reason or another
lost radio contact and were coming in blind. Following the
old cavalry tradition, they homed in on the sound of the
guns, knocking out or destroying two more M-13s, and by
1630 they were shooting up the convoy, which, as the sun
set, was a burning cauldron for over a dozen miles.

The British themselves were in bad shape. The Second RTR, for instance, was again almost out of ammunition and had only a handful of cruisers running. With so few tanks operable, there was a grave danger that Bergonzoli, now in overall command after Telera had taken a mortal wound, could find a way to break through Combeforce, which couldn't be reinforced due to a lack of tanks.

Bergonzoli wasn't giving up easily and kept up the pressure on Combeforce for most of the night. Tanks and infantry attacked through the convoy at around 2100 hours; they got in so close with the Rifle Brigade that Campbell's 25-pounders couldn't tell friend from foe and had to cease fire and look to their own security. A small group of tanks and truck-mounted infantry actually broke through the roadblock and escaped away south along the road. Then out of the dark and fog, a Lieutenant Kernan of 106 RHA materialized with two more 37mm portees and full ammunition. There were now 11 portees available to Combeforce plus C Battery, Fourth RHA, with what little 25-pounder ammunition remained to them. At midnight, the last Italian attack was attempted, but as they stayed bunch up they made a good target for moonlight shooting and were eventually broken up and captured.

On the morning of 7 February, things started off a little weird. The 2nd Rifle Brigade had set up a POW compound south of the roadblock. About 0400 two Italian tanks came puttering through the sand dunes and the Italian prisoners, who were guarded only by Platoon Sergeant Jarvis and a Private named O'Brien, scented freedom and immediately rushed the tanks, followed by two shouting Tommies. While the Italians swarmed over the tanks, the Englishmen fired their rifles into the vision slits, sending ricochetting slugs dancing off the inner walls and wounding several crewmen.

The side hatch of the lead tank opened up, and an officer took a couple of shots at Jarvis with a pistol. The lieutenant missed and Jarvis, wheeling and swinging, gave the unfortunate Italian a buttstroke to the head, ending the encounter as the tanker dropped unconscious to the ground. The crews surrendered and spent the remainder of the cold, wet, miserable night under the guns of their own tanks, whereas Jarvis and O'Brien enjoyed the relative warmth of the hulls.

Just after first light, at 0630, the Italian artillery opened up again, peppering the area, but it was obvious that they were shooting at random, with no forward control. Bergonzoli had managed to find a force of about thirty M-13s to spearhead his last desperate attempt to break out, and these came on with almost fanatical determination. The men of Combeforce were equally determined and the 106th RHA's portees went gun to gun with the M-13s while the infantrymen could only duck their heads and pray. This was not their kind of fight; when gun fights steel armor, flesh and blood can only cringe.

A Sergeant Gould played cool, staying hidden until a platoon of tanks had passed him, apparently free and clear, running for the border. Then Gould came out of cover, leveled his portee and killed all six tanks with rear shots into the engines. The 106th's commander, Major Burton, with his batman and a cook formed up a scratch crew for a damaged portee, repaired whatever was needed, and fought until the battle was over.

The Rifle Brigade always tried to show a touch of class and had, the night before, erected an officers' mess tent. This now, for some reason, began to attract the last of Bergonzoli's tanks, and they began to focus in on it, getting thoroughly mixed up with the infantry. Colonel Jock Campbell, desperate to stop this assault, finally obtained permission to use his 25-pounders' direct fire against the tanks while they were mixed up with the Second Brigade. Given permission by O'Connor, his crews opened up, using optical sights, and began to recycle the M-13s into scrap metal. . . . The last one rolled to a stop only yards from that officers' mess tent. This was the last straw, and white things began waving from all the Italian positions and vehicles.

By 0900, 7 February, O'Connor had achieved a rare thing, indeed, in military history: total annihilation of a force ten times his size. The radios sang with the message. O'Connor turned to Dornan-Smith in Creagh's HQ and said, "We'd better send a message to Archie. What shall we say?" Wavell being a keen sportsman, they decided on a hunting metaphor. "Fox killed in the open" was transmitted, and then the entire text of the battle was sent . . . uncoded . . . for Mussolini's express benefit. Then the celebration began.

O'Connor and his men began to survey their triumph and found that they bagged 25,000 prisoners, over 100 tanks, 216 guns, 1,500 assorted wheeled vehicles, tons of fuel and food, and last but not least General Tellera's private rolling bordello. When discovered, it consisted of a converted bus beside which the ladies were brewing tea and watching their conquerors with some interest. The mess tent was now bustling with captured viands and relays of guests, both Italian and British, were feasting in relays. Later on O'Connor was to apologize to the captured Italian staff for their rather crude treatment, to receive the understanding answer, "That's all right, we realize that you arrived in some haste."

Alas, that was the high point of the affair, for just days after the victory, O'Connor's proud, efficient, military machine was to be dismantled and fed piecemeal into an unwinnable cauldron in Greece and the Balkans. What no one seemed to know was that the first segments of the Afrika Korps were already in Italy getting ready to ship out to Tripoli. Rommel himself said later that if Wavell [actually O'Connor] had simply kept on going, no force available could have stopped him. There was only one understrength Italian division left between the British and Tripoli, and the city was garrisoned by five understrength and demoralized divisions.

Churchill, however, had other worries. The Germans were in Greece, the Balkans, and were planning an attack on Russia. As a result, Britain, thinking the desert war was a done thing, began to pull troops out of North Africa and disband the Seventh Armored into various internal duties. . . . On the morning of 14 February 1941, the First Panzers were offloaded at Tripoli.

When General Dornan-Smith, acting as an urgent messenger for O'Connor, arrived in Cairo he rushed to Wavell's HQ, and was ushered into the inner sanctum, where Sir Archibald Wavell swept an arm toward his map board that was now bereft of the Western Desert maps. Instead, the boards and walls were covered with maps of Greece. "You

see, Eric," Wavell said somewhat sardonically, "I'm planning my spring campaign."

Thus did Winston Churchill prove that although he was
great enough to be Churchill, he was no Marlborough. His
own chief of staff, Kennedy wrote, "nothing we can do can
make the Greek business a sound military proposition. . . .
In the Middle East, we must not throw away our power of
offensive action by adopting an unsound strategy on
Greece." Thus was victory thrown away and the war lengthened by two unnecessary years. Time after time in history,
a victorious general has had his triumph destroyed by a
politician.

In this case, the destruction was especially bitter. Only six
days after the victory at Beda Fomm, the 13th Corps was
disbanded and Cyrenaica Command set up. The Seventh
Armored was utterly scattered through Egypt on internal
duties, and its tanks were shut down and parked. O'Connor,
still fighting his well-earned ulcer, was assigned as general
officer commanding (GOC) British troops in Egypt. Out on
the border there was only the Green 2nd Armored Division,
along with a brigade of Australians under a General Neame,
also new to the desert.

The Brits were armed partly with captured Italian tanks,
so as to save wear and tear on their precious few cruisers
and Matildas. Theoretically, this was all quite in order as
the British were by then reading much of German signal
traffic. They knew that Hitler had given Rommel orders to
be ready to move by 20 April, at the earliest, so they figured
that they had plenty of time to rearrange their forces.

On 31 March 1941, the Panzers rolled with Rommel at
the head of the center column, running up O'Connor's old
track from M'sus to Mechili, and from Mechili to Derna,
utterly upsetting the 2nd Armored Division and the Australians. Neame, in near panic, called for reinforcements and
for advice from the old hands. On 3 April, with German
patrols all over the area, O'Connor arrived and proceeded
to set matters aright. According to all British sources, this
could not be happening, it must be only a reconnaissance in
force, for Rommel was not thought capable of a full offen-

sive as yet—but here he was headed for Tobruk at speed and in force.

Rommel's tanks were running out of fuel, but he was setting up supply columns and feeding them whatever they needed in order to catch up with the retreating British. The Brits, for their part, remembered how they outran the Italians, gathered their strength, and lashed back. "Here we go again," they thought, as they outran the Germans. Neame, however, was too shaken to take advantage of literally hundreds of stranded German tanks and halftracks. Worse, Rommel was no tyro and had one hidden advantage. He had a source of desert-wise tankers.

When the French surrendered, so did the French Foreign Legion, which was about one-third German. These Germans were quickly taken into the 5th Light Division, which was to be one of the core units of the Afrika Korps. As a result, what hit poor General Neame was not a bumbling Italian assault, it was a German chain saw. With all of the British generals confused and off balance, it was only natural that O'Connor should take the inexperienced Neame and go kiting off into the desert to gain the knowledge he so desperately needed.

On the evening of 6 April, they took a staff car and drove into the night, headed for their new HQ at Tmimi. Unfortunately for history, they took a wrong turn and got onto the Derna track just about the same time as the German Ponath Group. This was a regiment of motorized infantry in trucks with a few halftracks. Their mounted screen was motorcycles with machine gunners in side cars, and when the British driver recognized them and tried to turn around, he was killed and Neame and O'Connor were suddenly looking into the muzzles of Schmiesser machine pistols.

The first of the desert foxes had been put in the bag. He was not the first desert general to be nabbed, nor would he be the last, and the campaigns of O'Connor, Rommel, Claud Auchinleck, and others still have their lessons to teach . . . as do the stories of their troopers. Tankers, artillerymen, and infantrymen as well as aspiring young officers would do well to learn the lessons of history, before the texts are again written in blood, burnt tanks, and captured soldiers.

When Winston Churchill stopped O'Connor cold, and disbanded his army, he did exactly the same thing that was done to Matthew Ridgeway at the 38th parallel in Korea, and during the Watergate fiasco in the Vietnam period, where Richard Nixon was stripped of the power to enforce a won peace. It was also the exact same type of political malfeasance that stopped Norman Schwarzkopf cold in 1991 . . . and we are still paying the price for that one.

CHAPTER 26

Malaya, January 1942
BATTLE FOR THE MALAY PENINSULA

ODDLY ENOUGH, EVEN WITH THEIR MOUNTED SAMURAI TRA-
dition, the Japanese never developed a strong armored
force. There are only a few battles in which they put together any kind of large tank force and we have already
looked at one, near Nomonhan, Manchuria. While the Russians triumphed there, the shoe was on the other foot in the
Malayan campaign. The Japanese had a fairly cohesive tank
force and several inspired commanders. The British, on the
other hand, were a strictly prewar, infantry-heavy colonial
force, and it cost them dearly.

The reason the Japanese could launch their offensive,
strangely enough, was in Europe. When the Germans took
first Poland and then France with such demoralizing violence, France capitulated . . . taking all her colonies with
her. French Indochina, which we know as Vietnam, was simply handed to the amazed Japanese on a platter. When the
emperor's forces moved into Vietnam, the independent nation of Siam was put in a pretty fix.

Siam, or Thailand, was the only Southeast Asian nation
never colonized, but now it was literally surrounded and the
king made a very quick decision to sign a treaty of protec-

tion and nonaggression with Japan. Before much time went
by, Japanese transports were disembarking troops and
equipment into the ports of southern Thailand and making
plans to run the British out of the area, all the way down
to Singapore.

Colonel Shizo Saeki, Imperial Japanese Army (IJA), was
a horse cavalry officer who had distinguished himself in
many Chinese campaigns while serving in command of the
40th Cavalry Regiment. In mid-1941, however, he found
himself in command of a totally new unit, the Fifth Mounted
Reconnaissance Regiment of the newly formed IJA Fifth
Division of the 25th Army. The new regiment was thoroughly modern, for the times. In addition to the horse-
mounted companies, there were two truck-mounted motorized infantry companies, two tank companies, a machine gun
company, and a battery of quick-firing guns.

After taking jungle training around Shanghai for most of
November and early December 1941, the new unit shipped
out one misty night, westward toward the Malay Peninsula.
Imperial Japan, having managed to cut itself off from most
of its exterior resources, now had to acquire them the old-
fashioned way, by armed theft. Colonel Saeki's orders read:
"The 40th Regiment, minus its armored company, will land
in Southern Thailand at the harbor of Singora, and will proceed to the railway junction of Hat Yai."

The actual landing took place at 0300 hours, 8 December
1941. Because of the international date line, that was precisely three hours before the attack at Pearl Harbor. Surprise was complete as the Japanese force landed "like foam
from the crest of a wave." Negotiations between Japan and
Thailand not being complete, the local Thai garrison immediately attacked but was driven off.

Despite the presence of a strong Thai force, the critical
railway junction at Hat Yai was taken, and by the evening
of the 8th, 5th Division Headquarters had arrived, but there
was to be no rest for the cavalrymen. They learned that a
British motorized formation had crossed the Thai-Malay
border and was moving up to attack positions around the
town of Sadao. Saeki immediately set off through a rainy
night on a 30 km forced march.

As they approached the town, they were suddenly hit by rifle and machine gun fire, but the cavalryman's automatic reflexes saved them. An immediate attack into unknown jungle positions and incoming fire dislodged the Brits, who didn't intend to hold the ground anyway. Their mission had been to blow the bridges and ruin the roads, and this they did, holding up the mechanized portion of the Japanese forces. Saeki and his horsemen, however, weren't to be stopped and they dismounted, swam their horses across the little river, and kept on. By midnight of the 8 December, Saeki and his lead cavalry troop were 70 km inside Thailand and at the Malay border. Behind them, IJA engineers were working feverishly on the bridges as the tankers and other motorized troops waited. The battle for Malaysia had begun. The British, however, had seemingly stacked the deck against themselves.

Lieutenant General Arthur Percival, the officer commanding Malaysia under General Archibald Wavell who had overall command . . . including the battle against Erwin Rommel, was a staff officer, not a field commander. As such he simply didn't have the political clout to get the resources he wanted. Percival, as early as 1940, had requested new fighter planes but got only obsolescent Brewster Buffalos. He'd requested antitank guns and a pair of armored regiments, but was told that the jungles of Malaysia were tank proof. Nobody had ever, at that point in time, tried to run tanks in the green hell, but commercial bulldozers had no problem at all in simply removing such jungles as were in their way. The British "powers that be" had sent him a modest naval presence though, the battleship *Prince of Wales* and the battlecruiser *Repulse*. These ships did not have any antiaircraft guns mounted. . . . Nor did most of the capital ships of the era.

By late November 1941, the British defense of Malaya consisted of three divisions, two Indian and one Australian plus several independent regiments and assorted Indian regiments used for formal guard duties. The total was 88,000 men, more or less. Against this force, the Japanese were sending just 60,000 men . . . and 80 tanks. The only armor that Percival had was a few tracked Bren gun carriers and

ancient Lanchester armored cars armed with machine guns.
In other words, nothing modern and not enough of it.

The Japanese commander was a veteran field commander,
Lieutenant General Tomoyuki Yamashita. He also had three
divisions and assorted smaller units, but our interest is with
the tankers so we shall concentrate on the affairs of the iron
cavalry of Japan. They were, as Bryan Perrett says in his
excellent book, *Seize and Hold,* "Something of a Cinderella
force," who never met Prince Charming.

The green mountains of the Malay peninsula run north
and south and are impassable to any vehicle save a helicopter, which hadn't been invented yet. The terrain severely
channelized military activities and as in many other coun-
tries, a narrow-gauge steam railway paralleled the road. On
one side were green mountains, on the other, swamps and
jungles.

The prize, the reason for the invasion, was the rubber
industry along with some mineral wealth, including uranium.
Japan, when it declared war on the United States, had effectively cut itself off from its external mineral suppliers and
suddenly found a need for such things as steel, rubber, and
crude oil. As far as they were concerned, they were attacking for needed supplies and the Greater East Asia Co-
Prosperity Sphere was actually a series of Japanese tentacles
of conquest. Their initial campaigns had all been completed
in just four months, but were a bit behind schedule due to
a pair of American tank battalions on Luzon.

The British, on the other hand, were a bit stretched. They
had been fighting for two years on several fronts, and England was being bombed from airfields in France and Germany. They had been fighting in the Western Desert since
1940, and America, while it had been supplying much equipment, was only just into the war . . . with most of its Pacific
Fleet still in the muck of Pearl Harbor and its army still in
the training camps.

The main British colonial unit was the 11th Indian Division, backed up by the Argyle and Sutherland Highlanders,
whom we last met at the battle of Cambrai going into battle
with General Elles's tanks. This time the Highlanders would
be on the receiving end of a tank assault and they wouldn't

appreciate the experience. The 11th Division was broken down into three brigades, the 4th, 12th, and 28th. The 12th Brigade, which took the brunt of this assault, was composed of the 4/19th Hyderabad and the 5/2nd and 5/14th Punjabis, all Indian troops with plenty of experience. . . . So much experience in retreating that by the time of the battle of the slim river, 7 January, they were punch-drunk. The 11th Indian Division had just recently taken on a large percentage of recruits who were ill trained and whose British officers couldn't yet speak Urdu, the official language of the East Indian Company Army.

There had been a plan, code-named "Matador," to send the 11th Indian Division to southern Thailand to mount a preemptive strike, but the almost unbelievable slothfulness of the British command had held that back until Colonel Saeki's cavalrymen went right past the 11th Division. By the evening of 8 December, the Japanese were firmly ashore. . . . By the tenth, both the *Prince of Wales* and the *Repulse* had been sunk. Half the British air force in Malaya had already been shot down and the rest would go soon. Also, by 10 December, Colonel Saeki's cavalrymen had linked up with two companies of tanks, detached from the Army's Third Tank Brigade and put under a cavalryman's command. From now on things would start to tick, as Saeki had a reputation for drive and initiative, honed for years in China.

The Japanese Type 95 light tank was called in the parlance of the time, a tankette, meaning that at 8 tons, 110 horsepower, and a 37mm cannon, it was just barely a tank. The basic design of the tankette was a copy of a Vickers commercial tank of the 1920s which had been sold to many smaller nations, including Poland. Its frontal armor was barely one-half-inch thick and the quarter-inch side plating could keep out pistol bullets and mosquitoes, if they weren't too thirsty.

Of the three-man crew, the driver and machine gunner/mechanic sat in the hull while the tank commander had the hand-cracked turret all to himself. This meant that, in addition to running the crew and watching out for flag signals and flares from his commander (they had no radios), he also had to aim, fire, and load the cannon. There was one other weapon on the tanklet, a machine gun mounted in the rear of the turret, just in case someone tried to sneak up with a demolition charge. The little tank could go just 100 miles on a full load of gasoline. This was about normal for the times.

The Type 94 medium was introduced in 1934, and was considerably more modern. Weighing fifteen tons, combat loaded and powered by a Mitsubishi airplane engine, it could make 28 miles per hour and could expect to travel about 100 miles on 210 gallons of fuel. The four-man crew had a main gun of either 47mm or 57mm, which were both good infantry support weapons, and two machine guns, one in the hull bow and one in the rear of the turret. Again, there was no radio, communication being done by flags, flares, or messengers.

The problem with this type of communication, obviously, is hostile fire. Tanks are bullet magnets and anyone approaching one with a message probably won't make the last few yards. Flags have the same problem, just opening a hatch to stick out a set of flags risks the insertion of a hand grenade or a burst of machine gun fire ricochetting down into the hull.

As mentioned, the terrain channelizes combat. The fertile valleys were cut up into rubber plantations with plenty of side roads, and General D. M. Murray-Lyon, who first commanded the 11th, would no more set up a roadblock than he would find himself flanked and hit from the rear, sometimes by bicycle-mounted troops, which is an indication of the relative lack of mobility of foot infantry. There were several times that the Indians had to attack southward, through a Japanese roadblock in order to retreat.

Jitra and Changlun in northern Malaya had been defended by the 1/14 Punjabis of the 11th Division, along with the 2/1st Ghurka Rifles, but none of these troops had ever seen a tank before and just ten of the little beasts were enough to shatter their defense and put them on the run. The heavy rain was no help, of course, and the tankers had more mobility than the infantry. By now, Saeki had a company of truck-borne infantry and a detachment of combat engineers. . . . Apparently he and a few other Japanese officers had been studying the Germans.

Coming out of Changlun and the wreckage of the two Indian Battalions, his heart must have stopped for a moment. There in line across the road was a battery of 37mm antitank guns, unlimbered and with muzzles pointing right at him. . . . And the crews were taking shelter in the sheds of a rubber plantation from the heavy rain. They shot up the guns, machine gunned the crews, ground the trucks down under their treads, and kept on laying tracks.

And so it went, the British leapfrogging from one humiliating defeat to another in a vain attempt to stop a modern army which was attacking *into* supplies, especially food, bicycles, and fuel. As the Brits lost mobility, the Japanese actually seemed to be gaining. Unit after unit, terrorized by Saeki's armor/mech-infantry team, simply abandoned their heavier gear and took to the swamps where the tanks, they thought, couldn't go. Saeki's original horse scouts, however, although they aren't mentioned in British history, had to have been in there, keeping tabs on the situation. He was General Yamashita's eyes and lead element, and he was getting too much information too fast not to have mounted scouts out. This trick, the combination of tanks and horse cavalry, as we will see in Russia later on, is one of history's lost military techniques.

Finally, General Percival decided on a sudden pullback to a defensible line, that of the Slim River, halfway down the peninsula. On 4 January 1942, the 11th suddenly moved back, trading distance for time, to put up yet another set of roadblocks, this time "properly" prepared. They were intending to hold the line of the Slim River until reinforcements from Singapore could arrive and stabilize the situation. Up to now, the 11th had been taking all the punishment, but there were the 9th Indians and the Australians to help hold the line.

By the morning of 7 January, the Punjabis were setting up near Trolak village, north of a settlement named Kampong Slim, on the Slim river. They were preparing roadblocks and getting ready to blow the important bridges, but were bone weary and moving slowly. They were so tired that commanders failed to check their maps. The old road, which had followed the terrain and wove around hills and swamps, had been recently improved, regraded, and most important, straightened. Every one of those straightened sections had a still-existing spur (the old road) going around it—and the Japanese maps showed the old, curving road.

When they came to a roadblock, their maps showed them an automatic bypass. Not only that, the plantations were full of firm, dry-weather access roads, all passable by bicycles. By this time, the Punjabis, Hyderabads, and the Argyles had been fighting for over a month and were short of almost everything, including decent communications gear. They were not only understrength and undermanned, but because of language barriers they could not fully communicate with each other. . . . Or even with their artillery. Worse, the Japanese had complete mastery of the air. They also had the tanks, whereas the British and Indians had only a rapidly decreasing number of ancient Lanchesters—about equivalent to a World War I Rolls, just not as rugged.

The British had been retreating since the war began, and had now decided to make a stand north of the Slim River. At the time of the Japanese attack, the Hyderabad Battalion was in the process of laying commo wire, stretching barbed wire, building concrete-block forts, and laying their few anti-tank mines. The Japanese 42nd Infantry Regiment, a part of their Fifth Infantry Division, sent scouts and a probing force against the British on the morning of 5 January. After a light covering force of Indian soldiers had been driven off, the Japanese attacked the half-built positions of the Hyderabad infantry.

They were bounced back savagely and spent the next day scouting and probing the rapidly hardening defenses. The Japanese advanced guard commander, a Colonel Ando, wisely decided to wait for his main force to catch up with him. This force included a company of tanks from the lone tank battalion of the Japanese Fifth Infantry Division, commanded by a Major Shimada. They were equipped with three Type 95 light tanks and 17 Type 94s. The tanks were accompanied by engineers and infantry in trucks. This combination was to prove deadly.

In the meantime, there had been some changes in command on both sides. The Japanese advance unit was now commanded by Colonel Ando; the commander of the 11th Indian, General Murray-Lyon, had been sacked and replaced by Brigadier A. Paris, who seemed to be something of an improvement. However the 11th was about worn out, they should have been relieved in place by say, the Australians. This did not happen, and it may have cost Singapore, which hurt the British as much as Pearl Harbor cost the United States.

The Slim River blocking position was theoretically as good as could be found, with the land and mountains on the east and the swamps on the west—for once channelizing the seemingly unstoppable Japanese. Brigadier Paris had installed his 12th Brigade in three consecutive blocking lines, consisting of the 4/19 Hyderabads, the 5/2nd Punjabis, and the Second Argyle and Sutherland Highlanders. This regiment, it should be noted, is the old 93rd, the "thin red line" that halted the Russian cavalry at Balaklava. They were also the ones with the only platoon of armored cars in the division. Now it would be their turn.

Colonel Ando, commanding the Japanese 42nd Regiment, was listening to his senior tank officer, one Major Toyosaku Shimada, who had a bold plan. This was one of the officers who had been studying the Germans and his idea was the same as the one used by among others, U. S. Grant's "Hit 'em and flank 'em" philosophy. . . . Drill right through their obstacles, get into their rear, and *force* retreat.

At 0330 hours on 7 January, a short artillery and mortar barrage hit the Hyderabads position and then they heard the one sound they feared most, the clatter of tank treads. The truck-borne Japanese infantry came on with their tanks, and the Japanese engineers filtered through the fighting forces to clear the antitank obstacles by blasting. In the middle of all this, the tanks dismounted a few crew members who, after a fast consultation with the engineers, ground guided their tanks through the cleared area. The Hyderabads, having no antitank weapons except the mines, were forced to retreat, after calling artillery in on their own positions, which they quickly vacated. This cost the Japanese just a single tank and delayed them only a single hour.

Leaving one battalion of the 42nd Regiment back to com-

plete the destruction of the Hyderabad Battalion, Colonel
Ando swept on. Obviously, he was onto something. The little armor/engineer/infantry task force was the perfect bur-
glar's tool for this type of breaking and entering. By 0430,
the column had come down to the Punjabi's belt of defenses
and found them a bit more prepared than the Hyderabads.
The lead tank hit a mine, broke a track, and slewed to one
side thus blocking the road.

The rest of the tank company slammed up against this
cripple, bumper to bumper, and the Punjabis attempted to
take advantage of the situation with Molotov cocktails and
.50 caliber antitank rifles. The .50 caliber Boys rifle was a
bolt operated item that couldn't break the frontal armor of
the Type 94 tank, but it could get through the side plating.
Unfortunately, the woods were full of Japanese riflemen
who effectively kept the Punjabis from closing with the
tanks. The Japanese were discovering tank-infantry cooperation and although they didn't use it well themselves, they
knew how to break up British and American tank-infantry
teams for the rest of the war.

About this time a probing Japanese scout noticed that his
map showed a curved, not a straight road, and he began
looking for the old road. Eventually the scouts found the
loop road and suddenly the column of tanks reversed direction, ran back to the cut-off, and in a few minutes came out
behind the Punjabis. Instead of heading southward, though,
the Japanese, not wanting to leave a hostile force behind
them, took the time to engage the Punjabis with small tank-
infantry teams—for a period a series of swirling firefights
circled through the jungle and plantations.

By 0600, the Hyderabads had been nearly wiped out, and
the rear battalion of the Japanese 42nd had caught up and
hit the Punjabis in their new rear . . . this was their old front
line, the battle having turned a full 180 degrees. By now
the Japanese individual units were working like broken field
runners and there were over a thousand British and Indian
soldiers out of the fight: dead, captured, or heading south
with what they could carry.

The other Punjabi Battalion (5/14th) and the Highlanders
should have been warned and been getting set up. Tragi-

cally, no word had gotten to them and the Imperial jugger-naut hit them unawares. Major Shimada still had 16 tanks operational and most of his engineers and truck-mounted infantry were still with him. He was obviously on a roll. He also had an interesting feature in his overall plan. That was to leave a platoon of light tanks on the road behind his advance in order to mop up stray parties of British and Indian troops and to prevent any regrouping.

The Argyle and Sutherland Battalion had set up two road-blocks, hinging their flanks on impenetrable jungle, only to find an armored force that they did not know existed slam into their barricades even as infiltrating infantry, fresh off the trucks, hit them from their jungled flanks. The first road-block didn't stand a chance and the second lasted only a little longer. There were several Lanchesters at this barri-cade, but the Japanese tanks made short work of them too. Quarter-inch plate may keep out rifle bullets but a 57mm cannon is another matter entirely. To their everlasting credit, the Highlanders held the Japanese infantry longer than the Hyderabads and the Punjabis, managing to separate Shima-na's flying column from the main body of the 42nd Regi-ment. Regrettably, the sacrifice didn't do much good as the HQ of the 11th Division had not got its act together yet.

All this action had taken place on the highway bypasses north of the town of Trolak, which sits around a bridge over a tributary of the Slim River. British engineers were setting demolition charges when a platoon of tanks came howling down upon them, completely unannounced. Machine gun fire from the tank's bow guns and rifle fire from truck-mounted infantry scattered the engineers, and then the tank platoon commander, a Lieutenant Watanabe, leapt from his tank, sword in hand, and personally slashed the demolition wires. That bridge was saved for the Regiment.

Watanabe and his company commander, Shimada, now without communications or orders from Colonel Ando, were working on instinct. They still had their engineers or truck-borne infantry with them. They still had a dozen more or less operational tanks and that bridge over the Slim River was an almighty tempting prize. The river at that point, half-way down the peninsula, was wide enough to be a military barrier. Capturing it intact would speed the invasion possibly by months.

The time, shockingly, was only 0730 hours and General Paris had only gotten the word at 0630. Just time enough to get his reserve forces on the road to try and stop the rampage. Those reserves, the 5/14th Punjabis, were the last combat unit of the 12th Brigade, and they were marching UP the road toward the Trolak bridge.

With Watanabe's tank in the lead, what was left of the little task force began a race with destiny, heading for the Slim River bridge. Before they had gone many miles, they came upon the desperately marching Punjabis who in normal infantry fashion were trotting along both sides of a dusty jungle road. They had to have heard the engines and looked askance at each other. Suddenly there were a dozen thundering, bullet-proof armored monsters among them and their battalion was dying. Literally hundreds of men were machine gunned and shelled in a few horrible minutes. In less than half an hour, the Punjabis had ceased to exist as a military unit. They had been converted to armed refugees by 48 men in tanks. Horsepower and firepower against raw flesh is not a balanced equation.

General Paris had done what his military education told him was the reasonable thing. Upon getting that awful series of messages from the Hyderabads, the Punjabis, and the Highlanders, he ordered his 28th Brigade out of their rest area and into preplanned positions. Then he ordered their antitank guns to limber up and move forward to brace up the Highlanders. Under normal circumstances, this would have been enough, but Shimada and Watanabe were moving so fast that they ran head on into that gun battery while it was on the road, hooked up to its transport trucks, and completely unable to fire.

If there was any room to maneuver when the two units met on a jungled road, in the middle of rubber plantations, and in a swirl of refugees, Shimada would have swung his command tank off to one side and raised a series of flags to a prearranged pattern that meant: "Deploy on line, facing enemy forces." That done, the signal to fire would have been Shimada's own tank firing into the midst of madly working gunners as they disconnected their 40mm antitank guns and frantically swung them toward the onrushing tanks. Then with still no guns pointing at them, the tankers would have opened fire, first at the guns and then at the ammunition trucks. . . . Then they would have simply pushed the bleeding wreckage off the road and continued.

The 28th Brigade of the 11th Division was a Ghurka unit, with all that the name implies. Amazingly enough, they had not been told *why* they were ordered into position. The orders moving them hadn't specified any immediate threat so, like the 5/14th Punjabis, the 2/1st Ghurkas, the 2/9th, and the 2/2nd Ghurkas, they were surprised in march order and machine gunned and cannonaded before they could even start to fight. In just a few short hours, over half the fighting force of the 11th Indian Division had been converted to refugees—or just plain killed. Those not engaged were bypassed and left for the rest of the 42nd Regiment to mop up piecemeal. A small regiment was in the process of ripping the heart out of a full-sized division, because of one thing: Iron Cavalry . . . tanks in the hands of men who knew how to use them!

By now the tankers were far into the tender rear of the 11th Division, back where a soldier normally thinks he is safe. They were shooting up soft transport, trucks, cars, even bullock carts, driving everything off the road and creating havoc for the advancing 42nd Regiment behind them to finish off. They found two batteries of the 137th British Artillery Regiment in various stages of unreadiness and shot them up in passing. Watanabe, by now wounded, was still in the van, heading for that all-important bridge.

At 0830, the tankers hit the bridge and its defenders, who were hastily setting demolition charges. The defense weapons of the bridge garrison were an antiaircraft battery and its 40mm Bofers guns couldn't penetrate tank armor, as their shells were fused to go off on aircraft skins. The tankers shot up the guns and the crews scattered. Watanabe, in too much of a hurry and too far away to use his sword on the wires, used his machine guns to cut the wires from long distance, and then he tore across the Slim River bridge . . .

They'd made it. Now, what else could they get into while they still had fuel and ammunition?

Leaving two of the more battered tanks to guard the bridge until the rest of the regiment arrived, Shimada and Watanabe moved southward again, more cautiously this time. They had made their objective, they just wanted to see what was in the area that might surprise them. Coming around a bend, Watanabe—still in the lead tank, wounded but keeping his head up—saw death facing him. The Third Battery of divisional artillery, one with 4.5-inch howitzers, was setting up across the road, 700 feet in front of him and with its guns leveled and firing direct. A 70-pound explosive shell slammed directly into Watanabe's hull front, utterly destroying the tank and killing the crew. . . . There wouldn't have been much left of either tank or crew, but they'd had their run. If the Japanese tank force needed a hero, they had one.

Checked at last, the remaining tanks of Shimada's task force circled back to that all-important bridge. About an hour later, their infantry caught up with them. By midnight, the rest of the 42nd had arrived and the rest of the Fifth Division was on the move. The British were also on the move, southward and trying to reconsolidate what little they had. Of the 12th Brigade, only 400 men (100 of them High-landers) made it clear to British lines. Of the 28th Brigade, about 700 survivors were evacuated.

South of them were fresh Australian troops, but they were not coming up to be fed into a cauldron. Someone had learned a costly lesson and there was some digging going on. The British had always had enough mines and blocking materials to set up a barrier, they just hadn't taken the Japanese seriously enough. The had also been seriously depleted in manpower. At the Slim River battle, most of the battalions were at less than 70 percent of full strength and were exhausted from walking and fighting. Retreating under fire is the most difficult of military operations and they had been doing it for a month.

Eleven days after Slim River, at a little town named Bakri, the Japanese tried it again. They hit the mine barrier, which was deeper and better laid than usual, and they began to work through it. The engineers, probing by hand and digging out the mines, were reducing the barrier. The tanks were impatiently edging along behind the engineers and the infantry were waiting . . . when an Australian antitank battery that had been patiently watching for the tankers to trap themselves, opened up. In minutes, nine tanks died in flames and explosions.

Suddenly, the conquerors were the victims of their own confidence. They were inside the minefield, covered by guns, and couldn't maneuver. All they could do was die in place. Shimada's juggernaut had been stopped cold, but it would only buy a little time, for the British Army in Malaya was shot down to half-strength and would have to be evacuated and rebuilt before it would fight again.

Had the British made any huge blunders or was it just a case of historical inevitability? The only really stupid thing that one old tanker sees is that they dismissed Malaya as nontank terrain. This, with the example of the jungle tankers of Bataan and Guadalcanal clearly evident. Lord knows they had the tanks available in 1942, for half the 8th Army in North Africa was American equipped by then. A dozen or so M-3 mediums would have eaten Shimada and Watanabe alive. . . . If they'd been there. Nontank terrain is any place a tank cannot physically go, and the only way to find out is to try.

Afterword

Major Shimada, who had the possibility of becoming one of the world's great armor officers, earned a unit citation for his company and his actions. He was then made instructor in the Armored Department of the Japanese Military Academy. The appointment seemed carefully designed to remove him from mainstream command, which is probably a good thing, as he could have seriously crippled British efforts later in the war when they came back to Southeast Asia with their own tanks. He could have been their Guderian.

REFERENCE SOURCES
Seize and Hold, Bryan Perrett, Arms and Armor Press.

"A Study in Armored Exploitation," LTC Martin N. Stanton, *Armor* magazine, May–June 1996.
Famous Tank Battles, Robert J. Icks, Doubleday.
Tank Warfare, Kenneth Macksey, Stein & Day.
The Cavalry of World War II, Janus Piekalkiewicz, Stein & Day.

CHAPTER 27

Hitler Moves East

WHEN HITLER, EMBOLDENED BY THE SUCCESSES OF THE PANzers on other fronts, launched Operation Barbarossa into Russia, he took on the largest tank force in the world . . . if you believe Russian numbers. Hitler had good cause to think he could get away with this invasion for several reasons. First, of course, was intelligence. He probably knew roughly how many tanks the Russians actually had, instead of having to believe their boast of 20,000 combat machines. As has been mentioned earlier, the Russians had set up a training camp deep inside Russia, at which the Germans were allowed to practice in return for the transfer of technical expertise.

All the while, though, the Germans were studying both Russian tank maintenance habits and tactical habits, and they were somewhat underwhelmed. Their estimates were that as few as one-quarter of the ill-led Russian tank fleet would be operational at any given time due to the majority of their officers being purged during the 1930s. They also had the advantage of an excellent rail network across Europe and the use of captured tanks. Many of the Panzers that had launched out on Barbarossa were captured Czech

LT-35s and 38s, which the Germans redesignated the
PzKfpw35(t) and 38(t). They also had the use of several
hundred French Renault and Souma light tanks in the ten-
ton range.

At that time, no other nation had such a density of communications and the intensive armor/air cooperation as the
Germans. Most analyses of warfare seem to miss one salient
fact. A tank is only one-third of a combined weapons system. It's attending infantry, whether Panzer grenadiers,
mechanized infantry, or Desantniki, are its eyes and ears
and its protection against both rude strangers with shaped
charge weapons and magnetic mines. The third segment of
the team is aerial support, in this case the Ju-87 dive
bomber.

The Junkers bomber was one of only two vertical dive
bombers in the war, the other being the American Hell-
Diver. This is important because a vertical bomber with dive
brakes is much more accurate than a conventional glide
bomber or level bomber. For a commander, this means that
he can cut loose from his conventional artillery and move
up as fast as his fuel and supplies can keep up with him. It
takes *time* to set up an artillery park and much of the German artillery was still horse drawn. Again and again, this
problem would return to haunt them, especially when,
against all expectations, American trucks began to show up
by the thousands to free the Russians from draft-horse
speed.

The question that seems to baffle most people who study
the issue, however, is: Why did he do it, and what made
him think it was possible? Part of the answer lies in the
shared history of Europe and inner Asia. When a Russian
looks west, he sees the Knights Templars, Napoléon, and
lately, the Germans as Menace. All those historic invasions
are responses to a menace that has existed since the beginning of recorded history. Look back at Qadesh, 1275 B.C.
(chap. 2) and its chariot warfare, and even farther back
you'll find more military menaces coming out of inner Asia.

The chariot wheels were rolling as early as 3200 B.C. at
Ur of the Chaldees, long before the time of Abraham.

Armed mounted invaders, that we only know as Indo-Europeans, took down Sumer and Akkad around 2300 B.C.

The Hyksos shepherd kings came out of Anatolia around 1600 B.C. and established suzerainty over Egypt, creating the Fifteenth Dynasty out of the crumbling ruins of the Old Middle Kingdom.

Here then, is the key to the fears of European and Mediterranean peoples. Every time in known history that a civilization has grown fat and complacent, the warriors of the steppes have harvested them. When a European looks east, he feels the hoofbeats of the earthshakers: Huns, Magyars, Turks, Attila, Genghis Khan, Tamerlane, Alp-Arslan. . . . The names go back to legendary times. The semilegendary Cimmerian tribes existed until destroyed by the Scythian hordes who bested the Assyrians. Is it any wonder that Europeans fear the tumult that comes howling out of the grass seas and looming mountains of a world that the ancient Greeks called Barbaria?

Hitler moved east partly out of greed and megalomania, but partly out of fear of what Stalin was going to do with 20,000 tanks. Not long before Operation Barbarossa, Marshal Georgy Zhukov, fresh from his victory at Nomonhan, had been holding invasion-style maneuvers on the new border between Greater Germany and Russia, in what used to be Poland. He actually held military war games over the same land and roads that the Germans later used to invade Russia.

This could not have avoided making Hitler nervous, and the Nazi dictator may have thought he was only making a preemptive strike. Then, wonder of wonders, his spies brought news of a serious weakness in Russia's military posture. For centuries, the western border of Russia had been secured by a string of forts along the old Polish border. Now those forts were being stripped of their garrisons and weapons. The troops and guns were on the move from their old locations to the new forts planned down the middle of Poland. Dismantled and on the move, both troops and weapons were terribly vulnerable to a sudden, sneak attack. If ever there was a time to invade Russia, it was the summer of 1941. Hitler, still smarting from a defeat at the hands of the RAF, and with only sideshow wars going on in North Africa and the Balkans, he struck eastward.

The 22 June, blitzkrieg took the Russians completely by surprise and only a few of their tanks were anywhere near the border, let alone in a ready state. One of these somehow materialized in front of the little Lithuanian town of Rossienie and stopped most of an Army for two days. The Sixth Panzer Division was part of Army Group North under General von Leeb and its mission on D-Day was to capture Rossienie and the bridges beyond the city, which would give vital access over the Dubysa River.

On D+1, the division occupied the village and set up an occupying force. Then they split off two combat teams (CTs) and took the two bridges that were ill defended: CT-R took the northern bridge, and CT-S captured the southern one. The result—CT-R captured about 20 Russians, including a lieutenant, and sent them back to the rear for interrogation. After loading the Russians onto a truck, they were put under charge of only one German sergeant . . . a very large sergeant.

The truck was heading south toward the town and the terrain on either side was swampy, with a large patch of woods just halfway between the northern bridge and the town. As they entered the low, brushy woods, the driver saw a Russian KV-1 tank sitting across the road, exuding menace. As the truckdriver slowed down, the Russians saw their chance and jumped the German sergeant. Apparently several grabbed his arms while the lieutenant went for the submachine gun slung across his chest.

Prying his right arm free, the sergeant swung hard enough to knock the lieutenant and several other Russians down. Then he fired his Schmiesser into the now-panicked Russians, some of whom dove over the side and into the woods. Most, however, were killed and after dumping the bodies, the sergeant ordered his driver to return to CT-R at the bridge, where he reported the existence of the KV-1. During all this time, the tank had not moved, as its crewmen were busy cutting the telephone lines between 6th Panzer HQ and the bridgehead.

The Germans could not know that this one heavy tank

and a few Russian soldiers and civilians were all that was in those woods, and they began to set up a perimeter defense around the town. Both bridgeheads also began to set up defenses and wait for the anticipated Russian counterattack. And the tank did not move. Possibly it was out of fuel and had used its last few drops to come out of its hideout to block that road.

On the morning of 24 June, the Germans sent 12 supply trucks out of Rossienie toward CT-S and suddenly the tank began to fire. The KV-1 could easily be called the "Big Brother" of the T-34, with a weight of armor at 47 tons and a 76mm main cannon. In quick thundering succession, the tank blew up all 12 trucks and then sat silent, waiting almost insolently stretched across the road.

German recon patrols could find no evidence of an impending general assault so they set out to remove this obstacle. They tried to bypass the tank by going through the woods, but their trucks got stuck in the soft ground and were instantly attacked by the Russians in the woods. Later in the day, a battery of 50mm *Panzer Artillerie Kanone* (PAK) antitank guns was slowly moved out of the town under muscle power. The crews, all volunteers with blood in their eyes, steadily pushed their guns through brush and into camouflaged positions. Finally, the Germans were in place, just 600 yards from the KV-1, which seemed to take no notice of them. The battery commander decided that the tank must be abandoned but decided to open fire anyway.

The first round was a direct hit. As all four guns in the battery opened up, hit after hit was made, with the troops cheering like spectators at a shooting match. At each strike the solid-steel shot rounds made a brilliant white spark on the Russian armor. Still the tank did not move. At the eighth shot, all four PAK-50s revealed themselves and the turret of the KV moved just slightly. There was a flash of fire and one PAK-50 was blown from its mount, the crew either wounded or dead. Three more times that awful cannon spoke and the battery was in ruins. Two guns were destroyed, two more damaged. The crews had to be evacuated, and the guns left in place. The Germans decided to up the ante.

Later on that afternoon, an 88mm Flak gun (the word comes from the sound of an AA [antiaircraft] shell exploding in the sky) was pulled out of its position near Rossienie and towed up toward the tank, which was facing the northern bridgehead at the time. Carefully camouflaged with branches, the gun was towed to within 900 yards of the quiescent tank, and the gun crew began to set up for direct fire.

Suddenly the KV's turret swung 180 degrees, steadied, and began to fire, every shot a direct hit on the 88mm, which was thrown into a ditch and wrecked. The Russian crew had just been waiting for them to get within range, knowing that the 88mm, while limbered up behind a truck, couldn't hurt them. When the Germans tried to collect their dead, they discovered another fact about the KV-series tank. It had a bow machine gun, a coaxial machine gun, and another one striking out of the *back* of the turret. It could fire in three directions at once, and they couldn't move without its permission, except at night. The decision was made to do this the old-fashioned way, by hand.

Meanwhile, at the northern bridgehead, supplies were running low and after a quick radio consultation, the commander decided to attack from CT-R, which was now down to eating canned emergency rations.

That evening, CT-R's engineer company commander asked for volunteers. All 120 men stepped forward, eager to succeed where others had failed. The CO picked every tenth man and led the attack himself. Just after full dark, the men crept out, loaded with small charges of explosives. Gliding through the darkness past a small hill, they entered the woods and, after removing their boots and stacking them with other gear, crept up to the tank. Crouched by the side of the road, they held a whispered conversation and then heard noises from the other side of the low embankment. A form mounted the hull and tapped several times on the turret hatch which opened slowly. Apparently someone had brought food to the crew, for the German patrol began to hear the sound of flatware clinking on dishes as the hatch closed again.

By 0100 hours, things had settled down and the engineer

captain led his men up to the side of the tank and began to place one of his charges against one track and roadwheel. What he hadn't noticed was that the KV's tracks and road-wheel were solid steel and would need much more TNT than he carried. After lighting the fuse, the group slipped off. A few minutes later a violent explosion lit up the side of the tank, apparently bending quite a lot of metal, but they had to lay low for a time for all three machine guns were now sweeping the brush. After the Russians quit firing, the engineer captain led his men back to CT-R at the bridge-head, reporting doubtful success and one man missing. Shortly before daylight, there was another blast and another spate of machine gun fire, then silence until dawn.

Later in the morning, the commander of CT-R spotted a soldier walking past his HQ barefoot but holding a pair of boots in his hand. He immediately called the man to him. This, of course, drew the attention of all the men in sight, and they watched as the colonel told the man to explain himself. As the trooper talked, the colonel suddenly grinned and offered him a cigarette. This was the missing engineer from last night and the following is his report:

I was detailed as an observer for the detachment that was sent out to blow up the Russian tank. After all preparations had been made, the company commander and I attached a charge of about double the normal size to the tank track, and I returned to the ditch which was my observation post. The ditch was deep enough to offer protection against splinters, and I waited there to observe the effect of the explosion. The tank, however, covered the area with sparodic machine gun fire follow-ing the explosion. After about an hour, when everything had quieted down, I crept up to the place where I had attached the charge. Hardly half the track was de-stroyed, and I could find no other damage to the tank. I returned to the assembly point only to find that the detachment had departed. While looking for my boots, I found that another demolition charge had been left behind. I took it, returned to the tank, climbed onto it and fastened the charge to the gun barrel, in the hope

of destroying at least that part of the tank, the charge
not being large enough to do any greater damage. I
crept under the tank and detonated the charge. The
tank immediately covered the edge of the forest with
machine gun fire which did not cease till dawn, when I
was finally able to crawl out from under the tank. When
I inspected the effect of the demolition, I saw to my
regret that the charge I had used was too weak. The
gun was only slightly damaged. Upon returning to the
assembly point, I found a pair of boots which I tried to
put on but they were too small. Someone had apparently taken my boots by mistake. That is why I returned
barefoot and late to my company.

This was early in the war, of course, and various combat
skills had not been learned. Specifically, the Russians in
those woods should have been picketing that tank and there
should have been a tanker on watch in the TC hatch with
a submachine gun. . . . Also when you go after a 47-ton
main battle tank, haul all the explosives you can carry. The
KV was over an inch thick in most places, heavier on the
bow. Its main defect seems to have been clutch and transmission problems, which might be why it never moved. The
Germans had made three tries: Plan 1 had been the PAK
505, plan 2 had been the 88mm, plan 3 had been the night
raid. Now it was time for plan 4, which would have been to
bomb the tank out of existence. Unfortunately, the Stukas
were busy elsewhere. Okay, then, the Germans would go to
plan 5.
Plan 5 involved an elaborate deception, a full company of
Mk-IV Panzers and another 88mm, brought in from Rossienie while the Panzers maneuvered through the woods,
cleaned out the Russian infantry, and the partisans. The
company of tanks came out from the town, got on line between the river and the KV, and began to work their way
through the woods. This finally deceived the Russian crew
and they began to take potshots at the German tanks in the
woods. Since the KV-series tanks carried around a hundred
cannon shells, they could afford a lot of this.
Meanwhile the 88mm was setting up behind the KV and

very quickly put three shots into it. The main gun of the KV suddenly rose to maximum elevation and all activity ceased. The 88mm crew put four more shots into the KV and finally classified it as knocked out.

The Germans closest to the KV dismounted and walked up to the monster tank, very cautiously. To their great amazement, there were only two 88mm holes in the tank and five great dents. There were also eight blue marks where the 50mm shells had merely bounced off; there was no trace of a fire starting, although there did seem to be a slight dent in the gun barrel. Suddenly the gun began to move, slowly dropping down level. In great haste, one of the German engineers slipped a grenade through one of the holes made by an 88mm. There was a dull thump from inside the hull and one of the turret hatches flew off. The crew were all dead, of course, but this one lone tank had stopped the 6th Panzer Division for two whole days. This particular crew of Russians had obviously come to fight a war.

REFERENCE SOURCES

Small Unit Actions during the German Campaign in Russia, U.S. Army Center for Military History, Publication 104–22.
War in the East, Simulation Publications, Inc.
Tank vs. Tank, Kenneth Macksey, Salem House.

CHAPTER 28

Schneider's Rampage
JUNE 24, 1941

THE EIGHTH PANZER DIVISION, PART OF PANZER GROUP Four under General Erich Hoepner, crossed the border into Russian-dominated territory on 22 June, and rushed into the newly annexed Baltic nations of Estonia, Latvia, and Lithuania with the aim of converting them into German annexations before their Slavic conquerors could get settled in. Panzer Group 4 was the northern prong of Operation Barberossa and was ultimately aimed at the vital seaport of Leningrad. For a time, they had the easiest traveling.

Unlike Russia, the Baltic nations had excellent roads, but no armies to speak of. The defending Russians had been literally kicked out of the way, and by the morning of 24 June, the Eighth Panzer Division was approaching the towns of Dvinsk and Griva, on the Dvina River. In order to cross the Dvina, 8th Panzer had to take the two bridges that crossed the river, at that point 250-yards wide. Their problem was to be that the Russians were stiffening up as political leaders died and were replaced by honest soldiers.

The city bridges were the prize. One was a highway bridge that would take the ten-to-twenty-ton Panzers with ease. It was also guarded by a fort. The northern bridge was a railroad bridge and was considered secondary, although it would have been considerably stronger, being rated for 50-ton locomotives and coal trains. . . . It was also guarded by a fort. Knowing that the bridges were probably wired for demolition, the local regimental commander decided to use subterfuge. He sent for two young officers, the captain who ran the Division's lead element and Lieutenant Schnieder, CO of company C 59th Armored Engineer Battalion. At that point, only the Germans habitually kept engineer units that far forward, and it was one of the secrets of their stunning advances. Combat engineers were one of the lost secrets of blitzkrieg. The two mystified officers received this verbal order:

One platoon of Company C, divided into four assault detachments will launch a surprise attack against the two bridges at Dvinsk. The detachments will jump off at 0130 on 25 June, and head for the bridges in the four Russian trucks that the division captured earlier today. The Russians must be led to believe that the trucks are friendly, so that the assault detachments can get within striking distance of the bridges without being challenged.

Once the detachments have reached the bridges, they will immediately cut all cables leading to the bridges from both banks to prevent the enemy from setting off the demolition charges electrically, cut all detonating cords leading to the charges and defend the bridges against all Russian counterattacks.

The main body of Company C will also jump off at 0130, but will proceed somewhat more slowly so as to arrive at the bridges about 15 minutes after the assault detachments, which it will relieve. Company C will be followed by the division's advance guard, which arrive at the highway bridge at 0305. Since the highway bridge should be firmly in German hands by this time, the advance guard consisting of one armored infantry battalion and one tank battalion will cross over into Dvinsk and spearhead the division's northeastward advance.

Gentleman, I have confidence in your ability to execute this difficult mission successfully and wish you luck. If there are no questions, that is all.

Two young German officers had just arrived at a piece of military real estate called "Function Junction."

While the division advance guard was getting its act together, Lieutenant Schnieder made special arrangements within his company. The four Russian trucks were manned from his 4th platoon. Each truck got ten men armed with a machine gun, submachine guns, hand grenades, and wirecutters. The main body of Company C marched in the following order. The first and second Platoons, each equipped with special engineer tanks, which were modified Pz-IIIs with lifting cranes attached to their hulls, would follow the Russian trucks. Each tank would be carrying a heavy demolition charge.

Following them would be the normal vehicles of Fourth Platoon, seven halftracks armed with rocket launchers. Since the men of Fourth Platoon were in the assault trucks, only the drivers would be in the halftracks. The Company's Third Engineer Platoon was a bridge platoon and was employed elsewhere so it could not be used, but the Fifth Platoon would follow in their own trucks. At 0130, they moved out of their combat bivouac settling into a road-speed of 40 miles per hour. Three trucks headed for the highway bridge through the little town of Griva, and one split off northward along the river road, heading for the railroad bridge. Both units passed several Russian infantrymen, but were not challenged.

By 0215, the three trucks approaching the highway bridge were almost through the town and nearing a Russian guard post of about 50 men. At first it looked as if they would get through, but a Russian sentry flagged them down. There were several Russians standing on the approach to the bridge and the driver of the lead truck, which also contained the platoon leader, pulled over as if to stop. As the Russian sentry moved around to the passenger's side, the driver suddenly gunned the truck in low gear, double clutched into second, and roared onto the bridge, scattering the Russians and running over several in the process.

The second truck followed quickly and the stunned Russians ignored the vehicles and went to the aid of their injured comrades. . . . They had missed the third truck which had quietly stopped with its lights out while ten German engineers ghosted out into the dark. These men were half infantry and had double skills. On signal, they jumped the dazed Russians and killed them with knives and bayonets. During this time, the first truck and its crew had gotten through and was busily cutting wires. The second truck had stopped in the middle of the bridge, its men rushing back to help the outnumbered group from the second vehicle. Then they began to take small arms fire from the now alerted Russians on the north bank.

The two groups of wire and detonator-cord cutters had just barely finished their work when they began to take casualties from Russian 45mm antitank rifles and machine guns. A rousing firefight then ensued, and the Germans began to take heavy losses. Ten minutes after the initial assault, the Russian rear guard unit that had been left in Griva arrived and began to chew on the Germans from the southern end of the bridge. By 0240, the 30-man assault detachment had lost one officer, one NCO, three privates, and four wounded. Then, Lieutenant Schneider and the tanks arrived.

Company C's 1st and 2nd Platoons of engineer tanks fanned out north and south of the captured bridge and began to slam 50mm shells into the north bank, quickly silencing the AT guns. Ten minutes later, the halftracks arrived and were quickly manned by the survivors of the 4th Platoon and began to loft rockets into the city of Dvinsk, setting off many fires. By 0305, right on schedule, the division's advance guard began to stream across the bridge, but the Russians were being damn stubborn.

A German engineer trooper suddenly noticed a hissing trail of smoke. A Russian had crawled onto the bridge with a fuse lighter and attached it to a cut fuse, thus the whole bridge was only seconds from going up with the Panzers on it. The engineer quickly wrenched the fuse from the nearest charge while several other Germans quickly jumped on the Russian. Lieutenant Schneider, meanwhile, had another bridge to handle. He had sent just ten engineers to handle the railroad bridge, and the firing from that objective was picking up.

Taking his Second (Tank) Platoon and his Fifth (Engineer) Platoon, he now rushed toward the railroad bridge following the river road. The lone truck that had attempted the assault had been detected by the guards in the fort, perhaps warned by the commotion down in the town. Just as the truck turned onto the road, it began to receive small arms fire and was abandoned, burning, over 500 yards (a third of a mile) from the fort. Then all ten men began a difficult assault on a stone fort full of Russians. They were first pinned down by machine gun fire, and at that time the Russians, panicked by the German success in town, set off the bridge demolitions with a terrific crash.

As the smoke cleared, though, it appeared that the main structure of the bridge was intact, only the wooden structure and the railroad ties were burning. Apparently not all the charges had gone off, and there was still a chance to save the bridge. At 0330, Lieutenant Schneider arrived and took charge. There was still heavy small arms fire coming from the fort, but nothing serious, so Schneider ordered one of his engineer tanks to back up to the fort's steel gate and lower a 110-pound demolition charge from its cargo boom. Then the tank backed off and turned in place, facing its armored bow into the blast. When the smoke cleared, the gate was gone and the German engineers charged into the breach . . . only to face another wall and another gate, this one of steel. By this time, the bridge was burning heavily and the Russian fire from the fort was preventing the use of firefighting equipment.

Again an engineer tank backed up to the steel gate under heavy enemy fire and again the gate was blown off by a 110-pound charge of TNT. Again the Germans charged through alongside their tanks; this time a few Russians surrendered. There were still a few in the fort's inner citadel who refused to give up, and the engineers, tired of incontinent stubbornness, used shaped demolition charges and simply blew the Russians out. By 0400 hours, the fort was in German hands and the fire was quickly brought under control. Of the 100 Russians in the fort, 70 were casualties and 30 were prisoners. Two things the Germans had that the Russians did not: armor and audacity. The whole assault had taken only an hour and 45 minutes, from initial attack to completion. . . . And Schneider was just getting started on an armored rampage.

The German practice of keeping combat engineers far forward was one of the keys to their success. The ability to reduce obstacles and bridge gaps is key to the advance: specifically, the capability of taking an armored vehicle far enough forward, for example, to put large amounts of explosives in the right place or to lay a bridge from under armor before the enemy has time to react. By putting engineers under armor with combat vehicles, sometimes they can also take enemy units out without having to wait for reinforcements. . . . By late August 1941, Lieutenant Schneider had become a permanent part of the division's advance group.

By 28 August, the 8th Panzer Division found itself in a little town named Kignisepp, southwest of Leningrad. A disorganized Russian force had been defeated south of them at Luga and was attempting to reach safety in Leningrad, which was already embattled. At that time, the 8th Panzer's mission was to reach the Luga-Leningrad highway and attack the retreating Russians who would otherwise add to the Leningrad garrison. The pivot point seemed to be a town named Volosovo, where several important roads and a railroad junction formed a communications hub. Schneider, as usual, was at the head of the First Division column, but behind the point unit. The operational area was made up of mostly swampy, forested terrain that severely limited the maneuver space.

The 8th Panzer had moved out at 0400 hours on 29 August and had quickly taken Moloskovitsy, its railroad station and road junction. Then it ran into only light resistance that was brushed aside. By 1215 hours, the point unit was in the little hamlet of Kikerino and the lead column, led by Schneider was taking a travel break in Volosovo. One of Schneider's officers with a motorcycle messenger was keeping him in contact with the advance guard, but as he was about to order his company back on the road, several things happened at the same time.

First, he heard machine gun and antitank weapons firing from the northeast, then a slightly panicked truckdriver came roaring back form the direction of Kikerino and said that the column had been ambushed, *after* the point had gone past the woods east of Volosovo. At this time, Schneider ordered his two engineer tank platoons to assemble with his rocket platoon at Logonovo, a small outpost hamlet of Volosovo, while he drove off for a scouting trip. About a mile east of the Logonovo road fork and on the crest of a low ridge, he could see about three hundred Russian soldiers coming out of the woods between Logonovo and Gubanitsky. They were heading for the top of the same ridge on which he stood. Along the southern edge of the roughly triangular piece of forest, he could see at least one Russian machine gun pit and one antitank rifle covering the road where two trucks lay burning. In one truck, small arms ammunition was cooking off. Schneider assumed that what he was seeing was the vanguard of a locally hatched Russian counterattack.

Ordering his driver to return to the Logonovo road junction, he gave the following order to his assembled platoon leaders:

Company C will immediately attack the Russian companies approaching the ridge, disperse them and prevent any additional Russian forces from emerging from the forest.

The First Tank Platoon will deploy immediately along the Logonovo-Gubanitsky road, midway between the two villages, lay down a smoke screen when the rocket projectors fire their salvo, and drive to point "A" which is shown on your map, at the forest's edge. The platoon will protect its own left flank.

The Second Tank Platoon will assemble east of the road fork and jump off simultaneously with the first, directing its thrust toward point B.

The Fourth Platoon [halftracks with rocket launchers] will take up positions outside of Lagonovo and will fire a salvo of 24 rockets at the two aforementioned points. It will then close up with Second Platoon and annihilate the Russian forces caught between the ridge and the forest. The first squad of the 4th Platoon will remain in its firing position as a company reserve.

The 5th Platoon will proceed along the highway, de-truck at a point about 1000 yards east of the road fork, occupy that stretch of the road which crosses the ridge and form the right wing of the attack force. This platoon will also clear the southwest edge of the forest and se-cure the portion of the highway that borders the forest.

I shall be with the Fourth Platoon.

By 1300 hours, the Germans were almost ready and Schneider had driven north toward Gubanitsky to keep track of the Russians. By now they were coming down the west side of the ridge in good order with scouts out in front. Behind them came a few 45mm AT guns pulled along by their crews. Behind the advance line, two more Russian in-fantry companies were coming out of the woods, at both points A and B. Schneider was now seriously outnumbered, but he had the firepower. He had had a quick conference with the column commander at Lagonovo, and there would be plenty of backup if he got his tail in a crack.

Just as the Russians began to deploy that second wave, the first rocket salvo landed in it and smoke shells began to leap from the tanks' launchers, hiding the advance of the defiladed Panzers. The Russians stopped their advance and began to fire into the smoke. By the time the smoke began to thin, the tanks had reached the crest of the ridge and had pinned the attacking Russians down. Then the Russians began to clump up and retreat, which only made them better targets for the Panzer's machine guns.

The ill-trained, ill-organized Russians broke and left their guns in the road as the tanks rolled over them. The 5th Platoon, acting as Panzer grenadiers, trotted alongside the tanks, mopping up little pockets of resistance and taking prisoners. It seemed to be all over when the First Tank Platoon's leader radioed in that he was taking intense small arms fire and was being attacked in company strength from the direction of Gubanitsky. Schneider immediately committed his one "reserve" HQ tank and a 12-rocket salvo from his 4th Platoon's last pair of launchers. By this time, the First Platoon had swung its axis and attacked northward on line, beating this last ditch effort off. By 1420, Schneider could radio the march commander that the road to Leningrad was again safe for traffic. By evening of the 29th, the Eighth Panzer Division was engaging the Russian column and had cut the Luga-Leningrad road at the village of Sivoritsy.

Plans were immediately made to continue mopping up fugitive Russians and the division was to split into two columns during the night. The major force would be heading down toward Luga as a smaller element drove southeastward toward a larger town named Staro-Siverskaya. Schneider's part of this would be to advance and secure the town of Kurovitsky, which would prevent the Russians from getting any reinforcements through, provided it could be garrisoned in time. After supper and a short maintenance period, C Company moved out, still minus its bridge platoon, which was off repairing damaged spans so that supplies could keep up with the rapidly advancing Panzers.

The First Platoon led out with its Mk-IIIs and the Fifth Platoon in its trucks acting as Panzer grenadiers. They passed the little village of Kobrino without incident and by 2145 were in Kurovitsky. Suddenly a column of ten Russian trucks, full of soldiers, were pinned in the headlights of the lead tank, which immediately opened fire. One truck escaped the tank fire in the direction of Vryitsa, then two more got away down the road to Staro-Siverskaya. The remaining vehicles were shot up and by that time their passengers were long gone into a night so black that the Germans wisely decided to forego pursuit into those soft swamps. Instead Schneider began to prepare to hold his new village. . . . And incidentally catch up on his sleep. His men had been going since 0400 the previous morning.

The First Tank Platoon and one squad of engineers were to mine and block the two roads to the south. The Second Platoon, minus one tank, was to block the road to Vyritsa, with another of the Fifth Platoon's engineer squads out in front of it to act as an outpost. They also would be planting mines. Having set up his blocking forces, Schneider disposed the rest of the company around the village as a reaction force in case the Russians tried a night attack. . . . They did.

At 0015 on 30 August in a black, moonless night, the Second Platoon reported hearing tracked vehicles from the direction of Vyritsa . . . then silence. Forty-five minutes later a truck coming up the road from Staro-Siverskaya hit a mine, resulting in two Russian casualties and the capture of one wounded Russian officer. The rest of the soldiers escaped into the dark, looming Russian forest. At 0230, the Second Platoon again heard the rattle of Russian tracks, closer this time. More silence, then a shot and the Second Platoon radioed in that its officer had just been sniped. Thirty tense minutes later, First Platoon radioed that five trucks were approaching from Staro-Siverskaya. Things were getting a bit hairy.

The lead trucks were immobilized and seriously damaged by mines but the Russians had jumped off and were trying desperately to become invisible while German machine guns from four tanks tore into them. Finally that battle was terminated when two Mk-IIIs rumbled a short way into the woods and drove the Russians off with point-blank cannon fire. Then the village began to blow up in their faces.

Schneider's command post was northwest of the village, where he had put most of his minuscule reserve, and now he began to hear small arms fire. Then a motorcycle messenger arrived on foot, having had his cycle shot out from under him two blocks inside the town. Then the Second Platoon radioed that it was receiving fire from the eastern edge of the village. Apparently the Russians from all those blown trucks were infiltrating into the town. Schneider ordered the remaining squads of the Fifth Platoon to assemble at his command post and then to start combing out the village, from north to south.

Dawn was beginning to lighten the eastern sky when the 5th Platoon, with two tanks began to clean out Kurovitsly, house by house. They were met by fire from houses, stables, hedges, and haystacks. Each house had to be first hand-grenaded and then entered by men with submachine guns who had long since learned the tricks. First the grenade, then the man with the submachine gun rushes in and shoots at the furniture, where a wise city combatant will have been hiding from the grenade. Then you're through the room and maybe the grenade you left on the table will get the hold-outs. Some Russians played possum and had to be killed several times before the treatment became permanent.

It is an awful thing to shoot a corpse, just in case, and watch his eyes open in shock as a grenade rolls out of his hand. Each haystack had to be sprayed with bullets or set on fire. The engineers, though, had an advantage over most troopers. They carried a goodly supply of explosives and buildings that gave too much resistance were simply destroyed, along with their inhabitants. Any room that appeared too dangerous received a delay explosive shell from a tank, which first penetrated the wall and then went off inside the building. Outbuildings were simply crushed with the tracks and the survivors machine gunned. By 0600, resistance within Kurovitsky had terminated.

Then the external attacks commenced. Shells began falling in Kurovitsky from some unknown Russian gun battery. At 0745, the Second Platoon reported tank sounds from the direction of Vyritsa. Then Russian infantry emerged in company strength and in assault formation from the woods southwest of the town. The Second Platoon now reported that a KV-1 heavy tank was standing in the road, past the mine barrier, and shelling them, albeit inaccurately—this was the source of the random shelling of the town. It was getting sticky, but Schneider still had his artillery. He ordered the Fourth Platoon's rocket tracks to go to firing positions north of town and be ready to fire on both the tank *and* the western approaches.

Now the Fifth Platoon, Schneider's sole infantry source at the time, was still tired from combing out the town, but it found firing positions in houses, hedges, and barns in the western edges of town—just in time to meet the oncoming Russian infantry. The time was 0815 and nobody had had much sleep for over 30 hours. Now they were engaged on east, west, and south. Suddenly a heavy blast was heard from the Vryitsa road. The crew of KV had apparently dug out a few mines and tried to advance. All they got for their trouble was a blown track, and the Germans watched as the Russians got out of their tank, inspected the damage, and then got back in and resumed shooting . . . very inaccurately. Most of the shells went right over the village.

By now, 0830 hours, Schneider had been radioing desperately for help—to no avail. This was part of a larger Russian push, up from Luga, and the rest of the 8th Panzer had its hands full. The Russian infantry attacks from the south were becoming more insistent, and suddenly the KV's crew figured out what they were doing wrong, and they began to come much closer to hitting German positions. Schneider ordered his rocket tracks to eliminate this menace and a full salvo knocked out the Russian tank. Then the halftracks began to swing around to take on the infantry from the west, but the range had become too short for the rockets.

Schneider was up against it, and there was only one way to handle the situation. He quickly gave orders by radio, messenger, and voice to assemble all his running assets at his CP. Then he led a roaring column of tanks and halftracks out in a sudden feint, 500 yards out of town, up the road to Kobrino. This might have looked like a sudden retreat to the Russians, but suddenly Schneider took his column sharply left, and came up on the unprotected Russian flank, cannons thumping, machine guns chattering, and treads grinding. The charge of a tank platoon simply cannot be described, only felt . . . and feared. The Russians had been taken completely by surprise. Schneider led his charge triumphantly in a sweep around to the south of the town, driving the Russians off or forcing them to surrender. Fifteen minutes later, the vanguard of the 8th Panzer's southern task force arrived. The time was 0930. Schneider's rampage was over, but for others, the war was just beginning. When Joseph Stalin purged his army in the late 1930s he actually beheaded it. Now it was up to Georgi Zhukov to pull the fat out of the fire, and he used a totally unexpected, forgotten force . . . The Cossacks.

REFERENCE SOURCE
Small Unit Actions During the German Campaign in Russia, Center for Military History, Published number, 104–22.

CHAPTER 29

The Cossack Tankers

WHEN THE TANK WENT INTO BATTLE, IT WAS SOON FOUND OUT that it was not the invulnerable monster of H. G. Wells's fiction. Like any other weapon system, it had strengths—and weaknesses, one of which was its lack of close-in defense. The Germans soon found out that a bundle of hand grenades stuffed into the tracks could immobilize a British Mk-IV, if it were not accompanied by attendant infantry. At Flers-Courcelette, it was found out that even a 4.5 mile per hour tank would soon outrun an infantryman with a 70-pound "combat-necessities" pack.

The horsed cavalry should have been the natural combat companion of the tank, along with the airplane, but due to command dilatoriness in the person of General Sir C. T. McM. Kavenaugh, the English cavalry cantered gracefully out of history at Cambrai. In America, all through the lean years, cavalry tried gallantly to make the transition, but again, its commanders fought fanatically against "those rude mechanicals." There was one cavalry/tank exercise in the late 1930s when horse cavalry was sent along the roads in cattle trailers, in order to be able to keep up with the mechanized troops. The scheme worked, but it was a case of too little, too late. The die was cast for mechanization and eventually, modern combined arms.

The world's military leaders were beginning to see that a tank is only one-third of a combat team, the other two-thirds being infantry and air/artillery. There were, however, still problems to be ironed out. Artillery, for instance, was still mostly horse drawn or even if truck drawn, couldn't keep up with the tanks on rough ground. Infantry support was worse. Even on level ground, they limited the rate of march to 2.5 miles per hour and combat speed to a few miles per day.

The Germans solved part of the problem with Panzer grenadiers who rode in armored halftracks but still had to fight on foot. By perfecting the Ju-87/Panzer connection, they were allowed to cut loose from their artillery and move at tank speed. The Russians in their turn perfected the mounting of a special infantry called Tank Desantniki on the fenders of their tanks or on special trailers hauled by the tanks. This trick seems to have been invented in the Spanish civil war, but the problem remained. How do you keep up the pace of the battle once the infantry is dismounted?

What was obviously needed was an infantryman who was about nine-feet tall, and who could march 30 miles a night cross-country, and charge at 20 miles per hour alongside the tanks. Ideally he should also be able to carry his own rations, about a thousand rounds of ammunition, and a sack of hand grenades. If he could also be equipped with something that could break an inch of armor, that would also help . . . Impossible? No, we have just described a Russian Cossack. The Russians made Cossack cavalry into a giant tank-escort infantry, and they made it work because they had to. Necessity is the mother of invention, but the father is desperation.

The military genius behind this seems to have been one Georgi Zhukov, and the knowledge was earned the hard way, in the 1920s and 1930s of the interwar period. While the cavalries of the Western world were playing polo and theorizing between the wars, Russia was fighting a ferocious civil war. White Russian Cavalry was fighting Red Russian Cavalry, and they were using all the new weapons as they came out. They had also absorbed much western knowledge in the process. The little known British/American/Allied intervention in Russia from 1919 to 1922 introduced the Russians to tanks and they had already figured out water-cooled machine guns on horse-drawn carts. When they observed the German invention of the submachine gun, ideas began to percolate. Zhukov, remember, commanded tanks and cavalry at Nomonhan, and he was a cavalryman who had gone through the Russian civil war and survived the purges. All through the sudden and unpredicted German invasion named Operation Barbarossa, something was obviously working in his subconscious.

While Stalin's paranoia was probably a symptom of a basic maniac/depressive nature—a Russian medical institute still has his brain, pickled—part of his suspicion of the officer corps was of Czarist origin. When Red cavalry fought White, from 1919 to 1923, the Whites had the loyalty of the old officer corps and were slowly winning. Then Stalin and his henchmen kidnapped the families of many of the old officers and forced them to work for the Bolsheviks.

This worked but created some of the ill-will that led to the purges of 1937–1938. Those purges decimated the Russian officer corps but seemed to have missed the Cossacks who had been disbanded in 1923 after the Russian civil war. Around Joseph Stalin you had to have eyes in the back of your head, but Russia was up against the deadliest enemy in its history. When Zhukov convinced Stalin to reactivate the Cossacks, their leadership was intact, and they could handle tanks as well as horses.

All through 1941 and 1942, the Cavalry, which seems to have been about fifty percent Cossack, of mostly the Don tribe but Kuban and Kalmuk also, fought desperate rear guard actions against the Panzer armies. Open, maneuver warfare is much different than static trench warfare which is designed to protect real estate. On the open steppes and plains and deserts, the idea is to inflict so much pain on an enemy that he will hopefully either surrender his territory, or if he is the invader, go away and stop bothering you. This opens up a whole set of new weaknesses that are vulnerable to heavily armed cavalry. . . . Provided that the horsemen are protected by tanks. If infantry can work alongside tanks, the reasoning went, so can cavalry, at tank speed.

Simply put, there are only 300 or so tanks in an armored division and, less a tactical reserve, they are all up front killing the enemy. Nor were these the heavy tanks of later years, they were mostly Panzer-IIs and-IIIs, with a smattering of captured Czech and French hardware, all small tanks. And the Cossacks were towing antitank and machine guns on wheels, while mounted scouts were out on the land on which they had been raised, hunting for Germans.

Normally, a unit's reconnaissance troops find the enemy, who is also usually a discrete formation on the move. Then what is called a battle for information begins, as the scouts probe for strengths and weaknesses. Their reports, going back to mobile HQ, make it possible for the two opposing commanders to begin the battle proper. Unless the division is advancing on line with other divisions, it is possible to get around its flanks and start chewing on its soft, vulnerable supply vehicles, mobile shops, mess halls, and the like. The only military force back there is going to be the tactical reserve that any canny commander leaves to plug any losses or exploit any sudden gains. Colonel-General Oka Gorodovikov describes what could happen, less than two days after Germany invaded Russia.

From June 24–31, 1941, the cavalry detachment commanded by Major General Kryuchenkin was entrusted with the defense of the line at the Ikva River, in opposition to General Kliest's 1st Tank Army. On June 26th and 27th, the detachment defeated the 16th German Tank Division, smashed more than 40 tanks and a battalion of motorcycle troops and captured an antitank battery and a large number of guns. More than 1000 German soldiers were killed in this battle. . . . In August of 1941, several units of the 2nd Tank Army, of the much vaunted General Guderian—one of the theoreticians of tank warfare—began advancing from the district of Chausi and Kricney in the direction of Roslav, in an attempt to emerge behind the lines of our troops to the north of Roslov and surround them.

In their turn the flank units of Guderian's group were exposed to the attacks of our cavalry detachments commanded by Colonels Yakunin and Kuliev. Effecting a forced march under cover of night, the Soviet Cavalry at dawn on the 2nd of August, attacked Guderian's columns near Shumachi and destroyed 30 tanks, 50 machines with infantry and 2 trench mortar batteries.

As usual in these sweeping narrations, no mention is made of just *how* the work was done, but a look at the Cossack TO&E on page 398 shows quite well how it had to have been done. Those cavalry troops were hauling horse-mobile antitank guns with them. There were just too many Germans and too few Cossacks.

Although much of conventional historical writing is given to the glamour vehicles—the T-34, the JS series, the Panther, and the Tiger—most of that war was fought by the little tanks: the Panzer-IIs, IIIs, and IVs; the Russian BT series; and the T–70s. Gasoline fuel, however, makes most tanks very short ranged and dependent on fuel supplies. Many pictures show Panzers with as many as 20 gasoline cans mounted in racks on the turret tops and over the engine compartments. Gods, what a gift from heaven to an antitank gunner. One burst of tracers and it is all over.

That tactical reserve would have been traveling with its gas cans mounted, continuously topping the internal tankage off, ready at an instant to drop the cans at a collection point and to charge into battle. Into this situation rode a Cossack patrol with the smallest of their A-T weapons, the 14.5mm rifle, mounted on a pack saddle. The rifle was mounted so that it could be pivoted and fired right off the saddle by the trooper who was leading the pack horse. A half dozen shots out of a woods line would set three to five Panzers on fire and then the patrol would move out again.

They made mistakes, of course, and got shot up many times before they learned their lessons about the strengths and weaknesses of tanks. Those lessons were sent in long cables to the United States, where they were basically ignored. They were sent to one of the few connections the Russian cavalrymen knew in America, the old *Cavalry Jour-*

nal, which was in the process of becoming *Armor* magazine. (For the researcher, a full set, dating back to 1888, exists in the Library of Congress.) Horsed cavalry need not have died out and they could probably fill a role in today's limited wars . . . *if* the modern military mind will accept the fact that modern weapons do *not* eliminate the effectiveness of older ones. A bodkin point will still kill at 300 yards, and a horse will still outmarch a man.

Oddly enough, the Russian knowledge came directly from the American Civil War, and the exploits of J.E.B. Stuart, John Hunt Morgan, and Nathan Bedford Forrest, and the rest of the cavalry greats are still taught in Russia today. They have even adopted the American word *raid* into the Russian language.

What happened was this: Our Civil War was the first of the modern wars and our leaders knew it. After the war, they sent a large digest of events to every military college in Europe, where they proceeded to gather dust. Field Marshal Helmuth von Moltke, the German military genius of the age, said scornfully, "one armed mob chasing another, nothing can be learned from this." In Russia, however, the information fell into the hands of the descendants of Genghis Khan and the Tartars. In a way, the knowledge had come full circle, because the campaigns of the Khans were studied at West Point, along with those of Alexander the Great, Hannibal, Oliver Cromwell, and the Comanche and Arapaho. There should be little surprise at what happened next.

The semidisciplined Cossack cavalry had already given one European army a solid kicking around, that of Napoleon Bonaparte. French General Moran had this to say about them:

> These savage riders have no formations, no alignment, and do not present that precise regularity in movements which are so respected in our army. What a beautiful sight our cavalry presented when, glistening in the rays of the summer sunshine, it proudly deployed its slender lines on the shores of Lake Niemm. And how sad it is to think that these masterly evolutions which tired out

the horses, proved to be completely useless against these Cossacks whom everybody despised beforehand, but who nevertheless accomplished more than any other cavalry.

General Etienne Maurice Gérard had this to say:

The light cavalry which surrounds the enemy with an impenetrable veil of vigilance, which exhausts him, which always strikes weakness and almost invariably evades the counterblow, fulfills every goal that light cavalry should strive to accomplish. They come and break up like a mighty surf; they sting like hornets; and they disappear like smoke.

And this was *before* these men were exposed to Stuart and Forrest. The basic principle learned from the American experience was that once you have broken a hole in the enemy main line of resistance (MLR), go do something that will cause pain and make him weaken his main force to catch you. Prince General Golitzin expressed it this way, "The Americans transmuted into reality the cavalrymen's most celestial dreams, and our cavalry is the only one in Europe which can emulate them." This was because the Cossacks already had a tactic designed to break up a solid enemy line. One learned on the steppes but known by Erwin Rommel, who had also studied Stuart, Morgan, and Sheridan, as well as Genghis and Tamerlane.

The Cossacks used a peculiar assault formation called the "lava," which broke one of their regiments up into small groups that would flow over a formal battlefield, always harrying, always searching, always taunting the formal unit to charge into a trap. The trap would then close, bite off a chunk of the enemy, and then disperse before reprisal could trap it in turn. When they were attacked, they would break, fade back, and then strike the attackers' flanks, doing as much damage as possible, and then vanish. This naturally requires small-unit commanders of incredible independence, who are still capable of combining quickly to take advantage of a break in the lines. It also requires the use of light, mobile horse artillery. Heavy weapons on wheels go all the way back to Julius Caesar and Alexander who used them to break up hostile formations.

The problem was, this was all they did—fight the enemy's formal line. What they got from the Americans was the concept of the coup de main, the deep raid into the enemy's heart. . . . Once, late in 1941, a regiment of Cossacks got so far into the German rear that they came within minutes of nabbing Heinz Guderian himself.

When the Cossack national tactics were combined with the American experience and then ground through the cauldron of the Russian Civil War, something unique in the annals of war began to emerge. To quote one of its most effective proponents, Colonel General Oka Gorodovikov:

> In fact, the inefficient use of cavalry in almost ALL of the armies during the first world war, caused many shortsighted "theoreticians" to claim that cavalry was powerless against modern technique—that its role as an independent arm of troops was over. In this fallacious viewpoint, they contrasted the "new technique of war" with the former "purely sabre cavalry" instead of visualizing a rearmed cavalry with tactics adapted to conform with the new technical equipment.

This writer's grandfather, who rode into Mexico with General John Pershing, frequently commented on the "idiocy of using a thousand pounds of horse and man to carry a three-pound pistol and a big knife into battle." Only when dismounted and using their carbines could these troops deliver accurate long-range fire.

We've all seen the histories, we've all seen the old movie Westerns of carbine, pistol, and saber cavalry charges against Cheyenne and Comanche, Custer and Little Big Horn, ad nauseum; we've also seen the horrendous results of cavalry charging modern firepower. . . . So what did the Russians know that we, and the Germans did not? A close look at the eventual TO&E of a fully modernized Russian cavalry regiment is *very* instructive. What they figured out is that a horse can haul a lot more military impedimenta then an infantryman. If machine guns can cut down horses, they figured, horses can pull enough machine guns and small cannons to even the odds. Here is the TO of a Russian M-1943 Cavalry Regiment and the basic personnel roster that went to about twelve hundred Cossacks.

Four squadrons of 140 horsemen, armed with mostly submachine guns and rifles, but also carrying horse-packed 14.5mm AT rifles

One squadron armed with 16 heavy machine guns on carts

One battery of 76mm AT guns [This was the same gun used on the T-34 and KV-1 tanks. . . . It could break 3 inches of armor.]

One battery of 45mm AT guns, at 900 lbs each, capable of keeping up with cavalry and capable of breaking the front armor of a PZ-III

One squadron with 12 mortars, 82mm, on carts

One squadron .50 cal AA machine guns on horse-drawn carts

One signal troop, with horsepacked and horsedrawn radios

One reconnaissance troop

One pioneer troop

One chemical/sanitation troop

By parceling all this out to the individual cavalry squadron commanders, each original 140-man squadron suddenly became a functioning 250-man, horse-mobile, combined-arms unit capable of breaking tanks and calling in artillery and air support. In effect—due to the ability of horses to haul equipment, including radios—they had more combat power than an equivalent United States mechanized infantry company, and they had it with them. Form mid-1942 on, they also acquired U.S. 2.36-inch bazookas and issued them at the ratio of 76 per regiment, or one per Cossack squad.

What most historians miss is this: *Each Cossack division also included a regiment or two of T-70 light tanks that had a range of 230 miles, and could burn the same fuel as the German tanks.* While they were no better than the Pzk-II or the early Pzk-IIIs, they were under the command of Cossack cavalry commanders—not recently purged, demoralized Red Army regulars who were afraid for their lives . . . and with good reason. Under Stalin's orders, inefficient commanders were *shot* by the next higher rank, who in turn, had to watch their own backs. While Stalin didn't entirely trust the Cossacks either, for awhile they were all he had. Somewhat reluctantly, at Zhukov's urging, he turned them loose into history.

Recruiting Cossacks is not difficult, all you have to do is let them know that a war is in the offing and select the best of the horde that will appear. The difference this time, though, was that instead of a semidisciplined mob of cavalry, they had grown into a very well-organized, well-equipped modern force but with their old elan intact. In effect, they had been almost civilized and modernized, but there was still a large amount of the old buccaneer spirit left. They could still live off the enemy's land. This time, though, the plunder would be fuel and ammunition. When they went into the German rear, they were attacking *into* supplies, especially as they were living in Genghis Kahn's old fuel depot.

Since the knowledge has been lost, this may take a little bit of explaining. Modern barn and paddock-raised stock simply has never had the chance to develop the blood and nutrition systems that range horses develop naturally. This information, by the way, comes directly from the old mounted riflemen who marched from the 1845 Mexican War to Kansas, and then to Walla Walla, Washington, before the Civil War. It was put into the *Cavalry Journal* by the men who made the march. These men and horses campaigned from first grass to first snowfall with *no* support from outside.

Ask anyone who competes in endurance races or who raises Spanish mustangs, and you will find it is in the blood, the breeding, and the raising. An animal that has been raised, running at herd speed, on wild grass is an entirely different animal than one raised on oats and hay. In effect, the digestive and nervous system of the modern thoroughbred has been stunted by running on high-density fodder, while the mustang or Cossack mount is eating its natural food. This, combined with the need to outrun predators, hardens and toughens the animal, making it a perfect war mount. . . . It also makes cavalrymen out of the boys who grow up on horseback.

Time after time in history, there are accounts of cavalry units making 80- to 100-mile marches in 24 hours. Pull out your calculator and try this on. For a horse, carrying a rider to make 80 miles in a 10-hour day, how fast must that horse travel, on the average? A look at the old cavalry endurance records backs the statement and the calculation up. . . . That is until the cavalry got soft and spent more time playing polo and politics than exercising in the field. More than one ancient civilization has come apart because they couldn't solve the problem of nomad light cavalry. The "secret" was no more than high-endurance horses and hardened riders.

This was one of the things that broke the German's well-thought-out tactical formulas. They *knew* how fast marching foot infantry could get around their flanks. . . . So just what were those submachine gunners and AT rifles doing behind their flanks two hours before they were due? Simple, for each five or six men on the gun line, there was one mounted horse-holder in a gulch some place, holding the squad's cross-country transport while it refueled. One ambush later, the horse-holders would trot up, the AT gunners would re-limber their guns, the machine gun carts would guard the rear, and the Cossacks would exit laughing.

These were not just simple ambuscades either, they had studied Stuart and Sheridan and cut loose from their supply lines and lived off the enemy. Some of those raids lasted as long as 130 *DAYS!* The question naturally arises . . . what were they eating and what were the tanks running on? In a war, the supply of dead horses is constant, and since an animal usually dresses out to half of its live weight in meat, one horse could feed quite a few men. Fuel was stolen from the Germans or paradropped in, and alcohol distilled from potatoes made antifreeze for the radiators of the tanks. A running engine produces three very handy temperatures, one for drying meat, another for distilling alcohol, and a third to cook a pail of horsemeat and turnip stew.

They didn't always work out perfectly though, Civil War and Stalingrad experience or not, sometimes they got their signals crossed and a lot of men and horses died. Witness the raid of the 8th Cavalry Corps in 1943. The corps was commanded by Major General M. D. Borislov, and consisted of the 21st, 35th, and 112th Cavalry divisions, which had been in the Stalingrad breakout with the 5th Tank Army. In addition to the cavalry divisions, the corps also included the 148th Mortar Regiment, the 263rd Separate Cavalry Artillery Battalion, and the Eighth Separate Antitank Artillery Battalion.

By this time, the Russians had developed a tactical trait that caused the Germans no end of grief. Since the Panzer units normally traveled separated from each other, it was possible to get around their flanks. It was also possible to penetrate one of their formations with a sufficiently strong armored force and let a lighter tank/cavalry force into the soft inner core of the Panzer division or army. This, of course, would focus the attention of the German reserve commander on the interlopers.

The tactical system the Russians used was to send their light tanks in a spoiling assault on the reserve itself and draw it into an attack on the raiding tanks. Russian light tanks, however, were always a few miles per hour faster than the Panzers and could always break contact. They would lead the Germans straight into an antitank zone set up by the cavalry's horse-drawn AT cannons and fade to the flanks as the guns went to work. This was the classic "Lava" trap, worked with tanks as the bait. With this turbulence in the Panzer division rear, the German commander had no choice but to weaken his front line to deal with the marauders. . . . Then his front line would be attacked and broken so as to let the raiders out. The problem was in synchronizing the secondary Russian assault, as witness what happened on the 1943 raid.

The operation started out normally with the discovery of a weak spot in the German lines south of Voroshilovgrad. The target was a large railroad marshaling yard and communications center at Debaltsevo. In concept, it duplicated several of the 1863 Union cavalry raids that destroyed much of the Confederate railroad system near Vicksburg, but on a much larger scale.

As a military operation it was a spectacular success. It cost the Germans: 12,000 casualties, 28 tanks, 70 motorcycles, 50 guns, 35 mortars, 54 machine guns, 2 armored trains, 1 fuel train, 20 locomotives, 1 train with assorted combat machines, 1 train with aircraft, and 3 trains with military vehicles. In addition, six communications centers were destroyed, three railroad bridges were burned, and the rail line was cut in 56 places. Thirty warehouses with ammunition and foodstuffs were also burned. . . . Not bad for a unit that was supposed to have been out of date for half a century . . . if even *half* that report were true, it was a success.

On the way back, however, things began to come unglued. Their return was supposed to have been synchronized with a special Soviet offensive that was unfortunately delayed just long enough to allow the Germans to concentrate against the Seventh Guards. Specifically, they sent the 17th and 6th Panzer divisions and the 62nd Motorized Infantry Division. While men on horseback can for a time move as fast as a tank, they cannot do it for 120 miles, which was the cruising range of most German Panzers. Their exit plan was to attack eastward into the rear of the German lines near a place called the Shirokii Farm Region, which would at the same time be attacked by units of the Soviet Southern Front Command. This failed to happen and the cavalrymen had to face the now alerted, enraged German frontline forces just as two Panzer divisions ripped into their rear.

Antitank capability or not, when 300-odd tanks meet 12,000 horsemen on the open steppes, there can be only one conclusion. At that though, they only lost 1000 men and horses to the tanks and Stuka dive-bombers. It is a measure of the bravery of the Russian officer corps that among the missing were three general officers and four colonels. While the 7th Corps was badly hurt, it was not destroyed. The Red Army Order of Battle credits it with battles in the Kursk salient and in the full pursuit of the Germans through the Brandenburg Gate in Berlin in April 1945.

REFERENCE SOURCES

The Profession of Arms, General Sir John Hackett, Macmillan.

The Cavalry of World War II, Janus Piekalkiewicz, Stein & Day.

The Red Army Order of Battle, Robert Poirier and Albert Conner, Presidio Press.

Zhukov, William J. Spahr, Presidio Press.

U.S. Cavalry Journal Articles

"Cavalry on the Front," General Nikolai N. Golovine, Imperial Russian Army, July 1921, October 1921.

"The Campaign Horse," Major Emil Engel, May–June 1943.

"Soviet Cavalry, 1918–1943," General O. J. Gorodovikov, March–April 1943.

"Air–Tank–Cavalry," Colonel Alexi Ignatyev, November–December 1942.

"The Tank–Cavalry Team," N. Coretneff, January–February 1944.

"Tank Cavalry Tactics," Colonel V. Tereschenko, March–April 1944.

"Red Army Cossacks," in five parts. By Major Robert B. Rigg. September–October 1944, November–December 1944, January–February 1945, March–April 1945. May–June 1945.

"Raids in German Rear," Eugeny Krieger, September–October.

CHAPTER 30

Stalingrad Breakout

THE FIVE-MONTH AGONY OF THE SIEGE OF STALINGRAD WAS the laboratory for all city fighting during the rest of World War II, just as bloody Tarawa was the laboratory for all subsequent amphibious work. The reason that city fighting could be taught in our stateside combat courses is that all during that period the Russian War Department was cabling us information. The tank and infantry fighting skills learned at Stalingrad showed up in our *U.S. Cavalry Journal,* and the engineer knowledge was sent to our *Military Engineer* magazine. Sometimes it seems as if we will never stop finding out something new about that battle.

Just as war-gamers and historians think they have it all together, a new Russian formation literally materializes out of thin air . . . or out of the ground. From the middle of July 1942 to the spring of 1943, there were always at least two entire Russian Engineer armies working in that city, first getting ready, then in the actual fighting. The Russians knew exactly where the Germans were headed because for at least two years prior to the invasion, Stalin's government had been shipping vital war supplies to the Germans. Many of the tanks and airplanes that invaded Poland and France

and bombed England were running on Russian fuel produced at Baku on the shores of the Caspian Sea.

As a result, when Hitler turned east, and then began to
run low on fuel in front of Moscow, it was just about a
foregone conclusion where the Panzers would head next.
There was also a group of communist sympathizers inside
Reich headquarters who could always leak information.
Worse, the German Enigma codes had been broken by British experts operating at Blechly Park, just outside London,
and Winston Churchill was sharing vital German code messages with Stalin. The Russians only real problem, it seemed,
was that the great purges of 1937 and 1938 had all but decap-
itated the Russian army and time would be needed to repair
the damage with the few capable commanders who had survived. Fortunately there were enough.

When, in the summer of 1942, the Panzers rolled south,
their main intent seemed to be to head straight for the oilfields south of the Caucasus Mountains. The original intent
was merely to get close enough to the Volga to interrupt
the river traffic with artillery fire, but then things began to
get complicated. No competent commander, and the Germans were all very competent, will leave an armed fortress
full of hostile tankers behind him—and that was just what
the Russian engineers were making out of the City of Steel.
A look at the Russian Order of Battle for 1942 shows that
there were already two whole field armies in the area, digging in. If the Germans were to have a free hand with Baku,
Stalingrad would have to be taken, not bypassed.

The first stage of the attack, predictably, was artillery and
air bombardment. The Stuka dive-bomber wasn't particularly efficient for this as its bombload wasn't adequate. Simply put, it took too many sorties to get metal on target.
German siege artillery was much better and before too many
weeks had gone by, the city was semiruined. However, Russian engineers—about half of whom were galvanized miners
from the Donets mining region—were building forts out of
the rubble. Forts that were connected by the city's storm
drains, electrical tunnels, and sewers. Every one of them
would have to be dug out of its hole. Worse, there were
little tank/cavalry battles going on both north and south of

the city and winter was coming on. Lieutenant General V. I. Chuykov has this to tell us:

> The defenders of Stalingrad created a peculiar type of shock group as an instrument for street fighting. These groups are flexible maneuverable and strongly armed and equally valuable in attack and defense. . . . The very nature of urban fighting demands these stock groups, all street fighting is at close quarters. An offensive inside a city means the storming of fortified houses which the enemy has turned into firing points, strong points or centers of resistance. Here there is no opportunity for offensive operations conducted by large units, here it is the small infantry group [and its tanks] that dominates the scene. The small unit is best adapted for taking single buildings or blocks of buildings from the enemy, step by step. So, let us take a look at some of these groups of specialists.
>
> The first stage of urban fighting arises when the enemy has only just seized a section of a city and his defenses are still split up. At this stage, a small group such as an infantry squad may operate independently without immediate organic contact with the larger unit to which it belongs. The second stage arises when the enemy has settled down in the city, has been there for two or three months and has established an unbroken line of defenses, hanging together and secured by mines and a fire network. Under these conditions, it is useless for a small group to imagine that it can go, see and conquer.
>
> The shock group still remains small but now it operates as the spearhead of a larger group whose operations are planned down to the last detail. The success of the storming of the "Railwayman House," for instance, was decided by just three groups of men of six to eight each, but they were supported by 82 other fighting men of various military specialties. What we have to have is storm troops proper, reinforcement groups and support specialists. The detailed composition cannot be stated exactly, until the conditions are

known, so the commander must know his business. . . . And have a goodly selection of infantry, sappers and gunners.

The assault troops are lightly armed with grenades, submachine guns, daggers and even shovels sharpened to work as axes until comes the time for digging. They must be first inside and must be capable of signalling either with flares or radios. There are several ways of breaching the walls and a tank cannon is one of the best, the bigger the caliber the better. Failing that, a machine gun can make a loophole into which a 2 pound charge of TNT can be inserted. When it goes, you have no time, go through the wall, tommy gun the furniture, because that is where the occupants will be hiding. Grenade the next room, then go in shooting. Keep moving, shoot the walls, floors and ceilings. If you are caught reloading, go to your dagger or axe and kill him.

As soon as the shock troop leader signals, "I am inside," the reinforcement group enters. These are heavily armed. They carry light and heavy machine guns, anti-tank weapons, picks, crowbars and explosives. They necessarily include sappers who know how to break down walls. The reinforcement group is subordinate to the storming party leader who already knows the ground. Now the reserve storming troops come in and fill out the casualties and new storming parties can be formed. At the same time, snipers must be kept from windows and men put into the second story.

A tank can do this, it can make a breach in a wall and men can board from its turret into an upper story. . . . But they must be men who have been trained to work with the tanks or disaster can result. A tank can not protect itself closer than 30-odd feet from enemy sappers or hollow charge weapons. City fighting can eat tanks unless they are part of a team. Sappers are best for this.

However heroic a shock group is, if the operation is not well prepared, the commander will hope in vain for success. The storm must be prepared most carefully and calculated most accurately. Preparations are based on two things, careful study of the objective and elaboration of the Storm Plan. The study of the objective must provide a complete picture of the enemy's firing points and fire system. It must produce complete familiarity with the roads of approach and enable the commander to estimate the best time for the storm.

Reconnaissance also must give information about the nature of the defense, the thickness of the walls and obstacles, the position of entrances, concealed loopholes and ways of communication, on the directional sectors covered by enemy fire, on the mines and other artificial obstacles in front of the entrances, and on the fire expected from neighboring strong points. For instance, do they have a tank hidden out down the block? Is smoke and darkness better for cover? Some commanders prefer one or both. Smoke gives a warning of your intent but darkness can always be removed by flares.

Lt. Yenin, who broke into the "Railwayman house," had gained all this knowledge through days of careful study and then provoked the garrison into thinking his attack was coming from down the street. Then he switched directions and threw a storm of fire into all the revealed firing points, shocking the defenders into temporary incapability. From experience he knew that the Germans would have new gunners in those positions in three minutes. In that period of time, he was in. In 30 minutes, he owned the house and was fortifying . Be fast, be daring, never dawdle, never stay still in a house, always begin your own defenses. Reinforce, replace, and attack again.

The sapper, the combat engineer, is indispensable to city warfare but in Stalingrad the sappers had their own terrible, unseen front—underground mine warfare. Painstakingly, the sappers laid tunnels by the scores of meters, carefully figuring the angles and lengths, working quietly beneath the enemy's feet so as not to be discovered and countermined. This story comes to us, adapted from the *Military Engineer* magazine, which reprinted it from Soviet sources.

In Stalingrad, the first mine attack was carried out by two sections of sappers led by Vladimir Dubrove and Ivan Makarov. Their underground blow was directed against a large German strongpoint from where the enemy covered the Volga with his fire. At the beginning they went straight down and dug out a well to a depth of five meters. From there they dug a mine in the direction of the enemy. For fourteen days the sappers stubbornly gnawed into the earth by the light of glimmering oil lamps, losing all sense of day and night. . . . Let us see how sappers work, how they lay these underground mine galleries.

This street, about 20 meters wide, became the no-man's-land of the battle in the city. The house on the left was occupied by a Soviet garrison, in the house on the right were the Germans. Both sides were well fortified and had converted their houses into strongpoints, and they were waging a tenacious battle. The Germans placed powerful machine guns everywhere and created thick zones of fire on all their approaches. To take them by direct assault would be very costly, in lives which bore special knowledge. An underground mine attack was decided upon.

They started to tunnel from the basement of the Russian occupied house. In the first day of work, they were able to reach a large water pipe, break it open and lay the walls of the tunnel even further. This was a fortunate accident as the pipe was dry and it gave them a little air. The work was performed as follows: In front, in the stope, a sapper sitting on one knee broke down the earth with his spade. The one behind him raked back this earth so that it did not interfere with the miner. The men behind that one carried the earth in sacks and cartridge boxes. Later this was used to help fortify the Russian house and then refill the tunnel. The soil was easily dug and as the slope lengthened, vertical walls supporting overhead beams protected from cave ins. These were made of house lumber and close together so that it looked as if the gallery were step by step dressing itself with a wooden shirt. The gallery was

1.5 meters high and one meter wide. Two men could pass if they met.

As they got farther in, there was not enough oxygen to support an oil lamp and the miners, so charged batteries out of vehicles were brought down. Then the sappers improvised an air pump that worked like a blacksmith's bellows, but still the shifts had to be short as air was short. By the fourth day the gallery was 25 meters long, this meant that they had crossed the street and were UNDER the Germans. Now they worked doubly quiet, wrapping cloths around their feet. After ten days they could hear Germans above them almost constantly. They dug out a mine chamber and filled it with three tons of assorted scavenged explosives and then backed out of there. . . . Very carefully. From the mine chamber was stretched out a thin wire.

Then, working quickly now, out from under the Germans, under the middle of the street, they put in the cork. There is a trick here. The thickness of the plug must not be less than the thickness of the floor left under the enemy or some of the force of the blast will blow BOTH ends of the shaft . . . an unwelcome event and the ruin of the reputation of the sappers who are sensitive about such things. Word was sent off to the commander of the Russian garrison, who told his subordinate leaders that the time was at hand. Watches were synchronized and storming parties crept to preplanned positions.

Finally, all is in readiness and our sapper twists the handle of his blasting machine. Instantly the building across the street erupts in fire and thunder. . . . Good thing all the windows have long since been broken. The building is lifted up under the Germans, rearranged hideously, and dropped on them. When the bricks quit falling, the stormers are away, to kick the survivors out of the rubble. This was war in Stalingrad, and the Russians were losing. By 12 November 1942, the Russians held only a few blocks along the Volga, and they were losing their supplies to ice.

The ferry boats that had been supplying them, running

the gauntlet of German fire, were being cut to pieces by windowpane ice that chewed into their wooden hulls and dented steel hulls with larger flows. Until the ice became strong enough to support pack animals and light trucks, in a month or so, the Russians would be on short supply. This, General Frederick Paulus, in charge of Sixth Panzer Army knew, and he readied his Panzers for an assault. He never made it, for the Russians out on the steppes had been very, very busy.

As we have seen, the street fighting, even with tanks for breaking and entering, was desperate and bitter. All the time though, the Russians were preparing a master stroke. As a look at a map will show, Stalingrad sits between two rivers, the Volga and the Don, which bend together and almost enclose the town. During the extremely cold series of winters in the early 1940s, the rivers froze hard enough to support heavy vehicles, including smaller tanks. Farther north, at Leningrad, the Russians had actually built a highway across one lake. That ice was one of the keys to the Russian breakout. In early November 1942, the new winter ice was not yet hard enough to support light tanks, but it could support men . . . And horses.

Absent from history until now were the Cossack cavalrymen who swarmed through the deeply ravined suburbs in the lake district south of Stalingrad. As we have seen, these were not the pistol and saber slinging Western cavalry of earlier years, these men were armed with fully modern weapons, rifles, machine guns, and grenades. Their horses towed light cannon and machine guns, and they fought on foot as much as on horseback. Using existing references, it is possible to recreate one of these actions.

South of Stalingrad is a suburb named Minina and a raid was in progress. Cossacks fought in groups and detachments as well as in mass. They could do this because they enlisted by family group and with your senior uncle's eye on you, you will perform. Silently a group of men on horseback ghosted up a railway cut below a raised block of houses, some of stone, others of gingerbread wooden construction. A dog comes at

them and is bribed into silence with a bit of horsemeat.
A horseholder is given the reins of ten tall animals. . . .
These were not ponies. Ten men take a variety of weapons up a hill behind a German command post; two carry
semiautomatic Tokarev rifles, these are the snipers.
Eight men carry PPsh submachine guns with 70 round
drums, all carry grenades, two frags and one hollow-
charge ribbon grenade. The snow is drifting, making
vision tricky for both skulking Cossacks and half-frozen
German sentries.

Another party of Cossacks has been working through
the frozen gardens and shell-pocked lawns of the neighborhood, two of their horses tow a 900-pound 45mm
AT gun that can break the armor of the two Mk-III
Panzers parked on the sides of the house that the Germans had taken over as a CP. They hope the owners
are not in the house, but omelettes have to be made.
A third party, a mounted one, eases forward farther
down the block, leading a team of horses and a ta-
chanki, a short wagon that looks like an American
buckboard. It carries a water-cooled Maxim machine
gun and a goodly supply of ammunition, including more
grenades. Just now the water jacket is partly full of
vodka to keep it from freezing.

The two snipers with Tokarevs fade off to the sides
and the tommy gunners move forward. There is no discovery. Two ribbon grenades arc toward the tank's hull,
their long ribbons trailing out behind them so that their
cones will hit the tank and their hollow charges deto-
nate against the armor. Chaos and fire, the rest of the
men are shooting out windows and throwing grenades,
it is time to go. Now the AT gun is firing at the tanks
from down the block and the Maxim is ripping out long
bursts. The Mk-IIIs are on fire and smoke is coming
out of the house, German MG-34s are firing back, and
a block away, tank engines are starting. Now men are
skidding back down the bank to a horseholder in the
railway cut and the dog is barking wildly. With a clatter
of hooves and some nervous laughing, the Cossack platoon moves out smartly, to a rendezvous.

How effective was this type of fighting? Consider this information from Panzer Regiment 24 that fought in and around Stalingrad from 17 June to 10 November. They were part of the Fourth Panzer Army, which escaped the eventual cauldron. On 17 June, they had 169 operational tanks. By 31 October, they were down to 14 running tanks, with 33 total write-offs and the rest immobilized or in the process of cannibalization. They had, however, knocked out 273 Russian tanks, breaking down to a single KV–II, 31 KV–Is, 169 T–34s, 12 T–70s, and 60 T–60s.

Inferences can be made from this. First, the Germans who say that the first models of the T–34 were not invulnerable are right. Second, since the little T–60s and T–70s were always in company with horsemen, something obviously was working to protect the little buggers, and it was probably that they were inside a screen of mounted scouts. Meanwhile, weather and time were closing on the besiegers.

In front of the city, the German Sixth Army commanded by General Paulus, was entrenched and was supporting the street fighting. Behind the Sixth Army was General Hermann Hoth's Fourth Panzer Army. In order to attack across the Don River, the Russians had first to cross it in two places, to get behind the Sixth Army. At the time, they forced a bridge north of the Germans at Serafimovich, and were holding the bridgehead, but they now needed to get *back* across the Don at Kalach, and that bridge was wired for demolition and strongly held.

The plan was to attack in two pincers, bite off a chunk of the German forces, and then annihilate them. The northen pincer would be the 26th Tank Corps, a part of the Fifth Tank Army. The souther pincer was going to have to take a railroad bridge at Karpovka in order to cross the river. That unit, commanded by General Podin, was the 13th Tank Corps, a part of 51st Tank Army. Altogether the Russians had six complete armies in the Stalingrad area, some of them newly equipped with American machinery, such as the M–3 medium tank and the Bell P–39 Aircobra fighter which carried a tank-busting 37mm cannon in its nose that fired through the propellor hub. Many of them had been flown across Siberia by women pilots.

Most of this is known conventional history, but one group has been left out. Embedded in the military makeup of those tank armies were five complete corps of Don Cossacks with their own tanks and antitank weaponry. At full TO&E, a Russian cavalry corps stood at about 18,000 men, the vast majority of whom were mounted combat troops. As we already know, they towed antitank guns and machine guns on carts. Most important, each cavalry division had a regiment of T–70 light tanks in its TO&E. With a small logistic tail, each of those five corps could put 15,000 mounted men alongside the tanks. Each one with a submachine gun, six drums of ammunition, and a saddlebag full of hand grenades. First, however, that all important bridge at Kalach would have to be taken, and they decided to try trickery first.

It is fairly well known in military circles that all through World War II, the Germans and Russians, as well as the British and Italians, were constantly capturing and using each other's tanks. Their plan hinged on this. The Russians took five captured German Mk-III medium tanks and three standard German supply trucks and then turned the project over to a proven and resourceful officer named Captain Philipov. After putting the Mk-IIIs into the shops north of Stalingrad, overhauling them, and cannibalizing other tanks into them, the Russians had the equivalent of a German platoon. They put German-speaking Russian crews in the newly repaired tanks, and 60 tommy gunners plus demolitions experts from the sappers were put in trucks. Then they set out to launch Philipov into enemy lines.

At dawn on 19 November 1942, the Russians started the long road back from Stalingrad. They had been driven as far back as they needed to—they had traded space for time, they had their factories back behind the Urals, and there was a steady stream of military supplies coming from England and the United States. Now it was time to eject the invaders. The attack from the Serafimovitch bridgehead also served to hide Captain Philipov and his men who, somewhat nervously, were trying to pass themselves off as good little Nazis. At the time of the assault, his little platoon of captured tanks was hidden inside the larger Russian force.

The main northern pincer moved out on schedule behind the traditional artillery barrage and into a fog "dense as milk." The tanks rolled along then, as prearranged, partisans from the local populace rose from the ground and began to guide the tank columns down little-known byways and snow-covered roads. Behind the tanks, feeling their way along, were their giant dragoons, the Cossacks. The Red Army Order of Battle lists the Third Guards Cavalry Corps, the Third Line Cavalry Corps, and the Fourth Line Cavalry Corps under a General Pliyev as the attendant horsemen to the steadily increasing flow of tanks. . . . They had come across on the ice. One Russian author, N. Corotnev, says that this cavalry operation was deliberately left out of then-current history, as it was considered to be a state secret.

The first and second German lines of defense were smashed and driven back on each other in rapid succession. Seemingly, the icy roads were giving the Russians more trouble than the enemy. As the day wore on, the fog began to thin out; then the wind began to pick up and it started to snow. This was not an improvement. By afternoon, steering was by compass. Slowly, carefully, the Russians (disguised as Germans) picked their way through the fields and forests, now having to drive by headlights and stopping every once in a while to clean the snow off the vision blocks. Sometime after midnight, they stopped to refuel from the gas cans carried on the tank decks. A tank column was spotted going northward and scouts confirmed that it was German. It was left to its inevitable fate.

At daybreak, resistance began to stiffen up around the village of Perelasovsky, which turned out to be a German headquarters. It was stormed by tanks and infantry, and then surrounded and cut off by motorized units that got behind the village, trapped its defenders, and then had to beat off two counterattacks. By now Philipsov and his Russians had been going for over 30 hours nonstop in combat in a Russian winter, and they were in dire need of rest. The 26th Corps took a short respite in the village of Ostrov and sent out a fan of scouts toward the Don. Those scouts had two missions, find the German MLR, and find out what the situation was at the Kalach bridge.

The German main line turned out to be just 20 kilometers south of them and would be assaulted in the morning. Then they had the good luck to find an old woman who had come into Ostrov to buy food; upon questioning, she was able to tell them that the Germans at the Kalach bridge still hadn't tumbled to the importance of the thrust and that autos with headlights on were still crossing the bridge. . . . The Germans weren't even checking identity papers, probably because of the cold.

At 0500 Philipov took his column of German tanks off into a black, cold, whistling night with his headlights on, acting as if he belonged there. Half an hour later the main column moved out and by the middle of the afternoon the main German resistance had been smothered by a rolling carpet of steel and horseflesh. . . . And no word from Philipov. When the tanks broke through the German lines, the squadrons of Cossacks took off, pulling their 45mm antitank guns, putting a line of A-T guns between the Sixth Army and the Fourth Army. Later on, the heavier 76mm guns would arrive and after the horses had been led off, the Cossacks would begin to dig the guns in and surround them with machine guns and submachine gunners.

These cavalrymen were acting as dragoons, and they kept the two German armies from reinforcing each other. The area between Hoth and Paulus had suddenly become impenetrable, but this could still come unglued unless that bridge was taken. By 1700 hours, the tension in 26th Corps HQ was almost unbearable; most of the staffers had given Philipov and his volunteers up for lost. Then an electrifying message came through over one of the captured German radios. *He'd done it!* The bridge was theirs, but he was besieged.

The little detachment had driven straight through from Ostrov right to the Kalach bridge, fooling the Germans completely. They weren't even challenged by the sentry at the bridge gate. By the time the lead tank was halfway across, tommy-gunners were already dropping out of the trucks and taking care of the sentries. Frantically now, the Russian demolitions men were scrambling on the ice under the bridge, removing the demolition charges before some holdout German could blow their hard-won objective. Now they were under attack from both sides as retreating Germans on both banks tried to use the bridge, only to find "their own" tanks were being used against them.

By 1700, though, the lead column of the 26th Corps, commanded by a major Philipenko, came smashing through the dim, snowy day and relieved Philipov's tattered band of pseudo-Germans, who had been fighting all day against heavy odds, beating off one attack after another. (Those names cause confusion in Russian history books too.) The fight went on into the night and more and more Russian reinforcements were piled on until, sometime after midnight, the Germans began quietly to filter out of the area. The next morning, the column, with Philipov's little unit of "German" tanks still proudly in the vanguard of Philipenko's regiment, the town of Kalach was taken and stage one of the breakthrough was completed.

The southern pincer, made up of the 24th Tank Corps, rolled out from behind the chain of lakes that strings south from Stalingrad and stormed the German main base at the railway town of Abganerova. The military booty was reported to be enormous. Here again, the Cossacks began to stream in behind the tankers, spreading out across the land, suppressing strong points, and pursuing fleeing enemy soldiers. The cavalry units involved in the southern pincer were the Fourth Guards Cavalry Corps and the Seventh and Eighth Line Cavalry Corps. The cavalry commander was General Sapkin. Although details even now are somewhat sketchy, it is known that at the town of Marinovka, west of Kalach, the two arms of the pincer movement came together, trapping the German 6th Army. The Russians were now officially on the way to Berlin.

REFERENCE SOURCES

The Cavalry of World War II, Janus Piekalkiewicz, Stein & Day.

Tank War, 1939–1945, Janus Piekalkiewicz, Blandford Press.

The Russian Version of the Second World War, edited by Graham Lyons, Facts on File Publications.

The Red Army Order of Battle, Robert Poirier and Albert Conner, Presidio Press.

U.S. Cavalry Journal References

"Salvage and Supply of Tanks," A. Afonskyk, March–April 1943.

"Encirclement at Stalingrad," N. Corotneff, July–August 1943.

"Tactics of Street Fighting," Lieutenant General V. I. Chuykov, September–October 1943.

The Military Engineer References

"Underground Warfare," N. Nemchinsky, V. Yuriev, and Y. Galkin, June 1944.

CHAPTER 31

Red Army Sherman Tanks

WHILE IT IS A GENERALLY KNOWN HISTORICAL FACT THAT during World War II, America shipped some thousands of tanks to Russia, it was not until recently that any hard information on how those tanks were used became available. All existing material on the subject was very closely held as far as the Russians were concerned. The Soviets were loath to admit that they'd gotten any help at all in what they called the Great Patriotic War. Any films that have been released have been *very* closely edited to show only Russian tanks. The facts are that we shipped around 7,500 tanks to Russia, consisting of mostly M4A2 Shermans, a few M-3 Mediums, and several thousand light tanks, mostly M-3s and M-5s.

They were shipped over a variety of routes. Some came by sea to Tehran in Persia (now Iran) and were shipped overland up to Baku on the Black Sea. Others came across the Atlantic and were sent up through the Arctic Ocean to Murmansk and Archangel. Still others were shipped direct from San Francisco to Vladivostock to be shipped on the Trans-Siberian Railroad. Their story has only recently been told, by men who were there.

When America was jolted into World War II by the Japa-

nese, the lend-lease policy had already been set up to aid
Britain, and "Uncle Joe" Stalin immediately put in for his
share. He wanted communications equipment, tanks, and
trucks . . . in that order. The first tanks he got were the M-3
Light tanks, which were an instant hit. Here is what some
of the Russians had to say about them. The following report
comes right from Captain Valkov, a Russian tank commander who had been in a 600-tank battle.

> The American machines made an excellent showing in
> action. Take this light tank, it has splendid fighting and
> maneuvering qualities. In this respect it is fully as good
> as the Soviet light tank, which has a high rating. It is
> in many ways superior to the German tanks. We have
> had no reason, either, to complain of the speed or qual-
> ity of the American tanks. An especially good feature
> is that they operate well on any kind of fuel. Their
> mechanism is simple to handle and enables men to learn
> to handle them very quickly. What else can I say? Here
> is a tank that has covered a thousand miles without a
> single breakage or repair.

Although the tankers were almost uniform in their praise
of the "Amis," there was one universal tanker's complaint,
almost all these tanks burned much too easily due to their
gasoline fuel. The Russians had several diesel-fueled models,
and they also knew that the American Sherman existed in
at least one diesel version. At that point in history, America
was producing much of the fuel for the war and cracking
plants simply hadn't been invented yet. As a result, there
was a limit to the amount of diesel fuel available, and most
of that was going to the American Navy for small boats and
to the U.S. Marines who also had the M4A2. The Russians,
however, had the giant oilfields around Baku and could produce all the diesel they needed . . . as long as they could
hold on to the land.

At this point, it would be instructive to take a closer look
at just what made the A2 version of the Sherman different
from all other versions. For one thing, it had a 76mm high-
velocity gun that would penetrate much more armor than

the 75mm shorty on the normal models of the M4. That gun descended from the French 75, which had been around since 1898!!

Its other main difference was in the power plant. Instead of the normal Continental radial engine or the Ford GAZ engine, two marine engines had been used, and that was what made the difference. The 71-series of the GM engine is rather unique among diesels in that it is almost soldier-proof. Its injectors are what is called "unit injectors," and are inserted directly into the cylinder head rather than being driven by a separate, delicate, and expensive pump. The injectors are powered by a "rack" driven off the engine's camshaft. In practice, this means that when one fails, a tanker simply unbolts the hold-down clamp and replaces the faulty injector, just like changing a spark-plug.

The engine is also a two-cycle, supercharged item, which means more horsepower per pound of engine weight. When the piston nears the bottom of its stroke, it uncovers a series of air ports that allows a blast of high pressure air to blow the combustion products out of the exhaust valves that have just opened. Then the pistol comes back up and fuel is injected for another stroke. The engine is so rugged that some of the first 1934 models are still running. They are about 190 horsepower each; this necessitated putting two of them on a bull gear to get the needed horsepower.

This fact gave the A2 a fantastic tactical advantage . . . when one engine was shut off, it was the quietest tank in the world. Running on one engine in the snow, it made about as much noise as a jeep. This feature was to give the Germans much grief. One more feature of the Sherman was that it used a five-man crew. With four husky male bodies to pull maintenance on the vehicle, it was no trick to insert a female somewhere in the crew, and thereby hangs a tale.

The state of affairs in Russia in early 1942 is almost unimaginable to the Western mind. Bolshevism had brought the economy to its knees, Stalin's purges had all but eliminated the czar's professional officer corps. The Germans were invading and supplies were pouring in from the United States in a flood . . . thus, it took no particular extra devious-

ness to lose one tank. Legend has it that one Russian countess did exactly that.

Normally one would discount the legend of a woman tank
commander, but verifiable stories and photographs keep
popping up here and there. The legend begins in the purges.
The lady's husband, a Russian cavalry officer was purged
and executed for treason against Stalin, but the countess
managed to survive and to keep some of her family fortune
from the greedy hands of the nomenklatura . . . the numbered class of high party members who have been harvesting
Russia for 80 years now.

When the Germans invaded, she patriotically went to
work in a hospital, but then her brother fell before the German Panzers, then her oldest son was taken as a walking
bloodbank by the SS, and finally disappeared. Last, her
youngest son was captured and taken back to Germany as
slave labor. Her entire line was about to die out and the
lady, we'll call her Valentina, decided to do something about
it. Coming from a military family, she knew soldiers and
she'd been nursing some very strange tankers. The Emchisti:
M-4 in Russian is M-Chetyrye, and the short name for the
tank was the Emcha. The tankers who specialized in the
Sherman were thus called Emchistis.

The legend has it that Valentina simply bought a Sherman
on the black market, assembled a crew of veteran Emchistis
out of the hospital, and after losing their records, took her
brand new Sherman tank and went hunting for her son. A
few photographs have surfaced, and that story is still under
research. It will eventually fit in a future book. There are
more, many more tales of military derring-do than have
made the "official histories," and each has a lesson to teach.

As mentioned, the Russians were superbly happy with the
American hardware. Listen now to a Hero of the Soviet
Union, Colonel Dmitriy Loza, who went through the whole
war in a Sherman. These descriptions are taken from his
book, *Commanding the Red Army's Sherman Tanks*.

There can hardly be found another item of foreign combat equipment that experienced such severe testing by
the incredible dirt of the pulverized and obliterated

front line roads, the summer heat, the serpentine pathways and mountain passes of the Transylvanian Alps. . . . The tanks were forced to move hundreds of kilometers along railroad track embankments on the crossties.

The Sherman's armor felt the blows of the German antitank guns, Panzerfausts, and the main gun rounds of Tiger and Panther tanks. Sherman tanks were subjected to German air strikes and even withstood encounters with Japanese kamikaze air attacks. The Emcha raced like a whirlwind across minefields, was blown up on Fougasse [aimed explosive charge pushing scrap metal onto a target] obstacles and burned with fire. In sum, these tanks and their crews experienced it all.

The first time we pick up Colonel Loza is when he is having trouble unloading his tanks from flatcars near the town of Fasov, southwest of Kiev. Tanks were normally loaded end-on to flatcars, each tank rolling up a loading ramp at the end of a siding, and then (very carefully) trundling down the whole length of the train until each tank had a flatcar to itself. Since a Russian-style tank company has only ten tanks, this means that a short train can move the whole company, with a few extra cars for HQ, supply, and repair troops. The problem comes when there is no unloading ramp at the destination.

Some tanks, because of the way their transmissions are built, can "neutral steer," that is, drive one track forward and one in reverse and pivot in place. The Sherman cannot, and Fasov had no loading ramp. They had orders to proceed from the railroad station, but how to get the tanks off the flatcars? Finally, Senior Sergeant Grigoriy Nesterof agreed to demonstrate a method he had learned but didn't really trust. The method was to move just slightly forward with one track locked, coming dangerously close to tipping off the flatcar. Then the tank is reversed and the trick done with the other track.

Enough of this backing and filling and the 34-ton tank is sitting crossways on a now sagging flatcar with only a meter between its nose and the ground. With the engine idling, the driver slowly releases his steering bars and the hull creeps forward, tipping gently at first. Then faster, faster, and WHAM with a tearing of wood from the railcar's deck and a smashing jolt on the earth, the tank is unloaded. . . . Only two out of ten tipped over, but this was no problem.

The drill then is for two tanks to approach the one that is resting on its side, and attach tow cables across the hull. Then one gently pulls the tipped hull back upright while the second acts as a drag brake. Once the tank is upright, its internal stowage is checked, the oil and water levels are checked, and the batteries are inspected to see that none have come loose. Then it is fire up and go about your business. . . . Simple.

Despite being a tad top heavy and easy to tip, the Sherman has always had a reputation for good cross-country capability for two reasons, an extremely low gearing, tracks that can take sideslopes, and low ground pressure. Most of the M4A2s that were shipped to Russia seem to have had the newer, wider suspension system fitted, which lowered their pressure on the ground to about that of a man with a rifle. What this means is something the Germans never seemed to catch on to. Time and time again, they would anchor their flank on some "impassable terrain feature," only to have a group of Shermans slip around them and start putting shells into their vulnerable rears. Africa, Italy, Europe, and now Russia, the stories are there. . . . And still the Sherman soldiers on.

In late January 1944, the weather south of Kiev, around Zazhkov and Zvenigorodka, was foul. It rained during the day and snowed in great wet clumps during the night . . . the flakes were big enough to feel when they hit. Tanks had to be used to pull trucks through the mud and if they didn't work very carefully, they froze in place during the night. When a tank stops in warm mud and the temperature falls, the mud can trap the vehicle until thawed. This is not a good situation in which to find oneself in Tiger country.

Senior Lieutenant Gevorg Chobanyan was attacking straight ahead against the German-held town of Tynovka, on the morning of 26 January 1944, when one of his tanks was shot by a haystack. An antitank gun crew had cleverly concealed a PAK 50 antitank gun by building a false haystack over it, waiting for a Russian assault. One shot and the track of his left flank tank was broken. And the TC obviously didn't see his persecutor, but Chobanyan did. Just slightly he traversed his turret, and then his gunner blew the haystack and its gun up with one single HE shell.

They still, however, had to take the town of Tynovka, but the ground was too soft and muddy for tanks . . . or was it? Leaving another tank to stand by the cripple while its crew worked on the broken track, Chobanyan took his remaining eight tanks off north of the town—across a slippery, muddy, snow-covered field—and eased into a gulley that hid his tanks. The Germans weren't even looking that way; after all, this was impassable terrain, wasn't it? A tanker would have to be crazy to try to run in that muck. Having worked all tank-crew positions in combat, and in most climates, this writer agrees with the Germans, those Russians were crazy to try it, but it worked.

By the time Chobanyan was in position north of the town, he received the welcome news that his two tanks on the road were fully ready, two pairs of driver-mechanics had repaired the broken track while the turret crews kept the Germans busy.

The Russians had a rather unique system working back then, in that they attached a squad of infantry semipermanently to a given tank. These troops were an elite force and were called *Desantis,* or tank jumpers-off, and became effectively part of the tank's crew. They were armed with submachine guns and grenades. Now Chobanyan's jumpers-off came trotting back across the snow with the welcome word that the flank was clear, there were no guns pointed their way. It was time to go.

A green flare arced into the worsening snowstorm. Two tanks with their Desantis aboard rumbled slowly down the road, firing steadily to keep the enemy's attention. The other six Shermans crashed up out of the muddy gulch, letting go with their guns as soon as they cleared the ground level. It was a complete surprise to the Germans, whose guns were pointed down the road. Jerry's reaction time was extremely fast, however, and Chobanyan urged his men to top speed in order to get in among the houses before the A-T guns could be relaid. Minute by minute, the battle grew in violence.

The scattered groups of houses that made up the villages were now burning and white-clad figures could be seen dashing through the snow, smoke, and flames. Wooden houses were burning and stone buildings were coming down as tanks drove through them. . . . A tank driver has to be quite careful in this, as tanks don't do basements very well.

Senior Sergeant Markor'yants, driving for the lieutenant, spotted motion and turned his tank toward it. Two muzzle flashes marked the location of a PAK-50 and a solid shot suddenly ricochetted off the Sherman's turret!

The German commander, now aware of what was happening, shifted his men against the flanking group. Now the submachine gunners were dismounted or were shot off several tanks and, struggling through the mud and deepening snow, began to fall behind. The sudden, high-speed chatter of the newest German weapon, the MG-42, began dropping men in groups as the gunners spotted them. Now the antitank teams were filtering through the wrecked village.

An Emcha commanded by Lieutenant Alexsandr Sosnin tore through gardens and yards, scattering animals and throwing up two rooster tails of mud and snow. It was his first battle. He saw a group of Panzerfaust men coming at him with shaped charge weapons that could hole his armor. His driver slipped the tank behind a mound as the lieutenant frantically swung the turret with his override. The coaxial Browning MG cut a swath and as soon as the gunner saw the group, the main cannon fired. . . . End of problem.

Now a group of Germans with a machine gun and machine pistols began to shoot the Desantis off the tanks, driving them to cover. A young infantry officer, grimed by gun smoke, ran toward Sosnin's tank, shouting for attention. He'd found another pocket of Germans slipping around their flank. Turning sharply to the right, Sosnin ordered his driver to full speed and stunned the Germans with his charge. Several were ground up under the tank's tracks and half a dozen surrendered.

By day's end, Senior Lieutenant Chobanyan had his tail in a crack. The Germans had yet to be fully dislodged, they had reinforcements available, and night was fast falling along with more heavy globs of snow that were fast burying both forces. He could not bypass the village on the left because of a wooded area along the southern edge of the road. Knowing the Germans, that patch of woods would be infested with A-T weapons and the machine guns that would protect them. Nor could he advance much through the now destroyed, rubble-choked village. *Okay,* he figured, *we do it the hard way, infantry forward, tanks support as they can.*

As dusk fell, there was a fortunate letup in the snowfall and, for a short while, Chobanyan's gunners could see almost 200 yards. It was all they needed. While the Desantis were working their slow way forward, low on ammunition and almost exhausted, the tanks began to fire accurately at the Germans, using the excellent sights of the Shermans to spot enemy positions and remove them with precision fire. Methodically they blew up machine guns, ammunition carriers, and any place that looked like it could harbor a Panzerfaust crew. Infantry who have learned to work with tanks can "talk" with tracers, and a burst of tracers into a building would be followed by a cannon shell made in the United States.

Not having squad radios, the Russians had to resort to signal rockets. When the infantry, flapping clumsily in their greatcoats, reached the attack line, they sent up a green rocket, which was answered by a red missile—the command for the attack. After a fierce half-hour battle, the snow began to fall heavily again and the Germans, now depressed and tired, began to fade back to the east.

As the night wore on, the storm increased, covering the tanks until they looked like giant snow-draped boulders. Inside the tanks, the men were much warmer than would be expected because the Shermans each had a little two-cycle generator set behind the turret that kept the lights on and the hull heated. Before they shut down for the night, though, the Emchisti took the precaution of stuffing rags into their sights so that the snow would not fill them. . . . And a good thing they did, for the next morning they found themselves not over a hundred yards from a half-dozen more snow-covered lumps. They'd buttoned up and gone to ground with a company of German Tiger tanks for neighbors, but that's another story.

REFERENCE SOURCES

Commanding the Red Army's Sherman Tanks, Colonel Dmitriy Loza, Red Army, translated by James Gebhart, University of Nebraska Press.

M-4 Sherman, George Forty, Blandford Press.

Sherman, Richard P. Hunnicut, Presidio Press.

"American Tanks in Action in Southern Sector." Z. Ostrovkovsky, *U.S. Cavalry Journal,* November–December 1942.

CHAPTER 32

The Malay Plain, 1944

THE JAPANESE HAD SEEMED ABLE TO CRUSH ALL BEFORE them in 1942, but as Admiral Isoroku Yamamoto had warned Emperor Hirohito and General Hideki Tojo some years before, "I will only have a run of perhaps six months before America's giant industrial power begins to take hold." The Imperial juggernaut had seemed unstoppable. Pearl Harbor had been devastated, one island group after another annexed, Guadalcanal invaded, the Dutch and British East Indian possessions stripped from them, and Australia was threatened. It is possible to stretch an army too far, however. It should be remembered that Japan is about the physical size of California, and Germany about the size of Montana. They had to consolidate very quickly and they simply did not make it.

The Nipponese had been fighting in China and Manchuria for much of the 1930s, but the steady supply of war material across the Burma Road and the airflights over the Himalayas had kept the Nationalist Chinese in the war. With a good foothold in Southeast Asia, the Japanese were determined to cut that road, and after kicking the British out of their ancient domain of Burma (now Myanmar) were about to pull it off. At this point the question arises, Just what was Britain's reason for being in Burma? Trade and safety.

On New Year's Day, 1601, Queen Elizabeth I had signed the charter of the Honourable East India Company, giving them exclusive English trading rights with the East Indies and India itself. Gradually over two centuries, the East India Company took over much, but not all, of India, partly by trade, partly by diplomacy and outright trickery, and partly by military excellence.

The normal course of events would be for a given small principality—India was not a nation then—to begin trade with the company, which would stimulate the growth of wealth. Then several things could happen, and did, sometimes in batches. The maharaja in question would find himself the object of his neighbor's greed and find out that the competing French East India Company had equipped his aggressor's army with modern European weapons. Then he would apply for aid to the East India Company and the company's rapidly growing Sepoy army would bail the potentate out.

Or said maharaja could secretly arm and train his own army and then try to take over a holding not realizing just how big the company was, and find himself reduced to a puppet, paying indemnities to the company with his heirs in exile plotting revenge. . . . The company had simply shipped in an army hired from another principality and trained by British professional officers. Gradually, though, India was more or less united for the first time in hundreds of years, even though there are a hundred languages spoken on the subcontinent. The rail lines went in, the telegraph lines went up, and the Babu system of civil servants began to replace fickle rule by potentiate, nepotism, and favoritism. Naturally, India began to grow rich and her neighbors covetous, among them the Burmese.

As the wealth next door grew, so did the raiding, piracy, and outright land grabs. Finally, as the British were changing governor-generals, the Burmese marched a small army into Bengal and declared that what used to be India's most eastern province was now part of Burma. Lord Amherst, the new Governor-General, knew that if he permitted this, he would lose his position, reputation, graft, and perks. He picked Colonel Sir Archibald Campbell to lead an army of 10,000 Sepoys (or British-trained native soldiers, mostly from the area around Madras) on a punitive expedition. They sailed on a fleet of company ships in late March 1824, and took Rangoon at the mouth of the Irawaddy River. Two years of hard campaigning later, the royal family of Burma, itself only in place for 75 years, capitulated. The treaty was with the East India Company—not with Great Britain—and it gave the company ten million rupees worth of indemnities and assorted territories on the Burma coast.

Several more go-rounds like that and Burma was part of the British Empire. Gradually, the plantations and mines went in, the Dacoits (armed gangs of jungle mafia) were suppressed, and everyone began to get wealthy. The original Burmese system of civil servants had been pure corruption. A given district controller, for instance, was not given a salary but simply appointed and expected to squeeze the populace for his needs. This the British stopped. Roads, hospitals, and electric power went in as they were invented, along with telegraphs and telephones. In 1940, Burma had almost 2,000 miles of railroads and was beginning to achieve independent status in the Commonwealth. The pirates were about to become a nation. If there can be said to be a secret to the growth of empire, this was it. People who are getting rich do not revolt.

Then came war and the long push back to India. The Japanese took over, cut the Burma Road to China, and began to consolidate; they wanted minerals, oil, and plantation products . . . and they got them at gunpoint. Then came the long struggle of the Chindits ("Wingates's Raiders"), "Merrill's Marauders," and seemingly the whole empire. There were also Australians because their continent was on Japan's list for expansion; Americans because they had been ambushed and drawn into the war; and Indian troops who volunteered because they did not want Japanese domination. There were South Africans because they were of the Commonwealth, and there were East African Askaris because they were Somalis and there was a war on and this is what they did for a living.

The war, at least in part, was over airfields, to keep the
Japanese from disturbing work on the new Ledo-Stilwell
road, but mostly to evict the interlopers who had destroyed
what was a promising new nation and set its progress back
decades. And one of the weapons was a new tank, new but
already obsolescent in other wars. This was the M-3 medium
tank, created as a war expedient but surprisingly jungle worthy. In fact, the clumsy beast fought as if it had been designed for jungle *and* city work.

When America got dragged kicking and screaming into
the war, we didn't really have a war industry, although because Great Britain was in worse shape than we were, we
had been selling them better tanks than they could build.
Unfortunately, our own metal-working skills weren't yet up
to full output. Specifically, the biggest thing we knew how
to cast out of steel was a railroad driving wheel. We couldn't
cast a large turret, let alone a full-sized tank hull. At that
time, possibly only the Russians could do that, but we
learned quickly. Not quickly enough, however, for the Grant
tank. We could cast the turret but the first hulls were put
together like a World War I tank, with rivits, and they
looked like *big* erector sets on tracks.

It was known that there should be a main cannon of at
least 75mm, and we had those, some left over from the
"Great War." We just couldn't make a turret big enough,
so the gun was mounted in a sponson on the right front of
the hull. The little turret on top mounted a 37mm minican-
non with a coaxial machine gun. On top of that was a little
tank commander's cupola with another .30 caliber machine
gun. There were also a pair of machine guns mounted right
in front of the driver. The crew could open side hatches and
use tommy guns on the hostiles. They also had small ports
for pistols and hand grenades.

This crude tank was 18-feet long, 9-feet wide, and a little
over 10-feet high, depending on model and the amount of
junk the crew hauled with them. With all the armament and
armor, the tank weighed 31 tons and this created an instant
problem. . . . We didn't have any tank engines that would
push that weight 25 miles per hour. We did, however, have
a decent supply of aircraft engines, so the original Lee tank

(Grant was the British model) was powered by a 375 horse-power Wright radial airplane engine. Later on, when the need for airplane engines got a bit pressing, Chrysler pulled off one of the wildest mechanical innovations of the war. They took five 6-cylinder, 80-horsepower truck engines and bolted them up on a common crank case. The result was the A57, a 30-cylinder multibank engine. After the expected teething troubles, it worked surprisingly well, even with five water pumps and five carburetors. If you want to hear and see one of them running, rent the old Bogart movie, *Sahara*. They were a righteous beast.

The tank required seven men as crew, a driver, two on the cannon, three in the turret, and a radio operator. This automatically produced enough bodies for night watch, dismounted security, normal maintenance, and a few spare bodies to replace the wounded. There was also quite a lot of ammunition available compared to that of modern tanks, 178 for the 37mm and 80 for the 75mm, although crews could easily find room for more. In this machine, you could fight a serious war. Now let's look at its opposite number, the Japanese Type 97.

The ninety-seven or Chi-Ha was the best of the Japanese tanks. It had a crew of four and a diesel engine, a 47mm antitank gun that could penetrate the Lee, but vastly inferior fire controls. Its engine was just 150 horsepower and the tank weighed 15 tons, giving it poor crushing power. As the tankers were to learn, there is a minimum size for jungle bashing and house wrecking. Lee or Grant was just about right and the Chi-ha was a bit light in the butt.

On 8 August 1943, General William Slim and General Joseph Stilwell initiated Plan Albacore, the reconquest of Burma, and division after division of Allied troops, all supplied with shiny new American equipment, poured into the jungle. The Japanese did not go quietly. There were tank versus tank battles in those jungles, there were small detachments of Grants, Lees, Shermans, and the little M-3 Stuart light tanks filtering all through those campaigns.

In jungles where infantry fought tree to tree, where marauders and Chindits probed and raided behind enemy lines, the tank companies were spread thin, working as battlefield

bullies for the infantry, then backing out to a road or elephant trail and cutting over to the next trouble area to blow
bunkers with the 75mms, pop snipers with the 37s, and hose
down troops with their multiple machine guns.

In the Hukwang Valley, places with names like Shingbwi-
yang and Yupbang Ga ate men and tanks on both sides. The
Japanese, however, did not have the advantage of massive
resupply—that was their weakness. They had to hoard their
supplies for each counterattack and those supplies had to
come up from Rangoon, after crossing a sea increasingly full
of American, British, and Dutch submarines. The main goal
of Plan Albacore was the taking of Myitkyina, a port on the
Irrawaddy River. A secondary goal was to punch out of the
jungles of northern Burma and onto its central plain, which
would be at last, tank country.

On the 4 March 1944, the city of Walablum fell, and Mo-
gaung on 26 June. But now, the Japanese, having built up
a supply base at Meiktila, south of Mandalay, were striking
back in earnest. Something would have to be done about
that supply base and General Slim decided to send out a
classic tank raid. The Japanese, however, knew about those
tank regiments and would have to be fooled as to where
they were. What happened next was worthy of the European
generals, and done in a much harder context. When Myitkyina fell during the last week of July, 1944, the tanker's road
to Mandalay was opening.

All through the later months of 1944, there was frantic
rearranging and reequipping of troops, and now squadrons
of bombers and fighters were arriving. The man-to-man jungle fighting was mostly over by then and the men could
sense that the pace would be picking up. The Allies had a
full-field army in the area now, the 14th, commanded by
Lieutenant General William Slim. This army consisted of
two corps of soldiers, but the Japanese had three whole
armies . . . rather battered, understrength armies.

Of tankers, there was the 255th Indian Brigade commanded by Brigadier Claude Pert. It was made up of the
116th Regiment RAC (the Gordon Highlanders), the 5th
King Edward's Lancers, and the 9th Deccan Horse armed
with Sherman and Stuart tanks. The brigade also had the

16th Light Cavalry, two truck-mounted infantry battalions, and B Squadron, 11th Cavalry. This was the armored fist of IV Corps, which was commanded by Lieutenant General F. W. Messervy.

The XXXIII Corps, commanded by Lieutenant General Montagu-Stopford had the 254th Indian Tank Brigade, composed of the Carabiners of the Royal Armored Corps (RAC); the 150 Regiment (RAC), armed with Grants and Lee tanks; and the Seventh Light Cavalry with the little Stuarts. There were also two Squadrons of the 11th Cavalry, with Daimler armored cars. The only Japanese tank outfit in Burma was their Fourth Tank Regiment, and they had just 40 tanks.

Since Mandalay was a critical junction of railroads, river shipping, and what few usable roads there were, taking it would literally break the back of the Japanese occupation. There was just one problem. The Japs were in place with their backs to the Irrawaddy River, and they could cross it with ease and blow the bridges. The Allies, on the other hand, had to get a tank force completely *around* the Nipponese forces under General Hoyotaro Kimura. They had first to cross the Chindwin River, a tributary of the Irrawaddy, and then the great river itself. The Irrawaddy is miles wide in some places, shallow in many places, but fordable in none.

There had been some command problems and shifting during this time. General Ord Wingate, who had built the famed Chindit force, was dead in an aircraft crash, and his beloved force of modernized tribesmen had been taken over by Major General Walter Lentaigne. The problem was that Lentaigne did not have the clout to protect his rapidly tiring men from the demands of "Vinegar Joe" Stilwell, who desperately needed those men to keep the Japanese off his back while he finished his road. Finally, Chiang Kai-shek and Stilwell had a falling out, and at Chiang's request, Stilwell was recalled to the states.

Meanwhile, the last Chindit patrols in the Mandalay area had pinpointed the huge base at Meiktila, and Wingate just before he died had told Slim just how important that base probably was. The two Corps of the 14th Army were coming

down a long tongue of land formed by the loop of the Irrawaddy and its confluence with the Chindwin. The Japanese,
who were probably feeling a bit overused about now, suddenly pulled back all the way across the great river and set
up a long defensive line behind the river loop, through the
city of Mandalay and out into the eastern jungles. They were
intending to go back after resupply and left many of the
vital bridges intact, although mined, and this would help the
Allies immensely.

The XXXIII corps set up to keep pressure on Kimura,
who believed that the next British strike would be a direct
attack on Mandalay. This left IV Corps to make the strike
down the Chindwin and around Kimura's left flank. At this
time, Slim put "Operation Cloak" into effect. The IV Corps
area was pretty much immune to Japanese physical patrols
and the sky was full of American fighters based out of Im-
phal, 250 miles away in India. What the Brits did was send
out radio teams all over the area that IV Corps had occupied, with just enough light infantry to protect them, and
then they began transmitting a completely bogus set of
signals. . . . They used exactly the same trick that Yamamoto
had used to camouflage the position of his fleet just before
the Pearl Harbor attack, but the Japanese generals and ad-
mirals didn't communicate well enough for Kimura to have
known of that electronic double play.

There were just enough security breaks to allow the Japanese to break some of the codes and soon their delighted
intelligence officers were reporting that IV Corps was settling in and setting up a defensive position. Kimura began
to relax at just the time the 255th Indian Tank Brigade
was beginning to roll, under radio silence. In fact, General
Messervy was moving his whole corps, consisting of the tank
brigade, the 7th and 17th Indian divisions, and the 28th East
African Brigade . . . fighting Somalis under British officers.
While the Somalis had never worked with tanks before, no
one has ever had to ask a Somali twice to go to war.

At this point there had to have been some really creative
engineer work going on because the reports tell of tanks
crossing one of the world's widest rivers on log rafts powered by large outboard motors. After crossing the Chindwin

at Monywa, the tanks could move roughly 100-miles out of their 300-mile approach march on tank transporters. The engineers had used bulldozers, elephants, and muscle labor to get a road even that far. Some miles short of the small town of Pauk, they had to unload and continue on their own tracks. They were taking a circuitous route to avoid detection, and they were heading into trouble. Their destination was the city of Pakokku on the Irrawaddy, from where they would swing south and bring the tanks across at the narrowest part of the river, at Nyaunga.

There were Japanese allies south of Nyaunga, at the ancient city of Pagan, but these were of doubtful value. The Indian National Division had been recruited up from POWs and local Indians of doubtful value. There were also some turncoat units of the Burmese Constabulary in the area. But the only matter of concern was this: Would they report enemy movement to the Japanese, and would Kimura's intelligence believe them? Slim decided to throw a little more confusion their way.

The IV Corps was now coming down the west side of the Irrawaddy and the 116 RAC equipped with Shermans was ordered to take the Somali 28th African Brigade and go *past* Nyaunga, south to Seikpu. This caused a violent reaction from the Japanese because Seikpu was directly across the river from the Burmese oilfields at Chauk, and this gave Kimura the idea that whatever British units were in the area were headed for the oilfields. . . . More disinformation.

On the night of 13 February, the 7th Indian Division began crossing the river at Nyaunga on rafts and assault boats. All the Lee, Grant, and Sherman tanks of the 255th Indian Tank Brigade lined up on the shore and acted as artillery, firing HE and smoke shells into whatever hostile positions were over there. What gets left out of many books is that the 75mm shells were burning white phosphorous. They give off smoke all right, but all those pretty little orange sparks cannot be extinguished except by immersing them in water. Any human hit by them is literally burned alive, and if they rush out into the water, the HE gets them. The crossings were accomplished with few casualties.

Once the tanks were rafted across, the bridgehead began

to expand, but the tanks had to be put on full alert to
counter snipers with machine gun bursts and 37mm cannon
fire. That was another advantage of the Grant tank. The
turret gun could elevate to 67 degrees and there was a canister shell for that weapon that made it a perfect sniper buster.
Swiftly the beachhead expanded into a full crossing and soon
the whole corps was across. While the 17th Indian Division
prepared for the breakout with 255th tanks, the Seventh
Light Cavalry turned south to clean out Pagan. The Indian
National Division gave up easily, their political leader, one
Subhas Chandra Bose, having found that "Important political matters demand my attention elsewhere." But at Nyaunga, the Japanese fought stubbornly and retreated into
catacombs in the hills. When they refused to surrender, the
Brits sealed the entrances with explosives and went on with
their war. By now, General Kimura *had* to know that there
was a large force across the river and in his rear, but suddenly Slim punched him again, this time on the right flank
and center. Now XXXIII Corps was beginning to roll.

The Irrawaddy runs north from Mandalay and on 9 January, the XXXIII Corps's 19th Indian Division had crossed
the river and got on the same side as Mandalay, but 60 miles
north of the city. The river curves around the city and then
flows almost due west. On 12 February, the 20th Indian
Division crossed 40 miles downstream. Come 24 February,
the 2nd British Division would cross between the west-
ernmost Indian position and Mandalay itself. It should be
remembered, at this point, that the Japanese still outnumbered the Allied force by over three to one.

The 254th Indian tank regiment was split up into groups
of mixed armored units for each of the bridgeheads. Each
vehicle had its particular use. The little Daimler Dingo armored cars were four-wheel drive, armed with a machine
gun in a hand-cranked turret and would do about 60 miles
per hour on a road. They were nominally rifle proof, had
reasonable cross-country mobility, and could ford about a
yard of water. Normally they were teamed up with a group
of light Stuart tanks with 37mm cannons.

The drill was for the small Daimlers to probe ahead, keeping to low ground, maybe dismount a man or two . . . *If*

they had a third man on board, to crawl up a slope and glass the area for enemy activity. If it was spotted, the car would ease forward until only the top of its turret cleared the slope. The best place to do this, of course, was from behind a bush. All the time they would have been radioing for the Stuarts, which with more powerful radios, would have immediately contacted the nearest platoon of Grant or Sherman tanks.

Then with backup assured, the Daimler would put several long bursts out of its Browning machine gun into whatever looked interesting. If only rifle fire came out of the position, one or two Stuarts, usually with mounted infantry on board, would go take a look, as more trucked infantry dismounted and the scouting Daimlers went on looking for more business. Meanwhile, a mile or so behind them, the 105mm self-propelled howitzers called Priests would be setting up for business, if needed.

While all three bridgeheads got across the Irrawaddy with little trouble, Japanese resistance to further aggression was *fierce*. Under orders to give no ground at all, the Japanese commanders first launched wave after wave of fanatical attacks against the new British positions on their side of the river, only to find out that one does not rush a position full of tanks with three or four machine guns each, and one or two cannons firing canister, and white-phosphorous (WP) rounds. Several days of this and the hostiles had lost too many men even for Japanese sensibilities, and they sullenly began to dig in. They set up in villages and on the higher hills around them and waited, only to find out that the Brits had gone fiendish on them. They knew about those orders to give no ground. General Slim did not want to just defeat that army, he wanted to destroy it.

When a position in front of some little village warranted the effort, the Brits would set up camp to do murder. The tanks and probing infantry would ease into the bunker line. The infantry's job was termite patrol: keep the fanatics with the pole charges and the mines strapped to their chests from getting to the tanks. With the infantry about even with the rear of the hulls, and one talking on the intercom over the external phone, a tank would roll up to a bunker. Usually

these were made of a coconut log frame covered with sand
and, if time was available, fire-dried clay mixed with straw.
It takes more than a grunt can carry to get through that
oversized brick, and the tanks were perfect for the job.
While the Grant's cannon crew went on with breaking the
bunker, the turret crew would calmly beat up the side
trenches with canister, and put HE into windows, doors, and
whatever else looked attractive.

This would go on all day and into the night. Then the
Brits and their Indian allies would pull back, make camp,
wash up, and have a warm supper, and pull maintenance.
Meanwhile Ghurka scouts would be forward, listening while
the Japanese frantically repaired damage and replaced the
corpses with fresh gunners. Next morning, already knowing
the position and what the enemy had done during the night,
the tanks would roll in again and start over, with the infantry
standing guard. Sometimes this went on for several days,
not until the Japanese retreated, but until they ran out of
warm bodies. . . . The Japanese 15th Army was committing
suicide against tanks.

One M-3 Grant came through a field of low scrub with
its guns thundering, its cannon breaking bunkers, and its
turret raking the trees when it got boarded by two Japanese,
one lieutenant with a Nambu pistol and sword, one private
with an Arisaka rifle. The turret from a running mate powered over and a burst of coax ripped across them, dropping
the private off the hull even as the officer's sword plunged
into the body of the TC, who dropped into the hull, dead.
The officer followed his victim in and plunged the samurai
blade into the 37mm gunner and then was shot by the
loader, who had to put nine bullets into this madman to
stop him. . . . And the driver and the 75mm crew didn't
even know that anything unusual had happened, due to the
rattle of incoming fire and the thunder of the 75. This happened to a tank belonging to A Squadron, 3rd Carabiniers.

The battles went on. A tank would glide forward on
creaking tracks, engine ticking over slowly, and then be
blown sky high because, in a pit before it, a Japanese soldier
had been waiting with a 250-pound aircraft bomb and a rock.
When the tank rolled over the spider hole, the soldier hit

the bomb's primer with the rock and went to his reward. It did keep General Kimura's attention, though, and many miles south and west of him, more tanks were beginning to roll.

Kimura had figured out that the tanks were his major problem, and he called in his last ace in the hole, the 4th Tank Regiment with a strength of roughly 40 tanks. There were problems. On 19 February, a patrolling squadron of RAF Thunderbolt fighter-bombers spotted a flash of light from an imperfectly camouflaged Chi-Ha tank in a patch of jungle some miles east of Mandalay. They had apparently been coming back from a mission with unexpended ordnance, for they made an immediate air attack on the area and destroyed 14 tanks, or over a third of the Fourth Tank Regiment's strength.

Several days later, another company unwisely tried a daylight dash to Mandalay and got caught in the open by another flight of fighters and were shortly turned to burning scrap. In the end, only nine tanks seem to have gotten through to Mandalay, and they were only used as mobile bunkers instead of as a combined task force. Meanwhile, the bridgehead at Nyaungu had consolidated, getting enough supplies across the river to restock the tanks, and the Japanese holding force was simply shoved out of the way as an armored juggernaut exploded from the perimeter, heading east at speed.

The 17th Indian Division had split into its two brigades, the 63rd on the left or northern side, and south of it, in another column, the 48th Brigade also rolled its truck-borne infantry. The cutting edge was the light armored cars of the 11th and 16th Light Cavalry, behind them came the Sherman tanks of the Deccan horse and King Edward's Lancers. The 16th, it should be noted, was the only Cavalry Regiment commanded by an Indian, Lieutenant Colonel J. N. Chaudhuri.

Part way from the bridgehead to Meiktila, an attempt was made to take the town of Oyin, which was supposed to be a soft target, being only administrative troops, but there is no such thing as a "soft" Japanese installation. The admin troops promptly went kamikaze, prepared the old human

bullet unit that had been invented at Nomonhan, and began
to dive under the tanks with satchel charges. They destroyed
one Sherman, disabled another, and then were machine-
gunned by the bow gunners.

On 23 February, the commander of the 17th Indian, General D. T. Cowan, brought his two columns together at
Taungtha, which was a Japanese maintenance center for one
of Kimura's divisions, the 33rd. The city was overwhelmed
by superior forces, and its airfield was taken intact. Then
with both columns together on 26 February, the Royal Deccan Horse's Shermans closely following a probing screen of
Daimlers and Stuarts, launched a classic cavalry raid north
around Meiktila, and took its undefended airfield, clearing
the shocked defenders with relative ease.

By the 27th, the field was fit for heavy traffic and by 2
March, Cowan's 3rd Bridgade, the 99th, had been flown in.
The question that begs to be answered here, though, is: Just
exactly what was Japanese Imperial Intelligence doing just
then? Making origami birds?

This was the subject of an intensive investigation after the
war by one Takuo Isobe, and there is *still* some confusion
as to the actual chain of events. What seems to have happened is that, due to friction between the Japanese Army
and Navy, no one in Burma had ever heard of Yamamoto's
fake radio transmissions, and IV Corps' dummy radio net
north of the Irrawaddy River had completely taken the
Burma Area Command in. When a transmission from a Japanese observer near Nayaunga had reported a column of
2,000 vehicles, including 200 tanks, it was simply not believed. Worse, it was sent to the High Command, who ordered the telegrapher to remove one zero from the estimate.
When the 33rd Division at Taungtha reported the same column, they were reprimanded for exaggeration.

The city of Meiktila sits on a strip of land between two
lakes, one to the north, one to the south, and on the morning
of the 28th, while most of his force was advancing from the
west, Cowan launched the 255th Armored Brigade north
around the city to take it's main airfield. He caught the
defenders about half prepared, still digging their bomb pits
and planting mines.

While the classic tank terror may work on Europeans, it doesn't seem to quite affect orientals the same way. All they did, after being forced from the airfield to the east of the city and the open ground to the west, was to retreat into the city and dig in for the long haul. It took three solid days of hand-to-hand and muzzle-to-muzzle street fighting, and time after time a tank would have to assassinate a cluster of snipers, shoot through the firing slits of bunkers, or shoulder whole buildings out of the way while the infantrymen shot down the suicide bombers with pole charges, magnetic mines, or satchel charges. . . . But the job got done!

By now, with XXXIII Corps steadily grinding across the Mandalay Plain and his supply base at Meiktila full of marauding tanks, Kimura and his superiors were probably at wit's end and thinking about honorable hari-kiri, but for the moment they were trapped. The battle for Mandalay went on for 20 grueling days and seriously damaged the historic city. On 21 March, Kimura packed it in and ordered whatever he had left out of Mandalay, rounded up the troops around Meiktila—who were vainly trying to retake the place—and displaced south, very quickly. This was to be the beginning of a classic cavalry pursuit, almost all the way to Rangoon.

Forty miles south of Mandalay a railroad and a major highway cross, at the town of Pywabwe, and there Kimura and Honda thought that they might be able to hold long enough for aid to come from one or another of the two field armies supposedly still left in Burma. By road, rail, and foot, they retreated, quickly this time, not stubbornly as they knew that in order to hold tanks, they'd have to have time to dig ditches, set fields of fire, and plant mines. Too late, far too late, they were getting good at stopping tanks. Kimura's plan seems to have been to hold at Pywabwe long enough to restock, reequip, and then run straight south 300 miles to Rangoon to link up with any other remaining Japanese units.

Kimura had a bit of time to get underway because General Slim was doing some troop shuffling of his own, and reconfiguring his two armored brigades for pursuit. His plan was to head for Rangoon hell-bent and simply outrun Ki-

mura and prevent that link up. There was also a plan, code-
named "Dracula," that was considered a bit risky, but
maybe worth the gamble. It involved the classic American
style amphibian/paratroop operation.

Slim had two routes south available to him, and he determined that by now he'd gotten enough supplies and reinforcements to use both of them. The two tank brigades
would be his tools for breaking and entering the whole peninsula down to Rangoon. General Montague Stopford's
XXXIII Corps would move back to Pagan overland and then
head down the valley of the Irrawaddy. Their tank unit
would be the 254th Indian Tank Brigade. Messervy's IV
Corps, led by the redoubtable 255th Tank Brigade, would
face right about in place and follow the road and rail track
down the Sittaung Valley past and through whatever the
Japanese had in place. Stopford was to keep the pressure
on the oilfields, Messervy was to apply classic blitzkrieg.

Japanese General Honda and his Chief of Staff General
Rikichiro had barely gotten into place at Pyawbwe and
started digging in when it hit. Brigadier Pert had assembled
a spearhead composed of two squadrons each of Probyn's
Horse with Shermans and the 16th Light Cavalry with
Daimlers, also 6/7 Rajputs in trucks as backup infantry. He
also had a battery of self-propelled artillery (105mm) and a
company of engineers. This was the same kind of force the
Japanese themselves used in Malaya in their successful invasion in early 1942, but there was a *lot* more of much better equipment.

On 10 April, the main Japanese position at Pyawbwe was
holding against the 17th Indian Division and the Royal Deccan Horse, when Brigadier Pert suddenly came out of nowhere, turned the Japanese position's flank, cut into their
rear, and shot the blazes out of their supply area and ammo
dump. When that happened, the 17th Indian and the Deccan
Horse mounted up and began streaming south. The defenders were either ground under the tracks of Shermans, shot,
or ignored. General Rikichiro, after the war, said that the
appearance of those tanks in his supply dump was "most
unsettling." At the time, he and Honda and several others
of the staff were seriously thinking about ritual suicide.

Yamethin fell on 14 April, Pyinmana on the 19th, and Toungoo on the 22nd. A battle was necessary at Payagale where the defenders were Japanese engineers. The task force was now coming into paddy country and the engineers had flooded one. Not knowing that it takes several weeks for a flooded paddy to get too soft to support a tank, they did exactly what the Japanese engineers wanted. . . . They drove out into a killing ground and began to take hits from 47mm antitank guns and to roll over hastily planted mines. One Sherman rolled over a buried, command-detonated aircraft bomb that blew the engine and crew out of it, dropping the tank back on its turret top, completely upside down. More suicide squads armed with pole charges would wait until a Sherman rolled past, and then rush from behind the escorting infantry to ram their charges into a tank's tender rear. Still, the defense only slowed the onrushing armored force down to a total of 6 miles for that day.

The 255th rolled on with the infantry divisions rotating lead security behind them. At each bridge or critical road junction either a garrison of troops or engineers, whichever was necessary, was left behind. Now the early monsoon rains, called Mango showers, were beginning, and the British and the Japanese were rushing almost parallel down to Rangoon. The aerial resupply system that had been set up could no longer reach all the way from the north and the whole attacking force was put on half rations. Fuel was rationed and the tanks were in danger of running out. Both the M-3 Medium and the M-3 Light tanks burned aviation gasoline and had to compete with the aviators for fuel.

On 31 April, Pegu was assaulted and as the Japs retreated, they blew the road and rail bridges, only to have to watch the British engineers install an American engineered Baily Bridge and keep coming. Now Indian Lieutenant Colonel J. N. Chaudhuri was commanding the fighting van, which was made up of both recon elements, 4/12 Frontier Rifles and a Squadron of Shermans from Probyn's Horse, along with a battery of 105mm self-propelled guns. The Japanese, however, had been busy.

The only usable road was heavily mined, including the shoulders; many of the mines were command detonated by

fanatic stay-behind troops who had to be evicted one by one
before the engineers could disarm the bombs. Eventually,
the job was done and on 3 May, the force reached Hlegu
only to find that all the bridges had been blown and the
engineering job would require weeks of work. They had
come 300 miles in 3 weeks only to be stopped cold just 32
miles short of Rangoon.

The bitter taste of defeat was sweetened somewhat by
good news. Lord Louis Montbatten had launched "Operation Dracula," and Rangoon was already in Allied hands.
The 50th Indian Paratroop Brigade had been dropped on
elephant point and the 26th Indian Division had come
ashore to consolidate what the paratroopers had gained.
With a little mopping up, the campaign for Burma was effectively over. When the atomic bomb was dropped and Japan
capitulated, it was found out that the Imperial Army had
had 250,000 men in that campaign, but only 50,000 were still
alive to surrender. British losses had been 2,800 killed,
10,000 wounded, and around 30 tanks destroyed or
disabled. . . . But it wasn't supposed to have been "Tank
Country."

REFERENCE SOURCES

The East India Company, Brian Gardner, Dorset Press.
Seize and Hold, Bryan Perrett, Arms and Armor Press.
Famous Tank Battles, Robert J. Icks, Doubleday.
Burma, Won Loy Chan, Presidio Press.

Cavalry Journal References

"The Jungle Ain't Half Bad" November–December 1944.
"Victory in Burma," Charles Gardner, July–August 1946.

CHAPTER 33

Korean Ridge Runners

THIS STORY WAS TOLD TO THE AUTHOR IN LATE 1955 BY A cousin who lived it. Sergeant Barry Doyle of Rockford, Illinois, went into the army in early 1950 and was trained as infantry. However, when he got off the ship at Seoul, there was a first sergeant with a predatory gleam in his eyes waiting. As each group of soldiers came down the ramp he would ask for a man with mechanical skills and . . .

I knew better than to volunteer, but the thought of riding instead of walking appealed to me. As soon as the top soldier had five of us, he loaded us and our bags into a 3/4-ton truck and took off. After about an hour of bumpy roads, he deposited us in front of a squad tent beside which was parked a Sherman tank, which I already knew had no business in an infantry company, without a crew.

Top wasted no time. "This," he said, "was left behind by a retreating tank company, because it ran out of fuel. Now, it's got a big Ford GAF V-8 engine which runs on MoGas, so we dumped in a can and slid off with it before their retrieval party came back. . . . Mebbe they got reequipped because nobody's been looking for it. The sucker's got a 105 howitzer in the turret and we can get ammo from a buddy of mine who's in a battery that supports us. My operations NCO got us a set of manuals for it, and here they are."

He reached into the cab of the truck and pulled out a stack of manuals about three-inches thick, handed them to me and then floored us with the statement. "Corporal, you and these other four apes are now a tank crew, The tank's all fueled up and ammoed up. Take it over into that little valley south of here and learn how it works. Yer going into the line with us in one week!!"

After we'd gotten settled in, made our usual rounds to meet the supply NCO and the mess sergeant, and gotten connected with the company hierarchy, we drew a few cases of five-in-one rations, and settled down to reading manuals. I'd been made the TC by reason of my two stripes, and the others just kind of rattled around inside the tank and fitted themselves into place. Pretty soon, we'd figured out who went where and how his machinery worked. A guy who'd worked dozers in civilian life naturally took over the driver's job. We all played with that bow gun, because that tricky sucker didn't have any sights. We finally figured out that reloading the belts with double tracer would allow whoever got the BOG position to shoot from line of sight. He was supposed to be the assistant driver anyway, so they could swap off on long road marches.

There was a roll-crimper for the 105 ammunition, which came in two parts so a howitzer crew could make up charges for various uses. To start with, we loaded them up at full charge, all seven bags of powder in the cartridge and crimped 'em down. We sure as heck didn't want loose powder in the turret in combat. Just about the time Top was ready for us, we were ready too. . . . More or less.

When we went into the line, our job was as bunker buster and attack neutralizer. We got real popular, real quick. One thing we learned the easy way; by looking at wrecked tanks. Whatever it was that the Communists had out there could put a hole right in the front slope of a Sherman, which was only about two-inches thick at the bow. After a couple of close calls, we developed a trick which worked like a charm. There was a HEAT [high explosive antitank] round available for that gun, and we had our ammo sergeant draw a batch, and then we began to play with the powder charges.

The tank had a Browning machine gun mounted co-axially with the cannon and before long, we'd made up a few 105mm HEAT rounds whose trajectory exactly matched the co-ax. Then, when we spotted a T-34 or an assault gun, we'd get to some kind of cover and start peppering him with the co-ax. They'd ignore this, every time, until *WHAM,* the big one came hammering down. About half the time, it'd trigger their own ammo and blow the turret clean off . . . that was a real pretty sight. Sometimes they'd sit bouncing on their tracks and explode for an hour or two.

Another way we'd do it was when our infantry point men spotted a Korean tank, I'd injun up to him with a walkie talkie set to the tank's frequency and talk my tracer stream onto him from behind a hill and then *Wham* again. I could get farther out than the co-ax could reach though and since our new powder charge was close to the trajectory of a normal white phosphorous round, I could spot WP shells into the right area and then call in indirect fire HEAT shells and get him that way. We also found out that we could switch fuzes artillery style and a concrete penetrator fuze would put normal HE through somebody's hull too. It was kind of a mix and match, come-as-you-are war.

One time we had a little problem with a pair of T-34s. They'd stopped our infantry company and we got called out of the little town where we were living. We'd fixed up a house, made friends with the locals and gone over to straight artillery work, acting as a company howitzer, using the azimuth indicator and the gunner's quadrant. We groused a lot when the CO called us out, because then we'd have to set up all over again when we got back. When we got up to the line, though, we saw what the problem was. The Koreans were hid out so well that no one could find them. They were using machine gun ammo with no tracers and firing from inside things so no muzzle flash could be seen.

There was a hootch, a barn, and a few haystacks next to a real soft paddy that made us nervous as the rice was a real deep green. That meant that if you drove in there, you'd darn near submerge, and not being a regular tank outfit, we didn't have a tank retriever. We'd long since learned the tanker's automatic reflex in tricky situations. "If something don't look right, shoot it up and see what happens." We put a few shells in the bar and got only the normal explosion. We machine gunned the barn but nobody ran out. We blew the hootch, but got no reaction. Then my gunner put a stream of tracers into the haystack and they began to come out straight up. They were bouncing off something solid so we put a HEAT round in there and there was this god-awful explosion. We'd got the sucker.

Then the radio started yammering again. There was another one under a bridge in a few feet of water about two hundred yards west of there. We backed down off our little hill and cut through a patch of woods to check it out. The problem was, the only way we could get to him was to get down in the river with him and while were doing it, our one-inch-thick side would be exposed to his 85mm cannon and we'd be dead. While we were talking about it, the XO got on the air and called in an airstrike.

Man was that a pretty sight. Those Sabre Jets came screaming down with their .50s hammering, dropping bombs and shooting off rockets and plastering the whole area. When they flew off though, most of the bridge was still there with that T-34 still sitting there, still peppering our infantry with his machine guns and blasting off the occasional cannon shell when he'd spotted a machine gun.

About the time we'd resigned ourselves to jumping into that river for a gun to gun match, a voice came down over the air support frequency. Seems there was a Marine Corsair fighter, a leftover from WWII, coming back from up north with some unused ordnance hanging under his wings. I got on the exec's radio and told him what the problem was. "O-K Armor," he said in a Texas drawl that I'll never forget, "Ah see yer bridge, that's the one east of them three burning houses ain't it?" When we answered affirmative, he said, "O-K tanker, ah've got a couple rockets left—comin' on down, y'all spot for me." Up till now we hadn't even *seen* him, but now we heard that slow rumble of that big 2500 horsepower radial engine coming UP the river, BELOW the tree line!

Suddenly there he was, coming in with his engine roaring and his flaps about half down, he wasn't even doing much over a hundred miles per hour and that big prop of his was actually throwing spray off the water. His .50s reached out like fingers. He was using the same trick we used. As soon as he got a ricochet, he let go with one of those big five-inch rockets and that T-34 just blew the hellangone UP. We could actually see him wave as he lifted up out of there and back to a warm bed, and a hot meal on the *Valley Forge*.

Barry finished up with "Let that be a bit of advice, Ralph, if you ever get into a war and you have to call in air support, don't use jets, they're just too fast for accurate fire."

About a dozen years later, on the Bong Son Plain of South Vietnam, I did just that.

The Ridgerunners

This story, by Lieutenant Willard Coulton, appeared in *Armor* magazine, which had just converted from being the *U.S. Cavalry Journal* in its May–June issue, 1953. (It has been edited somewhat for brevity.)

In Korea, the tankers have learned a new lesson: how to climb ridges and fight from mountain tops. Tankers first took to the hills in force in the Mundung Valley in December 1951, when the 31st Infantry Regiment launched a bunker-busting operation. The Japanese had always built bunkers on the lower slopes of hills where they could get good grazing fire across the valley floor. But the Chinese Reds built their bunkers at the military crest and on the ridgetops; there they are dug into the rock, with log and dirt walls three feet thick. Tanks couldn't hit them effectively from the valley floor.

So the commander of the 31st decided to put his tanks where they could fire right into the enemy's teeth. In three days the 13th Combat Engineer Battalion slashed a road up the rear slope of hill 605. Then four tanks were moved into position on top of the hill— about 1000 feet straight up. The platoon leader spotted them where they could cover a battalion front and dug them in so only the turrets were visible. Within a week fifteen Chinese bunkers had been knocked out. Bunker building by the Chinese on their forward slopes came to an abrupt halt.

In the months that followed, tankers all along the front inched and winched their way to the ridgetops and the enemy found himself methodically blasted out of his hilltop strongpoints. At Mundung-ni, on Heartbreak Ridge, north of Kumwha, wherever an old line tanker would look at the high rock ridges and shudder, tankers are now facing the enemy on hills only a few hundred yards apart—across some of the narrowest, deepest valleys that have ever been fought through. At Kalbak-kumi, north of Inje, tanks at one time were dug in less than 200 yards from the nearest enemy position and in some sectors, our tanks are on the same ridges as the Chinese.

Retaliatory fires by the Chinese have been highly unsuccessful. They can't get close enough with recoilless weapons to inflict any damage, and they are extremely reluctant to use artillery for fear of betraying their positions. Further, any mortarman will tell you how difficult it is to lay a mortar round on the crest of a razorback ridge. . . . One communist did get in a lucky round, however. The 61mm shell whoomed smack down the turret of a 31st Tank Company Sherman. The crew members had just finished firing, and had crawled out of the tank. Nobody was hurt but the tank went back for major repairs.

The ridge-running tankers must cope with problems besides enemy mortars—problems that have no solutions in the book. More than one tank, attempting to negotiate a steep hillside, has gotten away from its driver and slid hundreds of feet down the hill in a shower of rocks and dirt. Tankers have learned the hard way how easily an M-4 will slip its tracks if you try to navigate a slope any way but head-on. One company lost a tank over the forward slope. The driverless M-4 plunged headlong into a Chinese outpost at the foot of the hill. The Reds poured out of the bunker and dashed frantically for their own lines. The tank rolled several times and plowed into a rice paddy, a total wreck. Seconds later the enemy opened up with mortars, automatic weapons, and even artillery. They probably thought a full-scale attack was in progress. . . . Sometimes the slope was so steep that every time the 76s were fired, the tank slid back downhill and had to be driven back up.

To help their Shermans claw up the mountain trails, the tankers put the center guides from wrecked M-26 Pershing tanks on the outside of their tracks, creating four inch grousers every five or six blocks apart. Then the tanks would climb like Mountain goats.

Ammunition supply was another problem, as trucks are useless on ice or muddy trails. The little weasel, with its high flotation and low gear rations was found to be the ideal ammunition carrier. It can lug 30 to 40 rounds of 76mm in fiber cases up the steepest roads. The ammunition problem is heightened by the fact that the high-climbing tanks are constantly in exposed positions. They can't maneuver, and their first round betrays their position to the enemy. As a result, they have to make it too hot for the Reds to bring up their low-slung 75mm antitank gun. "If you use enough ammunition, they won't have a chance to fire back," the commander of the 31st Tank Company said. "But if you run short, they start sneaking up those 75mm guns again."

The favorite weapon of the ridgetop tankers is the .50 Browning machine gun. One tank of the company mounts twin .50s, one feeding from the left, one feeding from the right. The same tank also mounts a .50 in the bow gun position. This enables the tank to reach across the valleys with power and accuracy never possible with the thirties. . . . Hilltop tactics do not necessarily call for close-in infantry protection. In fact, the infantry, normally some distance from the tanks being exposed, drew a lot of retaliatory mortar fire.

The tanks can protect themselves against infiltration because all the approaches to their positions are wired and mined. With this advantage, the tankers can protect each other with machine gun fire and can call in VT [variable time] fire to break up an enemy raid. (To a Vietnam tanker, this seems eerily familiar, but it was not taught, we had to go in blind.)

In most positions, the tanks could pull off their lofty roosts in a hurry if a pullout were ordered, but some of the roads up the mountains are so treacherous that tanks are swapped and left in position, when one tank outfit relieves another on line. The tankers gather up their personal gear and trudge down the hill to pick up another tank in the reserve area. One tank got caught on top of a hill when the rains came and the road was washed out behind it. The only way out was to dash through the enemy territory below.

Another rough problem is supporting infantry patrols. Forced to keep to the roads by the soft paddies, they have found out that the best method is to hold fast; they can support most patrols without budging off their ridgetops. Since most patrols operate within sight of the MLR, the tanks can give solid support with .50 and 76mm fire directly into the newly spotted Red bunkers with precision accuracy. Using their direct fire sights, they can actually walk the infantrymen right up to within 25 or 30 yards of the enemy. . . .

Perched atop sheer cliffs and crawling along the jagged peaks of razorback ridges, our tankers in Korea have dispelled for all time the notion that they are creatures of the open plains. Never again, perhaps, will this peculiar combination of factors occur: extremely rugged terrain, a static front, and an enemy who builds bunkers on hilltops. But if it does, you can rest assured that our tankers know how to take to the hills.

It did occur, with jungle, swamp, and caves added to the mountains, in Vietnam, and the tankers did it again, and always will. In RVN, however, the old link between armor and aircraft began to be forged into a more perfect partnership. There, for the first time in history, tanks began to fly, and the ammo and fuel problem was solved by helicopters. When Company A of the old 69th Armor was attached to an air-cavalry division with a sufficiency of cargo-carrying Ch-47s and a surplus of Hueys, magic began to happen.

CHAPTER 34

Vietnam and Dien Bien Phu

GENOCIDE IS NOTHING NEW IN THE ORIENT, AS A SHORT LOOK at its history will show. What has to be realized is that, like the Balkan area (where Yugoslavia used to be), Indochina is made up of literally dozens of warring ethnic groups who have been preempting each other's real estate and razing their cities since time immemorial. When the average American thinks of the war in Vietnam, the normal mental picture is of infantrymen in savage battle with pajama-clad guerrillas in nightmarish jungles, having to call in air strikes on elusive foes who simply wouldn't come to grips. Nothing could be farther from the truth. Our liberal media have done this nation a great disservice in romanticizing the Vietcong. In the process, the handwringers and settlers of "rules of engagement" also set the stage for the rape of Cambodia by the fanatics of Pol Pot.

When the word Vietnam is used, the mind usually calls up pictures of the Annamese people who are the refugees, the boat people, the remains of a defeated nation who are now scattered throughout America. In actual fact, the peninsula is a melting pot. During the war, we had to contend with the Annamese in the south, the Tonkins, a physically larger race, from the north, and several groups of hill tribes-men. There were about seven different groups of Monta-gnards, of which the Rhade in the central highlands was the largest. There were also the Mountain Chams, who hated everybody, because you see. . . . it was their land.

The Empire of Champa was the name of the people who inhabited the land that is now Vietnam when China was so young that it had not yet reached the sea that now bears its name. Ancient China was an inland nation that was having its troubles with horse raiders from the inner Asian plains. Indeed, a study of history shows an almost unbroken string of raiding horsemen driving the history of the civilized city-states and nations around that vast sea of grass.

Around 300 B.C. a tribe called the Hiung-Nu began to press on what is now China. These were the people who eventually caused the Great Wall to be built. But at that time there wasn't enough organization to resist them, and the peoples of China were driven south out of their ancient lands. This, of course, displaced the Annamese, and forced them down into Indochina, into the Empire of Champa. And they came a-conquering. With the Chinese hot behind them, they had no choice. Their own records tell of armies made up of orphans who had been raised as soldiers and knew no other life.

So history unfolded. Northern Vietnam was invaded by sea peoples of unknown origin who bred with the Annamese and created the Tonkins. The Tonkins, ever at war with China, were eventually discovered by French explorers. The Tonkins, impressed with "modern" French weaponry and military technique, invited them in as allies against the Chi-nese, and the rest is modern history. . . . And what were the Annamese doing just then? They were invading Cambodia, having detected a weakness in the then-decadent Khmer civilization.

At that time, Europe was going through the Industrial Revolution and had discovered a need for many new prod-ucts, such as tea, coffee, rubber, exotic woods, and all these could be produced in Indochina. With all the internal turbu-lence, the French had no real problem taking them over, and the land became a colony of France. In return for land dominance and trade, the French gave the various groups who made up their colony, modern medicine, railroads, industry, and even a modern alphabet—freeing them from the Chinese-based symbolic script. This made mass literacy possible. Most important, they began to open up their great universities to their colonials and in the early 1900s came one Nguyen That Thanh. Eventually he was recruited by the local French communists and became a friend of one V. I. Lenin. After a long, turbulent career, and a few name changes, he returned to his native Vietnam and began the struggle against the French, who were now seen as oppressors. In order to be accepted, however, and to disguise his communist affiliation, he had to disguise his past and change his name . . . to Ho Chi Minh.

France, like most other colonizing nations, expected to regain their possessions after World War II, but history was against them and they didn't realize it. Their Third World children were growing up and wanted to slip the leash. Hindsight is always 20-20, of course, but if the French had been content to elevate their prótegés to protectorate status and really teach them the skills of government, they would *still* be reliable allies. Instead, they tried to put the lid back on and actually plowed the ground for the crop of Marxists who grew into the political weeds which almost choked out civilization in Indochina.

First, they hired surrendered Japanese and rearmed them to police Vietnam until they could rebuild their colonial army. This was not calculated to cause good will with the Vietnamese people. Then, with the Japanese finally going home to rebuild a devastated nation, the French decided to send in their Foreign Legion. The legion at that time was more than half German and an officer was required to be fluent in two languages in order to command his troops. Unfortunately, the Vietnamese were chafing under the harsh rule of the French/Japanese police army and the Viet Minh were then receiving massive supplies from both Russia and China. Terrorism had become the favored tool of the northerners under Ho Chi Minh, and the famed trail was already bringing in such items as cannons and tanks.

In the early 1950s, while we were embroiled in Korea,

France decided that they needed to do something drastic to counter all this inimical activity—so they hired a full battalion of former German SS troops. This is known as overreacting. The result was that for three years and three months, the Viet Minh was on the run from one battalion of men who didn't know the rules of war. . . . They made them. In that period of time, the Battalion of the Damned virtually terminated action on the Ho Chi Minh Trail, killed 7,466 guerrillas by count, destroyed 211 Viet Minh bases with explosives, and liberated 311 political prisoners by force. Their history book, *The Devil's Guard,* is still in print, and is listed by the Library of Congress as fact, not fiction . . . liberal propaganda to the contrary notwithstanding.

In 1954, however, they were destroyed, not by firepower, but by the international, slightly leftist world press. Always, when the social engineers are losing on the battlefield, they resort to the press, the loudspeaker, and lately, the TV camera. When the Germans left, however, a small strike force, TF-G, was hired by the South Vietnamese government, which had just come into being. And the Russians had just shipped a small unit of tanks down the trail into the central highlands, which is good tank country. The scene was being set for eventual American involvement.

The French, however, with their hands still set in the mold of World War II, were just about to put their troops in harm's way, in a little valley west of Hanoi—Haiphong. Their idea was to "create an irresistible target and make the Viet Minh come out of the jungles and fight a formal battle." In so doing, they would inadvertently take the next step in the linkup of light armor and heavy airlift. Aircraft were not yet heavy enough to lift tanks entire, but those ships were definitely on the drawing boards and the battle of Dien Bien Phu only served to establish the validity of the concept.

Colonel T. E. Lawrence had initiated the concept in 1917. The British and French had used "air policing" in the interwar years and there had been sporadic attempts to supply tanks by air in World War II. There had even been a few tries to deliver tanks by air . . . all tactical failures. Korea was not a maneuver war, and no one seems to have used the existing helicopters for tactical supply. The French seem to have been the first to really fly tanks into battle.

Dien Bien Phu, 1954

While the French paras, the Legion, the Germans, and assorted tribal mercenaries were out in the jungles wearing down the Viet Minh, the French high command in Hanoi conceived of a master stroke. The complaint had always been that the guerrillas would not come to grips and would not "fight an honest war." Alright, the generals figured, let's set up a base in a vulnerable valley, surrounded by guerilla country, but with an airstrip that we can use for resupply. The concept was to use the base as a trap and simply suck the guerillas in and kill them. . . . They probably got their inspiration from General "Iron Tits" Matthew Ridgeway in Korea, who had figured out that he could kill Chinese faster than Mao could train, arm, and ship them. For him it worked, for the French, it did not.

The long narrow valley they picked was named Dien Bien Phu, and it has gone down in history as one of the greater blunders of the military art. There are, however, mitigating factors. For the tanker, there is this: there were 13 ex-U.S. M-24s there—which the French knew as Bison—that had been flown in to the base. This is the first-known time at which a significant force of combat-worthy tanks arrived by air—Air America to be exact.

Although the concept of delivering armor by air has been around almost as long as the tank itself, the reality had to wait for the development of ever-larger and more-efficient aircraft . . . and that event took place during the Vietnam War. Unknown and unsung, the marriage between light armor and heavy airlift was in its courting stages. The matchmakers in this case were Foreign Legion tankers with a flair for combat innovation, and wild-flying pilots with nicknames like "Earthquake McGoon, Cueball, and Doc Kusack."

Tanks and aircraft share one abiding need, a thirst for ever-greater amounts of raw power. The liberty aircraft engine of World War I, for instance, powered several generations of tanks, and the Wright whirlwind radial engine was the original powerplant of the M-3 Light Tank and the M-3 Medium as well as its famous descendant, the M-4 Sherman. As the Main Battle Tank was growing ever larger, its battlefield partner, the light scouting tank, was evolving more speed and heavier armament. There came a time in World War II when the scout tank, the M-24, weighing in at just 18 tons, sported the same 75mm firepower with which the Sherman had been born. As a matter of fact, that particular gun had been designed to fit in a B-25 bomber for antishipping use. That gun is still in service and has existed for exactly a hundred years.

By January 1954, when the Foreign Legion needed to move tanks by air, however, the large aircraft were still on the drawing boards, and all they had were C-47s, a few British Bristols, and fewer yet American C-119s. . . . What to do? They needed those tanks at Dien Bien Phu to make their trap work. Eventually some mechanic or loadmaster noted that while nothing they had could move a whole tank, the M-24 could be broken down into parts that a cargo aircraft would digest. The tanks could be disassembled by mechanics, with the crews helping, into tank kits and shipped to where they were needed.

One by one, the Bisons of the Composite Squadron, 1st Regiment of Legion Armored Cavalry were driven under the armored wreckers of an artillery unit to be stripped. First came the turrets, to be rolled into the Bristols. Then the engines and tracks went into C-47s and the hulls went into the big C-119s. Out at Fire Base Anne-Marie, the artillery wreckers were again used to lift and reassemble the tanks—and from 1 February to 7 May, those tanks fought almost every day, until the garrison quit fighting. . . . Dien Bien Phu never surrendered, it just quit fighting when the North Vietnamese Army (NVA) were in the camp raising their own flag.

What had happened to the war-weary French, however, was that their trap was inside out. They had thought to be the bait of an infantry trap, but they were on the end of a very long supply string that started in Washington, went through Paris, and then through Saigon and Hanoi. The Viet Minh, on the other hand, were getting weapons shipped by rail from China right across a border and through China, from Russia. What no one seemed to realize was that the man known as Ho Chi Minh had more connections to Lenin, Stalin, and Mao than he did to Vietnam, and he was using them for all he was worth.

From 1912, when he left to attend college in Paris, to 1941, he had never set foot back in his native land. Instead the man had been an international agent of the Communist movement and had even been jailed by Chiang Kai-shek, until bribed out by other agents in order to subvert Vietnam out from under the Japanese. As a result of these connections and the fact that Vietnam is strategically important for two reasons, the floodgates opened and the guns began to roll south. The characteristics of those Russian guns were critical—but first a look at two items of international interest.

Vietnam, as a piece of real estate, sits on the northern side of the Straits of Malacca. Any navy sitting in Cam Ranh Bay can prevent an American task force from getting from Tokyo Bay (or any other of our eastern bases) to the Persian Gulf. At that time, Russia was still coveting our Mideastern oil supply as well as the mineral treasures of Africa. The other fact has just recently become generally known, although most Vietnam vets knew it. There is about as much oil under Indochina as there was under Saudi Arabia. That is why China, the Philippines, and Vietnam are squabbling about the Spratly Islands. And we may *still* get sucked into that one. If Saddam Hussein is not neutralized, he will take over the Middle East, and we will have to go back to Vietnam.

Back in 1954, though, all the tankers knew was that they were part of a plan to grind the communists down into military insignificance. What they did not know was that their guns were outranged by the enemy's weaponry. A look at the guns will tell the problem. The French were armed with American 105mm and 155mm howitzers, eminently suitable for high-angle fire against jungle targets. The 105 will throw an 18-kg projectile 11.5 kilometers, or about seven miles. It was, and still is today, a good piece of light artillery. The 155mm gun which was in service with the French at that time, was a bit long in the tooth, though. It was an American adaptation of a French World War I model, and it could throw 43.4kg out to a range of 14.6km, which in artillery terms is quite respectable—if you aren't outranged and have observers with radios to spot targets for you.

The Russian 122mm field gun, on the other hand, will reach 24km with a 27.3kg payload—and that was what Ho's minions were equipped with. Simply put, the French were outgunned, outranged, outnumbered, and they had set up in a bowl surrounded by master artillerymen. When the enemy outranges you, you can't hit back and he can kill you at his leisure, as has been proved many times. The wonder is that the French held out at all, let alone three months. Worse was yet to come, for the French advantage of supplying by air was about to be canceled.

Unknown to apparently *all* intelligence services was the fact that the Viet Minh had very good antiaircraft capability. Before the French knew what had been done to them, their two airfields were ringed with an ever-increasing number of ever-larger weapons. Fifty caliber and 20mm autocannons were first, followed by 37mm and 40mm and up to 100mm AAA weaponry. The supply pilots were forced to run a gauntlet from the very start and then the Viet Minh gunners began to target the airstrip itself. When the communist artillerymen weren't shooting at planes, they were making the airstrip unusable. The trap had been sprung alright . . . on the trappers.

The squadron of 13 bisons became operational on 1 February 1954, and stayed operational, losing tank after tank until combat ceased on 7 May, after four months of continuous combat. Dien Bien Phu was an area of strong points, not a single hard perimeter. From Gabrielle on Hill 406 in the north, the position straggled down a long narrow valley. The main complex, Anne-Marie/Hugette/Francoise/Elaine, held the main airstrip and drew the most attention. Further south, past several villages, the strongpoint of Isabelle more or less protected the auxiliary airstrip just north of the town of Ban Hong Cum.

With two separate complexes, it was automatic that the besiegers would try to separate and isolate them, and that is what General V. Nguyen Giap's opening move was, an attempt on the road axis between Anne-Marie and Isabelle. The result was a savage riposte with the whole tank force and two companies of infantry. Each time the Viet Minh would cut the road, the tankers would open it up again. For a time, it actually must have seemed that the plan would work. Giap and "Uncle Ho," unfortunately, had a *lot* more firepower than anyone could have guessed. Against 16,500 defenders, there came an army of 54,000 backed up by 3,000 trucks and 300,000 coolies. There also came 144 heavy artillery pieces and several dozen World War II Katusha rocket launchers.

While the French had envisioned a set of little swirling mobile battles that would eat the enemy alive, what actually happened was World War I all over again, with the defenders living in dugouts and trenches under almost continuous artillery bombardment. Under these conditions, the French had exactly one maneuver element, the tankers. By the end of March though, those tankers were worn down a bit. Every tank had been holed several times, most of the crews were injured and swapping off to keep the running tanks fully crewed and spending what time they could cannibalizing parts off hopeless wrecks to keep their "runners" functional.

The tank unit had also been split up, with the main force at the northern encampment, but with a small reserve platoon down south at Isabelle. Those four tanks were under control of the Tank Company Commander, Captain Yves Hervouet, who by this time had both arms in plaster casts and was doing most of his fighting with a radio. On 28 March, the overall commander, Colonel Christian De Marie Castries, ordered an attack on the most dangerous antiaircraft position, a gun nest just west of Huguette.

What had happened was that the Viet Minh under cover of darkness were sapping trenches ever closer to the French positions and getting their guns ever closer to that vital airstrip. At 0600 hours on the 28 March, a platoon of three tankers under a Lieutenant Jean Preaud came howling out of Isabelle, linked up with what was left of four battalions of paras and tore into that trench and bunker complex.

The only warning the communists would have had was the sudden artillery barrage from the French position, an air strike, and suddenly the tanks were among them. Unlike later tanks, the M-24 had a bow gunner, who handled a machine gun right alongside the driver, and that one fact made the little 18-tonner a deadly infighter as the two men in the hull could take care of themselves while the three in the turret went to the aid of the infantry.

With the tracks grinding bodies as the bow gunner flushed them from cover, the 75mm cannon broke the walls of dugouts while the coaxial machine gun exterminated little groups of hostiles. Two tanks were quickly hit by rocket-propelled grenade (RPG) fire but kept on fighting. Any hull penetration that does not set a tank on fire or blow up something is not usually fatal and two or three men can still make a tank fight. In conditions that close, the gunner can't really see much anyway and is quickly put to work replacing the first wounded crewmen . . . usually the tank commander.

By 1500 hours, the communists had had enough. Suddenly they broke and headed for the surrounding jungle, leaving the French tankers and Paras standing in a battlefield littered with 350 enemy corpses, five 20mm antiaircraft cannons, a full dozen .50s, and assorted other badly needed battle plunder. Three operational tanks had allowed a heavily outnumbered force of Paras to break into a solidly entrenched enemy works, but that was the last attempt of its kind; there simply weren't enough running tanks to go around. . . . That kind of tank fighting, also, isn't taught anymore, and that lack is going to get somebody killed in the near future.

Dien Bien Phu, of course, will continue to be dissected by armchair tacticians for generations, but the question will always remain: "What if there had been a few more tanks and they had been allowed to go hunting?"

REFERENCE SOURCES

Dien Bien Phu, Howard R. Simpson, Brassey's Inc.
The Early Years, Ronald H. Spector, U.S. Center of Military History.
War in Peace, edited by Sir Robert Thompson, Harmony Books.
"French Armor at Dien Bien Phu," Captain Michael E. Woodgerd, *Armor* magazine, September–October 1987.

CHAPTER 35

The ACAV, Light Armor in Paddy Country

DURING THE PERIOD FROM 1953 TO 1965, THE WESTERN World was preparing for the expected confrontation with the conventional bogeyman, Russia. Every tank in the world seemed to have been designed for a Kursk-sized clash of armored hordes somewhere around Fulda Gap, West Germany. With the exception of the M-551 Sheridan, there was no light, amphibious combat vehicle in service in the U.S. Army. We had, however, gone through a series of amphibious Armored Personnel Carriers, or APCs. When we got snared into Vietnam's internal affairs, though, what we *needed* was a light tank that floated.

When we began to equip and train the Army of Vietnam, or ARVN, we sent the brand-new M-113, which was made by the same company, Food Machinery Corporation (FMC), that had manufactured the famed Alligator and Amtanks of World War II fame. The idea was for the APC to get to rifle range of a hostile formation and then disgorge a squad of infantry for the actual assault. The vehicle driver and gunner were to stay aboard and deliver support fire with the .50 Browning. At least that was American doctrine. The Viets, however, didn't quite see things that way.

There seems to be a foxhole gene in the Asian makeup.
Every war we have fought over there teaches us that given
any chance, an Asian soldier will do two things with shocking efficiency. Go to ground and build a tunnel works and,
secondly, set up for mortar fire. When we provided them
with the makings of a mechanized infantry company, we had
inadvertently given them portable foxholes. We thought they
were infantry, they thought they would rather be cavalry,
and by God, they were.

First thing they did was cut the number of crew on board
and add a couple of wing machine guns to complement the
big .50s. Then they simply moved their dunnage and rations
on board and set up housekeeping. They fought mounted
and began a series of amphibious patrols that cost the VC
and NVA horrendous losses. Thus was born the Armored
Cavalry Assault Vehicle or ACAV.

Of course, we had to send them "advisors," who were
actually out on "makee learnie," as the oriental term goes.
What the Viets had created, they were happy to teach the
big round-eyed men with all the money and hardware. There
was, however, a certain amount of culture shock. What follows is a condensation and adaptation of the experiences of
two U.S. officers who went through the Tet experience with
the Viets at the same time I was going through it in Pleiku.
The first voice will be that of Captain Kenneth P. Long,
who stepped out of a modern aircraft into a muddy Saigon
night full of tracers.

My arrival in Vietnam was a study in surrealism. The
time was the late 1960s, and the buildup in Vietnam
was still continuing. The airconditioned Boeing 707 descended through the black night, while outside the ship,
tracers, exploding artillery and flares could be seen on
the horizon. The feeling of personal helplessness was
amplified by the ensuing drive through Saigon's blackened streets where only ghostly images of people could
be seen through the windows of a bus which was driving
on blackout lights. Once the brief formalities at Koepler
Compound, a former French hotel complex, were over,
another short bus ride took us to the military airfield.

My personal assignment was to be an armor advisor to a Vietnamese cavalry troop, and after a caribou airplane ride to Dong Tam, the support base for the U.S. 9th Division, I received a standard briefing. Then I took a short, hair-raising helicopter ride to Support Team 75 HQ out in the Delta. After another unsettling briefing, another helicopter ride put me down in the base of the ARVN 6th Cavalry squadron, which was part of the ARVN 7th division, and immediate culture shock set in.

It should be noted at this time that we "advisors" brought a variety of American knowledge with us, but no combat experience, we soon found out that we were actually learning, not teaching. My ARVN counterpart had been sent through various Vietnamese military schools, including that of years of mechanized combat in the mushy, brushy lands of the Mekong Delta. The ACAV version of the then-new M–113 was basically a Vietnamese invention, not an American design. Our main operational area (AO) was to be the Ca Mau Peninsula and its main road artery up through My Tho, to Saigon, national highway number four.

Part of the advisory mission was to gain rapport with our Vietnamese counterpart but there were definite obstacles to overcome. "Rapport" implies friendship and that implies shared goals, interests and commonality of language. The basic lack of experience on the part of the incoming advisor, the complete lack of knowledge of the language, and the suspicion of the Vietnamese that the advisor was basically a snoop for MACV created an environment of distrust that took months to overcome.

Due to our lack of combat experience, the advisors became fire support coordinators and MEDEVAC facilitators for the Vietnamese, which did two things. First, it helped build the "rapport." Second, it helped provide battlefield survivability for both the advisors and the Vietnamese. This was no small advantage, for culture shock and a feeling of absolute aloneness were an ongoing part of life.

For individuals familiar with the normal American

supply system, to include showers, porta-potties, ice, rations, and sundry packs, the total lack of a support tail was a sudden jolt. The Vietnamese Cavalry lived mostly off the local economy, except for obvious military needs such as ammunition and spare parts. While the Vietnamese took much criticism for their non-reg maintenance procedures, in all fairness, it should be noted that their vehicle availability often exceeded that of an equivalent American unit. . . . Basically, they pushed wrenches instead of paper.

If the Vietnamese trooper excelled at anything, it was the maintenance of his equipment, there was always some cleaning going on, either of the track, weapons or individual equipment. During TET 1968, most damaged vehicles were returned repaired within 24 hours. There may have been an RPG hole or two in the hull, but the internal workings had been repaired and the track was operational. The only real problem was the lack of operational radios, but that was above troop level. After TET, the Direct Exchange system was implemented in the ARVN and things smoothed out, especially for heavy use items such as machine gun barrels.

The ARVN cavalry units had started out as Mechanized Infantry, but in operation both the vehicle and the T.O. changed. The M-113s had been modified to perform as combat vehicles, not battle taxis. In effect, they were used as amphibious light tanks which carried a few dismountable soldiers for close in work and security. They worked as a tank with an oversized crew, not as an infantry squad with a vehicle.

There were three ACAVs per platoon and three platoons per troop. The HQ section consisted of a command track, a maintenance track and a support section consisting of the wheeled supply vehicles. The ACAVs were armed with a .50 caliber machine gun and a pair of .30 caliber wing guns each. There was an 81mm mortar section, the occasional scrounged 57mm recoilless rifle, and a Rube Goldberg coffee grinder contraption which spewed out 40mm grenades. The primary problem seemed to be finding spare parts for the equipment, especially the non-TO&E items.

There was no mess section. Each track had an appointed cook. The requirement for culinary ability was not standard, therefore it fell to the newest or most hapless member of the crew to do the cooking. Formal rations were nonexistent, and food was either bought locally or carried along. Meat was carried in the form of live chickens in the M-113s, and this could create some problems, especially in combat. Grabbing an ammo box in a firefight might mean disturbing a laying hen, and sleeping in the tracks was impossible due to roosting chickens. Clutches of eggs tended to show up in the oddest places, such as duffle bags or G.I. helmets. Unofficial reveillie was usually provided by the resident rooster and "rooster etiquette" had some influence on vehicle parking sites. A really aggressive bird was considered a cash asset for the evening cockfights.

Breakfast was hot French coffee and soup. This usually came from soup shops set up along Highway Four and in some of the larger villages. Lunch depended on operational considerations. If an operation was pending, there would be a rush to the local bread shop where a loaf of hard crusted French bread would be slit down the middle and filled with a mix of roast pork, pepper sauce and other, usually unidentifiable, items. Each would be wrapped in last week's newspaper and placed on top of the vehicle's radio, so that it would be warm for lunch.

Fast food was also possible. Prawns could be bought from local fishermen and cooked on board while the vehicle traveled. The drill was to roast them on the exhaust grille of the Detroit Diesel which powered the M-113 and then pass them out to the crew, who dipped them in either a spiced brown bean paste or the ever-present bowl of nuc mam, a fermented fish sauce. Every track carried a bottle of this, continually added to and properly aged.

While on combat operations, lunch would usually mean a complete cessation of movement while the "cooks" scurried to nearby homes to buy, scrounge, or in known VC areas, liberate food. Fires were lit, rice cooked, and the meal consumed. The rice could also be kept warm by placing the pot in or near the engine compartment. Supper usually terminated the existence of one of the chickens, unless it was an unusually good laying hen or had become a pet. The almost invariable meal was soy-stirred chicken, rice, fresh cucumbers, a hot vegetable stew, a salad, and hot tea. The scraps were recycled to the chickens. With this ration method and considering that the M-113 could range over 475 kilometers on one load of fuel, patrols could last for a week or more, unless enemy contact was made. For extreme duration operations of course, a complete re-supply could be brought by just one CH-47. This included a 500 gallon 'blivit' of fuel, some rations, a medic, ammo, and the mail. . . .If the pilot was Vietnam-ese, some girls somehow got smuggled aboard.

Accommodations were spartian. Sleeping inside the track was inadvisable due to the chickens. Vietnamese crewmembers either used cots or strung up net ham-mocks while on patrol. If near a village, they would sleep in local houses, school buildings or warehouses—whatever was available. There was an ongoing acclima-tization due to the fact that in Vietnam there are exactly two seasons, hot and wet, and wet and hot.

Since most advisory teams had just two members, an officer and an NCO, usually separated by several hun-dred kilometers, sleep became a luxury and no more than three (interrupted) hours per night could be counted on. With nine operational vehicles out in three separate patrol areas, something always seemed to be going down. Sleep when it was possible, came during the hottest part of the day when both the ARVN and the VC seemed almost by mutual agreement, to shut down for a siesta.

Operations during the night usually involved the searchlight section. This was a pair of xenon searchlights of 75 million candlepower each. They were mounted on M–151 jeeps and were capable of both infrared and white light. They could be set for wide beam or focused to a point. During night operations, the advisor would have to coordinate the searchlights with operational units as they could be used to provide artificial moonlight. Since most nights were cloudy, simply aiming the beams at the area over the action provided acceptable illumination.

Radio traffic was the bugbear. During movement to contact, it was necessary to communicate not only with your own NCO, but with adjacent troops, the squadron HQ, the battalion advisors, and sometimes senior American advisors at divisional and province levels. Also needed was contact with artillery forward observers, airstrike controllers, Medevac birds, and helicopter gunships. Communications usually failed just when they were needed most, and the command track always looked like a porcupine with as many as eight aerials sticking out of its hull. This tended to attract VC bullets and during encounters of the most intense kind, these aerials were some of the first casualties. (Losing contact with several overlapping layers of command, however, is not detrimental to combat ops. . . . You just reconnect the radio that provides fire support to whatever antenna is left).

While combat operations were frequent, combat planning was not. The usual warning order consisted of being waked up with a hand on one's shoulder and the detailed command, "We go," from the reaction platoon CO. This generally meant that the advisor spent the next few minutes racing madly down the highway trying to match up a hastily drawn map overlay (transparent plastic sheet with a situation drawing on it) from the troop commander with his windblown map, and trying to read the result by flashlight. The next few minutes were usually spent on the radio trying to find out what was going on.

Intelligence of enemy activities was about as bad. It was not until the spring of 1968 that the 7th ARVN division commander began to use special funds to buy information from locals that some of the sweeps and operations began to bag large VC/NVA units. Prior to this, a report of VC activity would result in a hasty rush to contact which would find that the enemy had already left. The VC/NVA forces, however, were probing, testing and gathering their strength, for the Chinese new year, or TET period of national celebration was approaching. My Tho, the district capital and HQ of the ARVN 7th Division, was obviously on the NVA hit list.

This concludes the report from Captain Long who rotated out in mid-1968. The comments of Captain Cole, who was in the same area but possibly not in Long's chain of command, will take us through TET in My Tho.

Five days before the battle, which commenced on 31 January, the 6th Cavs 1st Troops, under Captain Nguyen Van Vinh, had returned to My Tho for R, R & R (Rest, Recuperation and Repair) after four months in the field. Almost immediately rumors of attack began to circulate, but as these had been around before, no one took them completely seriously. The American G.I.s, though, took note of an increased density of unoccupied military age males. "Those arrogant little bastards that look like they're measuring you for a coffin," being the usual description.

Higher command, both Vietnamese and American seemed oblivious and by 30 January, the troop's present-for-duty strength was down to about 50%, due to troop members having been given leave to visit relatives for the coming holidays. The duty troops who were resting and working on the tracks prepared to throw a Battalion TET party. . . . Then solid reports of guerrilla attacks in northern III Corps area started coming in.

General Trang, commanding the 7th Division, was a cautious individual and ordered 6th Cav to put a troop on alert in My Tho. With 1st Troop already being in place, 6th Cav ordered Captain Vinh's men to full alert and the preparations for parties stopped as the men streamed back to their tracks. The reason they could do this so quickly is that ARVN units were mostly locally raised and the men's homes were all within a few miles of the city. In effect, they were defending their homes from Northern invaders. By 1930 hours on the 30th, 1st Troop was in position along My Tho's main drag, Hung Vuong street, awaiting the onslaught.

My Tho sits in a bend of the Bao Dinh Canal, a dredged and maintained river. Hung Vuong Street runs straight north across a French bridge to the gate of the old French military compound which at that time, housed the Vietnamese 32nd Ranger Battalion. Shortly after 0400 on the 31st, 82mm mortars began to fall on the Ranger compound and by 0415, they were under heavy assault by the VC 261-B Battalion, and were calling for help. This resulted in 7th Division ordering 1st Troop to send a platoon of three ACAVs across the canal to beef up the Ranger's firepower. Captain Vinh was now suddenly down to six ACAVs and his command track. Apparently they got there just in the nick of time, as the Ranger commander now considered his situation to be desperate. The sudden arrival of three more .50s and nine .30 cal machine guns and assorted auxiliary weapons seems to have saved the day, for the compound never fell.

Shortly after 0500, the Troop's 2nd Platoon, stationed at three equidistant points around the city's traffic circle, reported infiltrators from VC 261-A Battalion working into the city and a savage firefight developed between the two forces. The VC were equipped with B-40 rockets, the predecessor to the famed RPG series of antitank rockets and the ground around the three tracks seemed to erupt with bursting warheads. The VC gunners, however, were thrown off by the hail of machine gun fire from the tracks and no hits were made. The 2nd Platoon was able to back up about one hundred meters eastward along Nguyen Trai Street.

At this time the VC were working forward and Captain Vinh suddenly ordered his Third, and last, platoon to advance northward on Truong Long Street, which ran north and south along the western side of the village. As they were approaching the traffic circle, they

began taking large volumes of automatic weapons fire
from VC in the buildings. Then the B-40 gunners, who
seemed to have an unlimited supply of rockets, opened
up and forced them to turn south, and take up positions
on Hung Vuong street.

At this point in time, 1st Platoon was still bracing
the Ranger perimeter, 2nd platoon was backed up into
Mguyen Trai St. and 3rd was licking it wounds on Hung
Vuong St. The 2nd platoon was the one which mounted
the 57mm recoilless rifle on one of its rear corners, on
a modified antenna mount, and the platoon leader put
it at the front of his column to keep the B-40 launchers
at bay. It seemed to be working, but the VC were steadily working through the twisted back alleys behind the
straight gridwork of the French designed streets.

Suddenly the vehicle took a direct hit on its left side,
and the crew were forced to evacuate the crippled
ACAV. Now more and more VC were arriving and the
firefight turned into a perfect hell of massed firepower
from the tracks and hundreds of man-to-man skirmishes. At the intersection of Hung Vuong and Nguyen
Trai Streets were a Catholic school on the northwest
corner and a hospital on the southwest corner. Suddenly, these were taken by the VC in an attempt to
surround the cavalrymen with firepower. First Troop,
however, was not about to give up. Time after time, the
Viets would dismount, flip a hand grenade into a newly
won VC position, and then follow it up with a personal
assault, under the guns of their own ACAVs.

They tried several times, throughout the morning to
extract the crippled ACAV, and finally Corporal Tran
Ngoc Ut decided to do it the hard way, by hand. Using
trees on the south side of the street, he flitted from
position to cover, always under fire from the VC, who
wanted that gun for their own use. Finally, he'd gotten
beside the vehicle and was protected from enemy fire,
for a few moments. At this time another ACAV rolled
forward, its engine rumbling and treads clicking on the
road. Its commander and gunners poured a tremendous
volume of fire into the VC positions in windows and

bullet pocked doorways. Corporal Ut now slipped around to the rear door of the track, entered and dismounted one of the .30s. Laying it across the commander's gunshield, he began raking the VC positions from another angle.

At this time, with the ARVNS gaining temporary fire superiority, the ACAV behind the 57mm track rolled quietly forward and two men slipped out the rear door with a pair of two cables. A tracked vehicle can only be towed efficiently if the cables are crossed, so there must have been an anxious few minutes under those two vehicles while a firefight raged above the men who were rigging the cables. Suddenly they were connected and two men squirted out from the south side between the tracks and before the VC realized what was going on, the ACAVs were back in friendly hands. . . . For this heroic action, Corporal Ut was promoted to sergeant.

By now things were getting a bit messy, as the city was full of milling refugees, whom the ARVNs made no effort to control. The ARVN 3rd Battalion, 11th Infantry Regiment, had arrived on foot, and the 3rd Troop of the 6th Cav had come in from their base on highway 4, farther to the south. By 0900, 3/11 had gotten into positions running across town, on Nguyen Trung Long Street near the Division TOC, and began to work northward. Now the civilians began to clutter the area, flowing into the ARVN positions dragging their dead children by the heels, and carrying their wounded grandparents. Unfortunately, no attempt at crowd control was ever made, and the VC/NVA force moved with the refugees, showing up at tactically uncomfortable spots at inopportune times.

By now 3/11 Vietnamese Infantry was on line and filtering northward through the city, with 6th Cav's ACAVs providing heavy suppressing firepower and the city's center was a shambles of refugees, firefights and burning buildings. The mass exodus effectively screened the withdrawal of the VC and here the official account makes an interesting comment.

"Guerrillas in green uniforms could be seen with-drawing toward the traffic circle and the rear of the school." Green uniforms would seem to indicate that a large percentage of the invaders were NVA, not VC. That would also explain the profligate use of RPG fire, as the canny VC were a LOT more cautious about their limited supplies.

By 1200, the enemy movement had been stopped and the VC had been driven from the hospital. By 1300, the 3rd Battalion was in a ferocious firefight in the corridors and classrooms of the Catholic school. The school battle lasted for four hours, with several of 1st Troop's tracks putting discrete bursts of MG fire into the classrooms in which the VC were trying to rally. At the same time the cavalrymen were taking intermittent fire from the buildings along Hung Vuong Street.

At 1700 hrs. the school's ground floor had been cleared and 1st Platoon, 1st Squadron with a company of 3rd Battalion began to work west along Phan Hien Dao St. They had, however, made a serious tactical mis-take. There were still hostiles in the upper stories of the school and the houses and shops along Phan Hien Dao street. They'd gone less than 150 meters before they began taking heavy fire from the second story win-dows and had to back out and regroup. Two more at-tempts failed, and by nightfall, the ARVNs were back to the traffic circle and the east side of Hung Vuong St.

At this point in time, the VC/NVA invasion held the area north of the city, less the Ranger compound, and the northwestern portion of the city. 2nd Troop, 6th Cav was stationary along Nguyen Trung Long St. 3rd troop, which had been off the map securing the Binh Duc Airstrip, had been relieved by a company of the U.S. 9th Infantry Division, and had moved south to se-cure the MACV compound, also west of My Tho. The various ARVN units started to settle in for the night, but peace was not to be.

The night battle started off with sporadic sniping from VC positions but the 9th Division had gotten some artillery FOS with night vision gear into place and was shelling the northwestern quadrant of the city, which was burning fiercely. At the same time, the VC were probing the ranger camp, and at 2400 they gave it their best shot. Unfortunately, the camp had two assets of which the hostile commander was ignorant. One was a jeep-mounted 75 million candlepower searchlight and the other was an orbiting "Spooky" gunship, an AC-47 with three 7.62mm Gatling guns.

When Spooky orbited in, the searchlight operator sent a tight beam straight up to locate the camp, and then switched to wide beam and dropped his fan to cover the invading forces. In the gunship, which the world knows as a DC-3, the pilot banked his big converted cargo plane and looking out of his left window, past a green illuminated reticle, made a subtle course adjustment. Soon the reticle was centered on the hundreds of little figures pinned in the beam and he thumbed the Gatling triggers, one after the other. With a deep bass roar, what looked like a solid death ray erupted from the firing ports of the ship. . . . The rest of the night was relatively quiet. There had, however, been some troop shuffling.

The U.S. 9th Division had a riverine force working along the Bao Dinh Canal and two battalions of these had rapidly marched overland and now began assaulting into the western sector of the city and began to drive the VC units north. Once they had shoved them up north a bit, 3rd Troop, 6th Cav. left their positions around the MACV compound and attacked southeast along Nguyen Phuong St., which entered the city from the northwest. Their objective was the city's bus terminal, which the VC were using as a HQ. Unfortunately, there seemed to be a lack of coordination and the troop attacked in a column without adequate recon and no artillery prepping.

They charged in a roaring stream, line astern, and all four platoons were hit by B-40 fire, with two tracks being knocked out in the first flurry of AT fire. These two were in the center of the column and 3rd Troop was effectively cut in half. The leading segment, losing two more tracks in the process. Of these four, two were destroyed by TACAIR and two were later retrieved. The other four of the lead element managed to drill through enemy resistance to 1st Troops positions along Phan Hein Dao St. The remaining seven tracks returned to the MACV compound to lick their wounds and re-ammo.

At this point, the American advisor to 3rd Troop told the ARVN commander that the next flight of F-100s would strafe the bus station. Immediately, VC were observed evacuating the bus station, so they must have been listening on Allied tactical frequencies. Due to the availability of captured radios, this was a problem all through the war.

During the night, the VC had filtered back into the school, and at 1500 hours on the first of February, 1st Troop with the elements of 3rd Troop which had fought their way through, were ordered to aid the ARVN 3/11th to again evict the VC. The two units must have been sharing lessons learned during the night, for this time they moved in concert, the ACAVs totally suppressing the enemy fire as the infantry rose up from behind the compound walls and assaulted directly into the ground floors. Then the cavalrymen drove straight into the courtyards and began firing directly into the rooms. A predetermined task force then began clearing the school while the rest of 1st Troop and the 3rd Battalion began to work back westward again down Phan Hein Dao Street.

This time, when they began to take fire, the Cav stopped, returned sniper fire with machine gun fire while the infantrymen swarmed the buildings and eliminated the second story snipers. For the next three hours, a slow, methodical period of delousing went on as block after block of occupied buildings were cleared. Time after time an ACAV would wedge itself through an alley and infantrymen would leap into second story windows, rolling grenades before them. There were still some problems though, the cavalrymen out in the streets and alleys were having trouble keeping exact track of the skirmishing infantrymen. This caused some near catastrophies until the platoon leaders of the 3rd Battalion began to send runners out to the ACAVs to keep them abreast of progress.

Another problem was the narrowness of the streets. The ACAVs couldn't pass each other, and if they got too far ahead of the infantry, the whole column would have to back up to allow the lead track to maneuver. There was a lot of bumping, clanging and cursing going on during the battle, as the metal monsters maneuvered in a city that many of them called home and were loath to destroy. . . . And just at sunset, they were ordered back to the traffic circle at Hung Voung and Phan Hien Dao for night positions, giving up 500 meters of hard won streets.

The VC seemed to be running out of warm bodies, though, and there was little activity during the night. The 3rd Battalion, 11th infantry was relieved by 3rd Battalion, 12th Infantry Regiment, but there was no relief for the cavalrymen. . . . As usual they were the only ones there. About 0400 on the 2nd of February, a small group of VC got back into the school and opened up on the infantrymen in the courtyard. Apparently, they'd not noticed the ACAV sitting in the shadows across the square and after several long, raking bursts and a dozen or so M-79 shells through the windows, the remainder of the night was quiet.

Dawn broke deadly quiet, no one moved—only watched with nervous bloodshot eyes as the sunlight filtered through the smoke. Captain Vinh, sensing that the enemy had pulled back, sent out foot patrols to make contact. When they failed to find hostiles, the Cav, supported by the new infantry battalion, moved cautiously out. When they passed the city reservoir, they had an anxious minute, spotting figures steadily advancing through the brush outside the city. Then they recognized foot patrols from the U.S. 9th Division. First Troop continued toward the bus station until it met the rest of the 3rd Troop which was again coming down

Nguyen Phuong St. from the MACV compound. The battle was over.

The ARVNs had lost 101 killed, 110 wounded, and there had been two ACAVs damaged but repairable, and three destroyed with weapons. The VC/NVA forces had lost 716 killed and 82 captured. They had also not overrun the city. The ARVN infantry and the 6th Cavalry had learned many lessons in this battle, including the need for combined arms, artillery support and the need for clearing buildings from the top down. As the months progressed, the VC would continue to lose more and more of the delta area as village after village was cleared by these roving ACAV, infantry teams. They fought bravely and skillfully for their country, and deserve better from history.

REFERENCE SOURCES

The foregoing was adapted from "A Black Beret's Vietnam Odyessey," an article in *Armor* magazine, by Captain Kenneth P. Long, January/February 1993; and "Armour in Urban Combat," May/June 1970, by Captain Larry K. Cole. Both men were advisors to the Vietnamese 6th Cavalry Regiment. At the time, the author was in combat in Pleiku in the central highlands, running tank and ammunition columns for Company A 1/69 Armor, 4th Infantry Division.

CHAPTER 36

When Tanks Began to Fly

IN ORDER FOR ARMORED COMBAT VEHICLES TO FLY, TWO things had to happen: First, the tank had to get a bit lighter; second, aircraft had to get a *lot* bigger. In the late 1950s and early 1960s, both things happened almost simultaneously. In the normal course of events one would assume that the 12-ton M-113 would have been the first armored vehicle to be lifted by the C-130 cargo aircraft, which is the military's workhorse. Tactical and political situations, however, have a way of unhinging human predictions. There is a "stretch" version of the normal C-130, designated as C-130H-30, or as it was called back in the 1960s, the C-133. The plane's normal payload is around 20 tons, depending on required range. . . . However, in emergency conditions a trade can be made.

Fuel weight can be swapped off for cargo weight, if one doesn't have to go too far, say from Saigon to Da Nang, South Vietnam. The political situation during that war was so unstable that periodic coups replaced elections. I personally remember having to guard a voting place during the fall of 1967, by parking my tank in front of the building to discourage Viet Cong interference. The practice was not new, and a common nickname for South Vietnamese tanks was "voting machines" and tankers were known as "coup troops." The first time tanks flew into combat was in Vietnam in 1966 to quell a mutiny. Colonel Raymond Battreall who was there, tells the story.

I'm writing to relate a historical milepost of Armor which could not be told before because the State Department disowned us at a rather high level of classification. Sufficient years have passed, however, that everything has long since been automatically downgraded. A routine notice of this historic movement appears in the USAF operational history of the Vietnam era.

From March into May of 1966, the Buddhist chaplains of the Army of the Republic of Vietnam's (ARVN) crack 1st infantry division incited their troops to open mutiny against what was perceived to be the Catholic-dominated government in Saigon. All operations against the enemy ceased, and the division began moving south against the I Corps headquarters in Da Nang. There was considerable anxiety that the Corps HQ might join the mutiny, for the commander and several key staff officers were Buddhists.

Organic to the ARVN 1st Division was the ARVN 7th Cavalry whose commander wanted no part of the mutiny. But he realized that no matter how it came out in the end, he and his squadron would still have to work with the division. He, therefore, obeyed the order to march on Da Nang with his three armored cavalry assault troops and one troop of M41A3 "Walker Bulldog" light tanks. But he seized every excuse to delay his movement and, in fact, avoided any contact with troops loyal to the government.

His intentions, however, were not known to Military Assistance Command, Vietnam (MACV) HQ because the Senior Corps Advisor, Marine LTG Lewis Walt, had restricted all advisors to their billets. His intent was to avoid U.S. involvement on both sides of the mutiny. Walt's order resulted in the loss of all communications with the units involved; MACV was, therefore, very much concerned about the armor threat to Da Mang.

4th ARVN Cav, headquartered outside Da Nang, also wanted to remain loyal, but was faced with the same dilemma of not knowing which way the Corps HQ would go. Its commander literally refused to answer the telephone or radio from Corps, thereby eliminating the need to take sides. Meanwhile, Prime Minister Ky had dispatched three VN Marine battalions to Da Nang by sea and was worrying about how to counter the armor threat, given the 4th Cav's uncertain status. He hit on the idea of sending 1st Troop (M41A3) 5th ARVN Cav, from Xuan Loc in III Corps to Da Nang. The only way to get it there in time was to airlift it, so he called on MACV for help.

As Senior Advisor Republic of Vietnam, Armor Command, I can only speculate as to how high up the decision was made, but one day in April I received instructions from MAC J-3 (MG William DePuy) to supervise the loading of 1/5 Troop aboard four USAF C-133s at Ton Son Nhut Airbase. I later learned that the C-133 was a "stretch C-130" with a lengthened fuselage. Its internal dimensions could accommodate two M-41s if we could get them inside without tearing the plane apart, and if we could keep the load balanced. We would have only 1/4 inch clearance on either side!!!

When the fully combat loaded tanks (fuel, ammo, rations and crew individual gear) met the aircraft, I gave the U.S. loadmaster their weight from the vehicle's tech manual. He labored with a slide rule and then told me where to place them inside. Having learned long before that the best way to load armor on a train is for the officers to lead the way to the loading dock and then get out of the way while the sergeants and the drivers did their thing, I gave the word to the ARVN platoon sergeants and stood back to watch. Everything went slowly but smoothly as each tank backed into the plane. This having been done and the tanks tied down, I asked the loadmaster where he wanted the crews to sit. He replied in horror.

"My God Sir, We can't take the crews, we already have waivers for the wing load and the floor load, and besides they'd screw up my center of gravity." I explained that the weight of the crews was included in the weight of the tank I'd given him, and he replied, "Well then, Sir, I guess they'd better ride in their tanks." And that's exactly what they did.

I admit to worrying as the first plane waddled out to the runway and to holding my breath as it started its takeoff roll, but it broke ground smoothly and disappeared to the north. We loaded the remaining aircraft. By the time the last was ready to go, the first had returned from Da Nang for a second load. Each plane flew two sorties and one flew a third to deliver the seventeenth tank. While this last tank was loading, at around midnight, a USAF sergeant tapped me on the elbow and asked if I was Colonel Battreall. He then handed me a TWX message which I read by flashlight.

It was addressed to me by name from the State Department in Washington and read: "You are interfering in domestic politics. Cease and desist forthwith." It was signed Rusk. For a split second, I contemplated a reply, asking the secretary what he thought we'd been doing all along, but descretion prevailed. Thinking of Patton's reaction when ordered not to seize Palermo during World War II, I said "Sarge, you didn't find me out here in all this darkness, noise and confusion, did you?" He thought briefly and replied, "No, Sir, I guess I didn't.' I told him to return to his office and I would be in to accept the message shortly. I waited until the last flight broke ground and then acknowledged receipt.

I recall wondering how Dean Rusk got my name and marveling that he thought a brand new LTC (I had barely five months in grade at the time) could marshal one fourth of the worldwide USAF inventory of C-133s and get every waiver in the book without considerable help from much higher pay grades. Nonetheless, we had accomplished the first combat operational airlift of tanks in the history of warfare. Oh sure, we had flown empty tanks around the airfield to prove we could do it on Strategic Army Corps mobility exercises, and we'd flown empty tanks over oceans when the delivery priority was high enough, but never before had we flown combat loaded tanks with crews ready to go into action on the other end. And that is just what 1/5 ARVN Cav did!! The M41s shown clearing the streets of Da Nang of mutinous elements were theirs.

I never did answer Secretary's Rusk's message, though I guess somebody did. Its classification and political sensitivity were such, however, that I felt constrained not to report this historic event at the time. But 28 years have passed, and it's about time for the armor community to learn what happened.

While it had been proven that light tanks could be flown into battle, there was another development that, even today, is little known. Not only were cargo aircraft growing, so were helicopters. The first time this was pulled off seems to have been in late 1967, the unit was the 11th (Blackhorse) Cavalry and the commander at that time should have been George Patton, Jr.

What happened was this: An armored cavalry assault vehicle (ACAV) commanded by a young sergeant who had not yet learned to read the paddy condition by the color of rice and dirt, got into some goop that was too thick to float in and too thin to run on and got buried to the driver's hatch. Some as yet unknown genius figured out that the weight of an ACAV matched the maximum overload lifting power of a CH-47 helicopter and after some figuring, arguing, and convincing, the stuck M-113 was lifted out and set on the nearby road.

This was probably the first time in history that this was done, but the only people who seem to have taken note were—the Russians. In 1977, Ethiopia and Somalia were having one of their periodic wars over the Ogaden province and both were, at the time, Soviet clients. For whatever reason, the Russians chose to back the Ethiopians and began to provide new tanks and around 11,000 Cuban mercenaries. There was also a Russian ground force of 1,500 technicians and security troops. The support was flown out of South

Yemen, Eastern Europe, and, using long range Anotov aircraft, even the Soviet Union.

Still, the Somalis seemed to be about to take the Ogaden,
which would have reduced Ethiopia by about one-third of
its land mass. Wanting to keep the status quo, General Vas-
ily Petrov decided to pull off a tactical heli-lift of tanks. The
old Soviet Union was still a bit sensitive about the ease
with which little Israel had beaten its Soviet-equipped Arab
enemies, and Petrov decided that a bit of overkill was
necessary.

The Somalis had come through the Ahmar Mountains by
way of the Kara Marda Pass and pushed into the Ogaden
as far as the town of Harar, which they were besieging. The
Russians were in the habit of giving obsolete weaponry to
their Third World clients and Petrov had 70 ASU-57 assault
guns at his disposal. These were little-tracked vehicles of
3.5-tons weight, armed with a 57mm antitank gun. They had
originally been designed for the USSR's airborne divisions
but had been superceded by larger weapons.

Petrov also had available 20 Mil-8 and 10 Mil-6 helicopters
with Russian pilots. On 5 March 1978, The Cubans air-as-
saulted the town of Genasene, 17 miles north of Jigjiga,
which was the Somali base. Once the town was held, all
70 ASU-57s were lifted in. Once they were organized, they
motored south and hit the Somalis in the rear, while the
rest of the Cuban force, mounted in APCs, hit them in a
frontal assault. The predictable result was a casualty list of
around 3,000, and three days later the Somalis agreed to
withdraw from the Ogaden.

Armored warfare had just gone three-dimensional. To the
conventional left, right, and double envelopments, must now
be added the vertical envelopment. To date, no army is seriously working on the concept of air-landing light armor with
heavy helicopters, but in the very near future, it will become
an urgent need. The terrorists, slavers, and drug czars that
we face today live in remote places and use weapons of
mass destruction. Even worse, Saddam Hussein and his ilk
have now stashed their munitions in places like Yemen, Algeria, and the Sudan, far out of reach of conventional forces.

Sooner than later, we are going to have to send the tanks by air mail.

REFERENCE SOURCES
Desert Warfare, Bryan Perrett, Patrick Stephens, Ltd.
War in Peace, edited by Sir Robert Thompson, Harmony Books.
"When Tanks Took Wings," Colonel Raymond Battreall, *Armor* magazine, May–June 1994.
"Achieving Dominant Maneuver," research manuscript by Professor Gabriel Boehler, Major William Schneck, and Ralph Zumbro.

CHAPTER 37

Puma Force

A KILLING MACHINE WAS BEING BORN, HIDDEN FROM PRYING eyes, in the back-maneuver area of Ft. Leonard Wood, Missouri. A dozen assorted models of the famed and time-tested Bradley fighting vehicles were sitting in a row, with men swarming around them. Although they still bore a family resemblance to the original chassis, there were differences. They looked somehow deadlier than even the Desert Storm–era Bradleys after which they had been patterned. Major Ulysses Tecumseh Butler, back from his last UN foray to the Middle East, was standing at one side of the line of highly modified tracks when the glitter of stars caught his eye. *Rats,* he thought, *this place was supposed to be brass-proof, now who the . . .* Then he recognized Puma Force's mentor, General Benjamin Weiss, accompanied by a gray-suited man whose studied anonymity said Defense Intelligence Agency (DIA) louder than words.

A sergeant, spotting the general at the same time, drew in a breath to yell "attention" but then remembered the rule—do *not* ever disturb men at work on machines—and quietly passed the word "brass aboard" to the troops.

"Welcome Benj," Butler began, a smile on his desert-burned face, but the smile died aborning when he saw the general's expression. The man looked like his best friend had just died, but as far as Butler knew, "The Hawke" Jimbo Franklin and the general's old buddies from his Vietnam days were all hale and hearty, some in the military, most out in industry someplace. "Sir?" was all he said, and the general, a smallish, wiry man with salt-and-pepper hair and a narrow gambler's mustache, nodded toward the office that took up one end of the hastily renovated World War II barracks. The two men left the line of vehicles and walked out from under the shed roof, crossed the carefully unmown lawn, and went up the stairs into the office. The new Puma base had been set up to look unused and uninhabited, and very few knew of its existence.

As the general sat and parked his attaché case, Butler wordlessly reached into a small refrigerator, withdrew a pitcher of iced tea, and poured two tall glasses. A raised eyebrow drew three fingers from Weiss, and Butler actually cringed. A three-shot problem was going to be a baddie. The man in the issue gray suit sat and said nothing. His eyes were concealed by sunglasses, and his head moved as he slowly scanned the room as if looking for hidden listeners. He had taken a small case out of a suitcoat pocket and erected an antenna. Neither man spoke until the bug scanner flashed the clear sign.

"Er, what's broken loose this time, sir, and can we go with the new gear? TF Puma is as hot and ready as you gentlemen tell me the old one was."

The general took a small sip, tasted the Yukon Jack appreciatively, and set off a verbal nuke. "We found one of Saddam's atomic/biological/chemical [ABC] caches in Sudan, Colonel; there's a terrorist assault forming, and we think Pan Islam is going to wreck a large number of Western cities while they take Saudi Arabia and get a lock on our energy supply. One of the Iraqi instructors at the site, which we found from satellite data by spotting the heat plume, had a car 'accident' a few days ago when his Zil command car went over a cliff and into a stream. Before he died, he did quite a lot of talking . . . about three days' worth, to be

exact. It is absolutely amazing how much information modern psychochemicals can extract.

"There's a round dozen of those missing Russian vest-
pocket nukes, several hundred gallons of Black Plague, and
ten tons of nerve gas in quart containers with detonators.
You are going to mobilize everything you can roll, load it
into C-130s, and self-deliver to Faya-Largeau, in northern
Chad. Your tactical birds will rendezvous with you and insert you on your own tracks, in the target zone. Any
questions?"

About halfway through the general's spiel, Butler had
stiffened up his own iced tea into what is called an Icepick
and looked questioningly at the man in gray, who smiled
for the first time and said, "Beer, please." Butler got him
one and then asked, "Just one thing, sir—can we take the
gloves off this time and do it the old-fashioned way?"

Weiss tried to smile, but it came off looking pained; the
man had too much worry in his mind to fully control his
face. "You tell him, Ellison," he said. The DIA man took
off his sunglasses, and even his eyes were gray. He was
about as average-looking a man as you'd expect and could
easily vanish into a crowd without a trace. He nodded his
head, but his face carried a question. "What's the 'old-fashioned way'?" he asked, and Butler answered, "Kill 'em all
and let God sort 'em out. . . . Or maybe Allah, in this case."

"That's what we had in mind, Colonel," Ellison said. "The
old term was, 'with extreme prejudice,' wasn't it?"

"Right, Butler said, "but as you can see, I am a major,
not a colonel." Weiss suddenly grinned and reached into his
briefcase, pulling out a certificate, a set of orders, and a pair
of the three diamond pips that denoted a United Nations
full colonel. "Try these on for size, Ulysses, and succeed in
this mission and we'll make it permanent. If you survive,
that is. The idea is to sanitize the chem and bio weapons by
blowing the nukes in place. They want a nuclear jihad?
They'll get an atomic crusade! These—people—now have
the capability to destroy Western civilization, and we have
to stop them or we have no future."

During this shocking disclosure Butler had first sent his
mind back over the final events of the twentieth century,

decided that the story was real, and then began to figure.
He sat quietly for a minute, digesting the information, and
then said, "All right, Benjamin . . . sir, we can do it, with
existing assets, but if we are to blow those suitcase nukes,
we'll need an atomic ordnance expert, and we don't happen
to have one on hand, but you'll have spotted that all . . . ?"

Ellison had raised his hand with a small smile and said,
"That's me, Colonel. The plan is to wire about three of
those little nukes, for simultaneous detonation, after the
chem and bio weapons have been stacked around them. I'm
basically a nuclear physicist who got into field work in Iraq.
I've worked at Los Alamos, Stanford, Berkeley, and a few
other places you don't want to know about."

"Speaking of which," Weiss said with a slight growl in his
voice, "the reason this is being done out here instead of
bringing you into the Pentagon is that we still can't quite
trust our security . . . for the same reason that we set up
Puma Force out here in the backside of an engineer base.
Remember back in the late nineties, a certain somebody
whose name we don't use anymore managed to get his surplus bimbos into supposedly secure areas, and we're *still*
finding very sophisticated bugs and computer-penetrating
software in the damnedest places. Somehow, there was a
virus planted in our mainframe, possibly during the year
2000 contretemps.

"We don't think they're tumbled to this operation,
though. You've got the usual carte blanche for supplies, and
there's the usual selection of available assets sending in liaison officers. The part of the U.S. Army that ain't politicized
is still the best fighting force on the planet, and the chairman
sends warm regards. Now, I've got to get back to the Puzzle
Palace, so give my regards to Coral and the ladies, bring
Ellison up to speed, and get rolling." After a quick round
of handshakes, the general was gone, driving his own rental
car for security, and two men whose destinies he'd just
linked were standing in the open, beside Ellison's small duffel bag, measuring each other. Each liked what he saw. Ellison's tight, compact, muscular build showed even through
the traditional Washington uniform, and Butler's lean, whip-
cord body and dark eyes made him look like an Arab in

uniform. He wore plain fatigues, not the traditional cammies.

" 'Coral'—Ladies, women out here?" Ellison asked in some shock as he reached down and picked up his duffel bag. "We have found," Butler said, "that if the atmosphere is set up properly, the ladies can actually help discipline. The trick is to keep the number small enough that the tomcat genes don't cut in. That way the men get real protective, and any woman who turns on the charm gets a quick transfer. . . . After being threatened with a *serious* court-martial on the basis of national security. We keep them in their own barracks, and Colonel Hawke's wife, Coral, ex-Mercier of French intelligence, is kind of a den mother and is setting up the program. So far, it works . . . and we're covered if we ever go public.

"The ladies are simply better at a lot of things than men, and our supply system is running like a dream. . . . First outfit I've ever seen where the troops actually volunteer for supply detail and KP. Okay, here's your room. This building used to be an NCO barracks back a few wars. Get into uniform and I'll give you the dime tour and introduce you around." In a very few minutes Ellison materialized in the motor shed, wearing fatigues and the insignia of a warrant officer fifth grade, which was about what Butler expected.

"I rode the TC slot in a Bradley in Two Sixty-Ninth Armor in Desert Storm, but there's obviously been some changes made, and the general said that you're now helicopter mobile. What's been done; we don't own a bird that strong?"

"No," Butler answered, a rather sly grin on hi face, "but there's a Belgian company named Skytech that owns a fleet of Russian Mi-26s, and everything they can lift is headed for Faya-Largeau right now. They sold a batch of them to Mexico some years back, but had to repossess them. They can deliver all our combat tracks five hundred miles in one lift."

"Oh, wow," was all Ellison could say, and then Butler began to point out what had been done to the Bradley hulls. Basically, the Bradley had evolved out of a need for something that would fight like a Vietnam-era ACAV and still deliver the troops. Instead of becoming an infantry battle taxi, it evolved into a light tank that carried a few dismounts. It had also gotten much heavier than design weight.

In order to combat this, the concept of a fiberglass composite hull built on steel wire armature had been created. Because the parent company, FMC, had wanted the sales, they'd been convinced by the general officer, who was their patron inside the military-industrial network, to volunteer a dozen hulls for an "unspecified combat test programme." The torsion bar suspension had been replaced by hydraulics, which gave more room and saved weight. The Cummins Diesel had not been installed. Instead, four Capstone turbo-generators sat in the hull, two just behind the driver and his assistant, who now had a bow gun and some sophisticated surveillance gear.

Two others were just ahead of the rear exit door that replaced the one-ton ramp. Electric motors drove the tracks and could be clutched over to drive water jets for amphibious operations. The weight of the hull was two-fifths of the original metal one, and its range was a bit more than a thousand miles on internal tankage. There were also racks on the stern for a pair of 55-gallon drums that gave the hull continental cruising range.

The original turret had been replaced by a composition model that carried a German 35mm chain gun that could fire a variety of munitions, including canister shells that could be set to go off at any distance. Atop the turret was a vicious little shock weapon: a 5.56mm Minigun that was controlled by either the TC's helmet or a small radar. "Missiles come in at around five hundred miles per hour," Butler explained to a somewhat bemused Ellison, "and a stream of armor-piercing slugs going into their noses really screws up their guidance."

Suddenly the technician grinned. "You remember that story in *Armor* magazine, back in ninety-two, about the Bradley that shot an Atol missile out of the sky? That was the two-three track in my platoon. Er—you said dismounts; how many grunts can you carry? Don't look like room for more than six in there, if that."

"Three is all we carry," Butler answered. "One for the tail gun and one of each side mount, but two tracks can put out six men, and these guys are kind of special. See that suit of armor over there?" Ellison turned his head in the indicated direction and goggled. The suit was more than eight feet tall, with enough kevlar, ballistic nylon, and ceramics to stop an AK–47 and 74 ammunition. "Jeez, what do you use for a powerpack? That thing must weigh a couple hundred pounds."

"The vehicle and the infantry are a designed combination," Butler said. "Scruggs, come over here and show the man." The suit, which had a peculiar rifle leaning against it, suddenly came to life and walked comfortably over to the two officers, where it towered over them like an adult over a ten-year old boy. "Here, hold this, sir," said a deep-toned, slightly gravelly voice, and the weapon was handed to Ellison, who looked it over with interest. It looked to be about 12mm magnum or .50 caliber, with a drum magazine and a grenade launcher on the muzzle. A huge pistol that used the same ammo hung from the weapons belt.

The man's hands, protected by titanium clamshells, reached up and twisted off the helmet, which had an eerie Darth Vader–ish look to it. Inside, the occupant looked to be the largest human Ellison had ever seen. "Meet 'Boarhawg' Scruggs, Ellison; his dad was the original Puma Force's top soldier." Ellison reached out a dubious hand and got the distinct impression that there was a machine in that suit, not a normal human.

"You know that there's a maximum size for enlistment?" Butler said. At Ellison's nod, he explained. "We just went back to the recruiting records and found us a couple hundred husky seven-footers. Look at the back of the armor." The giant obediently turned around, and Ellison saw two things. First, the suit had a compressed-air cooling and breathing unit, and second, there was a battle axe in a sheath across its shoulders. "Close combat and sheer psychological terror," Butler explained, and then turned to a normal-sized black soldier who'd materialized out of the group that had accumulated around their C.O. and the mystery visitor. "Sound officer's call, Washington, we're going to war." Tradition was strong in this resurrected version of a legendary tank force out of the past, and the clear notes of an ancient call stopped all action as every leader in Task Force Puma homed in on the bugle. Here would be adventure or death. Most of the soldiers were young enough to still believe in their own invulnerability. The older men, though, were resigned to the need to protect civilization from unheeding fanatics. . . . If it cost their lives, so be it, but they would not die alone; that they knew for certain.

Faya-Largeau, in the French-dominated African country of Chad, is a small desert city out of *Beau Geste*. It is far from the capital of N'Djamena, remote enough to be out of reach of most of the diplomatic corps and the few reporters who are interested in Africa. Most important, it has a large airport suitable for heavy cargo planes. By air route, it is exactly 450 miles from the Sudanese city of Kebkabiya. This settlement had long been known as one of the sinister slave marts of the Sudan, and it was rumored that even white women had been seen in its desert flesh bazaars, although most of the merchandise was southern Sudanese Christian blacks.

It was from the purchase of one of these that the story had come out, for when his new master, a diplomat of another Arab nation, took him to a UN hospital in N'Djamena, he was found to be suffering from mild radiation sickness. This had gotten the Americans interested, and now Colonel Ulysses Butler was sitting on the flight deck of one of the world's largest helicopters, watching his small armored force arrive on U.S. C-130s. The Belgian helicopters had arrived first and, because the area was already host to groups of French and Belgian military/technical representatives, had caused no disturbance. Nor had the steady arrival of C-130s, as the word had been let out that a desert exercise with the Foreign Legion armored cavalry was planned. There would be an exercise very soon, but it would be across a border instead of out into the sand seas.

An Mi-26 can make 187 miles per hour, unloaded, but with an armored, 15-ton slingload, 120 is much more realistic. And as the afternoon progressed, a lot of computer time in the field command center that the choppers had ferried in was devoted to several factors. The big ships could move

20 tons about five hundred miles, but they would be out of fuel at the end of the trip. The drill for this mission, then, would be to carry their 15-ton loads into assault position, with the ships carrying several more tons of disposable ordnance provided by Puma Force. Then they would shift to a hidden landing zone where a French helo would have already established a depot out of rubber bladders of fuel. The French, when they found out what was right next door and that their beloved Paris was on the hit list, became most cooperative. . . . And they also agreed to keep operational details at the lowest level. Paris, like Washington, leaks critical information like a machine-gunned water tower.

0100 hours, 1 May 2007: There was a sudden scurrying of men and a few women, and the big shops began their warm-up cycle. Generators were cut on, and then power was fed to the big Ukrainian D-136 turboshaft engines. With a pair of loud thumps, the engines caught, and now there was 22,000 horsepower available to the big 105-foot rotors. Almost lazily, the big ships lifted off their pads and spaced themselves in a rumbling, hovering line along the runway. Out of each of the C-130s, which had suddenly lowered their ramps, came a desert camouflage–painted Bradley light tank. Four men were perched on the top of each vehicle.

As the combat machines came under the hovering choppers, small FM radios went into action, and the TCs and the crew chiefs brought the vehicles ever closer. The connection between aircraft was four very thick nylon straps, each rated at 20,000 pounds breaking strength. Each strap carried one half of a Capewell-style locking device, while the other half, about eight times the size of a standard Capewell, was bolted to the Bradley's four lifting points. As soon as the connection was made, and the two intercom systems plugged into a receptacle on the Bradley, the radios were shut down.

The lead pair now began to roll forward, the Bradley rolling on its tracks, moving fast enough to allow the helicopter to use airspeed to aid the takeoff. To speed the assault landing, the crews would ride, Russian style, aboard their tanks.

0130 hrs: The ships were over the horizon, and all that was left was a small cadre of communications types, mostly women, a few clerks, the rear-area first sergeant, and a medical staff, all in field command modules set up in a miniature pentagon shape at one end of the Faya-Largeau airstrip. There was no security force as such. Each module had a General Electric Gatling/Stinger turret on top of it, crewed by a pair of very determined women in cammies.

0400 hrs: Command ship, Task Force Puma, second bird in the stream, was flying low and fast through a wadi between two mountains of the Jebel al Marra, western Sudan. Lieutenant Simon Epstein looked up from his console in the command truck. Alone of all the modified Bradleys, it carried no dragoon infantry—instead, a very compact commo/communications/command, or C3, installation. Remembering one of his father's comments on how fast C3 can become an abbreviation for Chaos Cubed, he keyed his mike. "Forty-five minutes out, Colonel. The satellite shows no vehicles starting up, Aurora surveillance cameras see no untoward activity. Jeez, I don't believe this resolution. If I see that guard on the ground, I'll be able to recognize him."

"Right, Ep," Butler answered, "now you know how your dad felt when he rode for the Hawke back in seventy-two." "Right, sir, he always said that 'only tracers will run the flutterbys off.' I just hope we survive this escapade; Pop'll eat this story like ice cream while Mom goes off and sulks." There was more of this desultory conversation in the paired vehicles until . . .

0500 hrs, Islamic ABC base south of Kebkabiya: A guard shook his companion awake, violently. "Allah save us, Iben, the sky and the ground are both shaking." The pair, one of whom had been dozing, looked around them fearfully. Then one shouted, *"AIIEE!!! Djinns in the sky,"* and picked up his field phone, which was wired into the command bunker back in the mountain. Rapidly, concisely, but with fear in his voice, he described what he saw. A giant helicopter with a tank underslung was coming up the valley, a valley in which no aircraft could land. A siren began to wail and a generator cut in. Antiaircraft sites began to power up.

Missile radars cut on, and parked ZSU-23-4 targeting radars began to pick up targets for their 23mm guns. Inside the helicopters, there was mad activity as radar spoofing beams went out and radar homing missiles left the newly mounted pylons on the big ship's sides. Then bombardment missiles, American-made 70mm Folding Fin Aircraft Rockets, began to pattern the area. A few missile sites got birds off, but now the antimissile Gatlings on the Bradleys themselves were firing.

Now the lead Bradley was down and running, its chain gun thundering. It had landed *inside* the mine-and-wire defensive belt. Butler listened to the intercom chatter between his driver and the big ship's crew chief. "Altitude oh-fifty and dropping" came from the helicopter, followed by "Rog, turbines lit off, and tracks turning—altitude oh-twenty, ground speed sixty and slowing—altitude oh-ten, ground speed thirty—that's a match, we got thirty on the tracks, set our ass down!"

Butler, who was watching excitedly from his TC hatch, felt the tracks bite dirt, saw the lines go slack, and felt the driver release the Capewells. All four released smoothly, and he took his hand away from the emergency explosive bolt switch. They were on the ground, inside a hostile installation in Sudan, and kicking ass; above them the big birds released a few more antiradiation missiles and raked the troop barracks with their rocket pods. One by one, the M-26s curved away, lifting over the mountain to a rendezvous in a deserted valley to refuel from a French Puma helicopter and await the call for pickup. Far above them in the African dawn, just visible as sunlit sparks, French Mirage/2000 jets circled slowly. This was supposed to be a surgical strike, but one never knows.

The combination of Russian maps, American and French satellite photos, and the DIA debriefing of the kidnapped terrorist officer had given them about as good a briefing as could be expec . . . ? "Colonel, you have got to see this," Epstein said urgently. "Look at what we just pulled off the real-time satellite, the new KeyHole 17." Butler, in no immediate danger and with his 11 combat tracks all joyfully wrecking preselected targets, dropped out of the TC hatch, leaving his gunner, a sergeant first class named DuBois from Lake Charles, Louisiana, to keep lookout. "Look at the scene, sir, I've got us in real time, right after the sun hit this valley. Look at the track I've got circled."

Butler was amazed; he seemed to be about 50 feet over the vehicle, and there was something oddly familiar . . . "Doobie, wave your left hand," he said over the intercom, and immediately the figure in the screen waved. "Well, I'll be dipped in . . . what did you do, Ep? I've never seen resolution like this!"

"We never had the codes for this satellite, sir, but when Dad heard about this run, he pulled in a few wires and fed me the keys; I don't think there's a blessed thing out there that I can't read." Butler's mind had been whirring. "Washington," he ordered his driver, "find us a hidey-hole and park. Ep, set that rig to cover this whole installation, and zoom periodically to each track; then transmit your codes over microlink to the rest of them. As each one clears its area and dismounts its dragoons, go to surveillance. . . . Beam one feed up to that French version of an AWACS, but *don't* tell him how to reach the source." Epstein, already punching keys and talking rapidly into a mike, only nodded.

Several aboveground bunkers in front of the access to the tunnels that went back into the mountain were holding out, and three Bradleys were parked in line in front of them. Nine very large, roughly human figures appeared between them, stalking forward with a purposely menacing gait. Most were not carrying rifles, only pistols, grenades, and—*axes?* A bedeviled Islamic warrior dumped the remaining half of his AK's magazine into the hulking figure, which wavered, flinched, and came on undaunted. The Islamic warrior fumbled for another magazine, changed his mind, and reached for a grenade, but too late. A stellate-edged axe split him from shoulder to navel.

A man beside him raised his own weapon but was shot down by a .50 caliber Grizzly pistol. Another of the giants slipped a finned tube over the muzzle of his pistol and shot a distant Sudanese, who dissolved in a pink mist. Someone inside the underground works decided enough was enough, and because all nine men were inside the minefield, he turned it on. Four of the giants were promptly engulfed by explosions, but when the dust settled, they were still there, albeit writhing in pain. Their kevlar had stopped the fragments, and their shock-mounted steel soles had deflected the blast. One of the men, while the others shot carefully into anything that looked like a firing slit, reached up and adjusted his helmet a bit.

Inside the helmet, the virtual display went slightly green, and Sergeant "Hawg" Scruggs grinned like a wolf. The mines, of slightly different composition from the ground, had just become visible. *Connie's gonna love this story; if I survive, that is,* he thought, and carefully began to shoot the mines in place. Around him, the others copied his actions, and suddenly the way to the armored door was clear. More and more of the dragoons, in their horrifically painted armor, began to storm up the cleared path as their Bradleys first deposited them and then turned to face outward. Soon two full squads of armored men waited outside that door while one Bradley, with its chain gun swinging around to aim, rumbled up.

The gun had a dual feed, one magazine full of depleted uranium armor penetrators and one with concrete penetrators. With steady concentration the gunner outlined the door in the living rock and then put a stream of uranium core slugs into the metal itself. Shredded and shot off its hinges, the barrier went down, and a smaller armored man, not one of the giants, lobbed a small object into the opening, an object that landed and gave off a whirring sound, sucking in and analyzing the air in the cavern. *"Gas—gas,* get tight," Ellison yelled, and shut off his air intake. He was now on internal air, a highly compressed bottle in the small of his back, and could live on it for only one hour . . . depending on his level of exertion.

Most of the men still relied on pistol, grenade, and axe, but there were always one or two in each group with the .50 caliber rifles and the high-yield grenades. Two by two, the armored suits began to move forward. Ellison stepped to the door, only to be grabbed by a dragoon. "And just who's gonna rewire them nukes if you buy it, Shorty?" came over his outside earphone, and he let the big men go forward. Now they were working on captured information, because the satellites couldn't see through solid rock.

No normal human could have survived that hell of booby traps, lethal gas, and explosions. As it was, six men were blown to pieces by shaped, armor-piercing antitank charges before they got through the outer defense zone. Shooting, chopping, and grenading, with wild battle yells blasting from their external speakers, the dragoons created a battle havoc not seen since Viking days. Nothing unarmored could stand before them, and soon the defenders were frantically scurrying deeper into their underground warren. Then, with a flying wedge of those very large men, whom he now thought of as Viking warriors, around him, Ellison was escorted proudly into the very pits of hell.

The terrorists had suicided by ripping the lids off the bubbling vats of everything from AIDS and anthrax to ebola and plague. The meter still read positive for nerve gas. They had only minutes left on internal air supply when a ribbon charge blew open the red door that held the atom bombs. . . . And a technician, wearing a rubber contamination suit with an air bottle, was just finishing activating one. Its timer read 30 minutes and counting down the seconds.

That, by Ellison's timing, was a bit close, but he'd been working with these timers since the first one had been captured. *Better me here than my family in Chicago next week,* he thought. "Relay this transmission exactly," he ordered, and spoke carefully and very distinctly. "I am in the bomb room, a fanatic has set one for thirty minutes, I am going to arm two more for sixty minutes, and then try to disarm and reset this one. I am sending nine of the twelve mininukes out with the advance guard. I strongly suggest you start to bring in the big birds at this time, Ellison out."

As the message was relayed from one suit to another along the rock passages, Ellison looked pityingly at the technician and noticed that he was a Russian, not a religion-driven Arab. "English?" he asked the man in the rubber mask and rubber suit. The man nodded, and Ellison tried his last gamble: "Life and a new name for that code." Almost frantically sobbing with relief, the man knelt at Ellison's feet and began punching a code into the keypad. Then he stood and gasped out a string of numbers. "I am almost out of air and couldn't have gotten past those rabid dogs out there anyway. Thank you for what little of life I have left."

"Okay" Ellison said. "I thought I was going to have to

cut the controls out of the circuit and hardware standard timers in place of them; thanks. Okay, guys, leave me an escort and get him and those bombs outa here, *Schnell.*" As the men left, he turned and knelt at the controls of the little aluminum suitcase. He barely noticed that as each giant left, he turned and saluted a man who was almost two feet shorter but had shown what he was made of. As the last of them cleared the ruined external door, Ellison caught up with them and, after checking his gas detector, opened his helmet and began to transmit.

"Puma Six, this is Alleycat, I'm out of the hole and it's resealed. I put a thermite grenade on the door and rewelded it. Plus we set a few other goodies around there. *No*-body is gonna get into that bomb room. We got only forty-five minutes from right *now* to get hooked up and outa here." The sky began to vibrate, and he looked up to see the ships coming in and the tracks lining up. Limping a bit, and exhausted to semihelplessness, he let one of the giants tow him to Butler's command track. A sudden blast of explosion-driven decontamination foam covered him, and then he was picked up and literally thrown into the vehicle. As he tumbled through the back door, an anxious French voice was coming from a speaker.

"They have sent a battalion of T-72 tanks from the base at Kebkabiya, my American friends," the voice said. "Their internal communication is in Iraqi, and they will be arriving in about forty minutes. Can you handle them or shall we air strike them?"

"No need," Ellison began to gasp out, but was waved to silence by Epstein, whose predatory grin was again in evidence. In the background, the unit's recall beacon was playing *"We gotta get outa this place / if it's the last thing we ever do"* over the admin link, which got into every radio in Puma Force.

Vaguely, Ellison heard Butler answer, something like, "One of their personnel may have activated an atomic weapon. Go to angels forty ASAP, and return to base," and then he passed out from sheer nervous exhaustion. The last thing he remembered was a series of clanks and a swaying sensation.

Like live things, the big Russian choppers leapt a range of mountains and thundered down into a preselected wadi behind them. Only seconds remained as the last Bradley was unhooked and its bird sat down behind it. Then the land shook and a new sun rose, flashed briefly, and then, with a God-awful *thump,* the outgoing pressure wave went by overhead, knocking down a few rocks. Then the land itself began to complain as small landslides threatened the tankers and airmen cringing in the wadi.

"Alright, crank 'em and haul our asses outa here," Butler snapped into his command link, as his crew began to hook up the Mi-26 that had sat beside him with its turbines idling. "We need to be up and gone before the return wave comes back and things start to fall out of the sky." He was cutting things rather fine, because the atmosphere rebounds from an explosion like a giant spring, and you don't want to be on the deck when the rolling ground wave comes back. Up and just off the ground they flew, until they could see the ground wave approaching, rolling dust, rocks, and the occasional camel or donkey before it.

Then, rising only enough to clear the worst of the ground effect, the birds rode over the wave and slid back down to flying low. There were rocks in the sky, falling in a large pattern. No one wanted to be overly high when a boulder knocked their ship out of the air. At that, only two ships went down, staggering as boulders hit them, and both were salvageable. Two aircrewmen and one tank commander died, but the rest walked—or staggered—away. Only one Bradley needed track repairs, and those were done on the spot by crewmen, men periodically stopped and looked back in awe at the fireshot mushroom that loomed over what had been a threat to their civilization.

0600 hrs, 2 May 2007, Faya-Largeau airfield, Chad, Africa: Most of Puma Force was gathered in the cavernous hold of an Mi-26, looking at a worried little blond TV news anchor who was pointedly oozing concern as she reported an atomic blast "somewhere in the western sector of the Sudan."

Several retired colonels had been brought on as technical consultants, and a UN monitoring team was already on the spot, over Sudanese protests. The consensus was that the terrorist groups had been practicing a dry run, and some would-be nuclear suicide bomber had inadvertently set one off. Speculation was rife about exactly how many of the bombs had gone off, and Benjamin Weiss, Jeremy Hawke, and Salomon Epstein, who had flown in for the finale, were congratulating their military heirs.

"That's about as clean as you can get," Colonel Jeremy Hawke was saying, "You didn't even leave tread marks behind, and there's no trace of chemical or biological weapons."

"Yeah," Epstein said from where he stood, congratulating his son, "and talking about making war support war, what are you going to do with those lovely new nuclear bombs you . . . rescued?"

"We hadn't thought much about that yet," General Weiss said, the corners of his mouth twisting wryly. "No doubt somebody will figure something out for them."

20 February 1998 CNN, Baghdad: *"Saddam Hussein is reported to have moved much of his supply of chemical and biological weaponry out of Iraq and hidden it in remote places in Yemen, Libya, and the Sudan."*

This book has covered, in vast leaps, 3,332 years of history, from the first fully recorded battle in human history to what *will* happen in our near future. There is *no* escape from the last scenario. Narcoterrorists are already in our cities, and half of Islam seems determined to tear down Western civilization. Only the time remains in doubt.

There is a good possibility that military action as much as a natural catastrophe caused the dark age that took down the Egyptian, Minoan, and Mycenaean civilizations. We know that corruption and decadence opened the doors to the fall of Rome and the beginning of our own history. The question that now has to be asked is this:

Will we face the task that history has set us and slap these barbarian hordes back into their cages when the world calls for help? Or will our nation and generation be cursed for all time because our savage descendants worship ancient gods with arcane names like FoMoCo, GenMo and

MaBell . . . instead of sailing ships between the stars? But, have we been this way before?

> It was a single projectile charged with all the power of the universe. An incandescent column of smoke and flame as bright as 10,000 suns rose in all its splendor. It was an unknown weapon, a gigantic messenger of death, which reduced to ashes the entire race of the Vrishnis and the Andhakas. . . . The corpses were so burned as to be unrecognizable, their hair and nails fell out, pottery broke without apparent cause and the birds turned white. After a few hours all foodstuffs were infected. To escape from this fire, the soldiers threw themselves in streams to wash themselves and all their equipment.
> —FROM THE MAHABHARATA, the epic poem of India, not translated into English until 1840

REFERENCE SOURCES

Final Warning, Robert Kupperman and Jeff Kamen, Doubleday.

America the Vulnerable, Joseph Douglass Jr. and Neil C. Livingstone, Lexington Books.

The Roots of Counterinsurgency, Ian F. W. Beckett, ed., Blandford Press, London.

The New World Order, Pat Robertson, World Publishing.

The War Against the Terrorists, Gayle Rivers, Stein & Day.

Alchemists of Revolution, Richard E. Rubenstein, L. B. Taurus.